ULTIMATE X-MEN

THE TOMORROW PEOPLE

WRITER
MARK MILLAR

PENCILS
ADAM KUBERT
ANDY KUBERT

INKS
ART THIBERT
W/ DANNY MIKI

COLORS
RICHARD ISANOVE
W/ BRIAN HABERLIN

LETTERS
RICHARD STARKINGS
& COMICRAFT'S
WES ABBOTT

ORIGINAL SERIES EDITOR
MARK POWERS

EDITOR IN CHIEF
JOE QUESADA

PRESIDENT
BILL JEMAS

ULTIMATE X-MEN VOL. 1: THE TOMORROW PEOPLE. Contains material originally published in magazine form as ULTIMATE X-MEN #1-6. Third printing 2003. ISBN# 0-7851-0788-6. Published by MARVEL COMICS, a division of MARVEL ENTERTAINMENT GROUP, INC. OFFICE OF PUBLICATION: 10 East 40th Street, New York, NY 10016. Copyright © 2000 and 2001 Marvel Characters, Inc. All rights reserved. $14.95 per copy in the U.S. and $23.95 in Canada (GST #R127032852); Canadian Agreement #40668537. All characters featured in this issue and the distinctive names and likenesses thereof, and all related indicia are trademarks of Marvel Characters, Inc. No similarity between any of the names, characters, persons, and/or institutions in this magazine with those of any living or dead person or institution is intended, and any such similarity which may exist is purely coincidental. **Printed in the U.S.A.** STAN LEE, Chairman Emeritus. For information regarding advertising in Marvel Comics or on Marvel.com, please contact Russell Brown, Executive Vice President, Consumer Products, Promotions and Media Sales at 212-576-8561 or rbrown@marvel.com

10 9 8 7 6 5 4 3

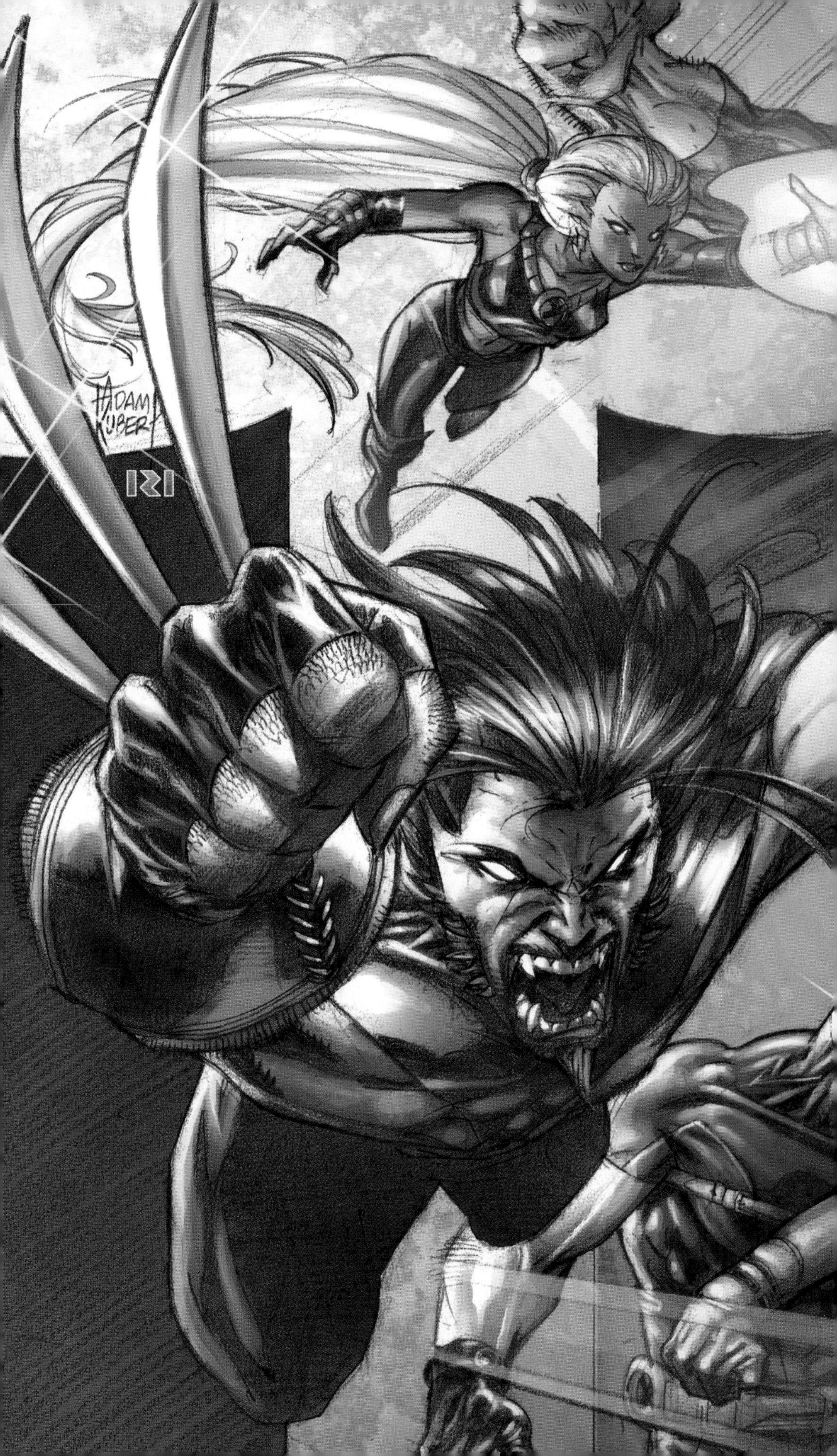
ADAM KUBERT

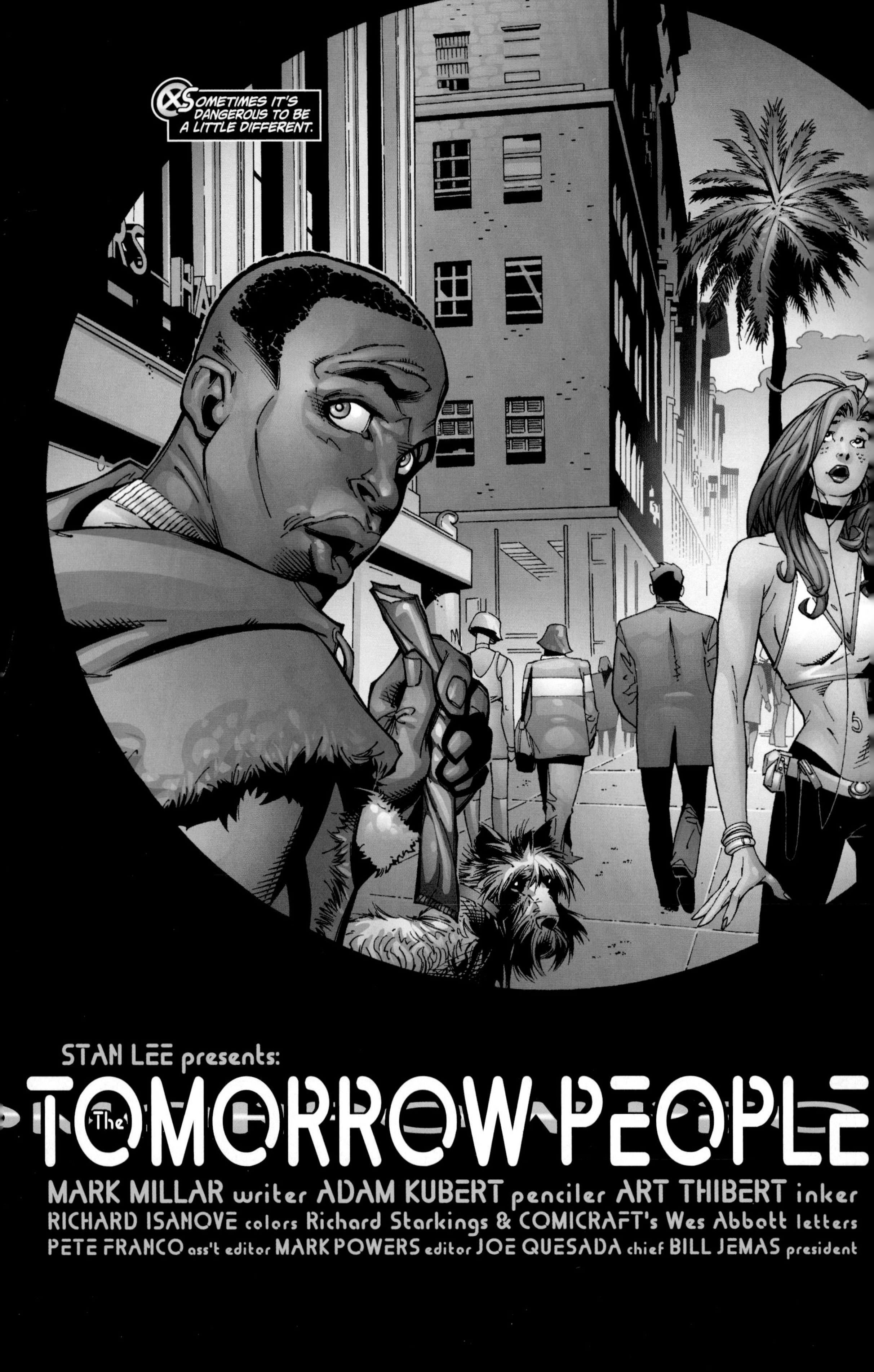
SOMETIMES IT'S DANGEROUS TO BE A LITTLE DIFFERENT.

STAN LEE presents:

The TOMORROW PEOPLE

MARK MILLAR writer ADAM KUBERT penciler ART THIBERT inker
RICHARD ISANOVE colors Richard Starkings & COMICRAFT's Wes Abbott letters
PETE FRANCO ass't editor MARK POWERS editor JOE QUESADA chief BILL JEMAS president

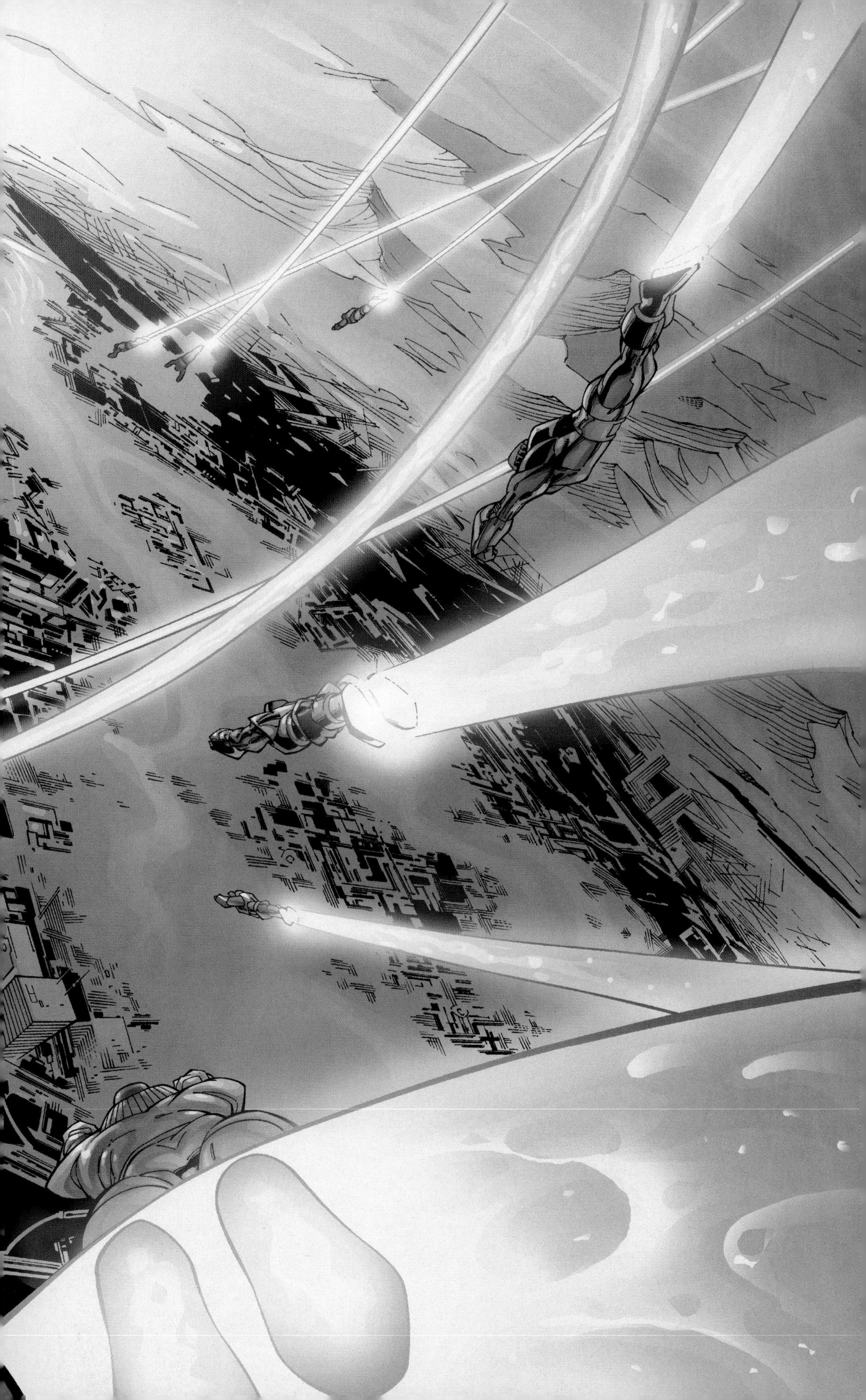

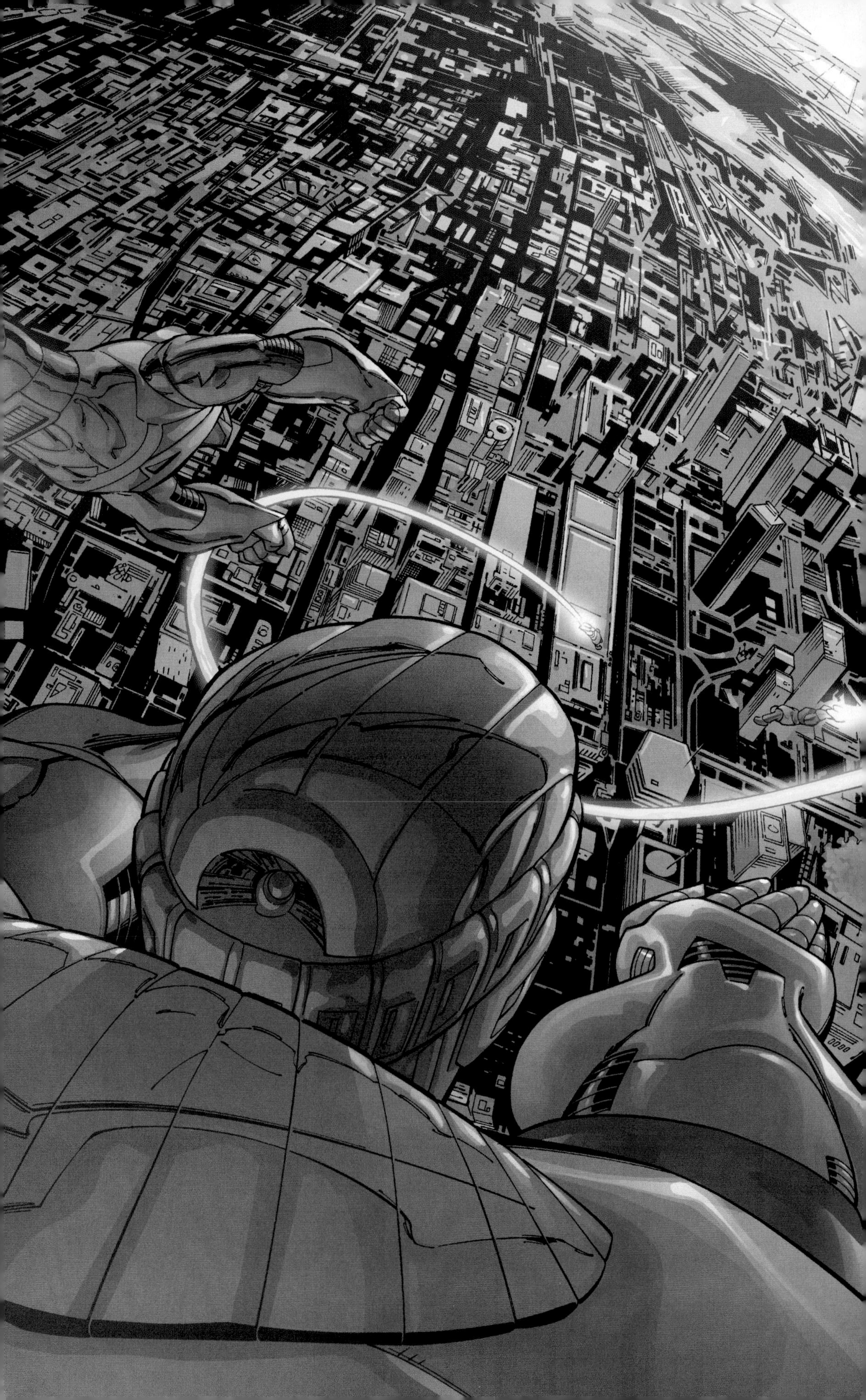

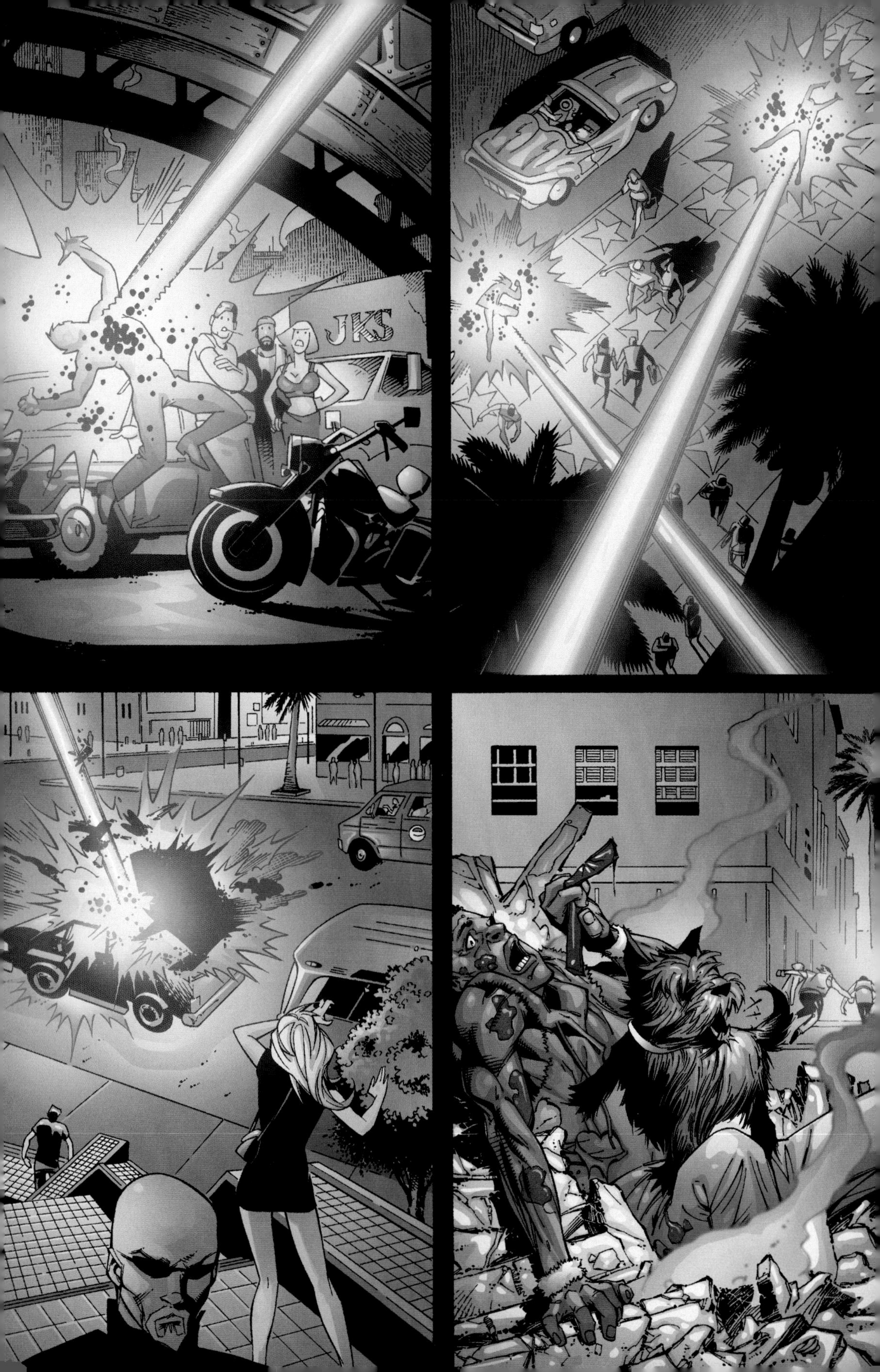
JKS

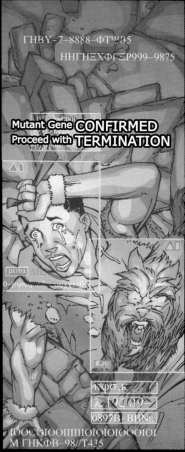

ГНВУ-7-8888-ФТᴪ95
НΗΓΗΕΧФΓΞΡ999-9875

**Mutant Gene CONFIRMED
Proceed with TERMINATION**

Κφσ.κ
λ.19./99
0897B-BBNε
Ι00Ϲ0Ι00ΙΙΙΙΙΟΙΟΙΟΟΟΙΟΙ
М ΓΗΚФΒ-98//Т435

CRUNCH

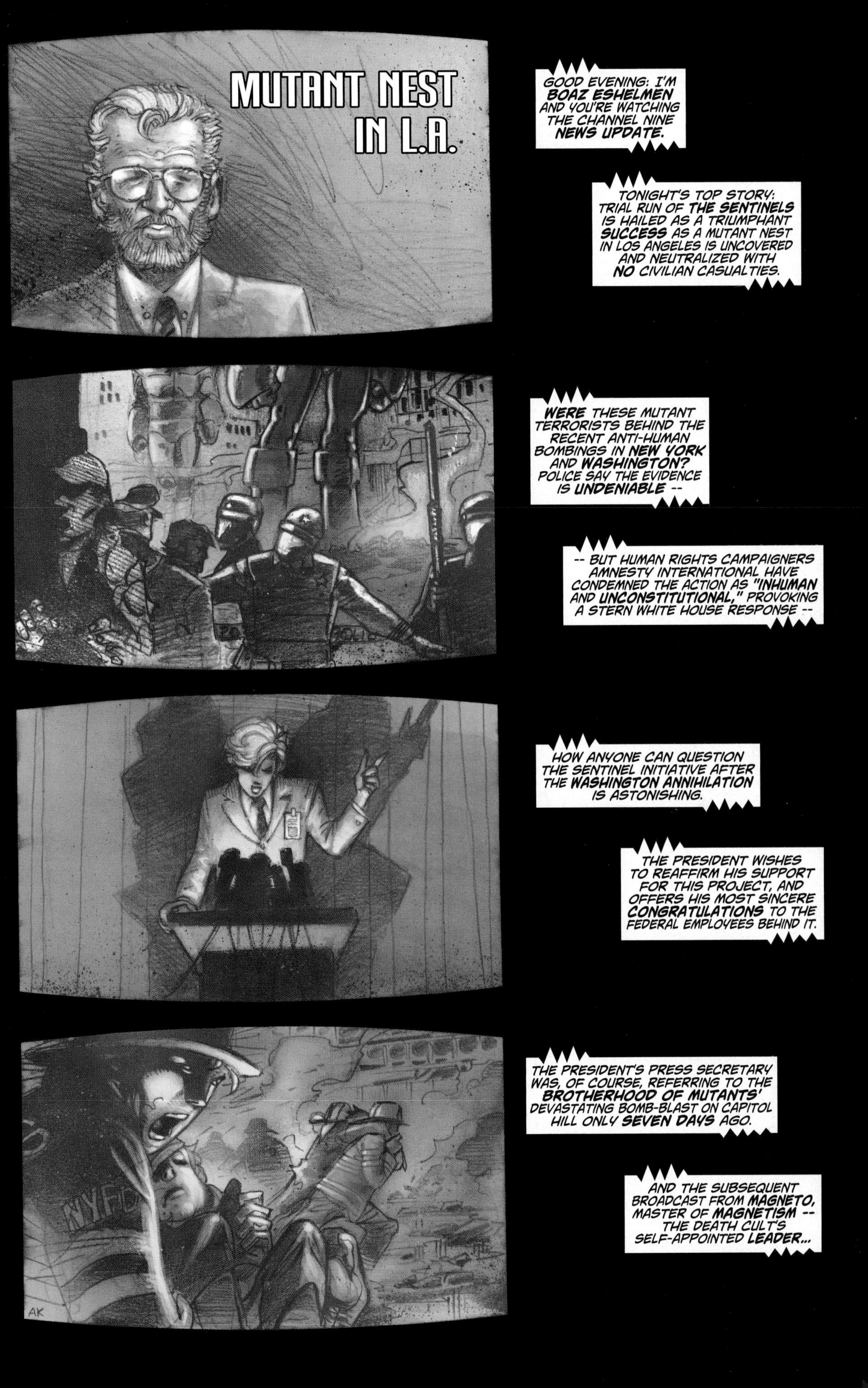

MUTANT NEST IN L.A.
GOOD EVENING: I'M BOAZ ESHELMEN AND YOU'RE WATCHING THE CHANNEL NINE NEWS UPDATE.
TONIGHT'S TOP STORY: TRIAL RUN OF THE SENTINELS IS HAILED AS A TRIUMPHANT SUCCESS AS A MUTANT NEST IN LOS ANGELES IS UNCOVERED AND NEUTRALIZED WITH NO CIVILIAN CASUALTIES.
WERE THESE MUTANT TERRORISTS BEHIND THE RECENT ANTI-HUMAN BOMBINGS IN NEW YORK AND WASHINGTON? POLICE SAY THE EVIDENCE IS UNDENIABLE --
-- BUT HUMAN RIGHTS CAMPAIGNERS AMNESTY INTERNATIONAL HAVE CONDEMNED THE ACTION AS "INHUMAN AND UNCONSTITUTIONAL," PROVOKING A STERN WHITE HOUSE RESPONSE --
HOW ANYONE CAN QUESTION THE SENTINEL INITIATIVE AFTER THE WASHINGTON ANNIHILATION IS ASTONISHING.
THE PRESIDENT WISHES TO REAFFIRM HIS SUPPORT FOR THIS PROJECT, AND OFFERS HIS MOST SINCERE CONGRATULATIONS TO THE FEDERAL EMPLOYEES BEHIND IT.
THE PRESIDENT'S PRESS SECRETARY WAS, OF COURSE, REFERRING TO THE BROTHERHOOD OF MUTANTS' DEVASTATING BOMB-BLAST ON CAPITOL HILL ONLY SEVEN DAYS AGO.
AND THE SUBSEQUENT BROADCAST FROM MAGNETO, MASTER OF MAGNETISM -- THE DEATH CULT'S SELF-APPOINTED LEADER...
NYFD
AK

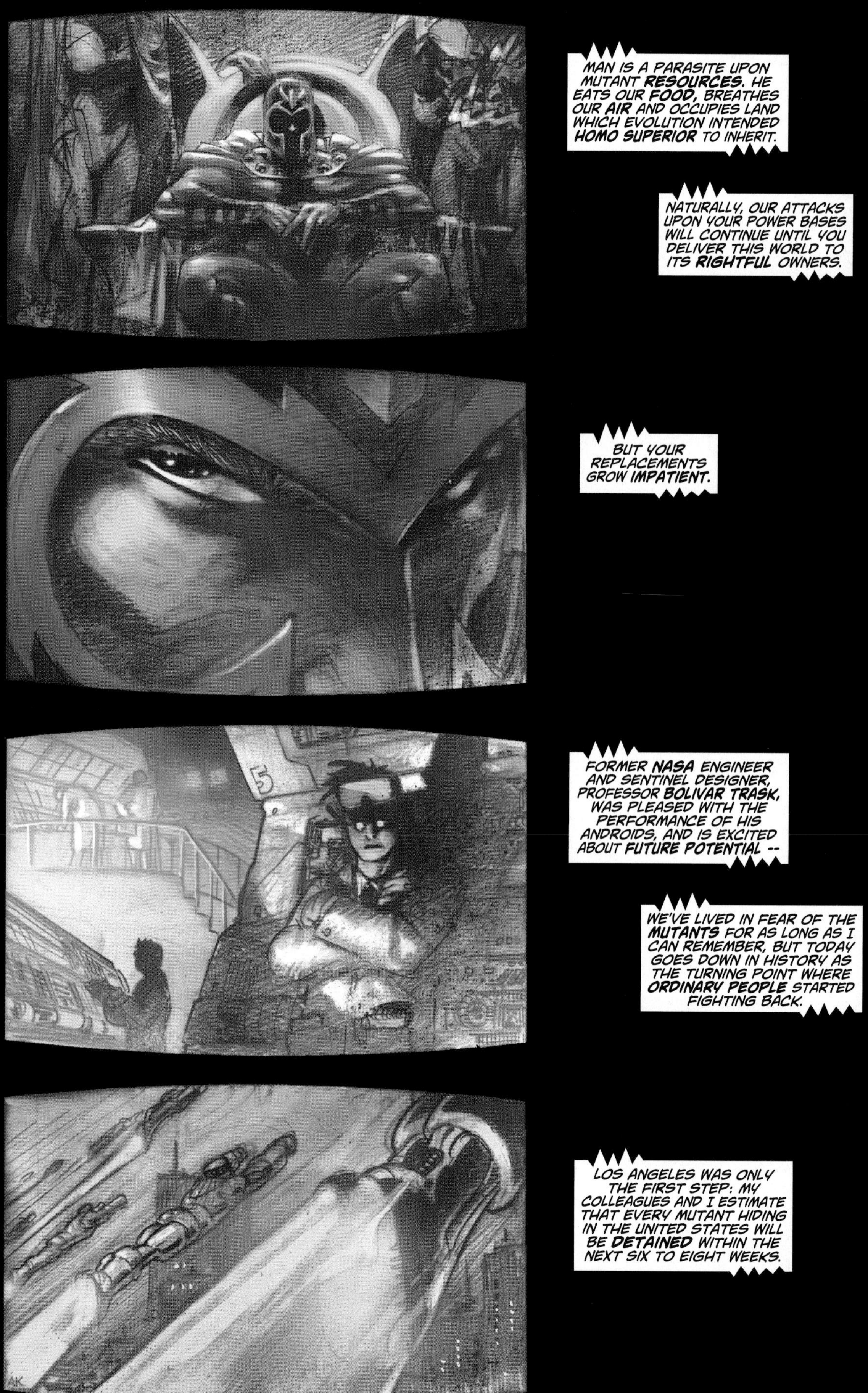
MAN IS A PARASITE UPON MUTANT RESOURCES. HE EATS OUR FOOD, BREATHES OUR AIR AND OCCUPIES LAND WHICH EVOLUTION INTENDED HOMO SUPERIOR TO INHERIT.
NATURALLY, OUR ATTACKS UPON YOUR POWER BASES WILL CONTINUE UNTIL YOU DELIVER THIS WORLD TO ITS RIGHTFUL OWNERS.
BUT YOUR REPLACEMENTS GROW IMPATIENT.
5
FORMER NASA ENGINEER AND SENTINEL DESIGNER, PROFESSOR BOLIVAR TRASK, WAS PLEASED WITH THE PERFORMANCE OF HIS ANDROIDS, AND IS EXCITED ABOUT FUTURE POTENTIAL --
WE'VE LIVED IN FEAR OF THE MUTANTS FOR AS LONG AS I CAN REMEMBER, BUT TODAY GOES DOWN IN HISTORY AS THE TURNING POINT WHERE ORDINARY PEOPLE STARTED FIGHTING BACK.
LOS ANGELES WAS ONLY THE FIRST STEP: MY COLLEAGUES AND I ESTIMATE THAT EVERY MUTANT HIDING IN THE UNITED STATES WILL BE DETAINED WITHIN THE NEXT SIX TO EIGHT WEEKS.

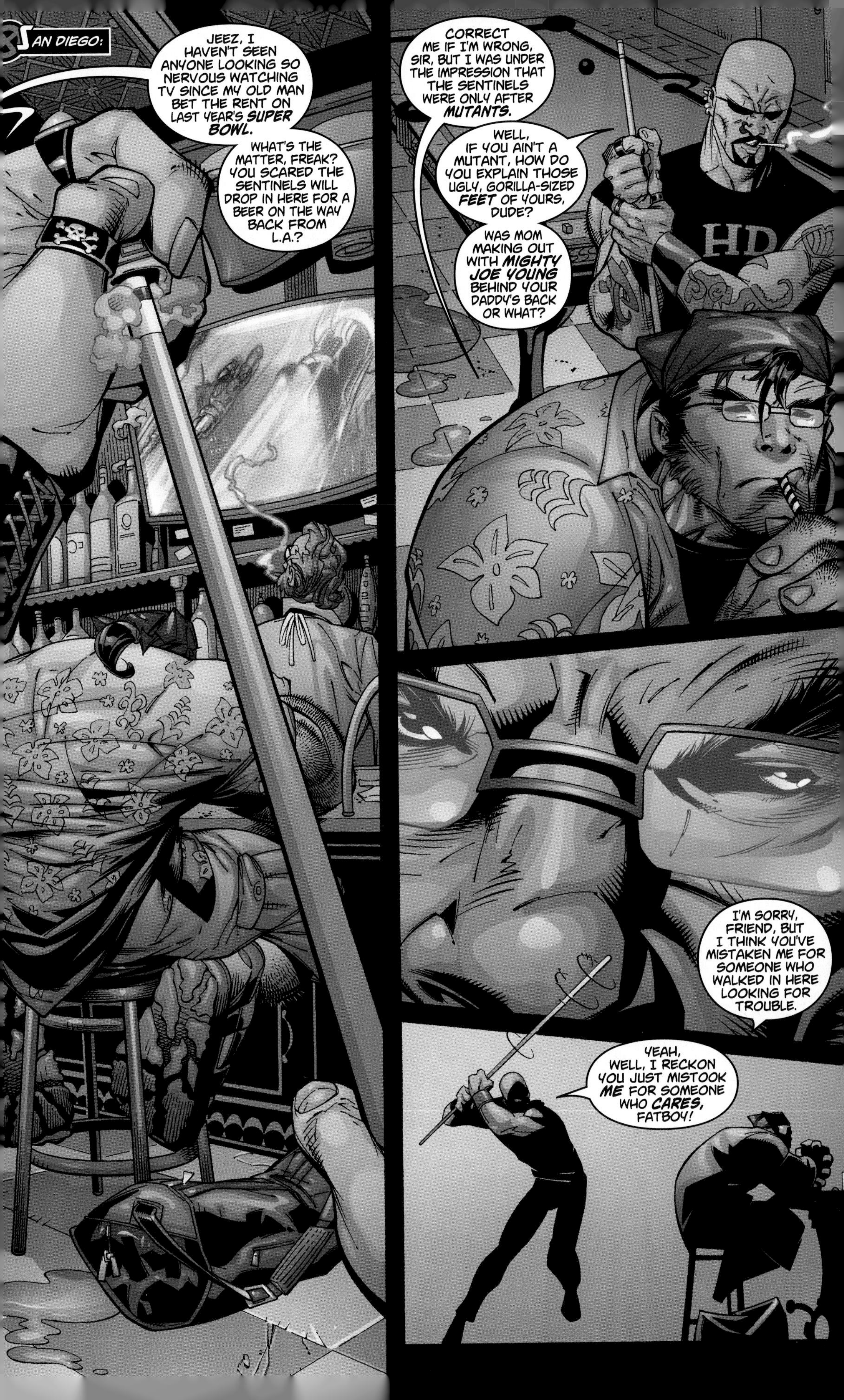
SAN DIEGO:
JEEZ, I HAVEN'T SEEN ANYONE LOOKING SO NERVOUS WATCHING TV SINCE MY OLD MAN BET THE RENT ON LAST YEAR'S SUPER BOWL.
WHAT'S THE MATTER, FREAK? YOU SCARED THE SENTINELS WILL DROP IN HERE FOR A BEER ON THE WAY BACK FROM L.A.?
CORRECT ME IF I'M WRONG, SIR, BUT I WAS UNDER THE IMPRESSION THAT THE SENTINELS WERE ONLY AFTER MUTANTS.
WELL, IF YOU AIN'T A MUTANT, HOW DO YOU EXPLAIN THOSE UGLY, GORILLA-SIZED FEET OF YOURS, DUDE?
WAS MOM MAKING OUT WITH MIGHTY JOE YOUNG BEHIND YOUR DADDY'S BACK OR WHAT?
HD
I'M SORRY, FRIEND, BUT I THINK YOU'VE MISTAKEN ME FOR SOMEONE WHO WALKED IN HERE LOOKING FOR TROUBLE.
YEAH, WELL, I RECKON YOU JUST MISTOOK ME FOR SOMEONE WHO CARES, FATBOY!

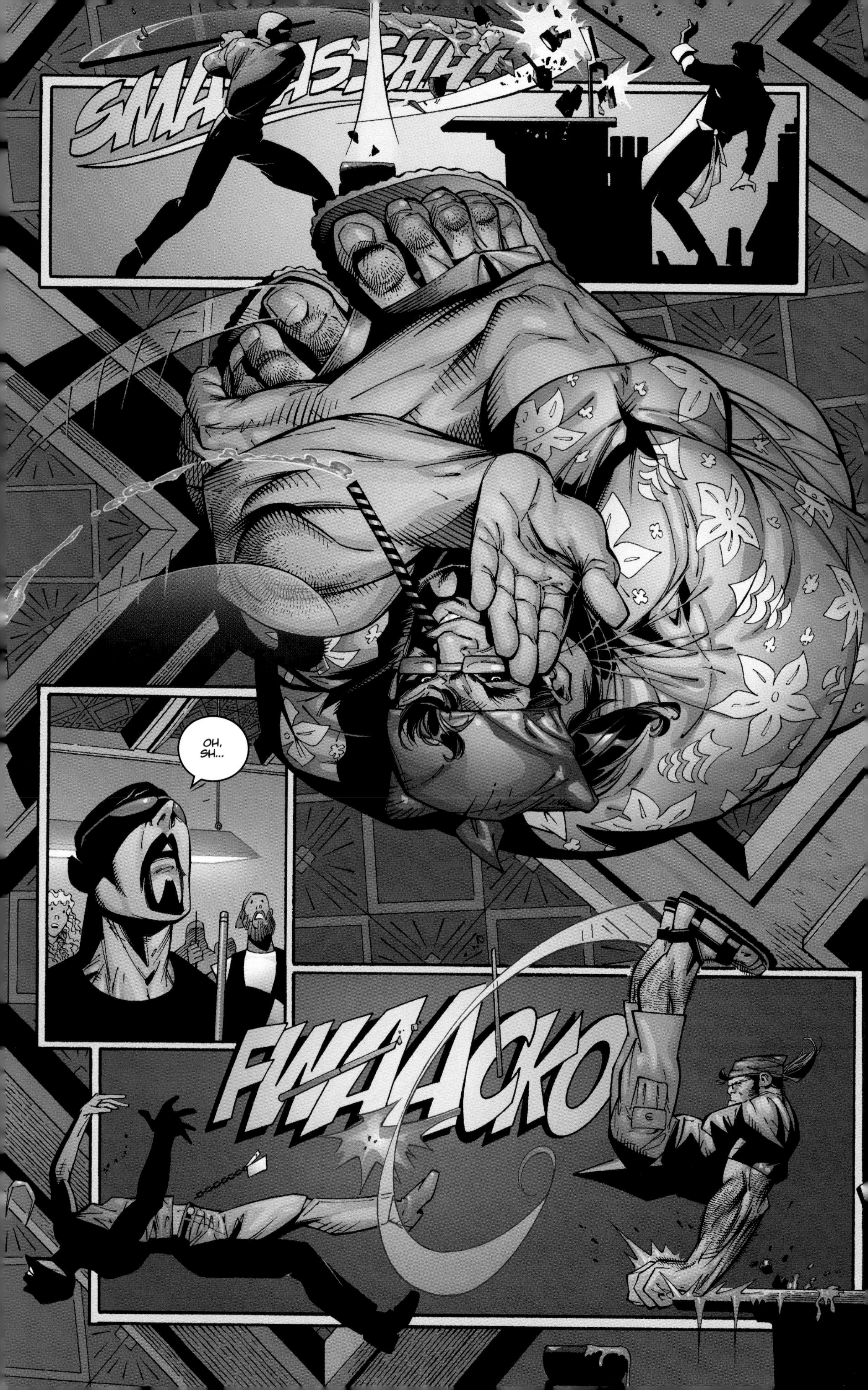
SMASHSHH!
OH, SH...
FWHACKO

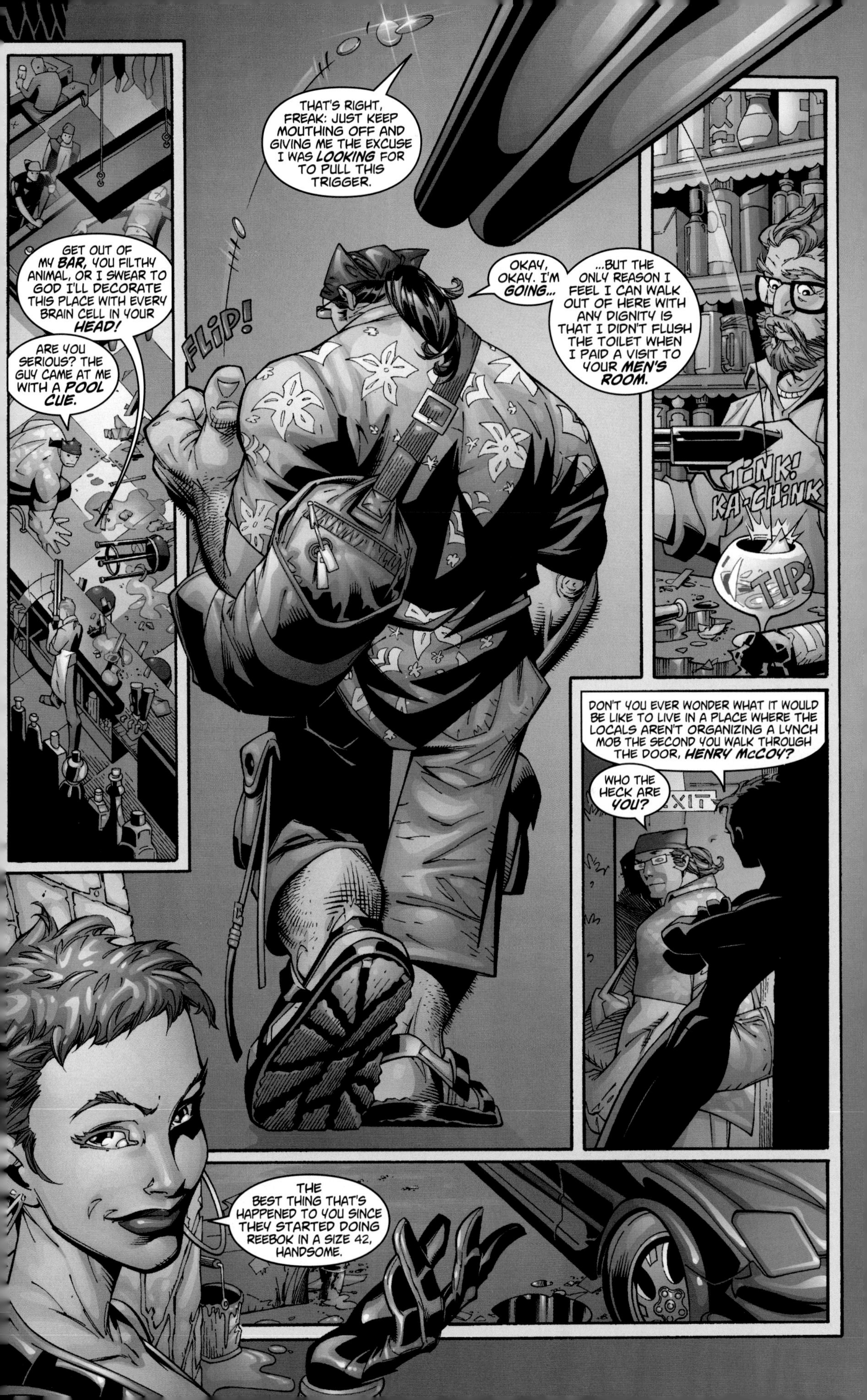

THAT'S RIGHT, FREAK: JUST KEEP MOUTHING OFF AND GIVING ME THE EXCUSE I WAS LOOKING FOR TO PULL THIS TRIGGER.
GET OUT OF MY BAR, YOU FILTHY ANIMAL, OR I SWEAR TO GOD I'LL DECORATE THIS PLACE WITH EVERY BRAIN CELL IN YOUR HEAD!
ARE YOU SERIOUS? THE GUY CAME AT ME WITH A POOL CUE.
FLIP!
OKAY, OKAY. I'M GOING...
...BUT THE ONLY REASON I FEEL I CAN WALK OUT OF HERE WITH ANY DIGNITY IS THAT I DIDN'T FLUSH THE TOILET WHEN I PAID A VISIT TO YOUR MEN'S ROOM.
TINK!
KA-CHINK
TIP
DON'T YOU EVER WONDER WHAT IT WOULD BE LIKE TO LIVE IN A PLACE WHERE THE LOCALS AREN'T ORGANIZING A LYNCH MOB THE SECOND YOU WALK THROUGH THE DOOR, HENRY McCOY?
WHO THE HECK ARE YOU?
THE BEST THING THAT'S HAPPENED TO YOU SINCE THEY STARTED DOING REEBOK IN A SIZE 42, HANDSOME.

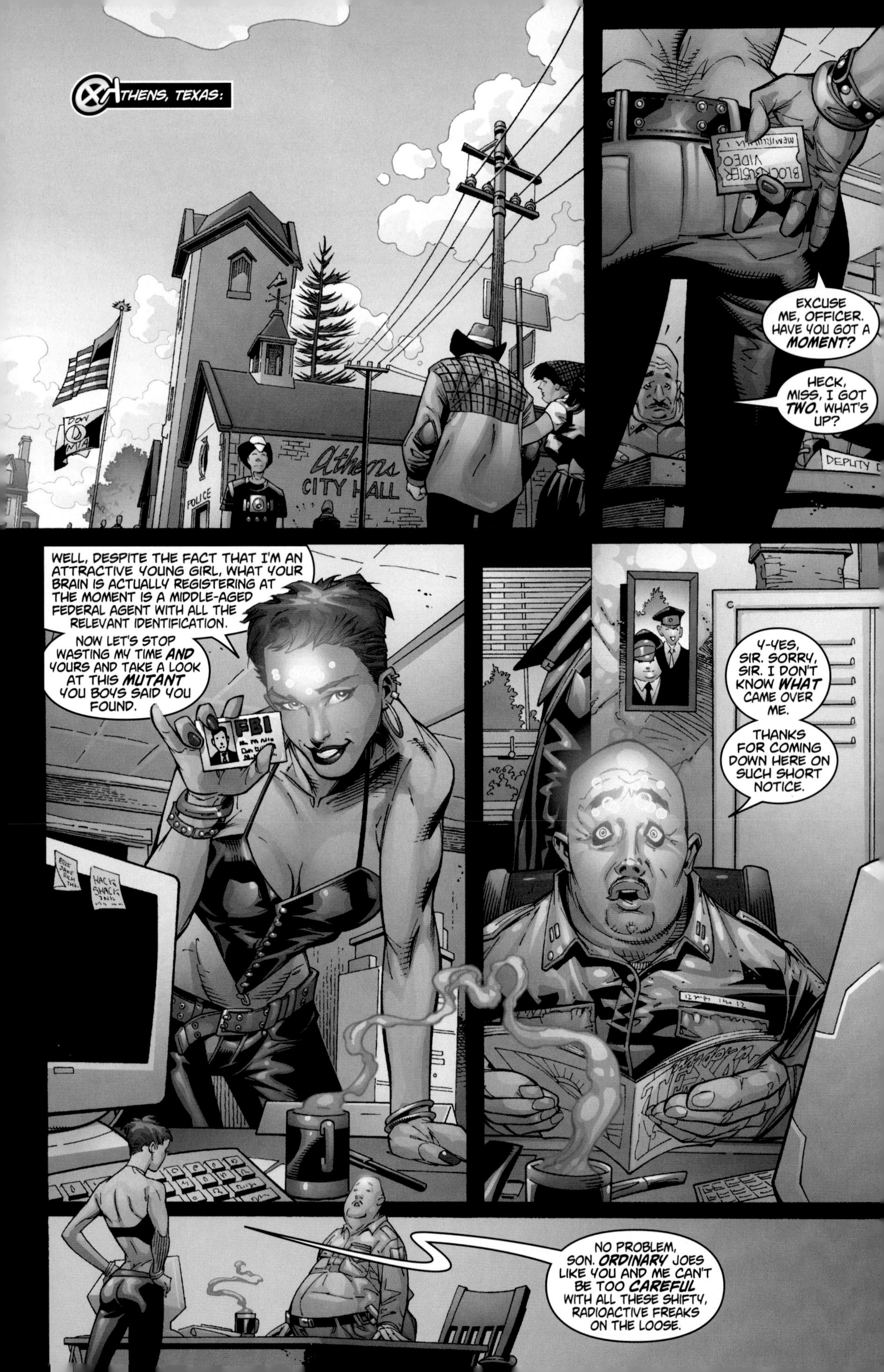
ATHENS, TEXAS:
ATHENS CITY HALL
POLICE
BLOCKBUSTER VIDEO
MEMBERSHIP
EXCUSE ME, OFFICER. HAVE YOU GOT A MOMENT?
HECK, MISS, I GOT TWO. WHAT'S UP?
DEPUTY
WELL, DESPITE THE FACT THAT I'M AN ATTRACTIVE YOUNG GIRL, WHAT YOUR BRAIN IS ACTUALLY REGISTERING AT THE MOMENT IS A MIDDLE-AGED FEDERAL AGENT WITH ALL THE RELEVANT IDENTIFICATION.
NOW LET'S STOP WASTING MY TIME AND YOURS AND TAKE A LOOK AT THIS MUTANT YOU BOYS SAID YOU FOUND.
FBI
Y-YES, SIR. SORRY, SIR. I DON'T KNOW WHAT CAME OVER ME.
THANKS FOR COMING DOWN HERE ON SUCH SHORT NOTICE.
HACK SHACK
NO PROBLEM, SON. ORDINARY JOES LIKE YOU AND ME CAN'T BE TOO CAREFUL WITH ALL THESE SHIFTY, RADIOACTIVE FREAKS ON THE LOOSE.

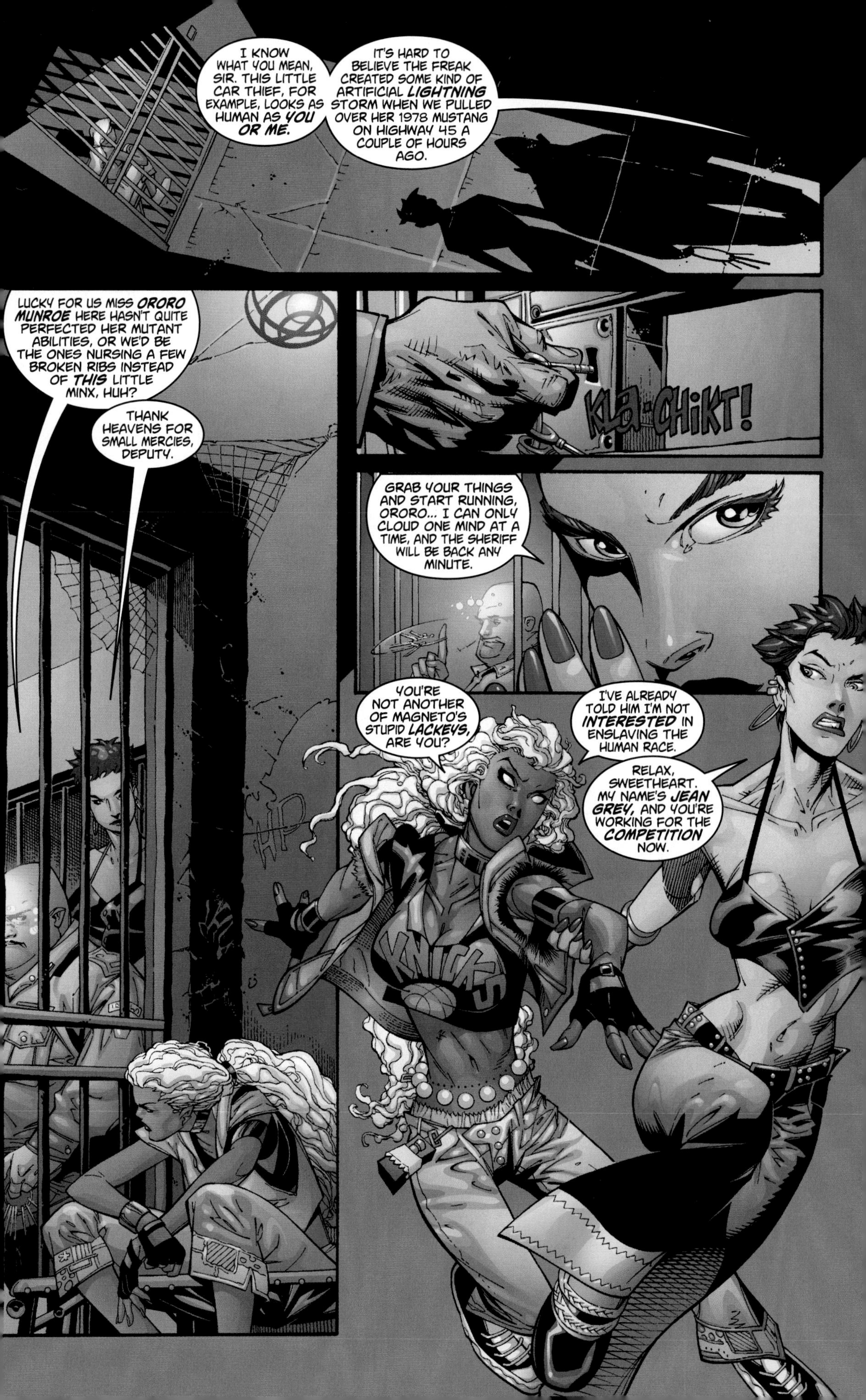

I KNOW WHAT YOU MEAN, SIR. THIS LITTLE CAR THIEF, FOR EXAMPLE, LOOKS AS HUMAN AS *YOU OR ME.*
IT'S HARD TO BELIEVE THE FREAK CREATED SOME KIND OF ARTIFICIAL *LIGHTNING* STORM WHEN WE PULLED OVER HER 1978 MUSTANG ON HIGHWAY 45 A COUPLE OF HOURS AGO.
LUCKY FOR US MISS *ORORO MUNROE* HERE HASN'T QUITE PERFECTED HER MUTANT ABILITIES, OR WE'D BE THE ONES NURSING A FEW BROKEN RIBS INSTEAD OF *THIS* LITTLE MINX, HUH?
THANK HEAVENS FOR SMALL MERCIES, DEPUTY.
KLA-CHIKT!
GRAB YOUR THINGS AND START RUNNING, ORORO... I CAN ONLY CLOUD ONE MIND AT A TIME, AND THE SHERIFF WILL BE BACK ANY MINUTE.
YOU'RE NOT ANOTHER OF MAGNETO'S STUPID *LACKEYS,* ARE YOU?
I'VE ALREADY TOLD HIM I'M NOT *INTERESTED* IN ENSLAVING THE HUMAN RACE.
RELAX, SWEETHEART. MY NAME'S *JEAN GREY,* AND YOU'RE WORKING FOR THE *COMPETITION* NOW.

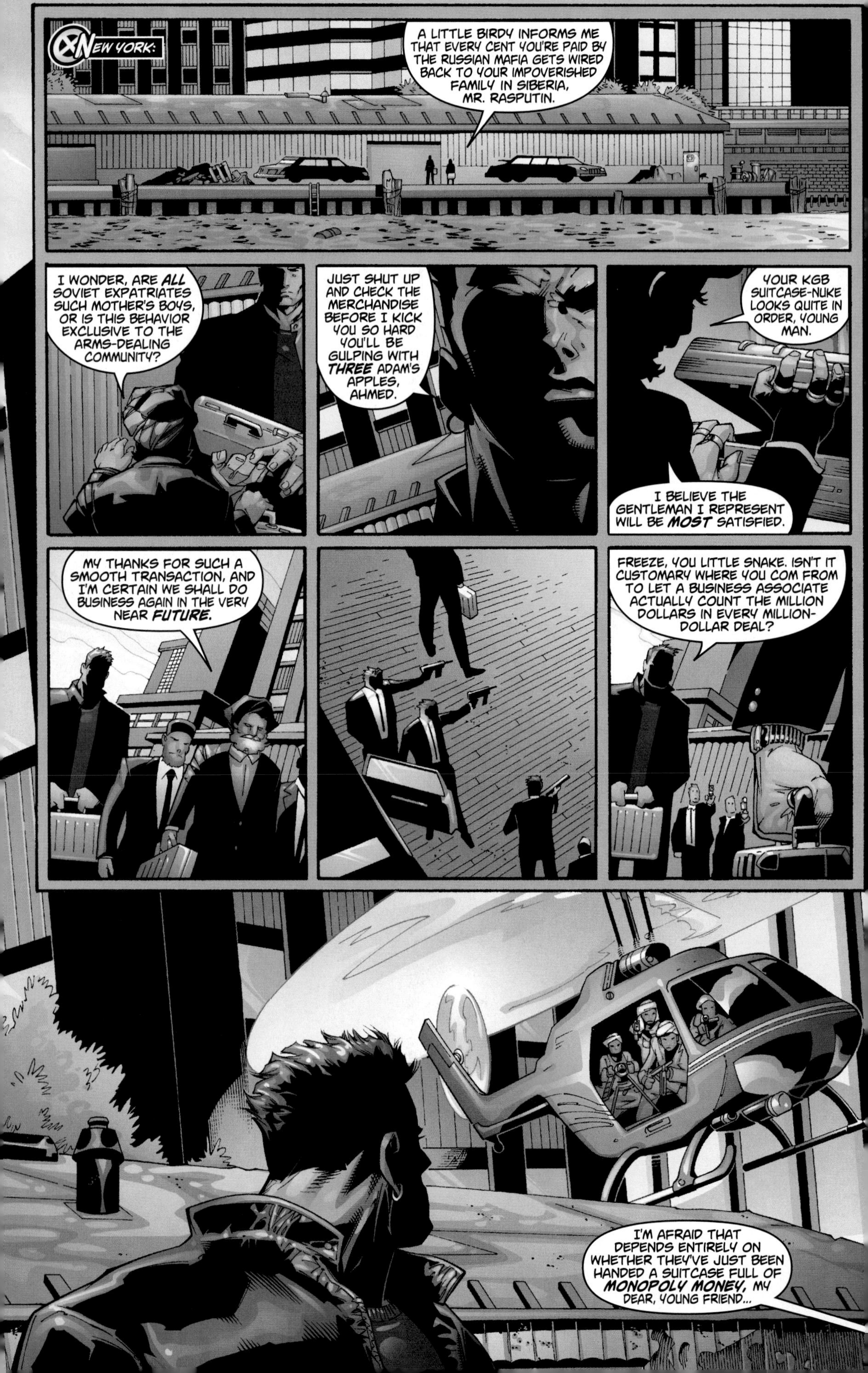
NEW YORK:
A LITTLE BIRDY INFORMS ME THAT EVERY CENT YOU'RE PAID BY THE RUSSIAN MAFIA GETS WIRED BACK TO YOUR IMPOVERISHED FAMILY IN SIBERIA, MR. RASPUTIN.
I WONDER, ARE ALL SOVIET EXPATRIATES SUCH MOTHER'S BOYS, OR IS THIS BEHAVIOR EXCLUSIVE TO THE ARMS-DEALING COMMUNITY?
JUST SHUT UP AND CHECK THE MERCHANDISE BEFORE I KICK YOU SO HARD YOU'LL BE GULPING WITH THREE ADAM'S APPLES, AHMED.
YOUR KGB SUITCASE-NUKE LOOKS QUITE IN ORDER, YOUNG MAN.
I BELIEVE THE GENTLEMAN I REPRESENT WILL BE MOST SATISFIED.
MY THANKS FOR SUCH A SMOOTH TRANSACTION, AND I'M CERTAIN WE SHALL DO BUSINESS AGAIN IN THE VERY NEAR FUTURE.
FREEZE, YOU LITTLE SNAKE. ISN'T IT CUSTOMARY WHERE YOU COM FROM TO LET A BUSINESS ASSOCIATE ACTUALLY COUNT THE MILLION DOLLARS IN EVERY MILLION-DOLLAR DEAL?
I'M AFRAID THAT DEPENDS ENTIRELY ON WHETHER THEY'VE JUST BEEN HANDED A SUITCASE FULL OF MONOPOLY MONEY, MY DEAR, YOUNG FRIEND...

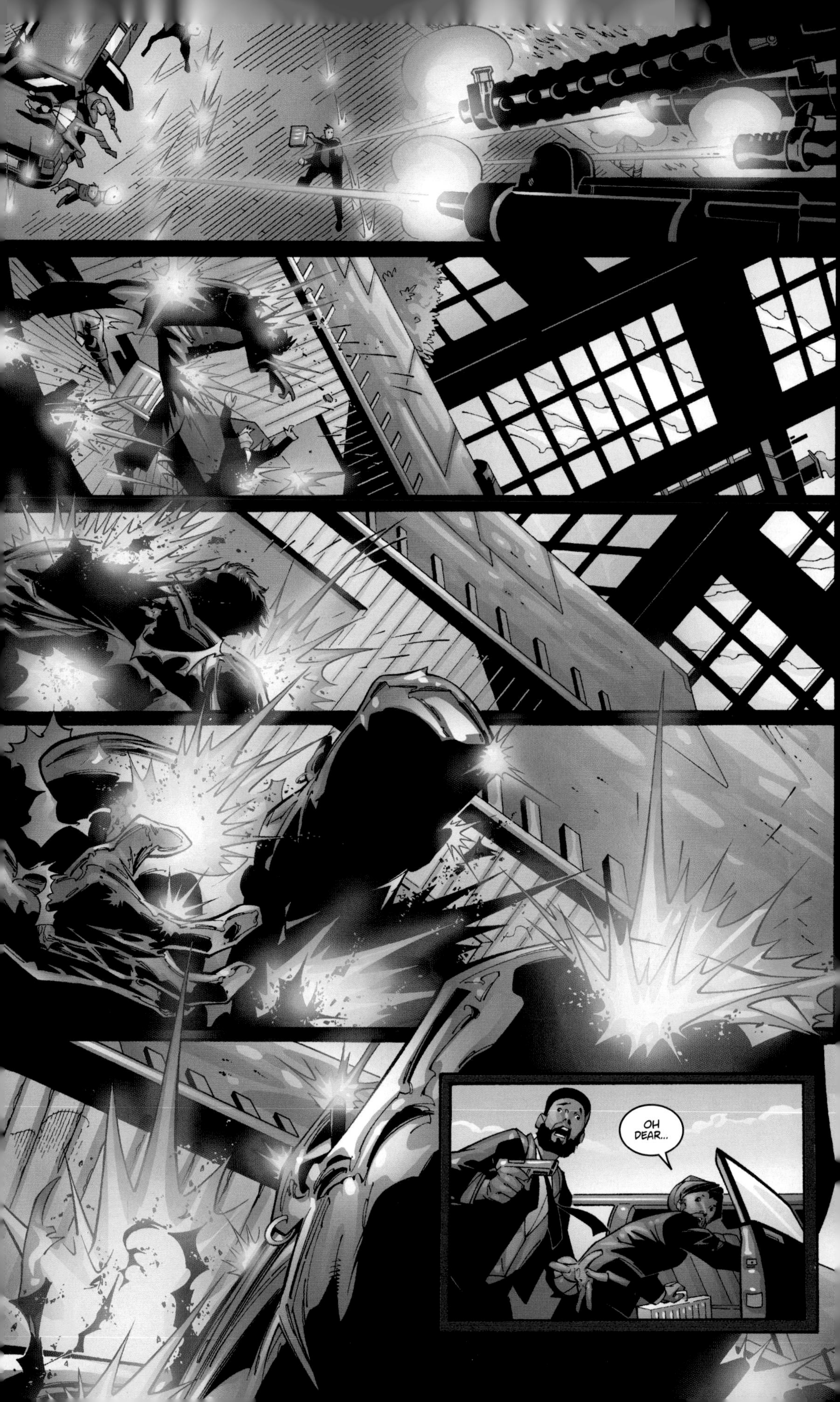
OH DEAR...

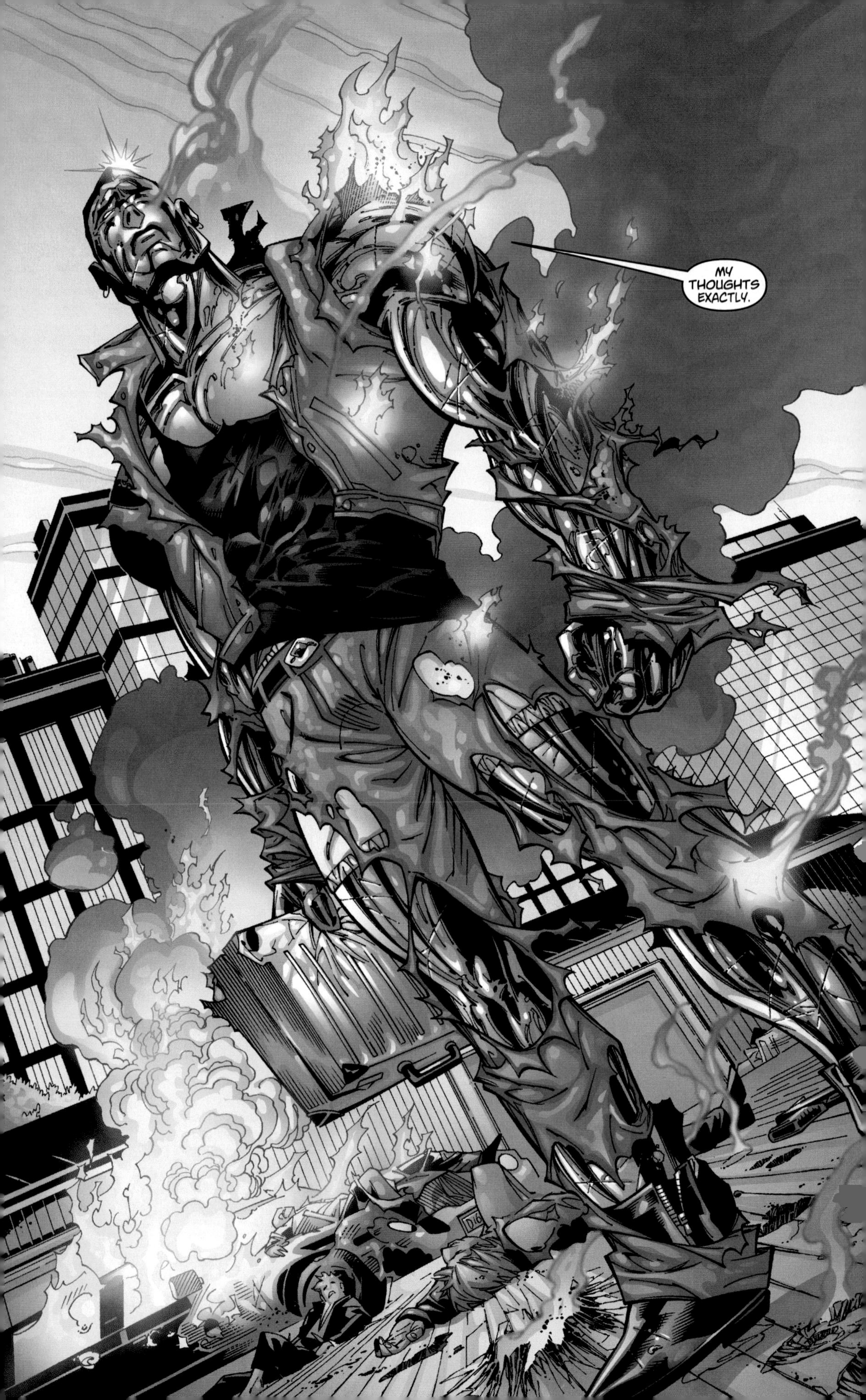
MY THOUGHTS EXACTLY.

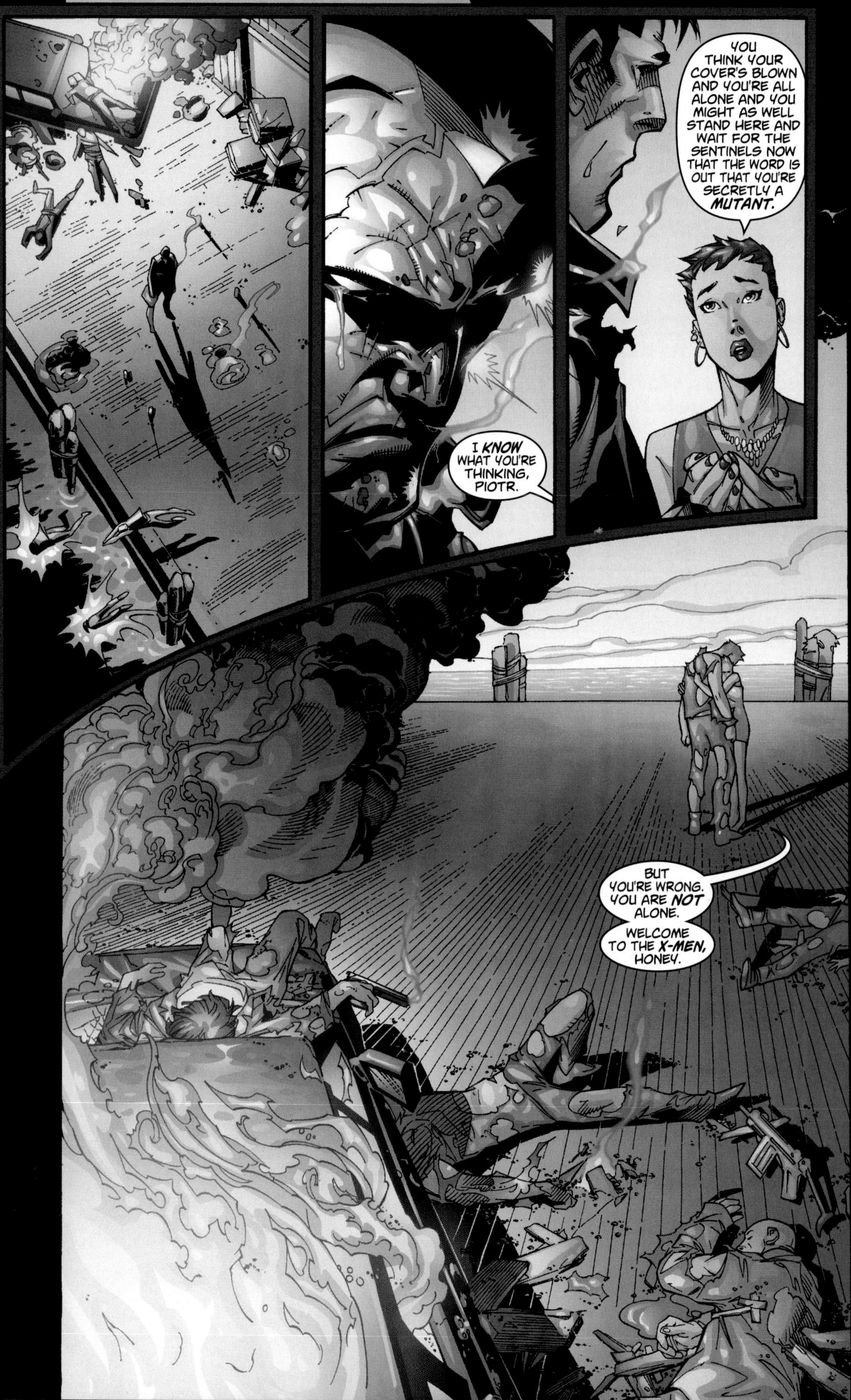
I KNOW WHAT YOU'RE THINKING, PIOTR.
YOU THINK YOUR COVER'S BLOWN AND YOU'RE ALL ALONE AND YOU MIGHT AS WELL STAND HERE AND WAIT FOR THE SENTINELS NOW THAT THE WORD IS OUT THAT YOU'RE SECRETLY A MUTANT.
BUT YOU'RE WRONG. YOU ARE NOT ALONE.
WELCOME TO THE X-MEN, HONEY.

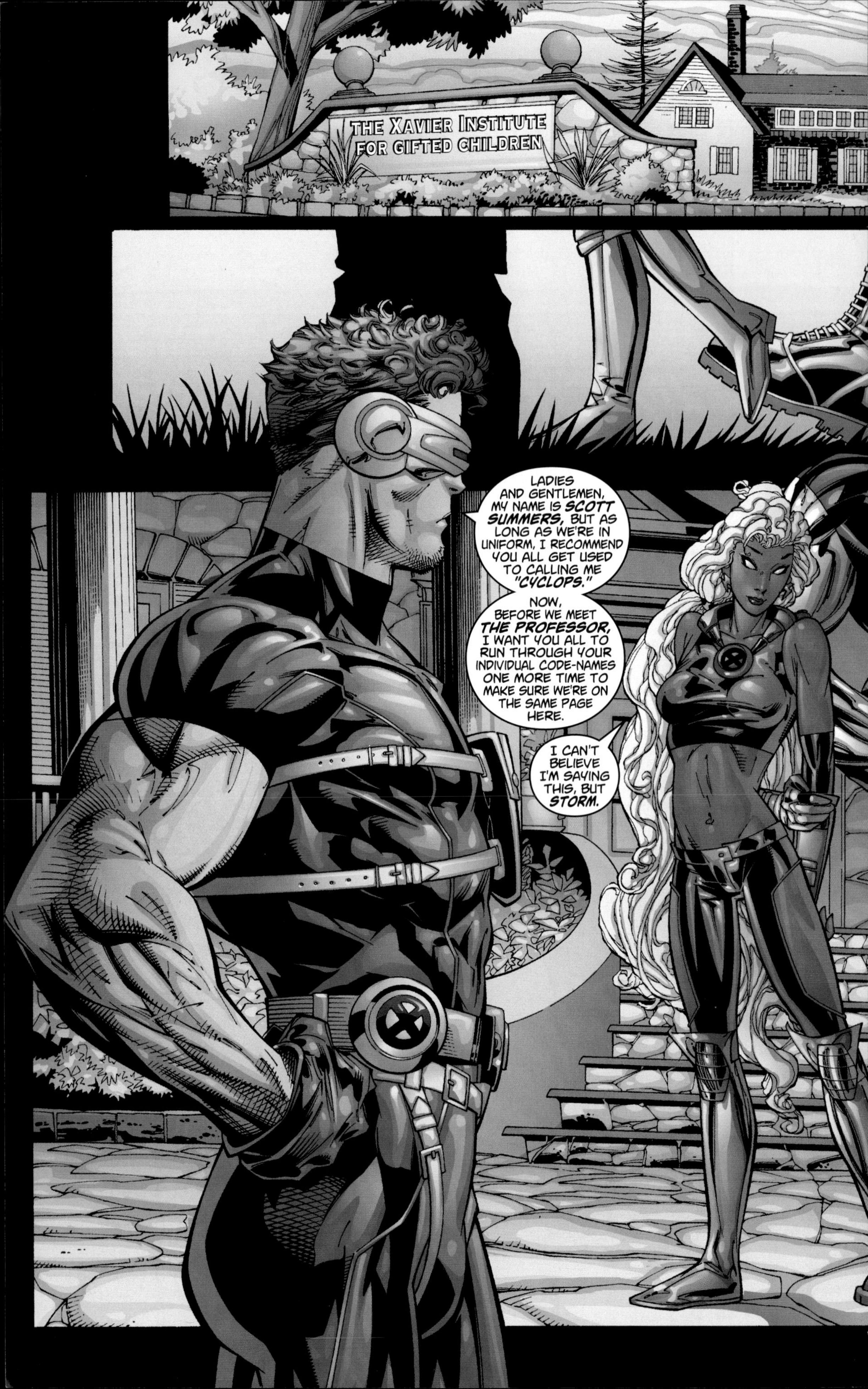
THE XAVIER INSTITUTE FOR GIFTED CHILDREN
LADIES AND GENTLEMEN, MY NAME IS SCOTT SUMMERS, BUT AS LONG AS WE'RE IN UNIFORM, I RECOMMEND YOU ALL GET USED TO CALLING ME "CYCLOPS."
NOW, BEFORE WE MEET THE PROFESSOR, I WANT YOU ALL TO RUN THROUGH YOUR INDIVIDUAL CODE-NAMES ONE MORE TIME TO MAKE SURE WE'RE ON THE SAME PAGE HERE.
I CAN'T BELIEVE I'M SAYING THIS, BUT STORM.

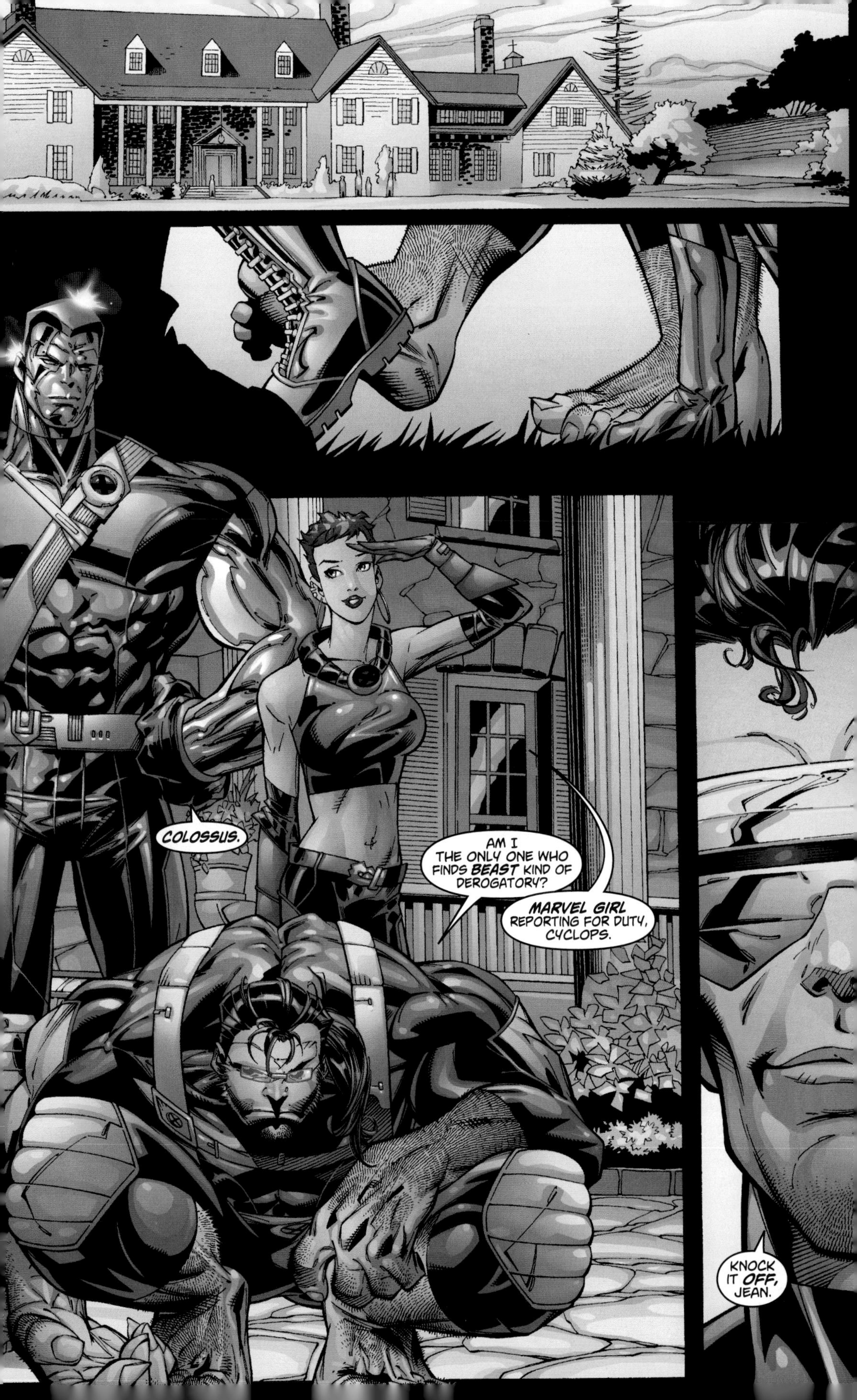
COLOSSUS.
AM I THE ONLY ONE WHO FINDS BEAST KIND OF DEROGATORY?
MARVEL GIRL REPORTING FOR DUTY, CYCLOPS.
KNOCK IT OFF, JEAN.

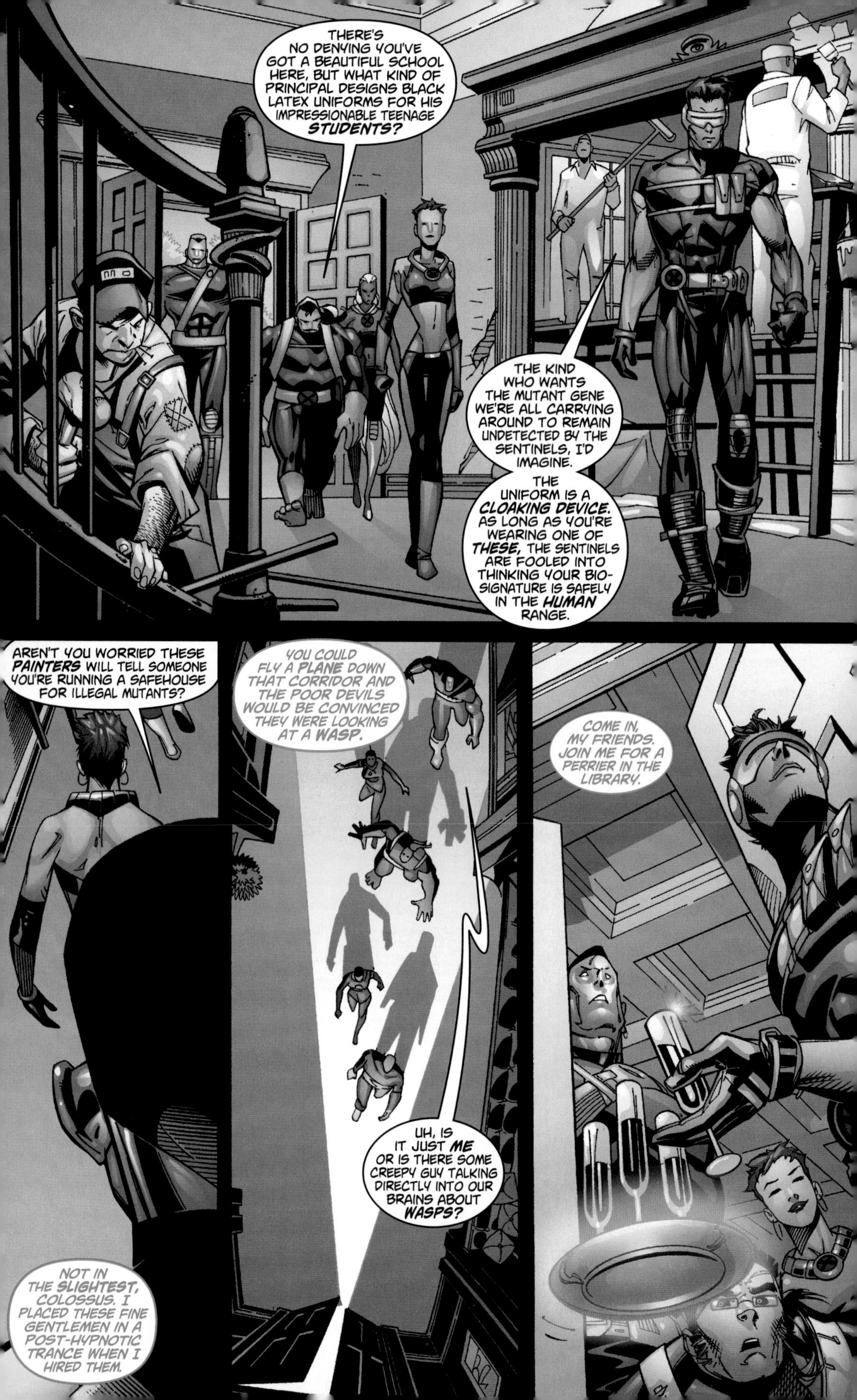
THERE'S NO DENYING YOU'VE GOT A BEAUTIFUL SCHOOL HERE, BUT WHAT KIND OF PRINCIPAL DESIGNS BLACK LATEX UNIFORMS FOR HIS IMPRESSIONABLE TEENAGE STUDENTS?
THE KIND WHO WANTS THE MUTANT GENE WE'RE ALL CARRYING AROUND TO REMAIN UNDETECTED BY THE SENTINELS, I'D IMAGINE.
THE UNIFORM IS A CLOAKING DEVICE. AS LONG AS YOU'RE WEARING ONE OF THESE, THE SENTINELS ARE FOOLED INTO THINKING YOUR BIO-SIGNATURE IS SAFELY IN THE HUMAN RANGE.
AREN'T YOU WORRIED THESE PAINTERS WILL TELL SOMEONE YOU'RE RUNNING A SAFEHOUSE FOR ILLEGAL MUTANTS?
NOT IN THE SLIGHTEST, COLOSSUS. I PLACED THESE FINE GENTLEMEN IN A POST-HYPNOTIC TRANCE WHEN I HIRED THEM.
YOU COULD FLY A PLANE DOWN THAT CORRIDOR AND THE POOR DEVILS WOULD BE CONVINCED THEY WERE LOOKING AT A WASP.
UH, IS IT JUST ME OR IS THERE SOME CREEPY GUY TALKING DIRECTLY INTO OUR BRAINS ABOUT WASPS?
COME IN, MY FRIENDS. JOIN ME FOR A PERRIER IN THE LIBRARY.

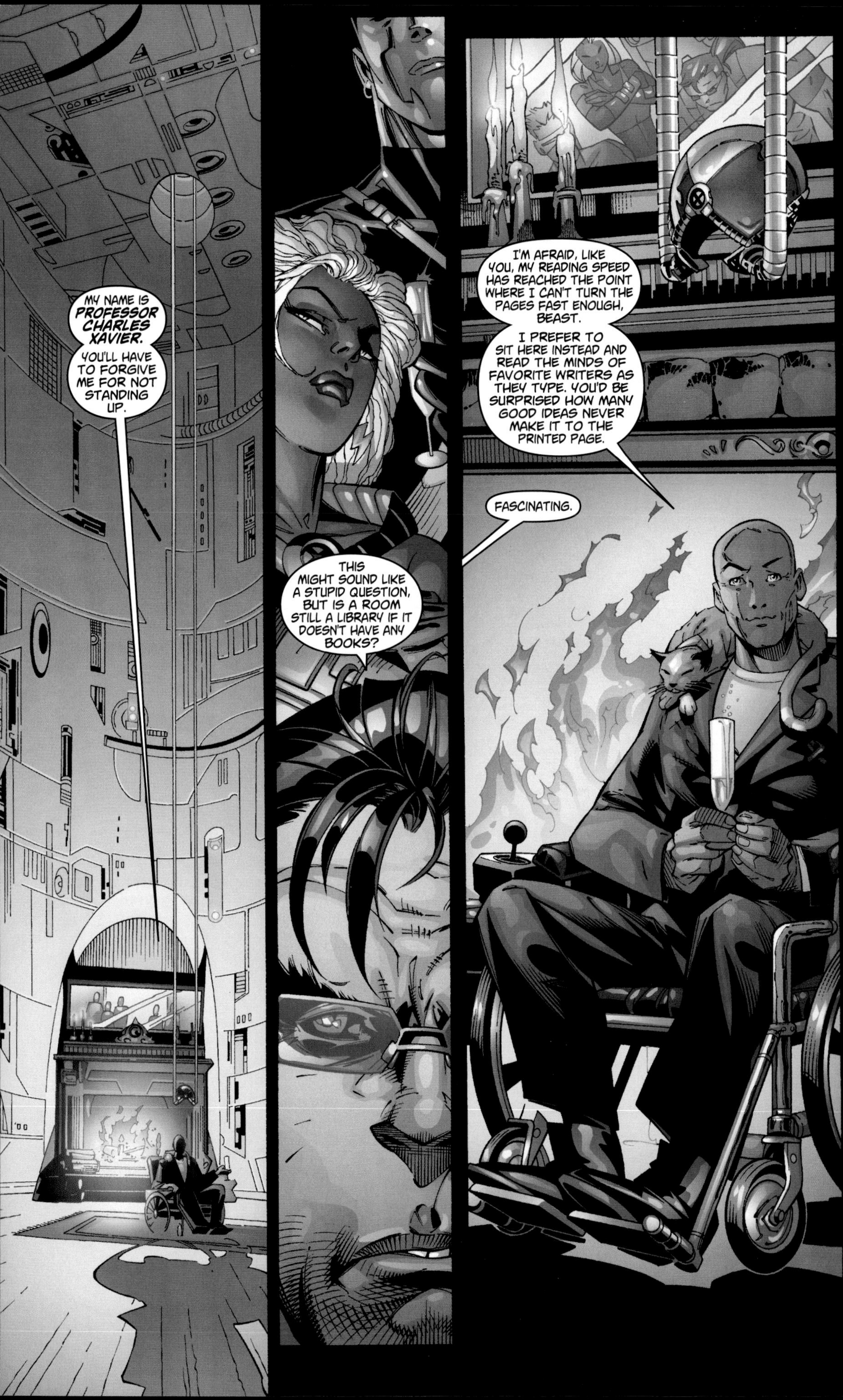
MY NAME IS PROFESSOR CHARLES XAVIER.
YOU'LL HAVE TO FORGIVE ME FOR NOT STANDING UP.
THIS MIGHT SOUND LIKE A STUPID QUESTION, BUT IS A ROOM STILL A LIBRARY IF IT DOESN'T HAVE ANY BOOKS?
FASCINATING.
I'M AFRAID, LIKE YOU, MY READING SPEED HAS REACHED THE POINT WHERE I CAN'T TURN THE PAGES FAST ENOUGH, BEAST.
I PREFER TO SIT HERE INSTEAD AND READ THE MINDS OF FAVORITE WRITERS AS THEY TYPE. YOU'D BE SURPRISED HOW MANY GOOD IDEAS NEVER MAKE IT TO THE PRINTED PAGE.

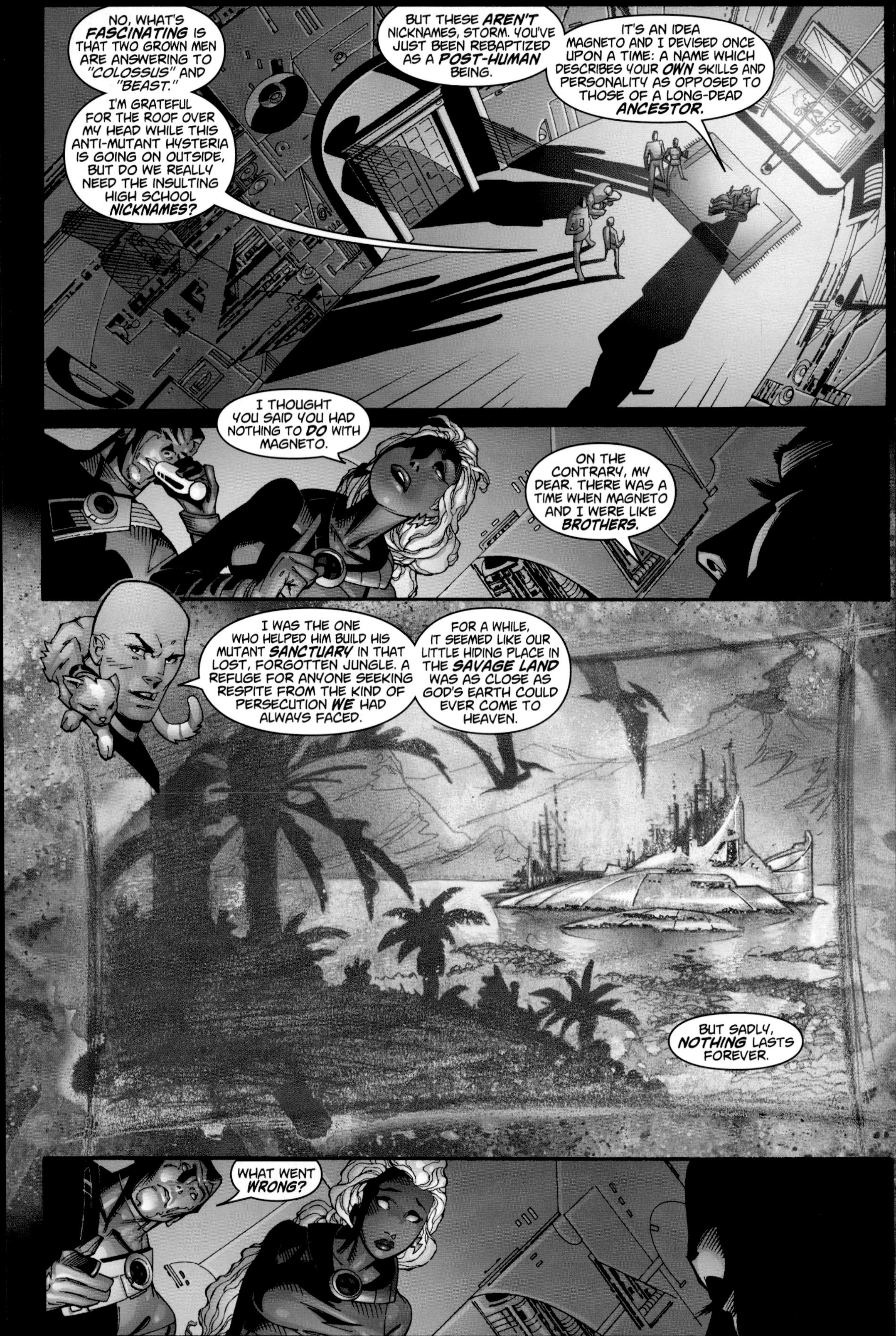
NO, WHAT'S FASCINATING IS THAT TWO GROWN MEN ARE ANSWERING TO "COLOSSUS" AND "BEAST."
I'M GRATEFUL FOR THE ROOF OVER MY HEAD WHILE THIS ANTI-MUTANT HYSTERIA IS GOING ON OUTSIDE, BUT DO WE REALLY NEED THE INSULTING HIGH SCHOOL NICKNAMES?
BUT THESE AREN'T NICKNAMES, STORM. YOU'VE JUST BEEN REBAPTIZED AS A POST-HUMAN BEING.
IT'S AN IDEA MAGNETO AND I DEVISED ONCE UPON A TIME: A NAME WHICH DESCRIBES YOUR OWN SKILLS AND PERSONALITY AS OPPOSED TO THOSE OF A LONG-DEAD ANCESTOR.
I THOUGHT YOU SAID YOU HAD NOTHING TO DO WITH MAGNETO.
ON THE CONTRARY, MY DEAR. THERE WAS A TIME WHEN MAGNETO AND I WERE LIKE BROTHERS.
I WAS THE ONE WHO HELPED HIM BUILD HIS MUTANT SANCTUARY IN THAT LOST, FORGOTTEN JUNGLE. A REFUGE FOR ANYONE SEEKING RESPITE FROM THE KIND OF PERSECUTION WE HAD ALWAYS FACED.
FOR A WHILE, IT SEEMED LIKE OUR LITTLE HIDING PLACE IN THE SAVAGE LAND WAS AS CLOSE AS GOD'S EARTH COULD EVER COME TO HEAVEN.
BUT SADLY, NOTHING LASTS FOREVER.
WHAT WENT WRONG?

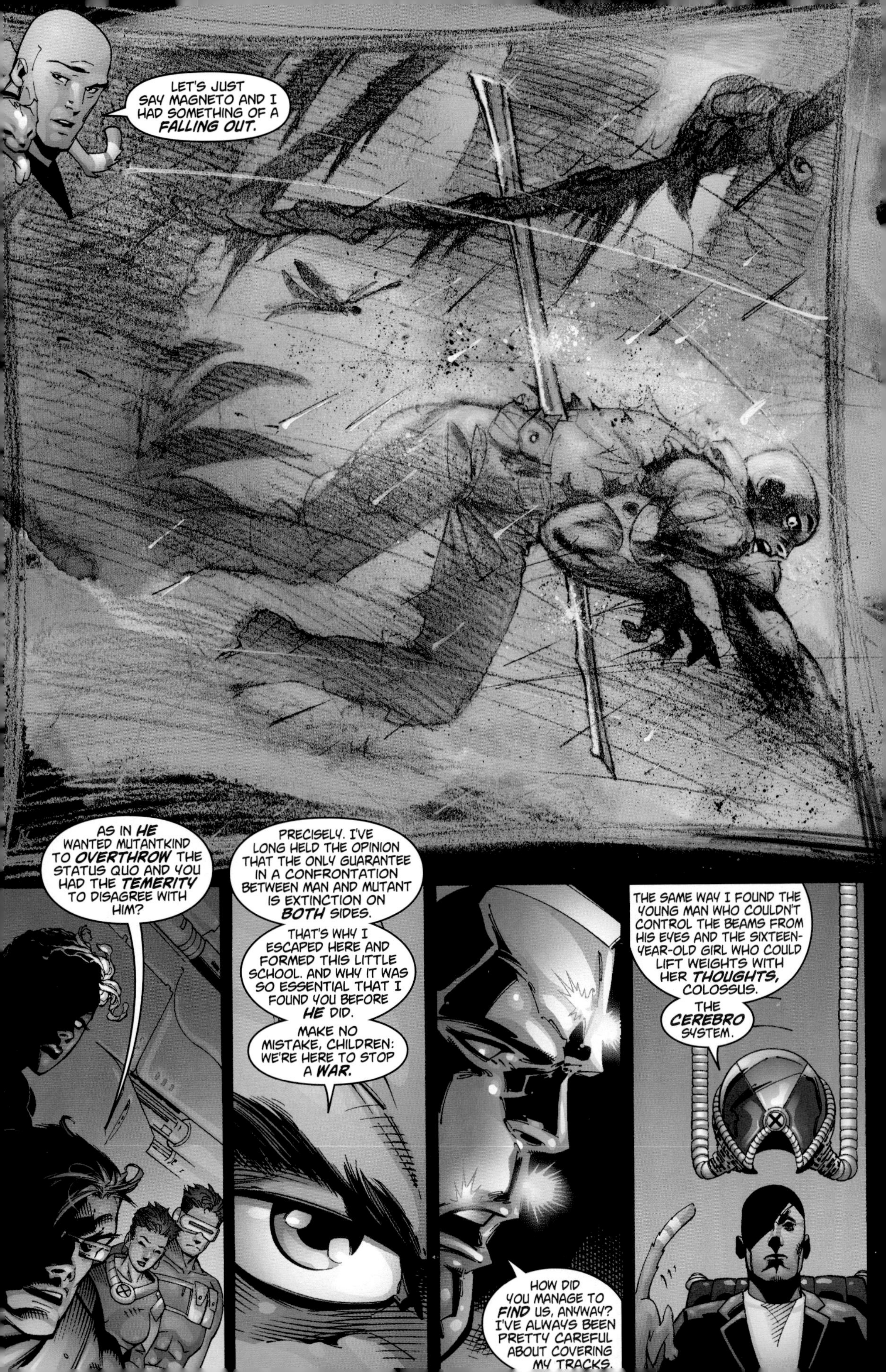
LET'S JUST SAY MAGNETO AND I HAD SOMETHING OF A FALLING OUT.
AS IN HE WANTED MUTANTKIND TO OVERTHROW THE STATUS QUO AND YOU HAD THE TEMERITY TO DISAGREE WITH HIM?
PRECISELY. I'VE LONG HELD THE OPINION THAT THE ONLY GUARANTEE IN A CONFRONTATION BETWEEN MAN AND MUTANT IS EXTINCTION ON BOTH SIDES.
THAT'S WHY I ESCAPED HERE AND FORMED THIS LITTLE SCHOOL. AND WHY IT WAS SO ESSENTIAL THAT I FOUND YOU BEFORE HE DID.
MAKE NO MISTAKE, CHILDREN: WE'RE HERE TO STOP A WAR.
HOW DID YOU MANAGE TO FIND US, ANYWAY? I'VE ALWAYS BEEN PRETTY CAREFUL ABOUT COVERING MY TRACKS.
THE SAME WAY I FOUND THE YOUNG MAN WHO COULDN'T CONTROL THE BEAMS FROM HIS EYES AND THE SIXTEEN-YEAR-OLD GIRL WHO COULD LIFT WEIGHTS WITH HER THOUGHTS, COLOSSUS.
THE CEREBRO SYSTEM.

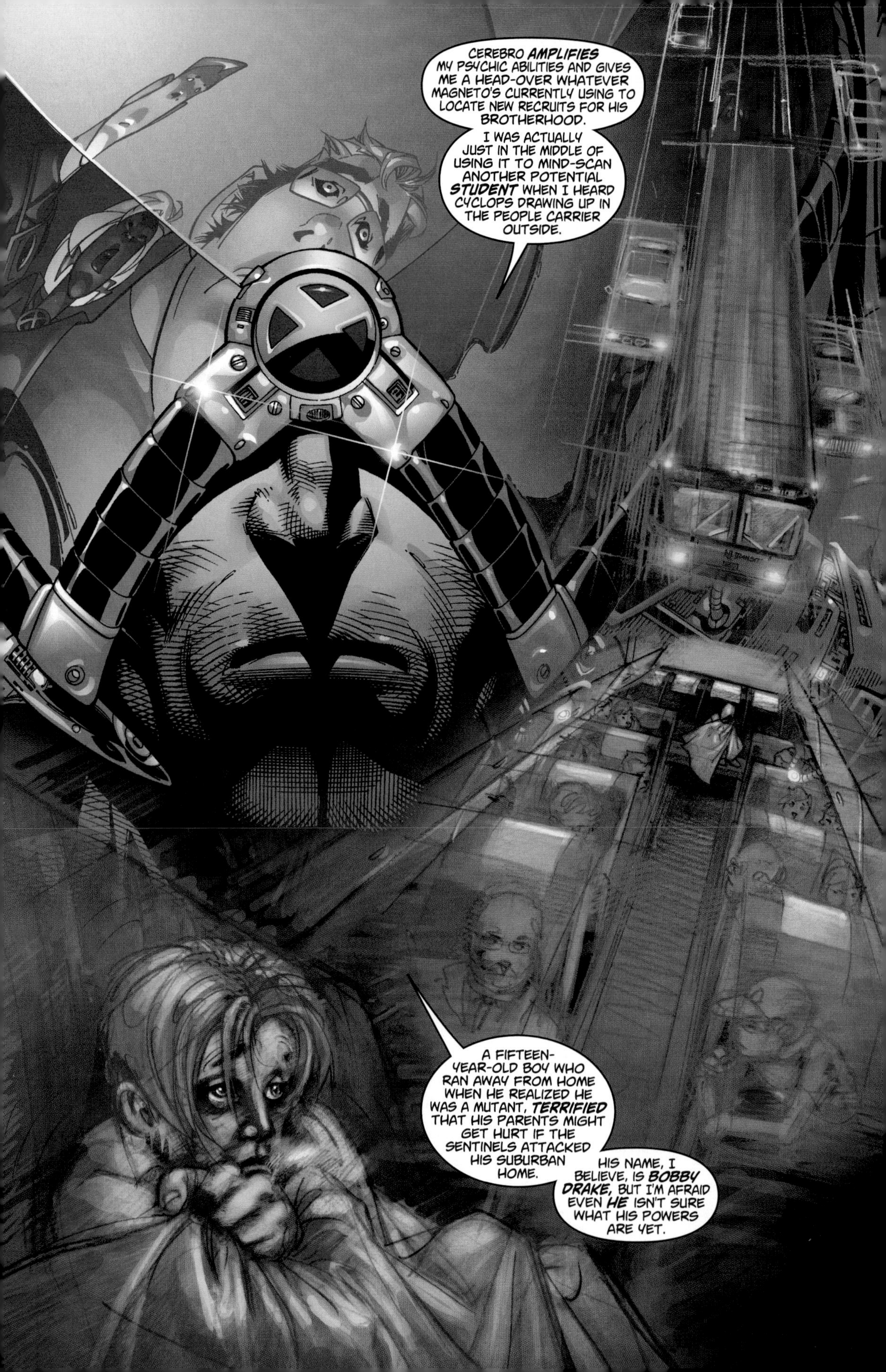
CEREBRO AMPLIFIES MY PSYCHIC ABILITIES AND GIVES ME A HEAD-OVER WHATEVER MAGNETO'S CURRENTLY USING TO LOCATE NEW RECRUITS FOR HIS BROTHERHOOD.
I WAS ACTUALLY JUST IN THE MIDDLE OF USING IT TO MIND-SCAN ANOTHER POTENTIAL STUDENT WHEN I HEARD CYCLOPS DRAWING UP IN THE PEOPLE CARRIER OUTSIDE.
A FIFTEEN-YEAR-OLD BOY WHO RAN AWAY FROM HOME WHEN HE REALIZED HE WAS A MUTANT, TERRIFIED THAT HIS PARENTS MIGHT GET HURT IF THE SENTINELS ATTACKED HIS SUBURBAN HOME.
HIS NAME, I BELIEVE, IS BOBBY DRAKE, BUT I'M AFRAID EVEN HE ISN'T SURE WHAT HIS POWERS ARE YET.

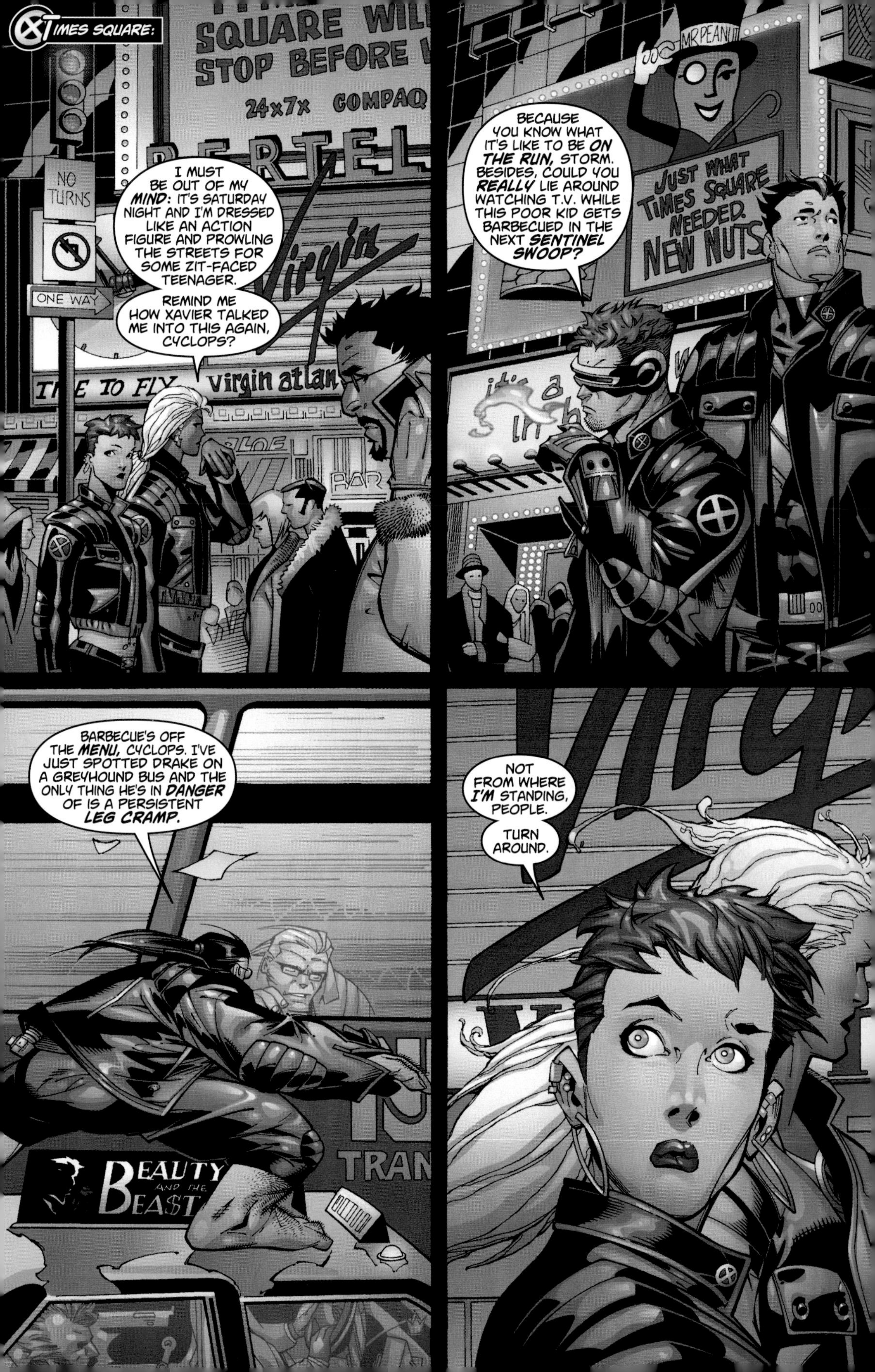

TIMES SQUARE:
SQUARE WILL
STOP BEFORE
24x7x COMPAQ
NO TURNS
ONE WAY
I MUST BE OUT OF MY MIND: IT'S SATURDAY NIGHT AND I'M DRESSED LIKE AN ACTION FIGURE AND PROWLING THE STREETS FOR SOME ZIT-FACED TEENAGER.
REMIND ME HOW XAVIER TALKED ME INTO THIS AGAIN, CYCLOPS?
virgin atlan
BAR
MR PEANUT
BECAUSE YOU KNOW WHAT IT'S LIKE TO BE ON THE RUN, STORM. BESIDES, COULD YOU REALLY LIE AROUND WATCHING T.V. WHILE THIS POOR KID GETS BARBECUED IN THE NEXT SENTINEL SWOOP?
JUST WHAT TIMES SQUARE NEEDED. NEW NUTS
BARBECUE'S OFF THE MENU, CYCLOPS. I'VE JUST SPOTTED DRAKE ON A GREYHOUND BUS AND THE ONLY THING HE'S IN DANGER OF IS A PERSISTENT LEG CRAMP.
BEAUTY AND THE BEA$T
TRAN
NOT FROM WHERE I'M STANDING, PEOPLE.
TURN AROUND.

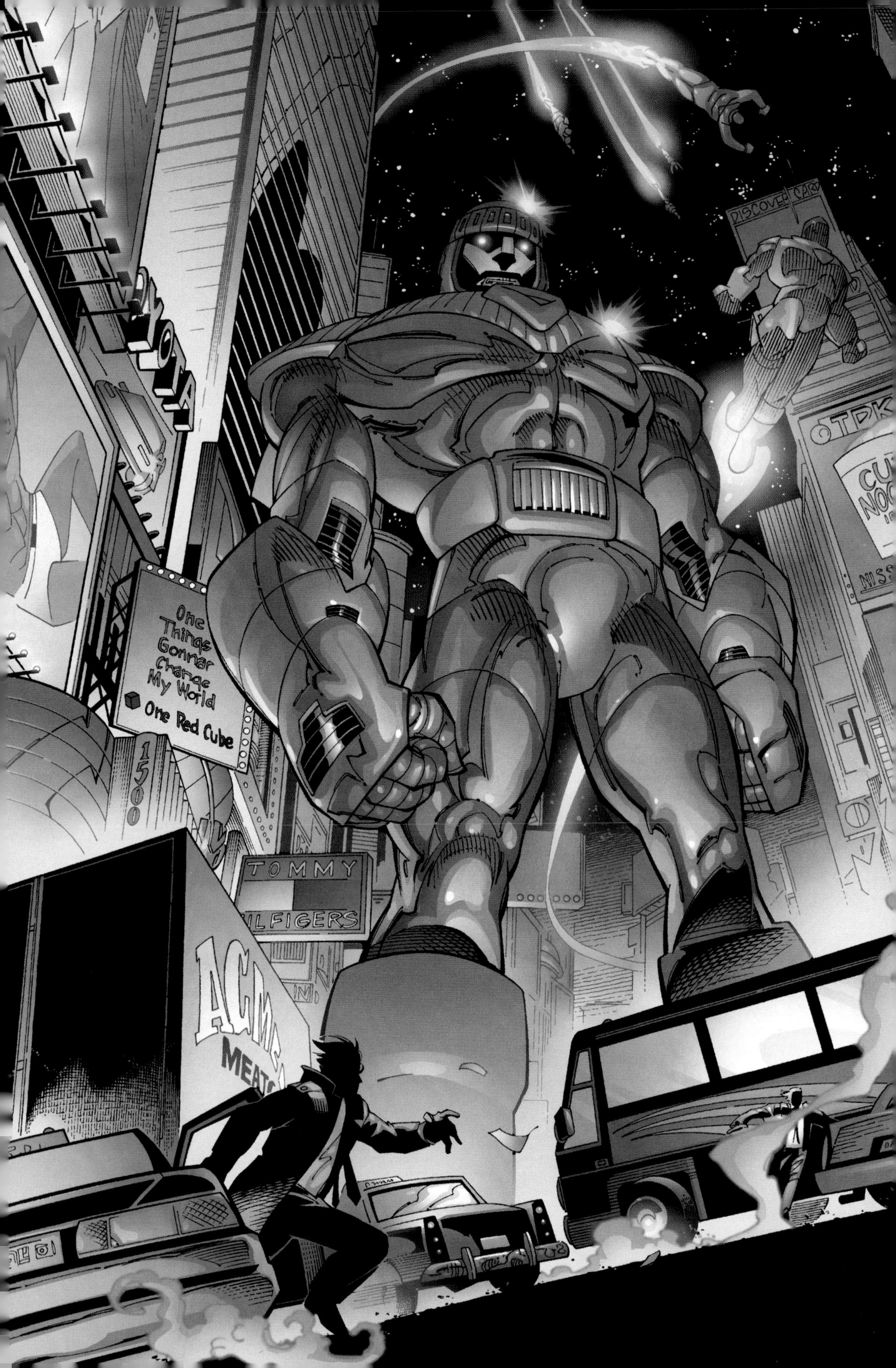

One Things Gonnar Change My World
One Red Cube
1500
TOMMY
DISCOVER CARD

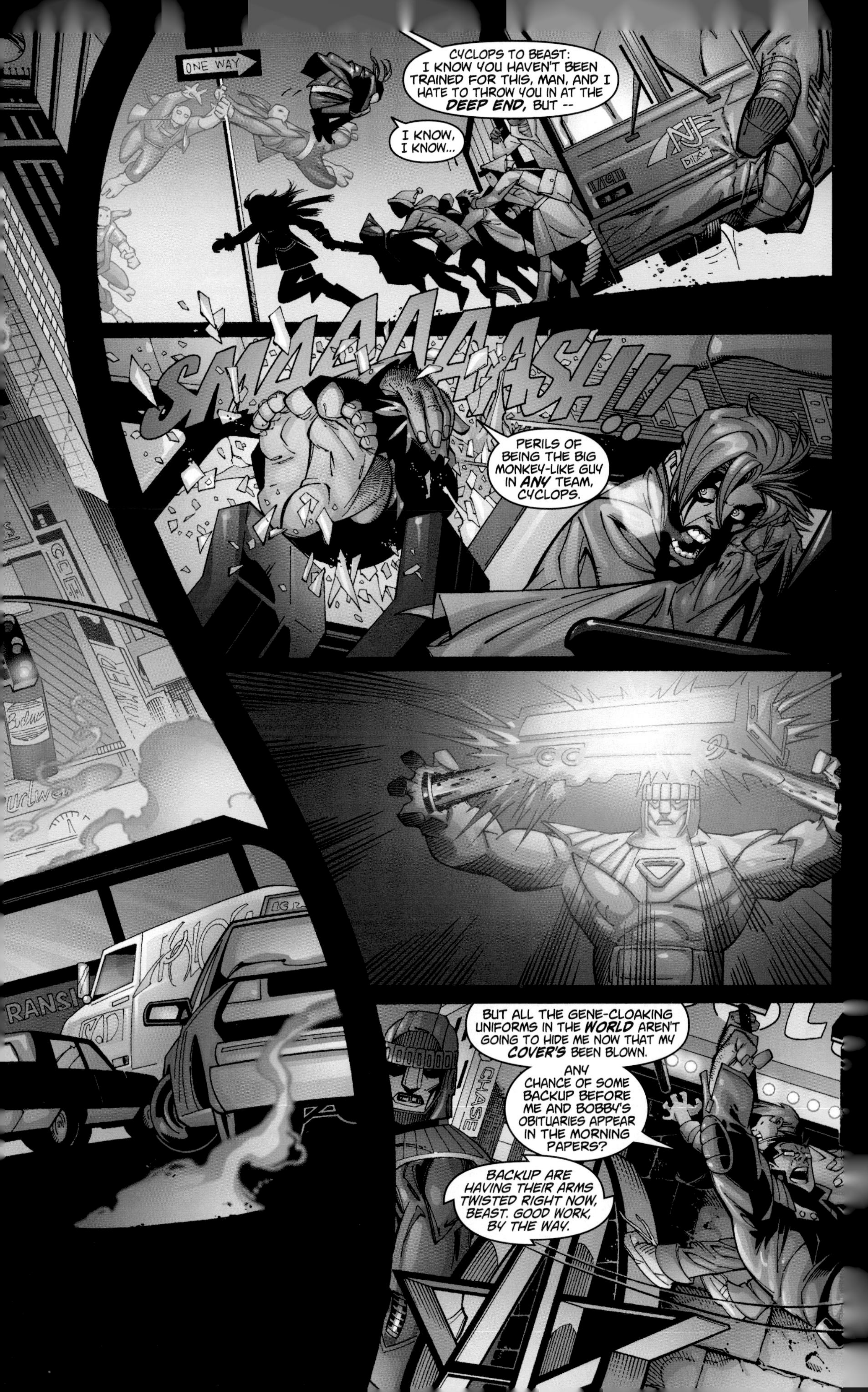
ONE WAY
CYCLOPS TO BEAST: I KNOW YOU HAVEN'T BEEN TRAINED FOR THIS, MAN, AND I HATE TO THROW YOU IN AT THE DEEP END, BUT --
I KNOW, I KNOW...
SMAAAAASH!!!
PERILS OF BEING THE BIG MONKEY-LIKE GUY IN ANY TEAM, CYCLOPS.
BUT ALL THE GENE-CLOAKING UNIFORMS IN THE WORLD AREN'T GOING TO HIDE ME NOW THAT MY COVER'S BEEN BLOWN.
ANY CHANCE OF SOME BACKUP BEFORE ME AND BOBBY'S OBITUARIES APPEAR IN THE MORNING PAPERS?
BACKUP ARE HAVING THEIR ARMS TWISTED RIGHT NOW, BEAST. GOOD WORK, BY THE WAY.
CHASE

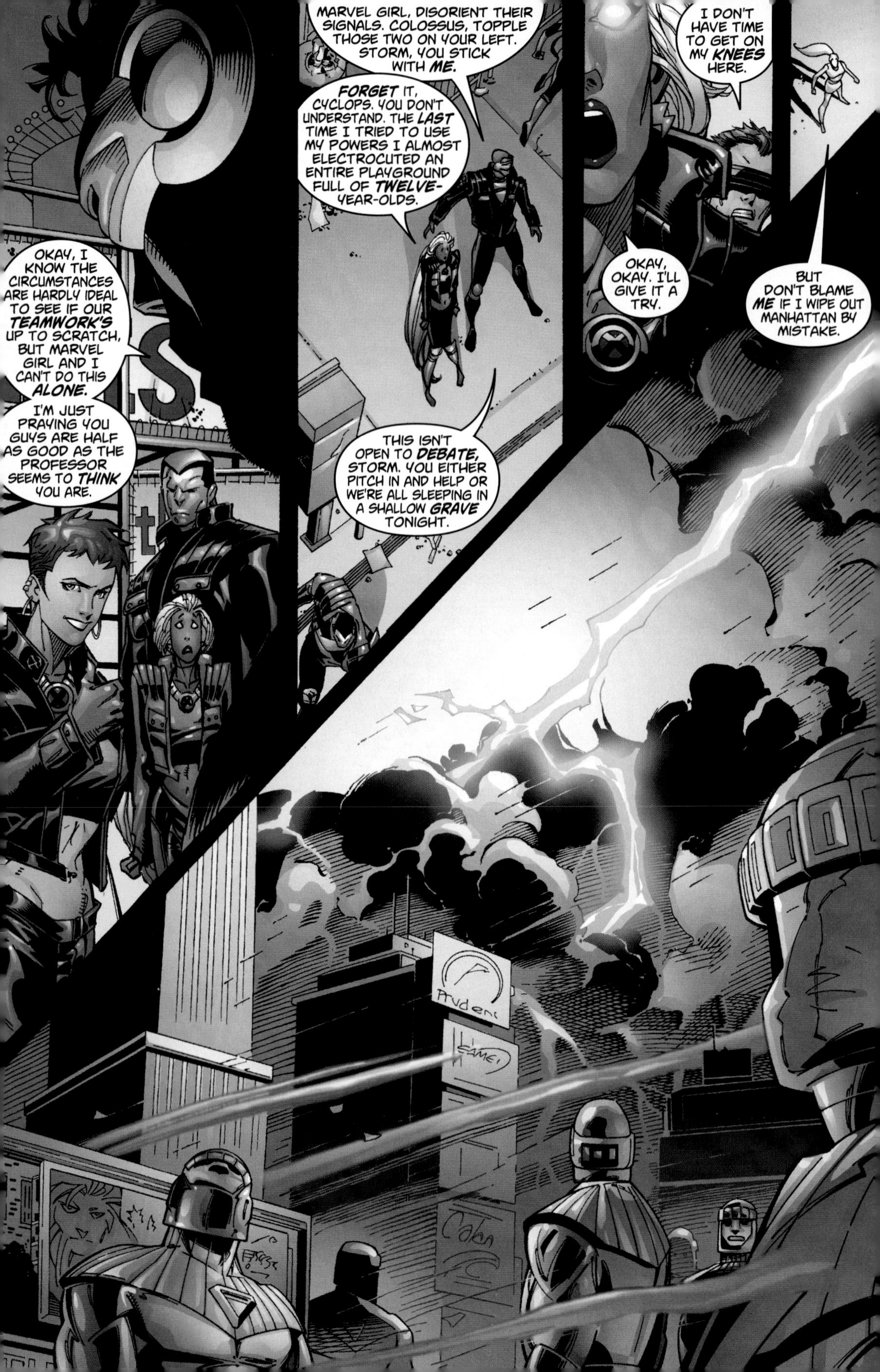
MARVEL GIRL, DISORIENT THEIR SIGNALS. COLOSSUS, TOPPLE THOSE TWO ON YOUR LEFT. STORM, YOU STICK WITH ME.
FORGET IT, CYCLOPS. YOU DON'T UNDERSTAND. THE LAST TIME I TRIED TO USE MY POWERS I ALMOST ELECTROCUTED AN ENTIRE PLAYGROUND FULL OF TWELVE-YEAR-OLDS.
THIS ISN'T OPEN TO DEBATE, STORM. YOU EITHER PITCH IN AND HELP OR WE'RE ALL SLEEPING IN A SHALLOW GRAVE TONIGHT.
I DON'T HAVE TIME TO GET ON MY KNEES HERE.
OKAY, OKAY. I'LL GIVE IT A TRY.
BUT DON'T BLAME ME IF I WIPE OUT MANHATTAN BY MISTAKE.
OKAY, I KNOW THE CIRCUMSTANCES ARE HARDLY IDEAL TO SEE IF OUR TEAMWORK'S UP TO SCRATCH, BUT MARVEL GIRL AND I CAN'T DO THIS ALONE.
I'M JUST PRAYING YOU GUYS ARE HALF AS GOOD AS THE PROFESSOR SEEMS TO THINK YOU ARE.

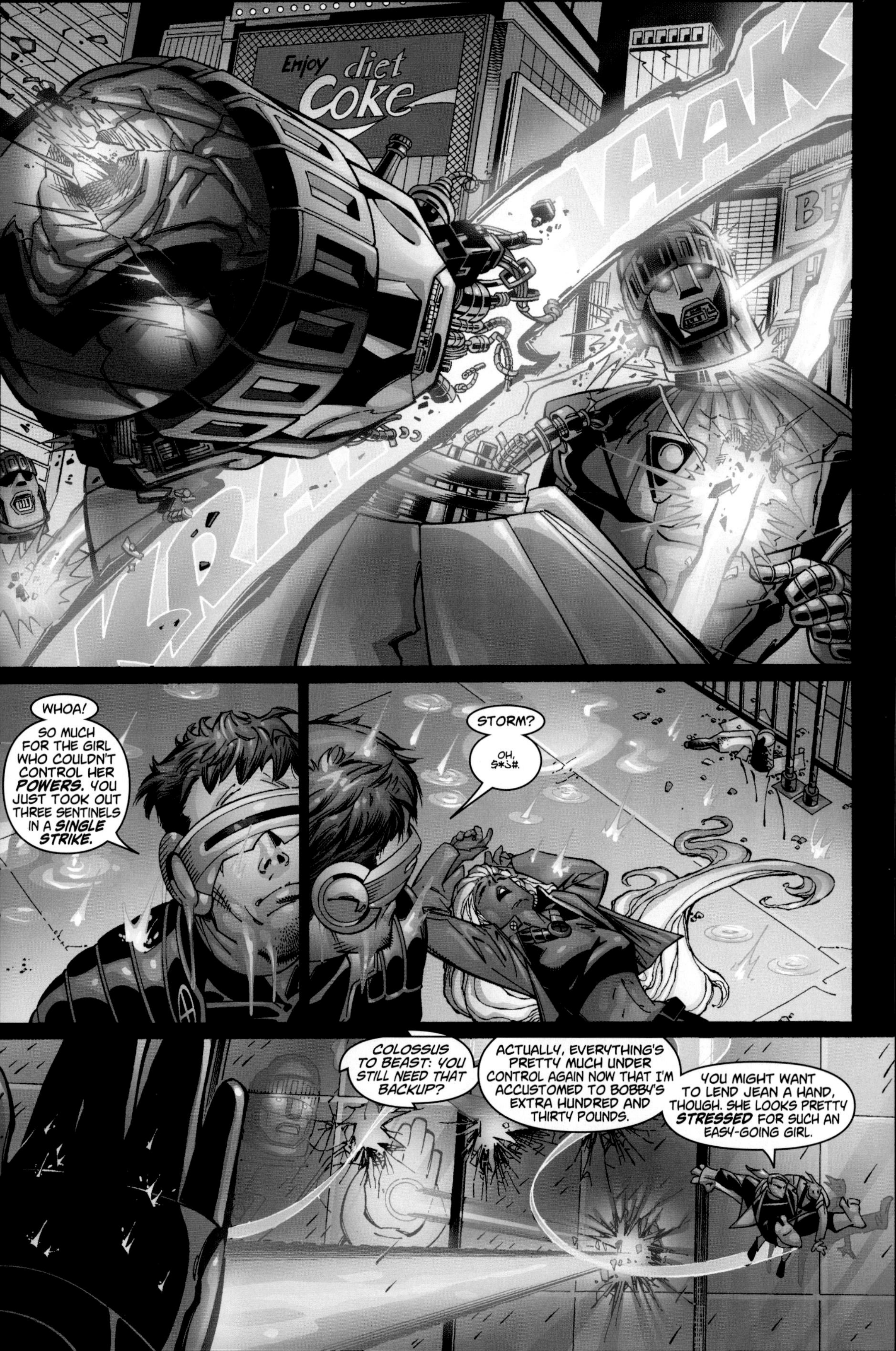
Enjoy diet Coke
WHOA!
SO MUCH FOR THE GIRL WHO COULDN'T CONTROL HER **POWERS**. YOU JUST TOOK OUT THREE SENTINELS IN A **SINGLE STRIKE**.
STORM?
OH, $*!#.
COLOSSUS TO BEAST: YOU STILL NEED THAT BACKUP?
ACTUALLY, EVERYTHING'S PRETTY MUCH UNDER CONTROL AGAIN NOW THAT I'M ACCUSTOMED TO BOBBY'S EXTRA HUNDRED AND THIRTY POUNDS.
YOU MIGHT WANT TO LEND JEAN A HAND, THOUGH. SHE LOOKS PRETTY **STRESSED** FOR SUCH AN EASY-GOING GIRL.

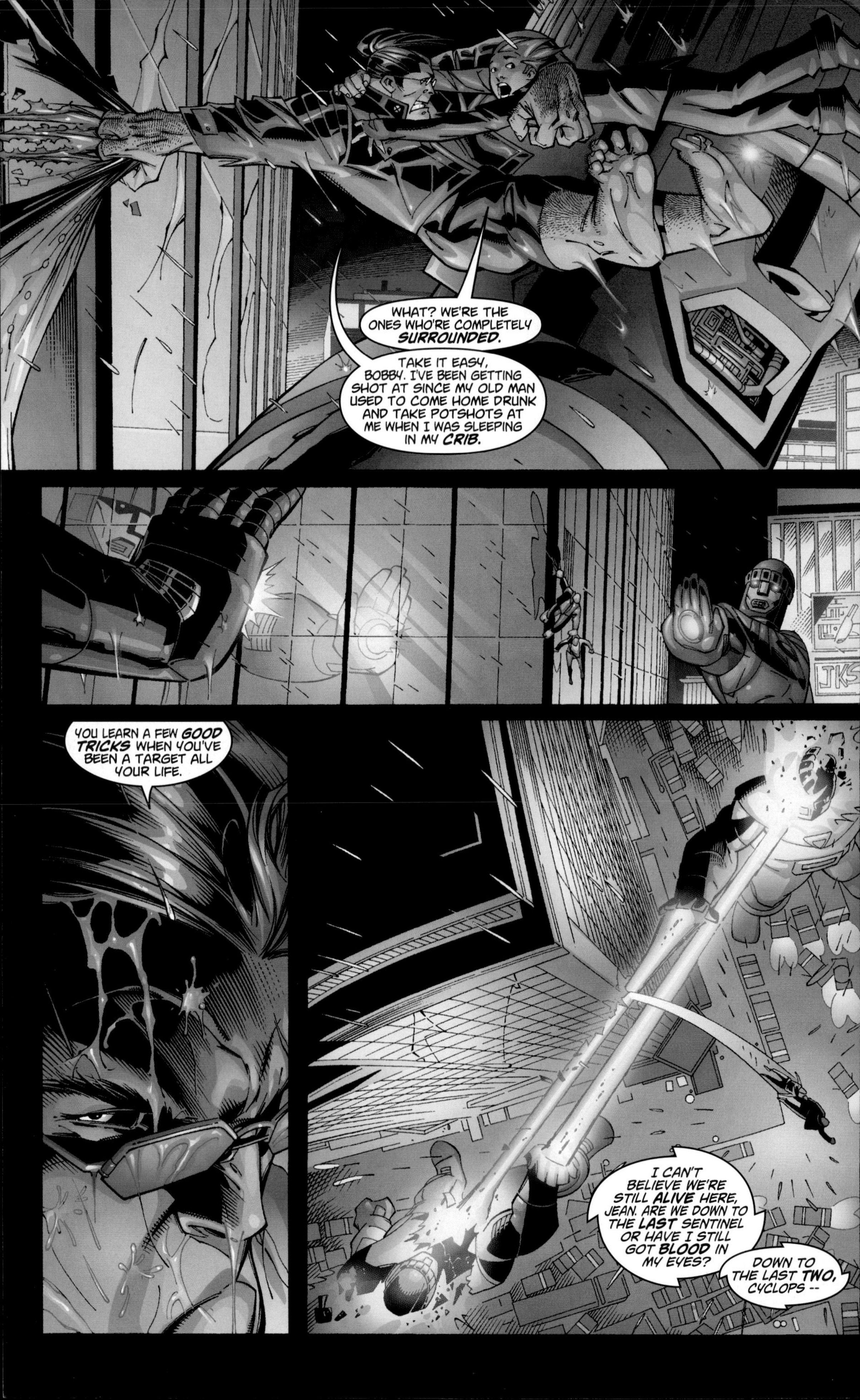
WHAT? WE'RE THE ONES WHO'RE COMPLETELY SURROUNDED.
TAKE IT EASY, BOBBY. I'VE BEEN GETTING SHOT AT SINCE MY OLD MAN USED TO COME HOME DRUNK AND TAKE POTSHOTS AT ME WHEN I WAS SLEEPING IN MY CRIB.
JKS
YOU LEARN A FEW GOOD TRICKS WHEN YOU'VE BEEN A TARGET ALL YOUR LIFE.
I CAN'T BELIEVE WE'RE STILL ALIVE HERE, JEAN. ARE WE DOWN TO THE LAST SENTINEL OR HAVE I STILL GOT BLOOD IN MY EYES?
DOWN TO THE LAST TWO, CYCLOPS --

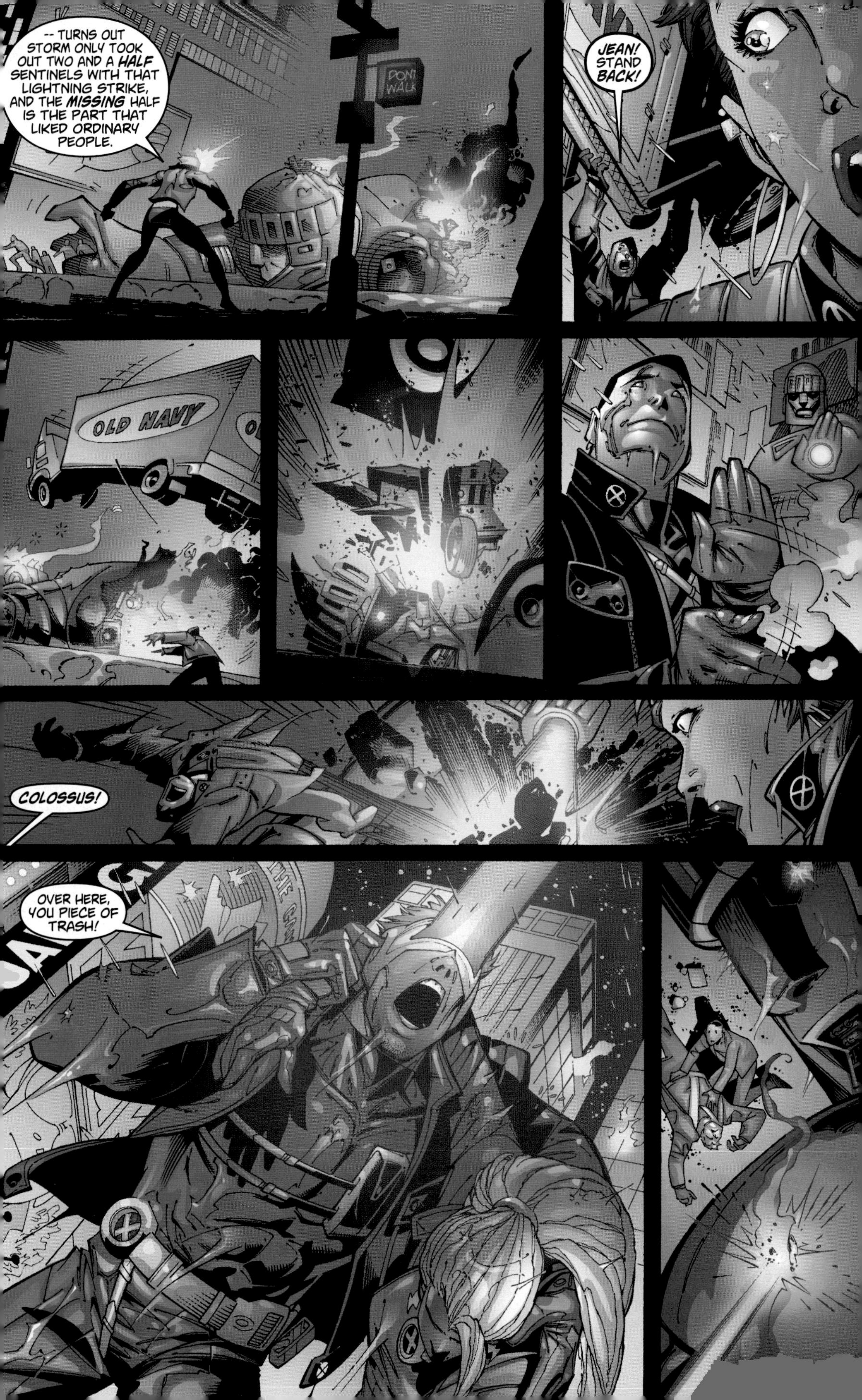
-- TURNS OUT STORM ONLY TOOK OUT TWO AND A HALF SENTINELS WITH THAT LIGHTNING STRIKE, AND THE MISSING HALF IS THE PART THAT LIKED ORDINARY PEOPLE.
DON'T WALK
JEAN! STAND BACK!
OLD NAVY
COLOSSUS!
OVER HERE, YOU PIECE OF TRASH!

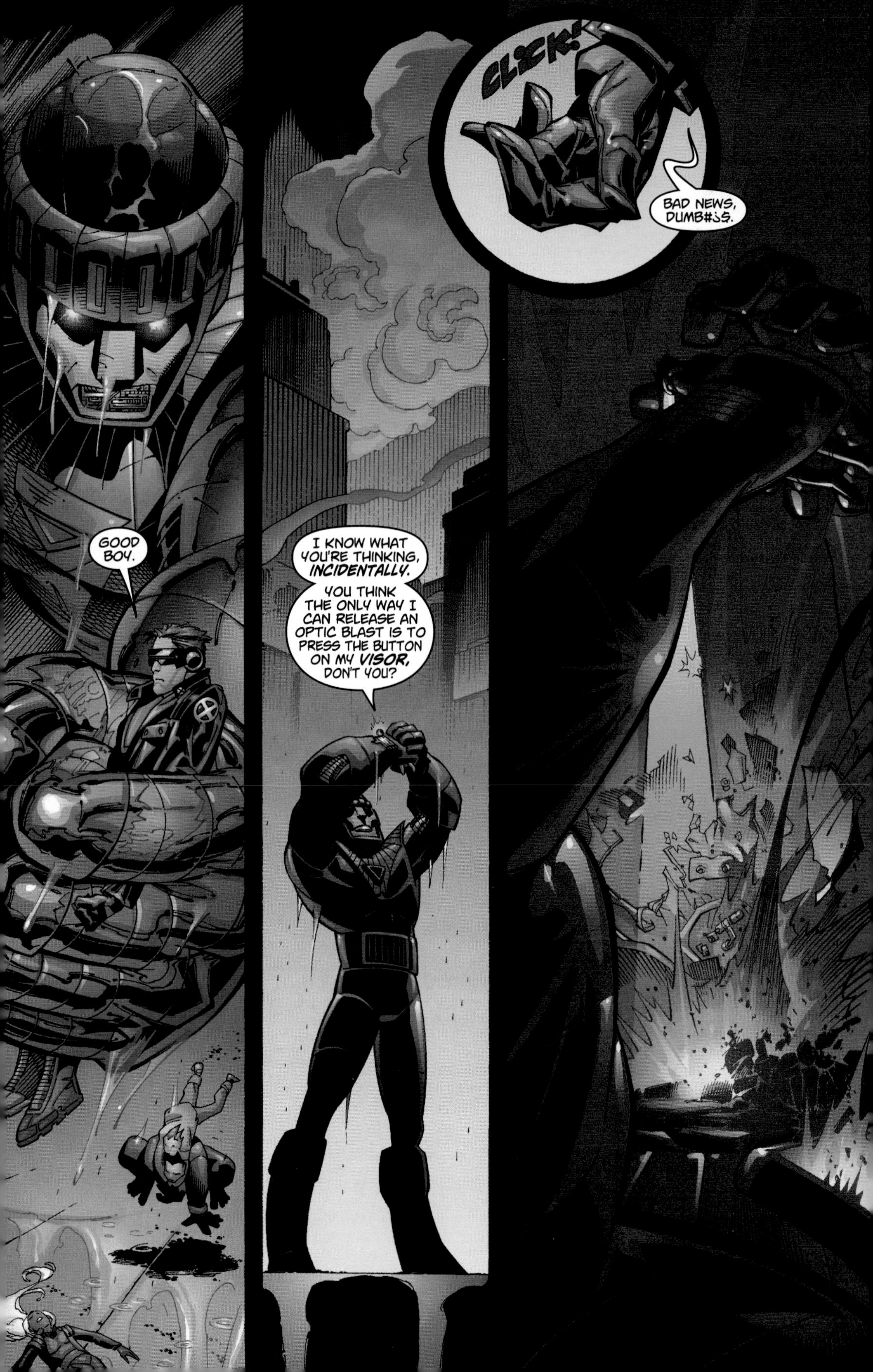
GOOD BOY.
I KNOW WHAT YOU'RE THINKING, INCIDENTALLY.
YOU THINK THE ONLY WAY I CAN RELEASE AN OPTIC BLAST IS TO PRESS THE BUTTON ON MY VISOR, DON'T YOU?
CLICK!
BAD NEWS, DUMB#$S.

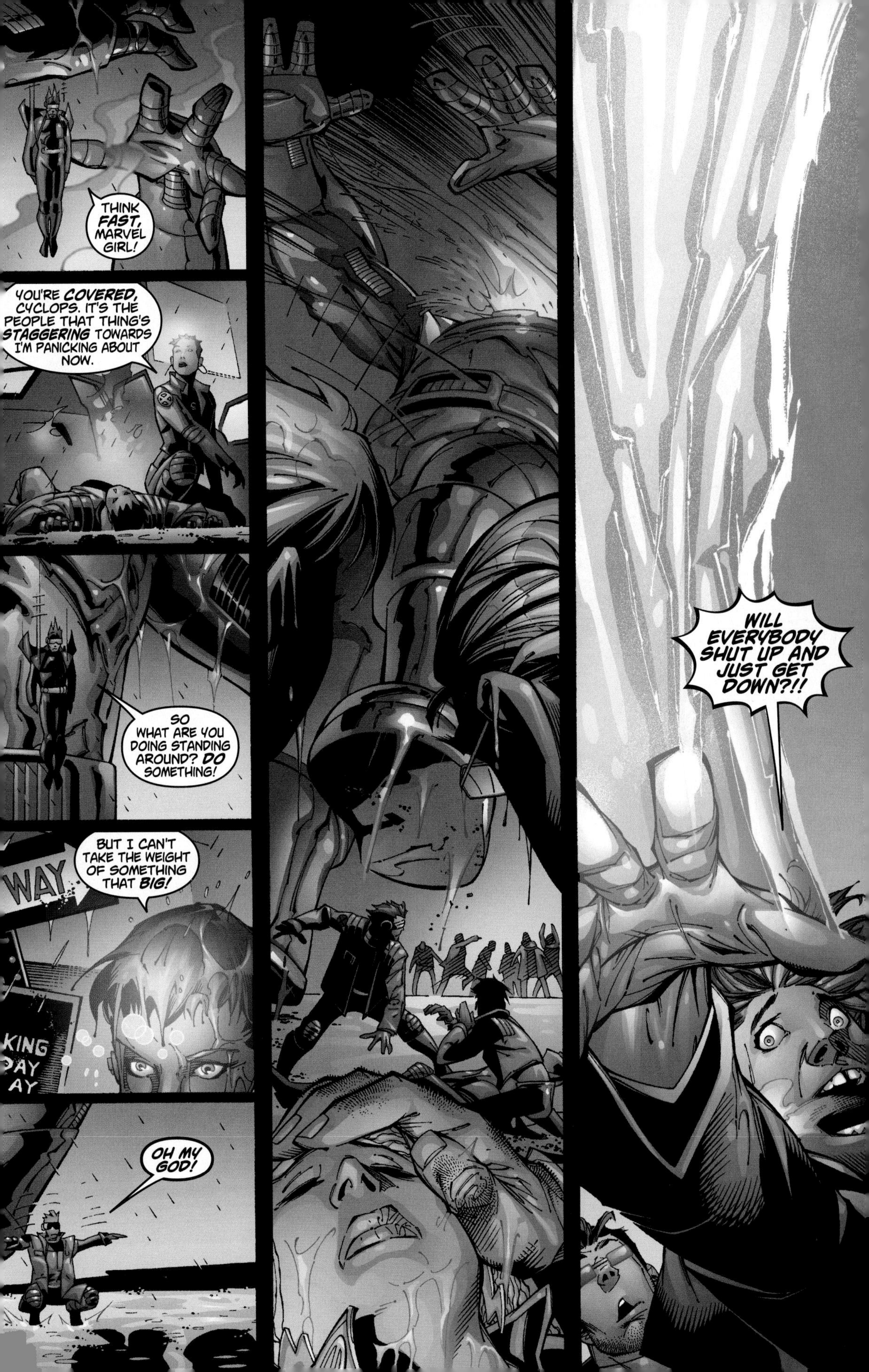
THINK FAST, MARVEL GIRL!
YOU'RE COVERED, CYCLOPS. IT'S THE PEOPLE THAT THING'S STAGGERING TOWARDS I'M PANICKING ABOUT NOW.
SO WHAT ARE YOU DOING STANDING AROUND? DO SOMETHING!
BUT I CAN'T TAKE THE WEIGHT OF SOMETHING THAT BIG!
WAY
KING
PAY
AY
OH MY GOD!
WILL EVERYBODY SHUT UP AND JUST GET DOWN?!!

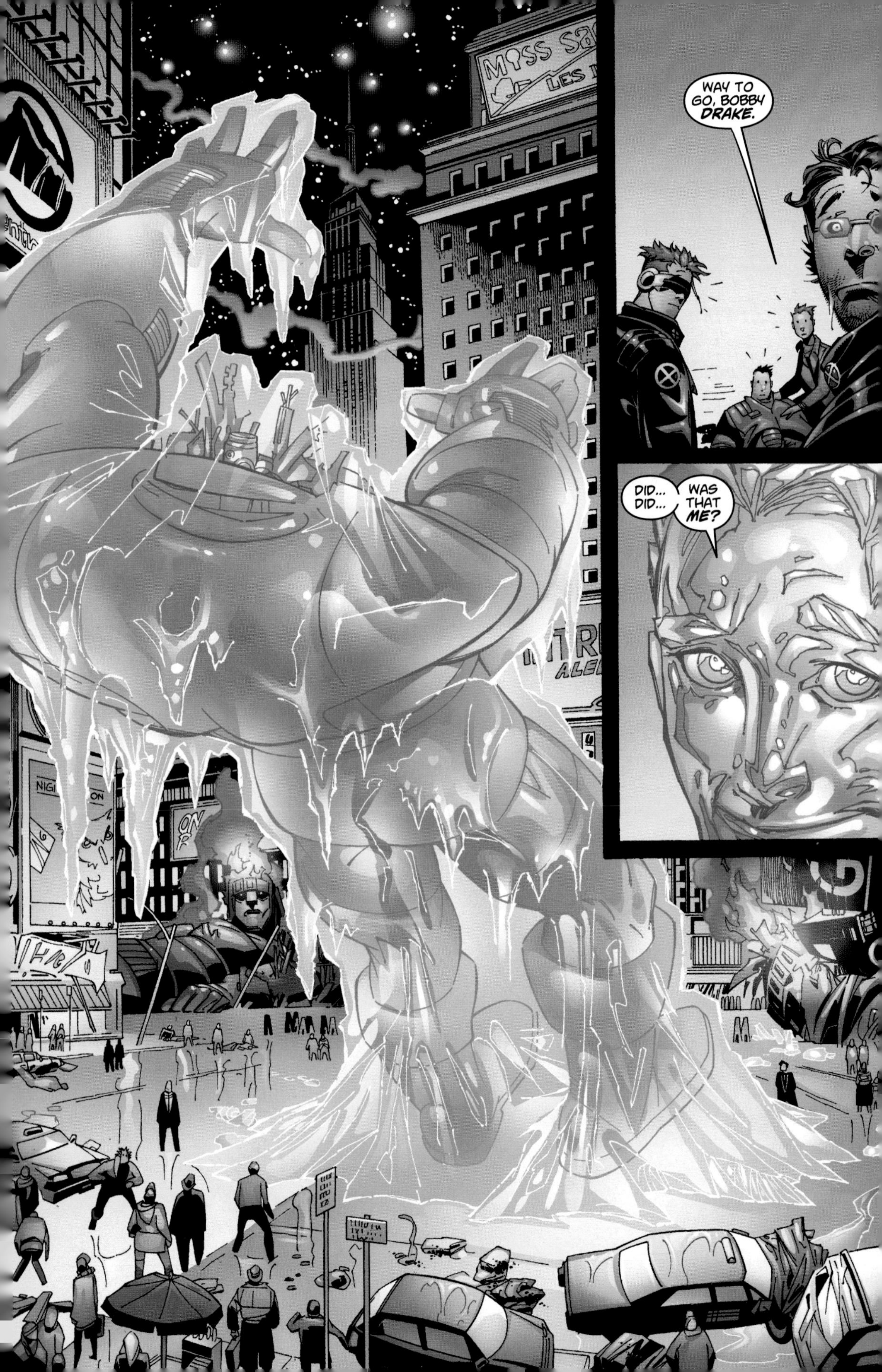
WAY TO GO, BOBBY DRAKE.
DID... DID...
WAS THAT ME?

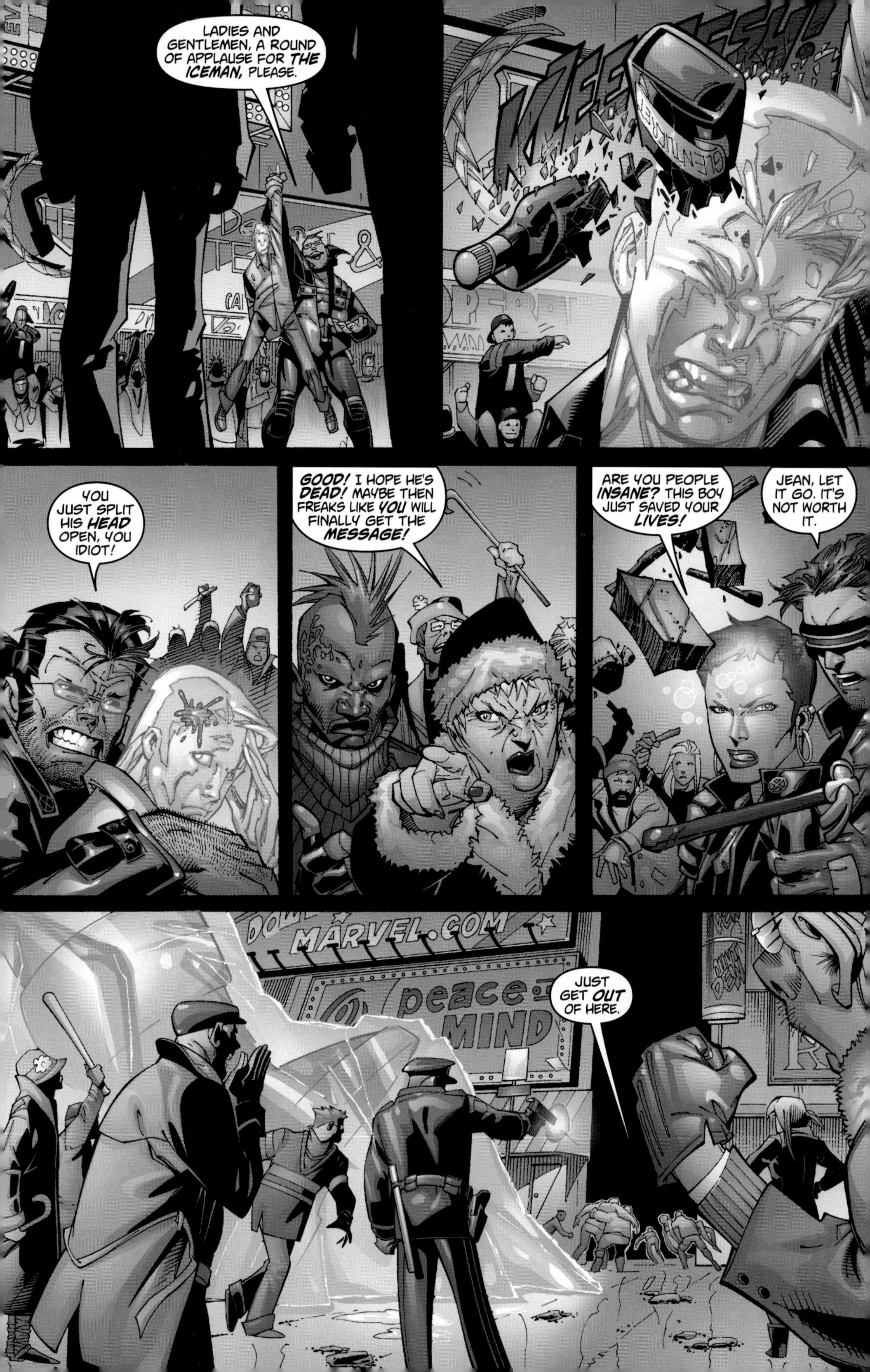
LADIES AND GENTLEMEN, A ROUND OF APPLAUSE FOR THE ICEMAN, PLEASE.
KKZEESSSH!
YOU JUST SPLIT HIS HEAD OPEN, YOU IDIOT!
GOOD! I HOPE HE'S DEAD! MAYBE THEN FREAKS LIKE YOU WILL FINALLY GET THE MESSAGE!
ARE YOU PEOPLE INSANE? THIS BOY JUST SAVED YOUR LIVES!
JEAN, LET IT GO. IT'S NOT WORTH IT.
MARVEL.COM
peace MIND
JUST GET OUT OF HERE.

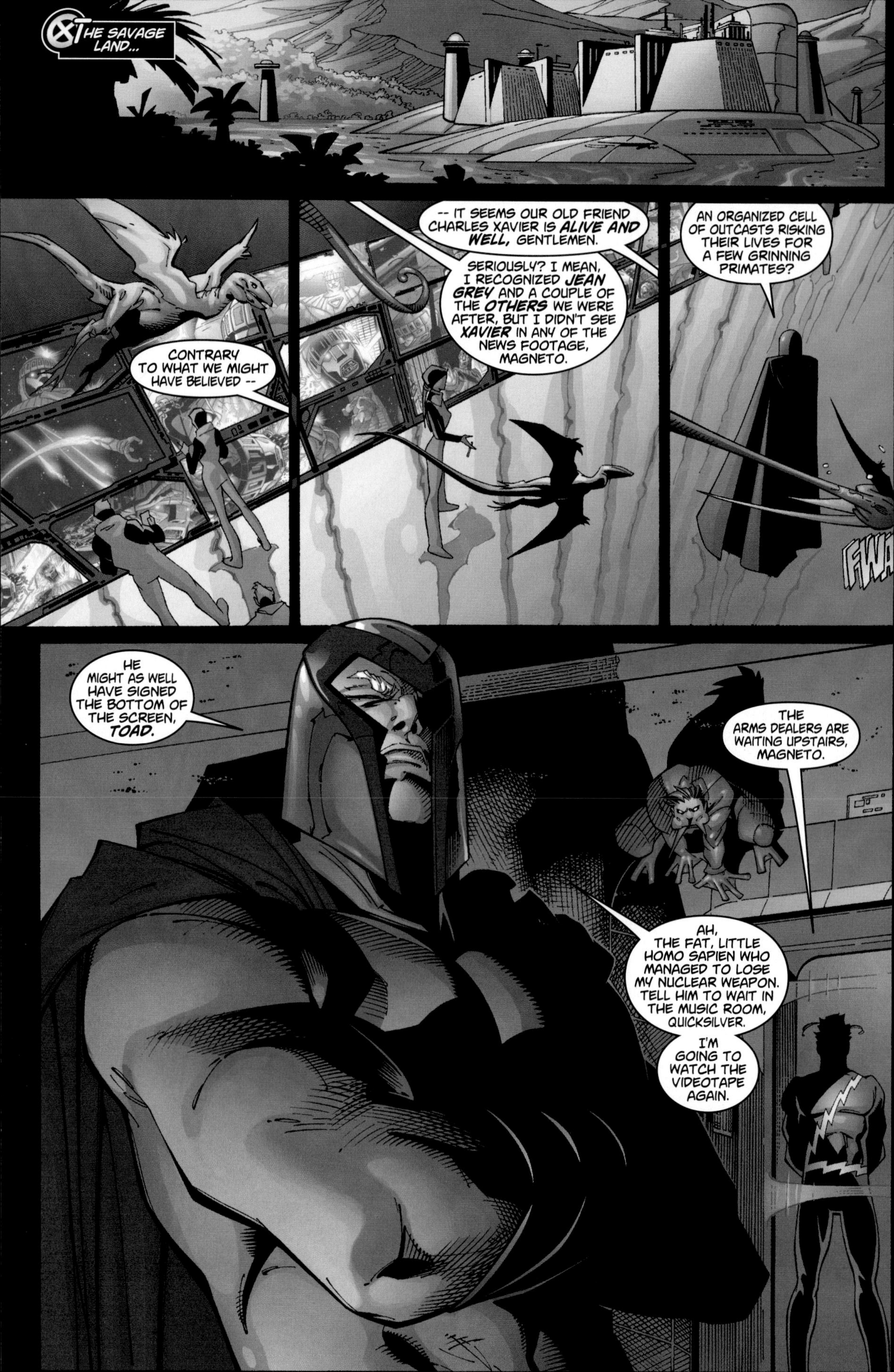
THE SAVAGE LAND...
CONTRARY TO WHAT WE MIGHT HAVE BELIEVED --
-- IT SEEMS OUR OLD FRIEND CHARLES XAVIER IS ALIVE AND WELL, GENTLEMEN.
SERIOUSLY? I MEAN, I RECOGNIZED JEAN GREY AND A COUPLE OF THE OTHERS WE WERE AFTER, BUT I DIDN'T SEE XAVIER IN ANY OF THE NEWS FOOTAGE, MAGNETO.
AN ORGANIZED CELL OF OUTCASTS RISKING THEIR LIVES FOR A FEW GRINNING PRIMATES?
FWA
HE MIGHT AS WELL HAVE SIGNED THE BOTTOM OF THE SCREEN, TOAD.
THE ARMS DEALERS ARE WAITING UPSTAIRS, MAGNETO.
AH, THE FAT, LITTLE HOMO SAPIEN WHO MANAGED TO LOSE MY NUCLEAR WEAPON. TELL HIM TO WAIT IN THE MUSIC ROOM, QUICKSILVER.
I'M GOING TO WATCH THE VIDEOTAPE AGAIN.

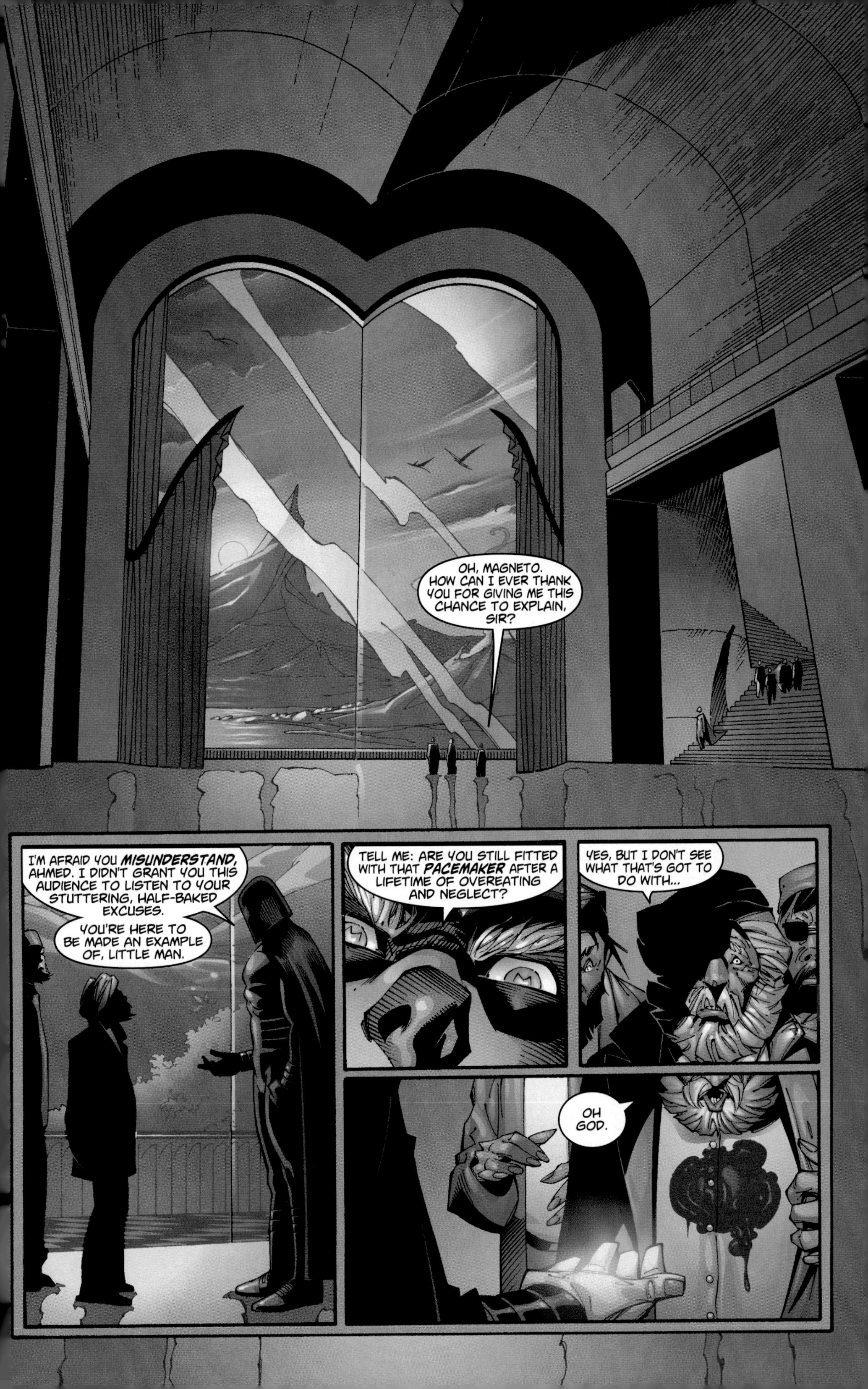
OH, MAGNETO. HOW CAN I EVER THANK YOU FOR GIVING ME THIS CHANCE TO EXPLAIN, SIR?
I'M AFRAID YOU **MISUNDERSTAND,** AHMED. I DIDN'T GRANT YOU THIS AUDIENCE TO LISTEN TO YOUR STUTTERING, HALF-BAKED EXCUSES.
YOU'RE HERE TO BE MADE AN EXAMPLE OF, LITTLE MAN.
TELL ME: ARE YOU STILL FITTED WITH THAT **PACEMAKER** AFTER A LIFETIME OF OVEREATING AND NEGLECT?
YES, BUT I DON'T SEE WHAT THAT'S GOT TO DO WITH...
OH GOD.

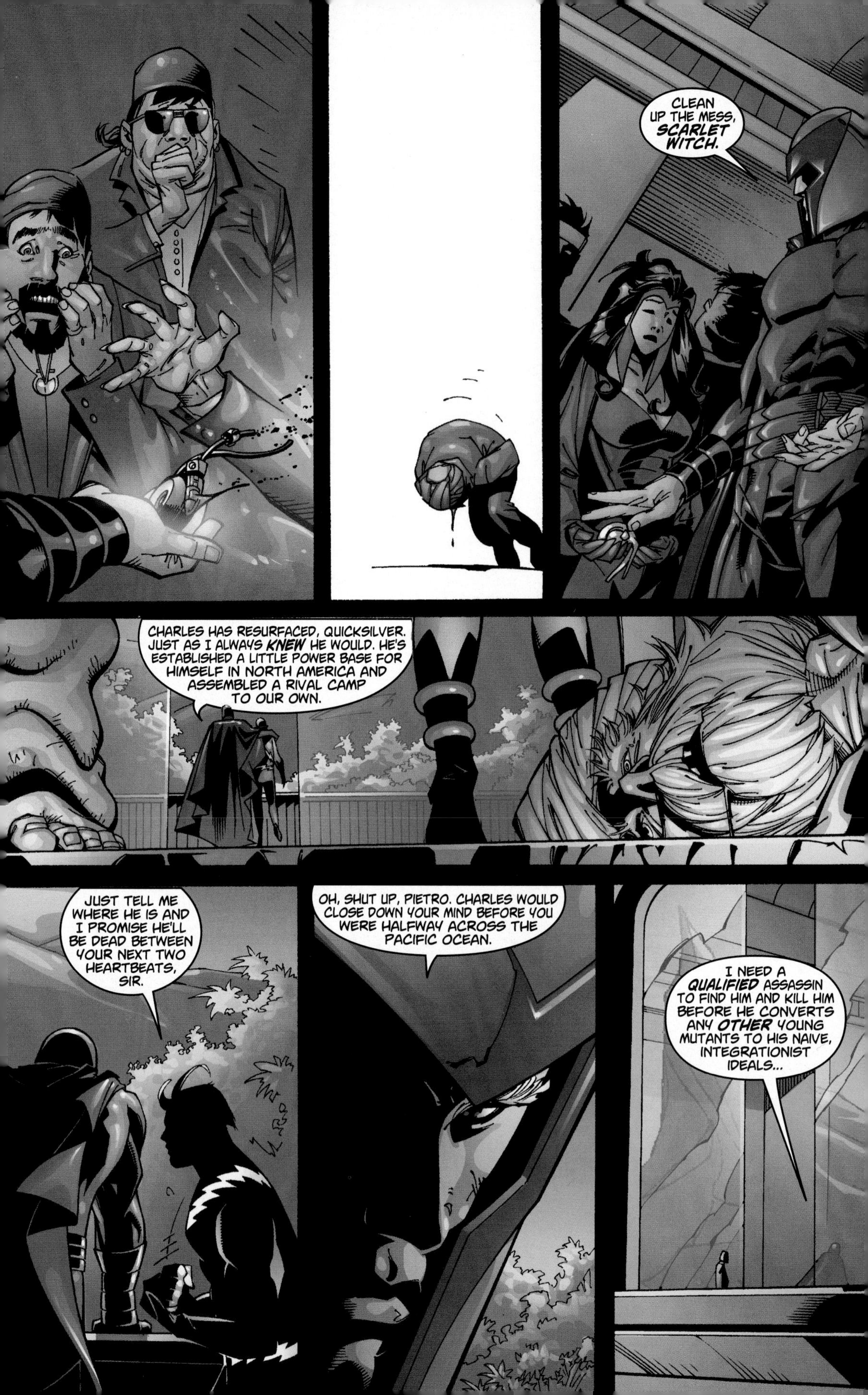
CLEAN UP THE MESS, SCARLET WITCH.
CHARLES HAS RESURFACED, QUICKSILVER. JUST AS I ALWAYS KNEW HE WOULD. HE'S ESTABLISHED A LITTLE POWER BASE FOR HIMSELF IN NORTH AMERICA AND ASSEMBLED A RIVAL CAMP TO OUR OWN.
JUST TELL ME WHERE HE IS AND I PROMISE HE'LL BE DEAD BETWEEN YOUR NEXT TWO HEARTBEATS, SIR.
OH, SHUT UP, PIETRO. CHARLES WOULD CLOSE DOWN YOUR MIND BEFORE YOU WERE HALFWAY ACROSS THE PACIFIC OCEAN.
I NEED A QUALIFIED ASSASSIN TO FIND HIM AND KILL HIM BEFORE HE CONVERTS ANY OTHER YOUNG MUTANTS TO HIS NAIVE, INTEGRATIONIST IDEALS...

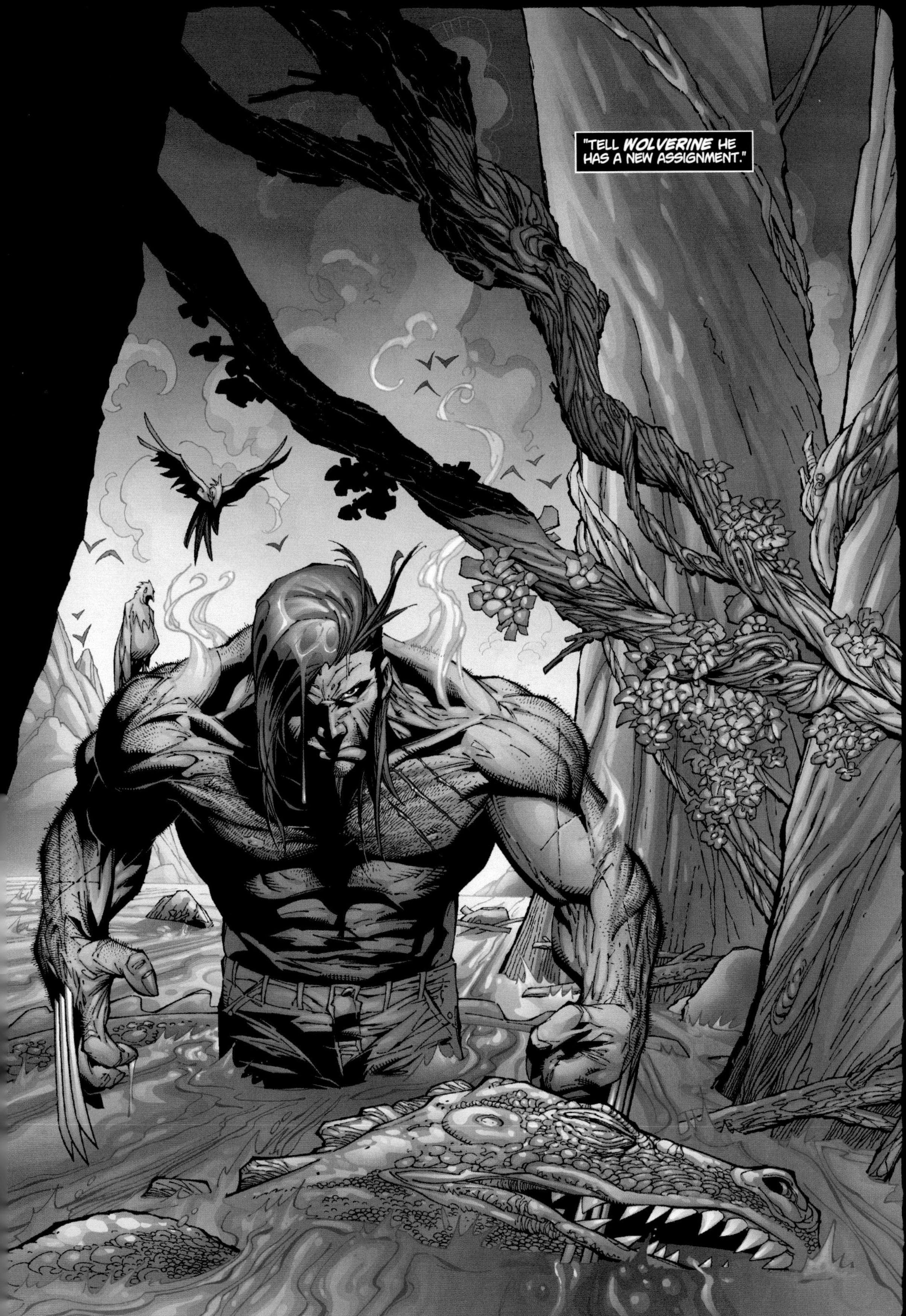
"TELL WOLVERINE HE HAS A NEW ASSIGNMENT."

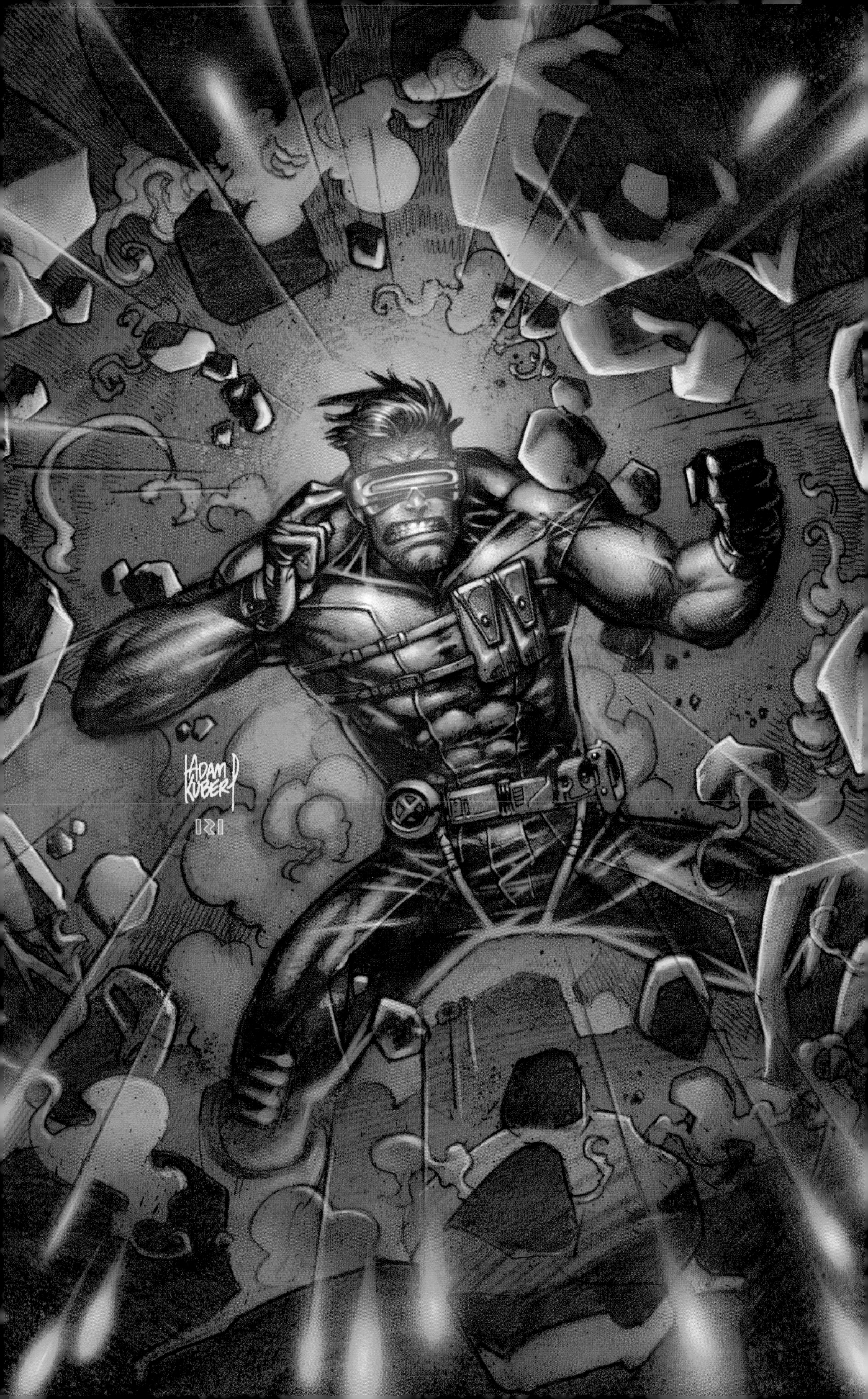
ADAM KUBERT

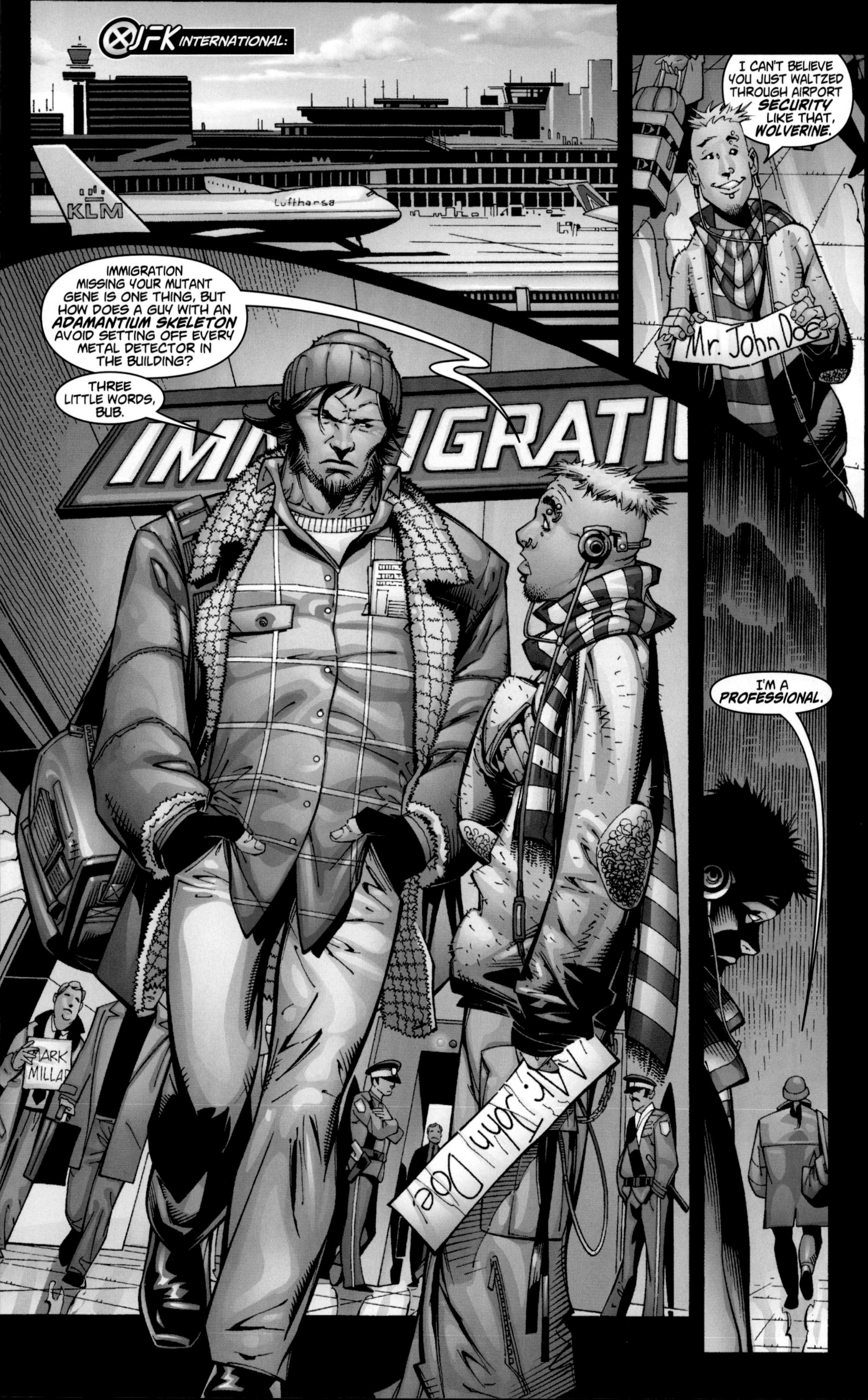
JFK INTERNATIONAL:
KLM
Lufthansa
I CAN'T BELIEVE YOU JUST WALTZED THROUGH AIRPORT SECURITY LIKE THAT, WOLVERINE.
Mr. John Doe
IMMIGRATION MISSING YOUR MUTANT GENE IS ONE THING, BUT HOW DOES A GUY WITH AN ADAMANTIUM SKELETON AVOID SETTING OFF EVERY METAL DETECTOR IN THE BUILDING?
THREE LITTLE WORDS, BUB.
I'M A PROFESSIONAL.
IMMIGRATI
MARK MILLAR
Mr. John Doe

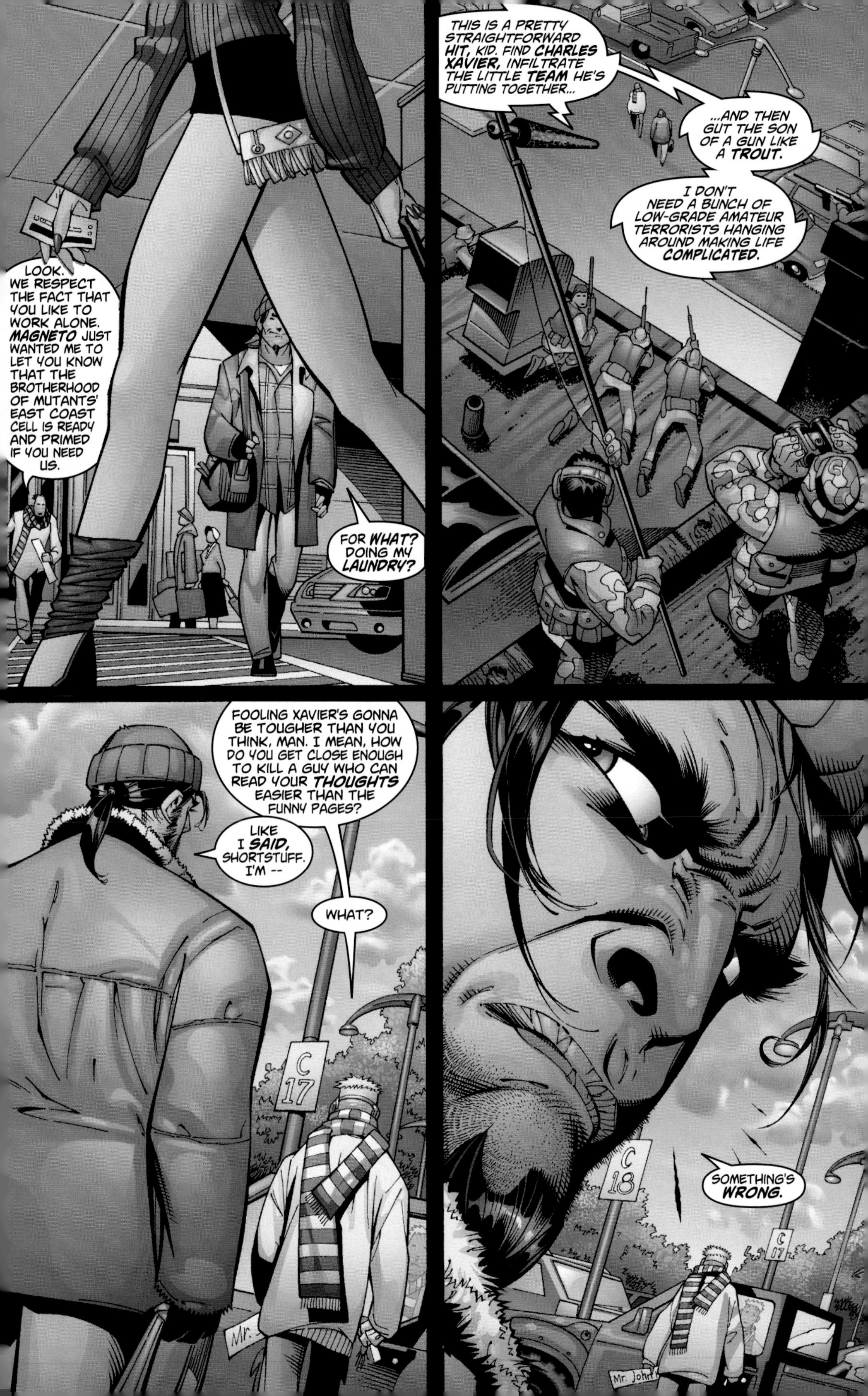
LOOK. WE RESPECT THE FACT THAT YOU LIKE TO WORK ALONE. MAGNETO JUST WANTED ME TO LET YOU KNOW THAT THE BROTHERHOOD OF MUTANTS' EAST COAST CELL IS READY AND PRIMED IF YOU NEED US.
FOR WHAT? DOING MY LAUNDRY?
THIS IS A PRETTY STRAIGHTFORWARD HIT, KID. FIND CHARLES XAVIER, INFILTRATE THE LITTLE TEAM HE'S PUTTING TOGETHER...
...AND THEN GUT THE SON OF A GUN LIKE A TROUT.
I DON'T NEED A BUNCH OF LOW-GRADE AMATEUR TERRORISTS HANGING AROUND MAKING LIFE COMPLICATED.
FOOLING XAVIER'S GONNA BE TOUGHER THAN YOU THINK, MAN. I MEAN, HOW DO YOU GET CLOSE ENOUGH TO KILL A GUY WHO CAN READ YOUR THOUGHTS EASIER THAN THE FUNNY PAGES?
LIKE I SAID, SHORTSTUFF. I'M --
WHAT?
C 17
SOMETHING'S WRONG.
C 18
C 17

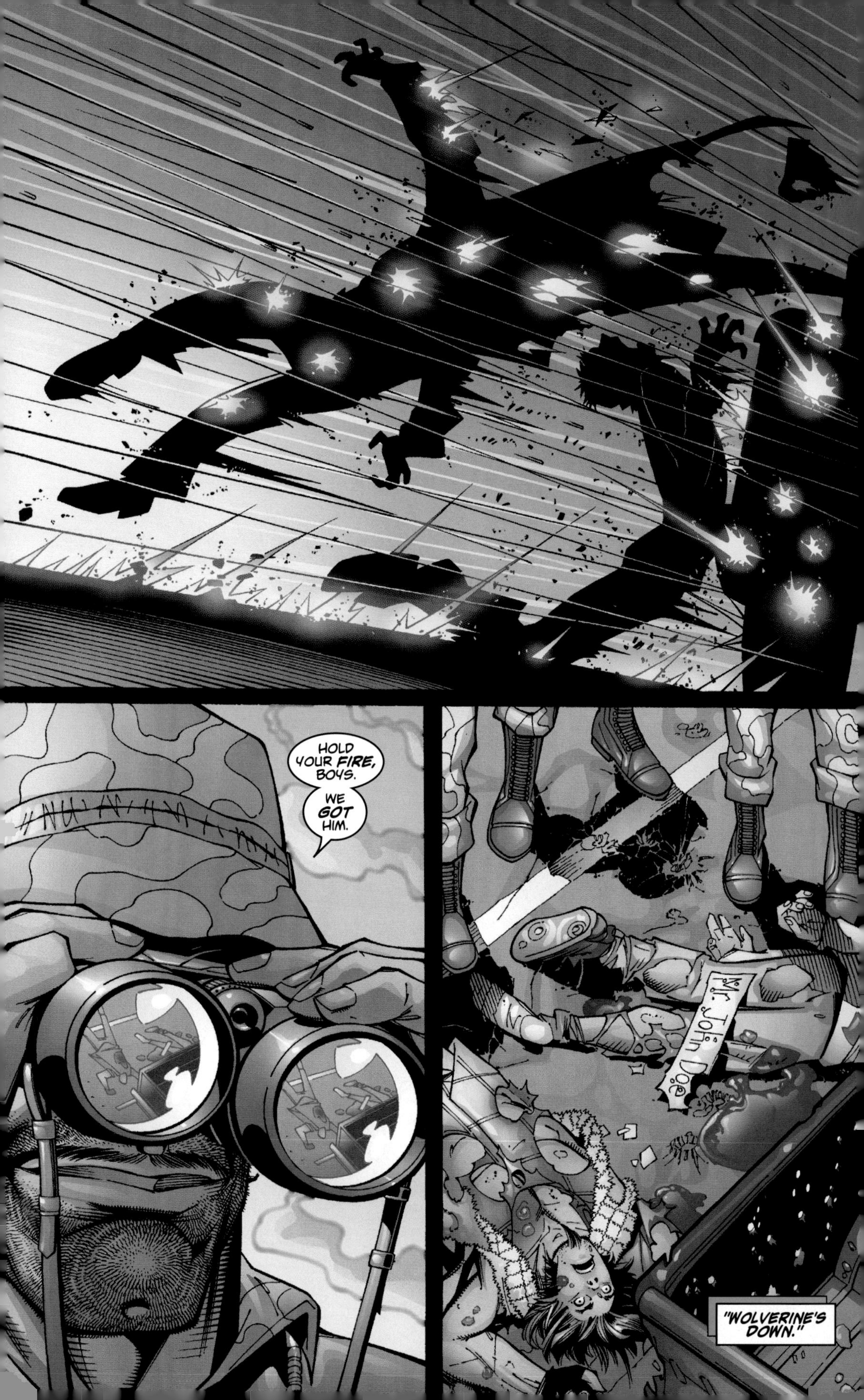

HOLD YOUR FIRE, BOYS.
WE GOT HIM.
Mr. John Doe
"WOLVERINE'S DOWN."

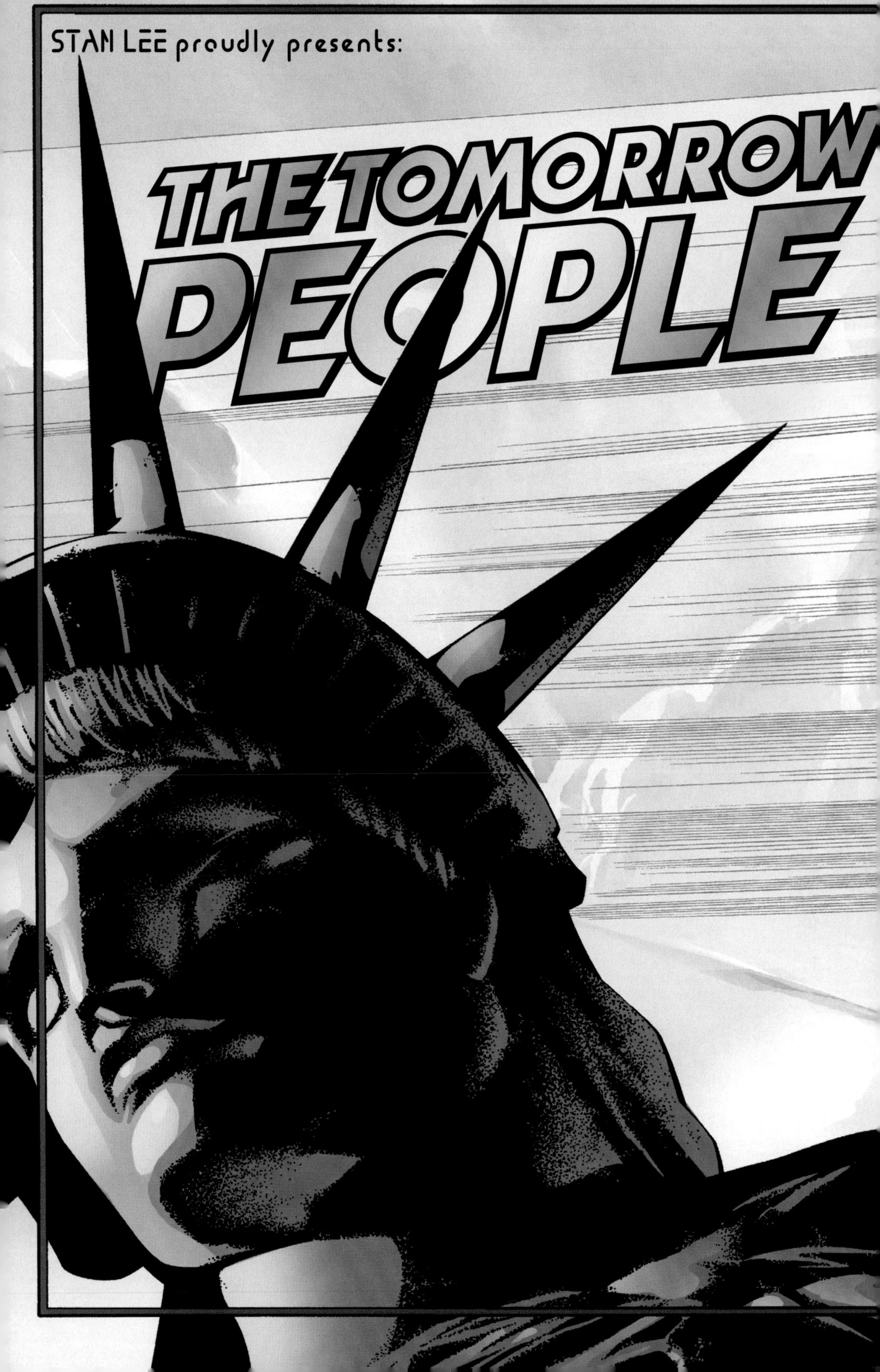
STAN LEE proudly presents:
THE TOMORROW PEOPLE

PART 2 OF 6
MILLAR KUBERT THIBERT
ISANOVE & WHITE COMICRAFT
FRANCO POWERS
QUESADA JEMAS

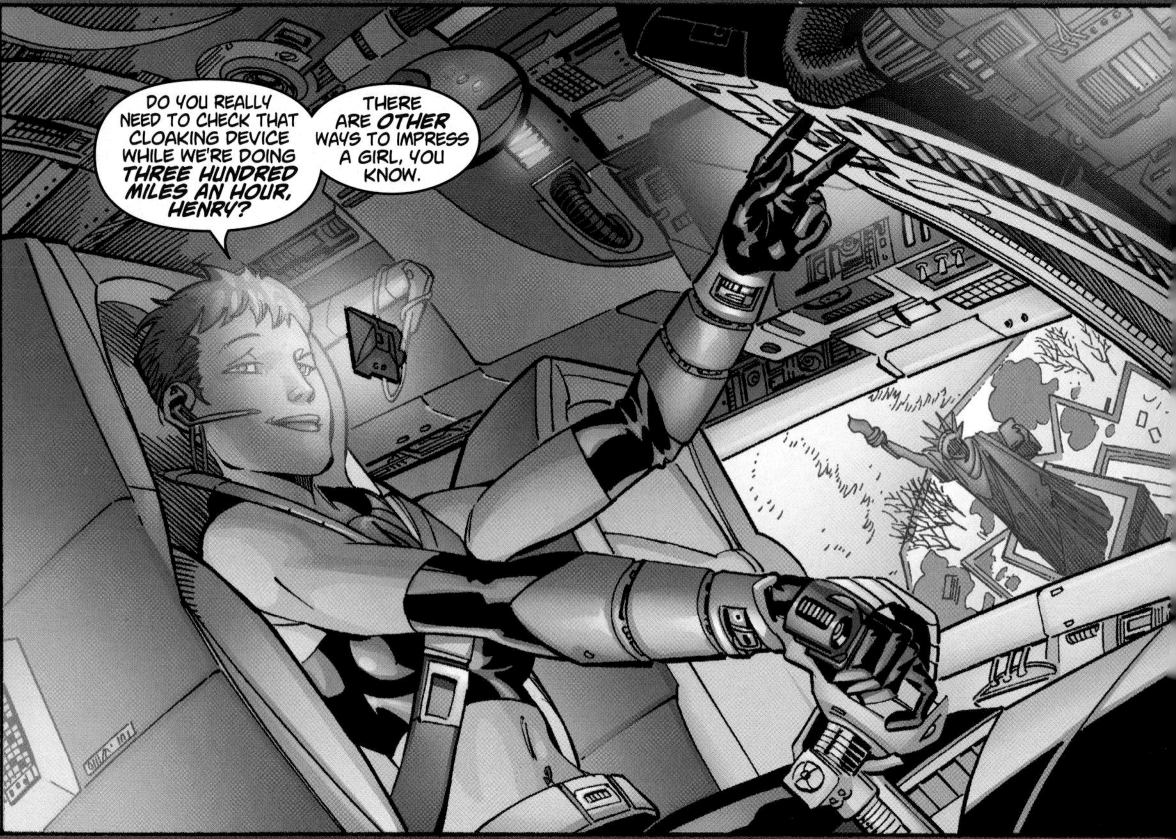
DO YOU REALLY NEED TO CHECK THAT CLOAKING DEVICE WHILE WE'RE DOING THREE HUNDRED MILES AN HOUR, HENRY?
THERE ARE OTHER WAYS TO IMPRESS A GIRL, YOU KNOW.

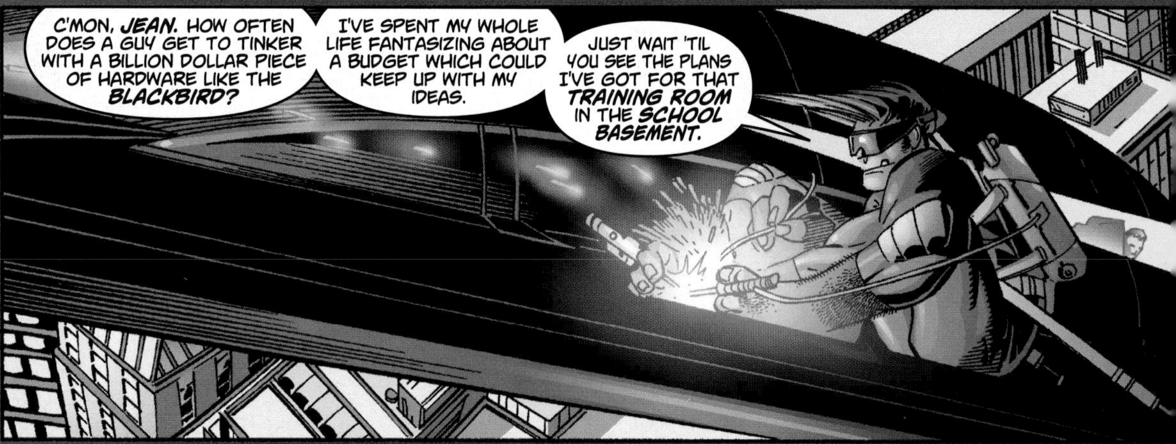
C'MON, JEAN. HOW OFTEN DOES A GUY GET TO TINKER WITH A BILLION DOLLAR PIECE OF HARDWARE LIKE THE BLACKBIRD?
I'VE SPENT MY WHOLE LIFE FANTASIZING ABOUT A BUDGET WHICH COULD KEEP UP WITH MY IDEAS.
JUST WAIT 'TIL YOU SEE THE PLANS I'VE GOT FOR THAT TRAINING ROOM IN THE SCHOOL BASEMENT.

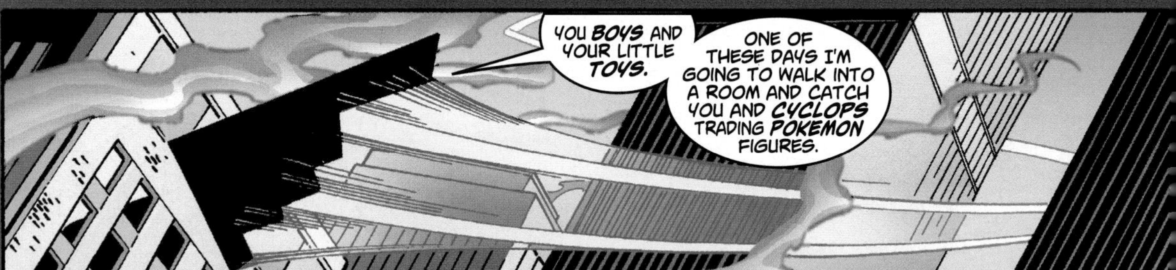
YOU BOYS AND YOUR LITTLE TOYS.
ONE OF THESE DAYS I'M GOING TO WALK INTO A ROOM AND CATCH YOU AND CYCLOPS TRADING POKEMON FIGURES.

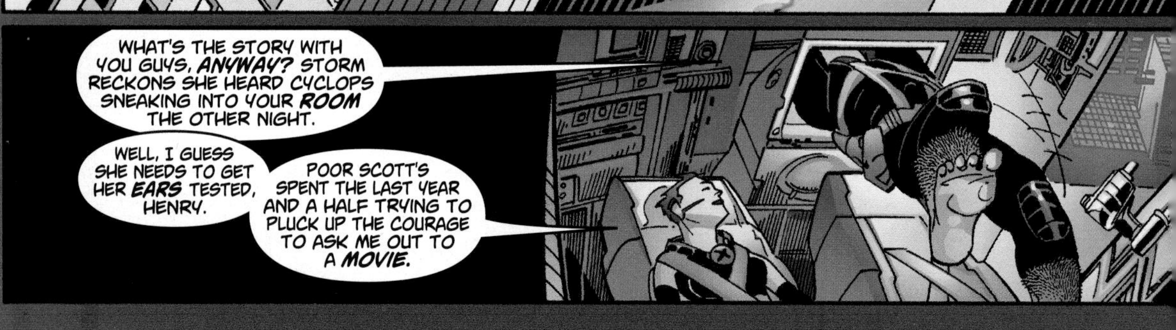
WHAT'S THE STORY WITH YOU GUYS, ANYWAY? STORM RECKONS SHE HEARD CYCLOPS SNEAKING INTO YOUR ROOM THE OTHER NIGHT.
WELL, I GUESS SHE NEEDS TO GET HER EARS TESTED, HENRY.
POOR SCOTT'S SPENT THE LAST YEAR AND A HALF TRYING TO PLUCK UP THE COURAGE TO ASK ME OUT TO A MOVIE.

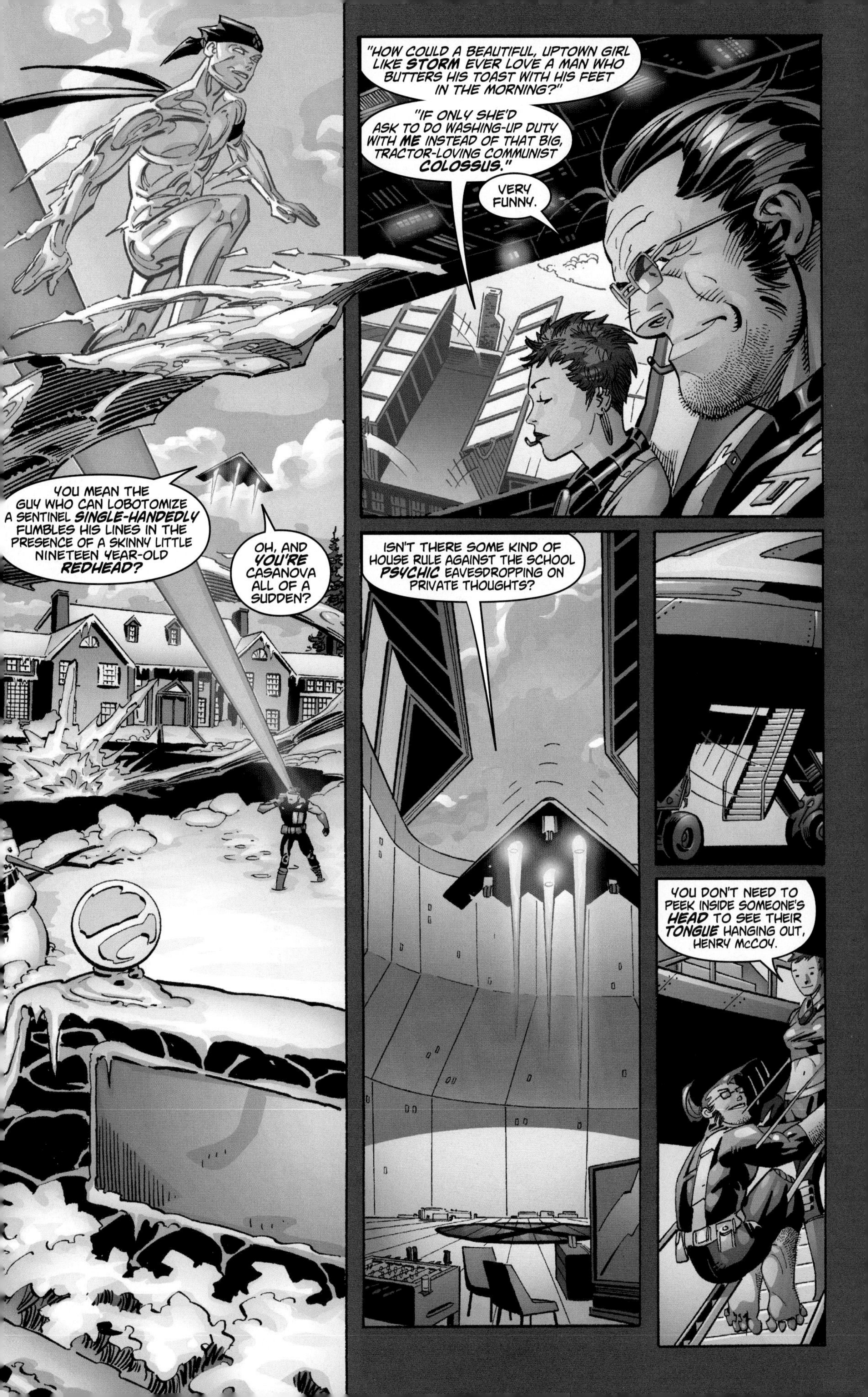
"HOW COULD A BEAUTIFUL, UPTOWN GIRL LIKE STORM EVER LOVE A MAN WHO BUTTERS HIS TOAST WITH HIS FEET IN THE MORNING?"
"IF ONLY SHE'D ASK TO DO WASHING-UP DUTY WITH ME INSTEAD OF THAT BIG, TRACTOR-LOVING COMMUNIST COLOSSUS."
VERY FUNNY.
YOU MEAN THE GUY WHO CAN LOBOTOMIZE A SENTINEL SINGLE-HANDEDLY FUMBLES HIS LINES IN THE PRESENCE OF A SKINNY LITTLE NINETEEN YEAR-OLD REDHEAD?
OH, AND YOU'RE CASANOVA ALL OF A SUDDEN?
ISN'T THERE SOME KIND OF HOUSE RULE AGAINST THE SCHOOL PSYCHIC EAVESDROPPING ON PRIVATE THOUGHTS?
YOU DON'T NEED TO PEEK INSIDE SOMEONE'S HEAD TO SEE THEIR TONGUE HANGING OUT, HENRY McCOY.

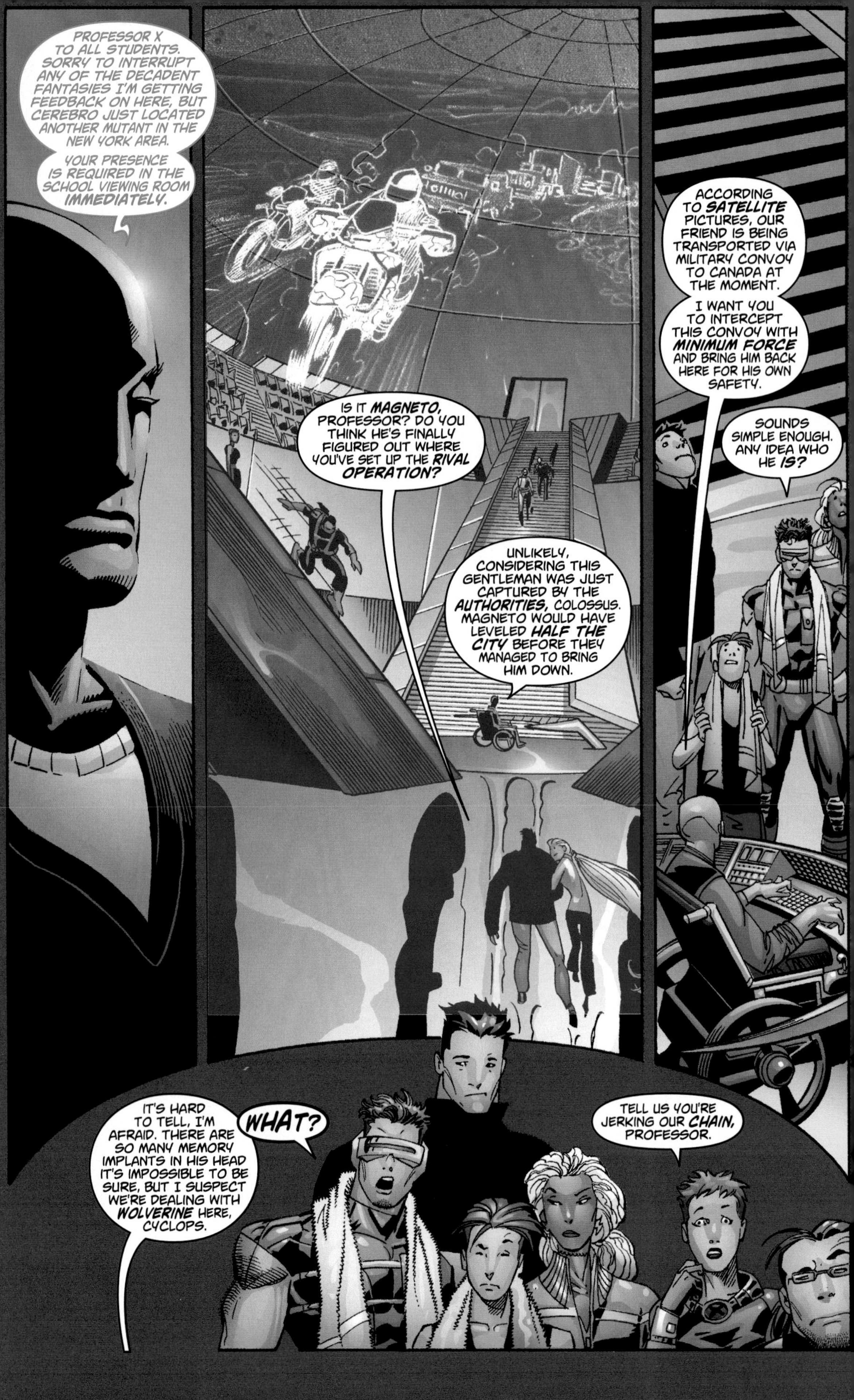
PROFESSOR X TO ALL STUDENTS. SORRY TO INTERRUPT ANY OF THE DECADENT FANTASIES I'M GETTING FEEDBACK ON HERE, BUT CEREBRO JUST LOCATED ANOTHER MUTANT IN THE NEW YORK AREA.
YOUR PRESENCE IS REQUIRED IN THE SCHOOL VIEWING ROOM IMMEDIATELY.
IS IT MAGNETO, PROFESSOR? DO YOU THINK HE'S FINALLY FIGURED OUT WHERE YOU'VE SET UP THE RIVAL OPERATION?
UNLIKELY, CONSIDERING THIS GENTLEMAN WAS JUST CAPTURED BY THE AUTHORITIES, COLOSSUS. MAGNETO WOULD HAVE LEVELED HALF THE CITY BEFORE THEY MANAGED TO BRING HIM DOWN.
ACCORDING TO SATELLITE PICTURES, OUR FRIEND IS BEING TRANSPORTED VIA MILITARY CONVOY TO CANADA AT THE MOMENT.
I WANT YOU TO INTERCEPT THIS CONVOY WITH MINIMUM FORCE AND BRING HIM BACK HERE FOR HIS OWN SAFETY.
SOUNDS SIMPLE ENOUGH. ANY IDEA WHO HE IS?
IT'S HARD TO TELL, I'M AFRAID. THERE ARE SO MANY MEMORY IMPLANTS IN HIS HEAD IT'S IMPOSSIBLE TO BE SURE, BUT I SUSPECT WE'RE DEALING WITH WOLVERINE HERE, CYCLOPS.
WHAT?
TELL US YOU'RE JERKING OUR CHAIN, PROFESSOR.

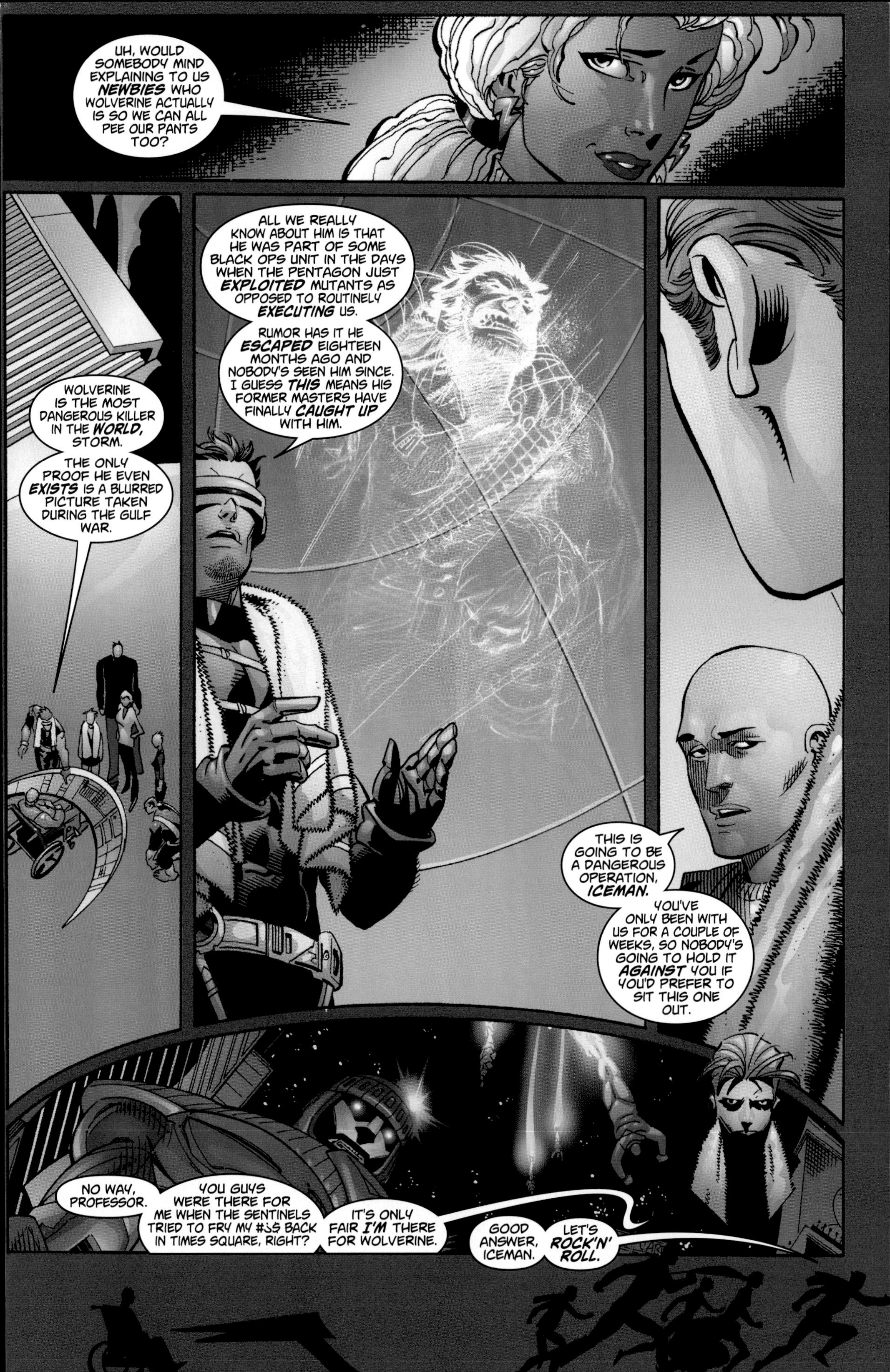
UH, WOULD SOMEBODY MIND EXPLAINING TO US NEWBIES WHO WOLVERINE ACTUALLY IS SO WE CAN ALL PEE OUR PANTS TOO?
WOLVERINE IS THE MOST DANGEROUS KILLER IN THE WORLD, STORM.
THE ONLY PROOF HE EVEN EXISTS IS A BLURRED PICTURE TAKEN DURING THE GULF WAR.
ALL WE REALLY KNOW ABOUT HIM IS THAT HE WAS PART OF SOME BLACK OPS UNIT IN THE DAYS WHEN THE PENTAGON JUST EXPLOITED MUTANTS AS OPPOSED TO ROUTINELY EXECUTING US.
RUMOR HAS IT HE ESCAPED EIGHTEEN MONTHS AGO AND NOBODY'S SEEN HIM SINCE. I GUESS THIS MEANS HIS FORMER MASTERS HAVE FINALLY CAUGHT UP WITH HIM.
THIS IS GOING TO BE A DANGEROUS OPERATION, ICEMAN.
YOU'VE ONLY BEEN WITH US FOR A COUPLE OF WEEKS, SO NOBODY'S GOING TO HOLD IT AGAINST YOU IF YOU'D PREFER TO SIT THIS ONE OUT.
NO WAY, PROFESSOR.
YOU GUYS WERE THERE FOR ME WHEN THE SENTINELS TRIED TO FRY MY #$$ BACK IN TIMES SQUARE, RIGHT?
IT'S ONLY FAIR I'M THERE FOR WOLVERINE.
GOOD ANSWER, ICEMAN.
LET'S ROCK'N' ROLL.

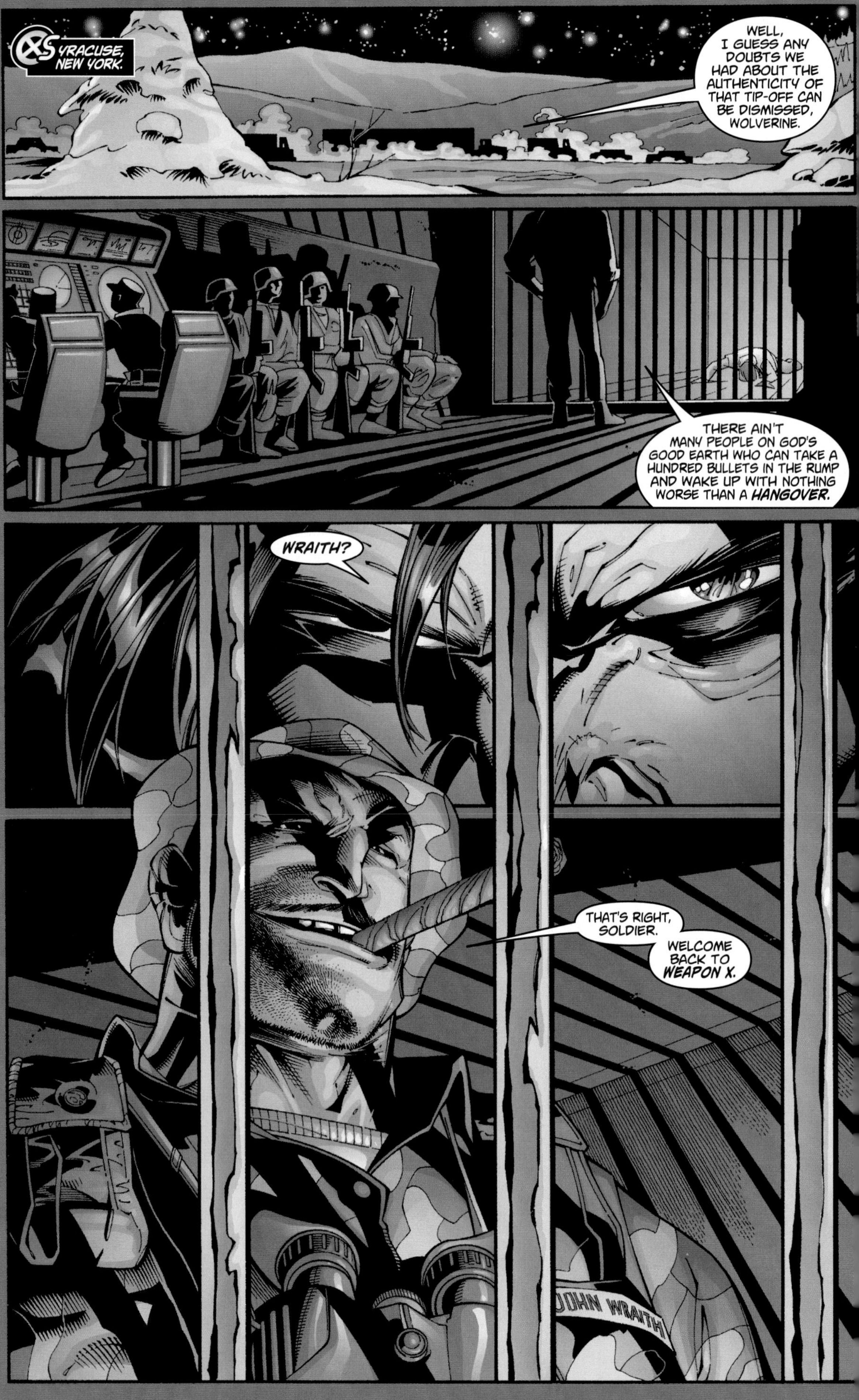
SYRACUSE, NEW YORK.
WELL, I GUESS ANY DOUBTS WE HAD ABOUT THE AUTHENTICITY OF THAT TIP-OFF CAN BE DISMISSED, WOLVERINE.
THERE AIN'T MANY PEOPLE ON GOD'S GOOD EARTH WHO CAN TAKE A HUNDRED BULLETS IN THE RUMP AND WAKE UP WITH NOTHING WORSE THAN A HANGOVER.
WRAITH?
THAT'S RIGHT, SOLDIER.
WELCOME BACK TO WEAPON X.
JOHN WRAITH

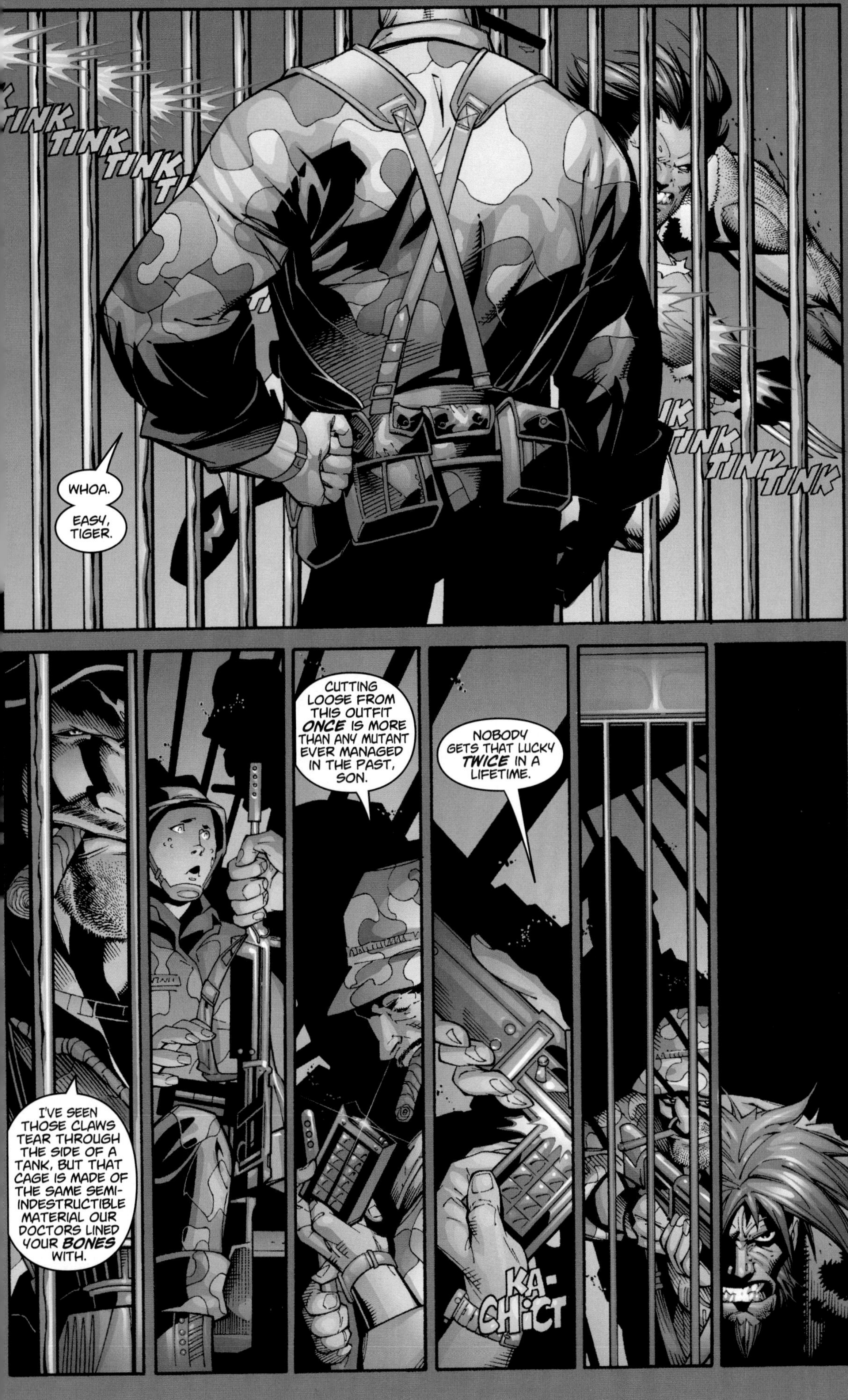
TINK TINK TINK
WHOA.
EASY, TIGER.
TINK TINK TINK
I'VE SEEN THOSE CLAWS TEAR THROUGH THE SIDE OF A TANK, BUT THAT CAGE IS MADE OF THE SAME SEMI-INDESTRUCTIBLE MATERIAL OUR DOCTORS LINED YOUR BONES WITH.
CUTTING LOOSE FROM THIS OUTFIT ONCE IS MORE THAN ANY MUTANT EVER MANAGED IN THE PAST, SON.
NOBODY GETS THAT LUCKY TWICE IN A LIFETIME.
KA-CHICT

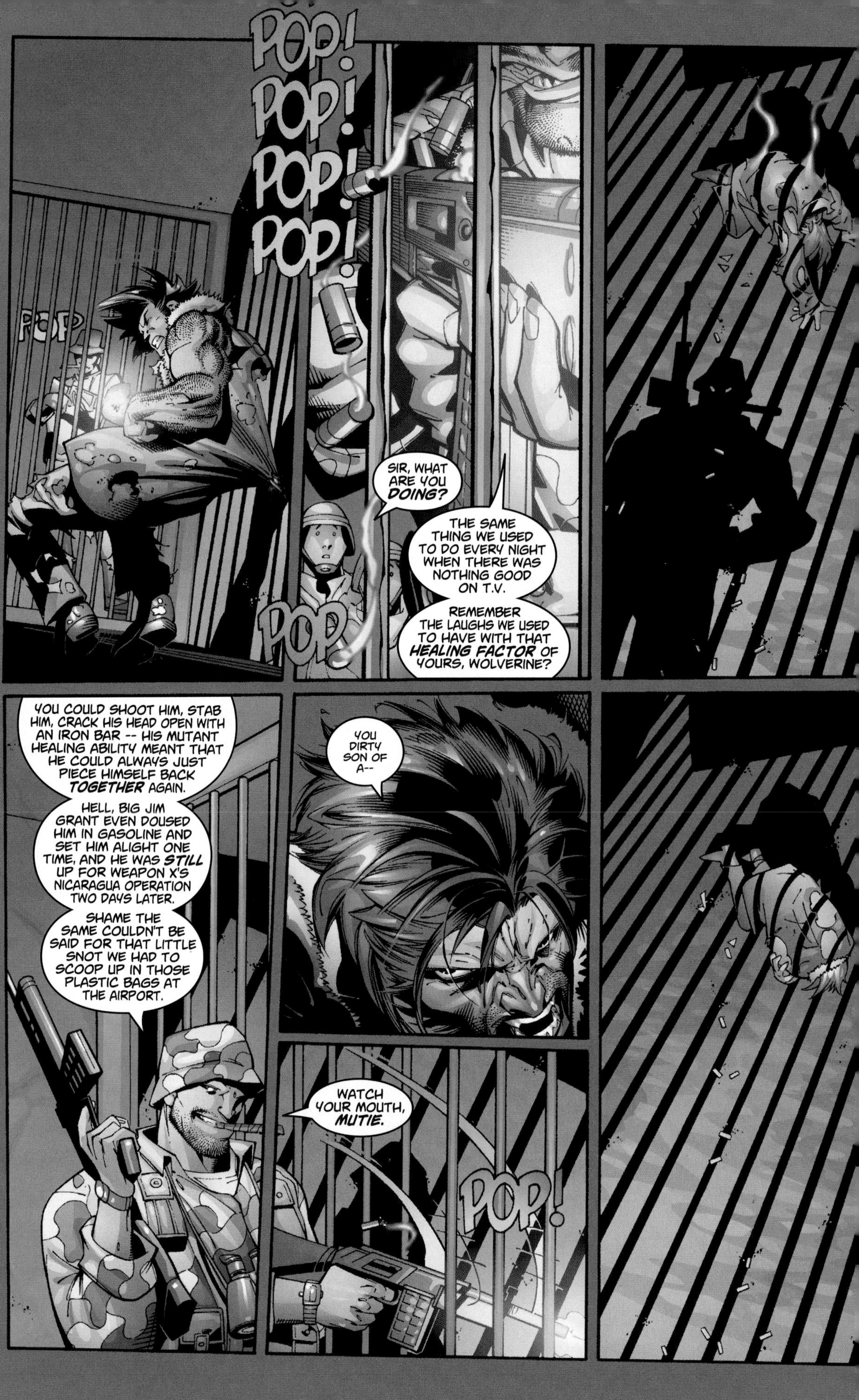
POP! POP! POP! POP!
POP
SIR, WHAT ARE YOU DOING?
THE SAME THING WE USED TO DO EVERY NIGHT WHEN THERE WAS NOTHING GOOD ON T.V.
REMEMBER THE LAUGHS WE USED TO HAVE WITH THAT HEALING FACTOR OF YOURS, WOLVERINE?
POP
YOU COULD SHOOT HIM, STAB HIM, CRACK HIS HEAD OPEN WITH AN IRON BAR -- HIS MUTANT HEALING ABILITY MEANT THAT HE COULD ALWAYS JUST PIECE HIMSELF BACK TOGETHER AGAIN.
HELL, BIG JIM GRANT EVEN DOUSED HIM IN GASOLINE AND SET HIM ALIGHT ONE TIME, AND HE WAS STILL UP FOR WEAPON X'S NICARAGUA OPERATION TWO DAYS LATER.
SHAME THE SAME COULDN'T BE SAID FOR THAT LITTLE SNOT WE HAD TO SCOOP UP IN THOSE PLASTIC BAGS AT THE AIRPORT.
YOU DIRTY SON OF A--
WATCH YOUR MOUTH, MUTIE.
POP!

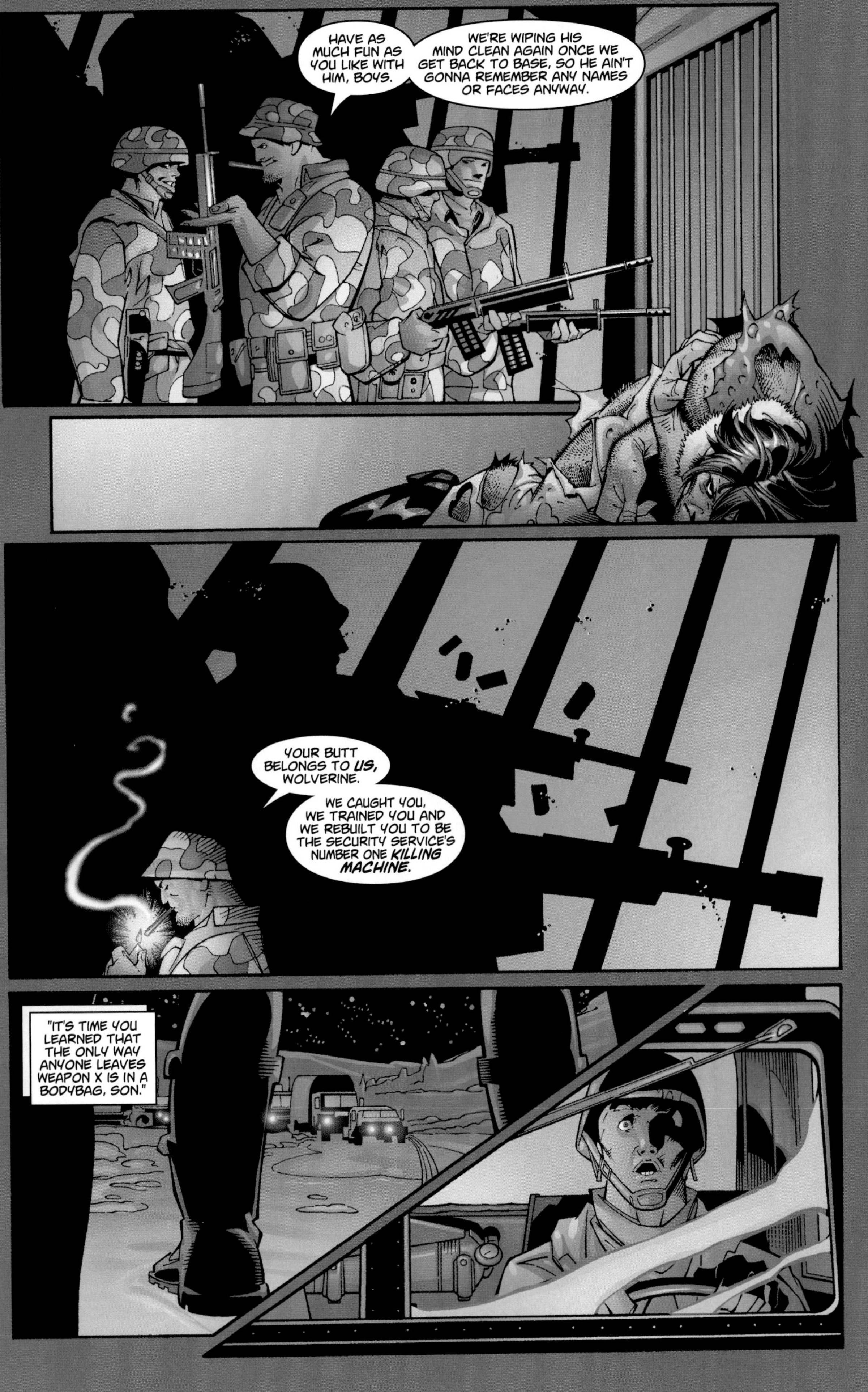
HAVE AS MUCH FUN AS YOU LIKE WITH HIM, BOYS.
WE'RE WIPING HIS MIND CLEAN AGAIN ONCE WE GET BACK TO BASE, SO HE AIN'T GONNA REMEMBER ANY NAMES OR FACES ANYWAY.
YOUR BUTT BELONGS TO *US*, WOLVERINE.
WE CAUGHT YOU, WE TRAINED YOU AND WE REBUILT YOU TO BE THE SECURITY SERVICE'S NUMBER ONE *KILLING MACHINE.*
"IT'S TIME YOU LEARNED THAT THE ONLY WAY ANYONE LEAVES WEAPON X IS IN A BODYBAG, SON."

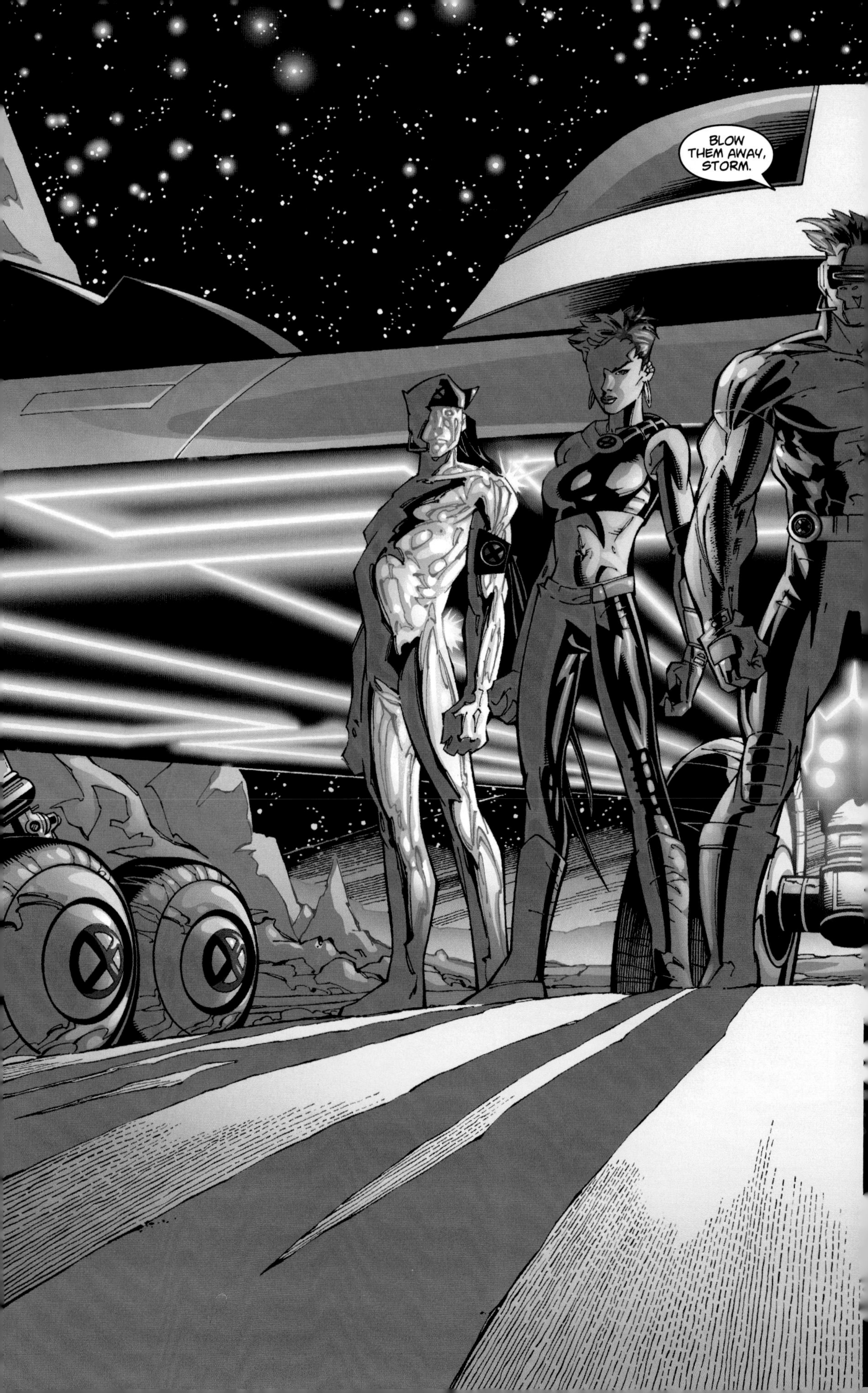
BLOW THEM AWAY, STORM.

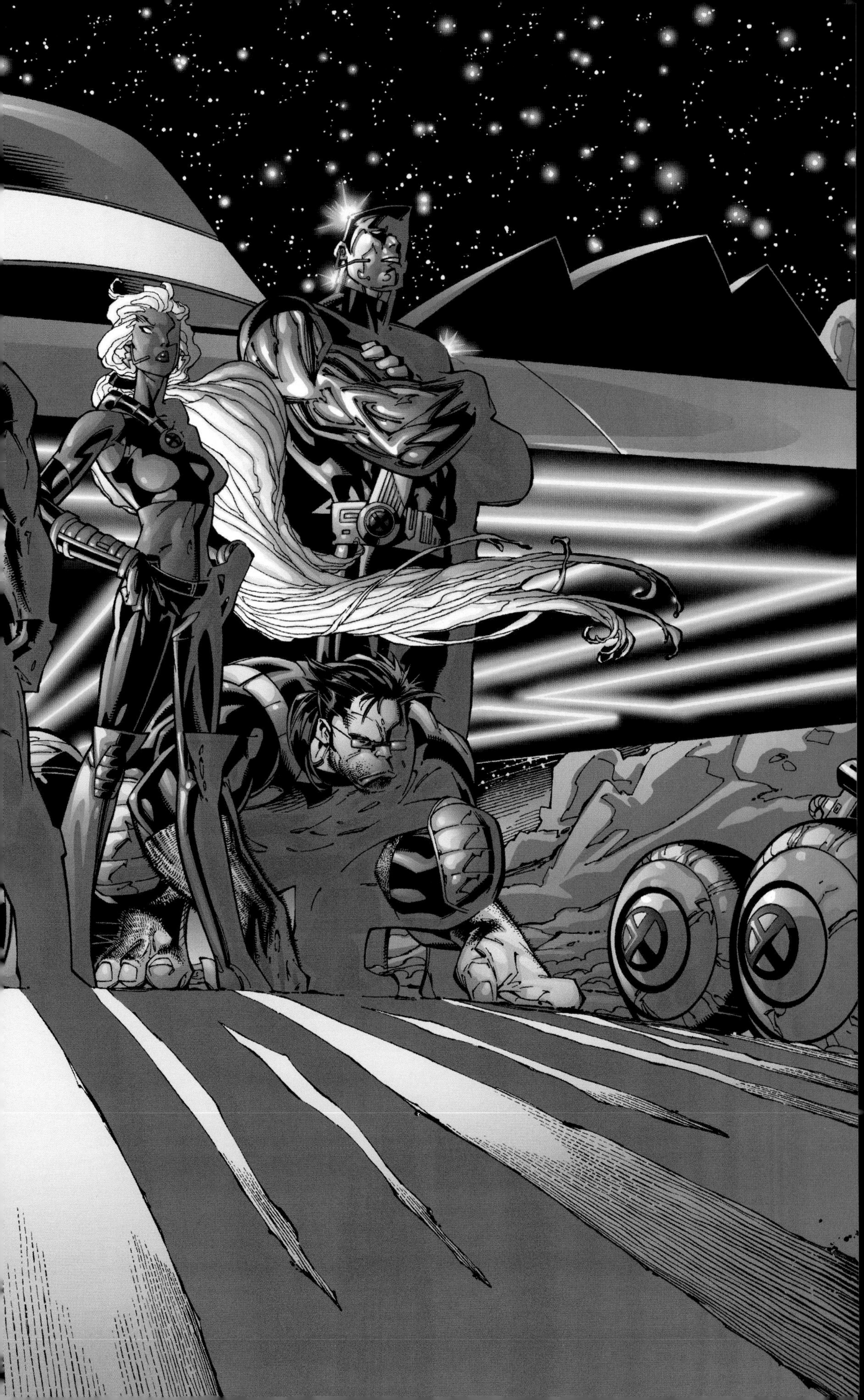

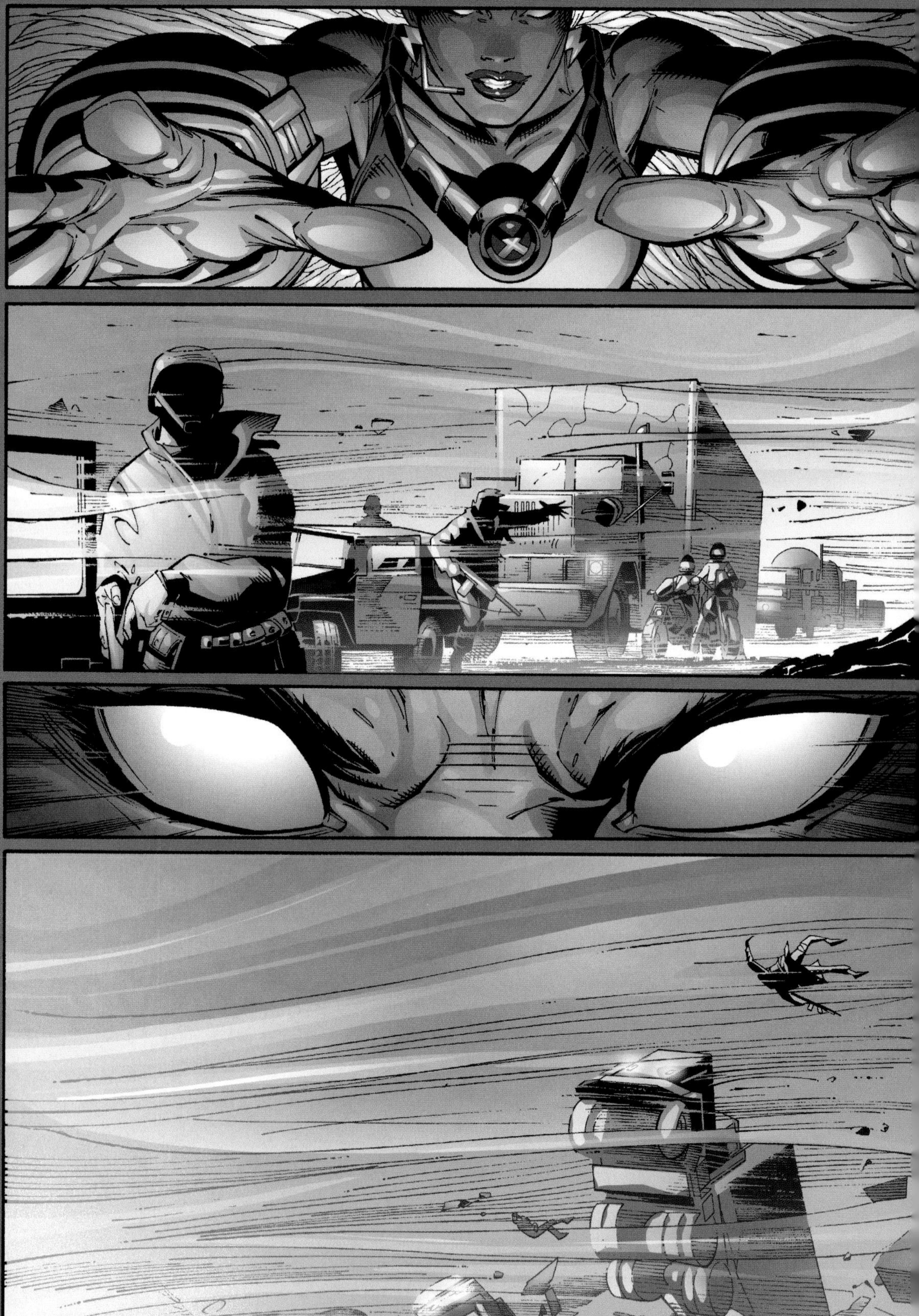

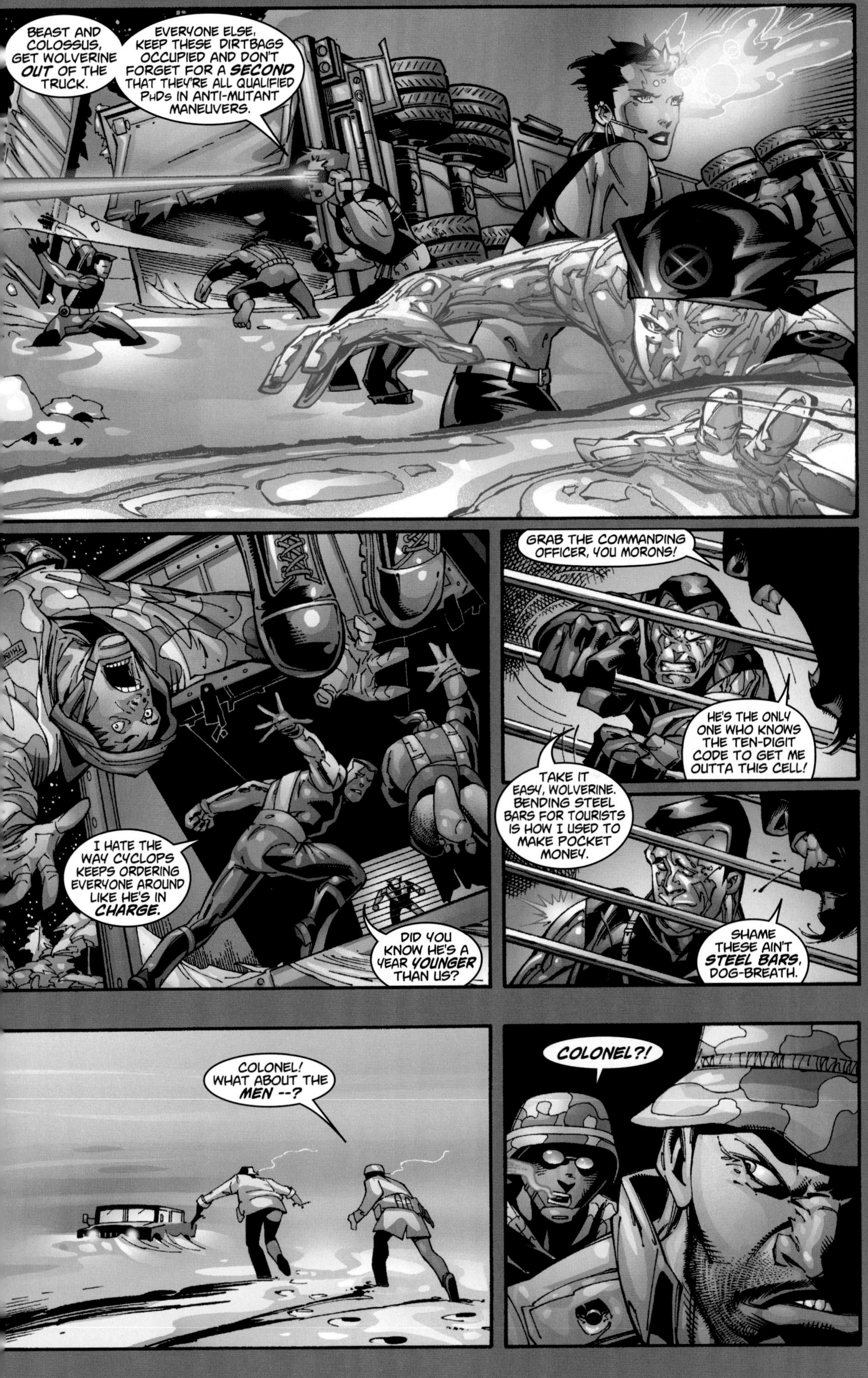
BEAST AND COLOSSUS, GET WOLVERINE *OUT* OF THE TRUCK.
EVERYONE ELSE, KEEP THESE DIRTBAGS OCCUPIED AND DON'T FORGET FOR A *SECOND* THAT THEY'RE ALL QUALIFIED PhDs IN ANTI-MUTANT MANEUVERS.
I HATE THE WAY CYCLOPS KEEPS ORDERING EVERYONE AROUND LIKE HE'S IN *CHARGE*.
DID YOU KNOW HE'S A YEAR *YOUNGER* THAN US?
GRAB THE COMMANDING OFFICER, YOU MORONS!
HE'S THE ONLY ONE WHO KNOWS THE TEN-DIGIT CODE TO GET ME OUTTA THIS CELL!
TAKE IT EASY, WOLVERINE. BENDING STEEL BARS FOR TOURISTS IS HOW I USED TO MAKE POCKET MONEY.
SHAME THESE AIN'T *STEEL BARS*, DOG-BREATH.
COLONEL! WHAT ABOUT THE *MEN* --?
COLONEL?!

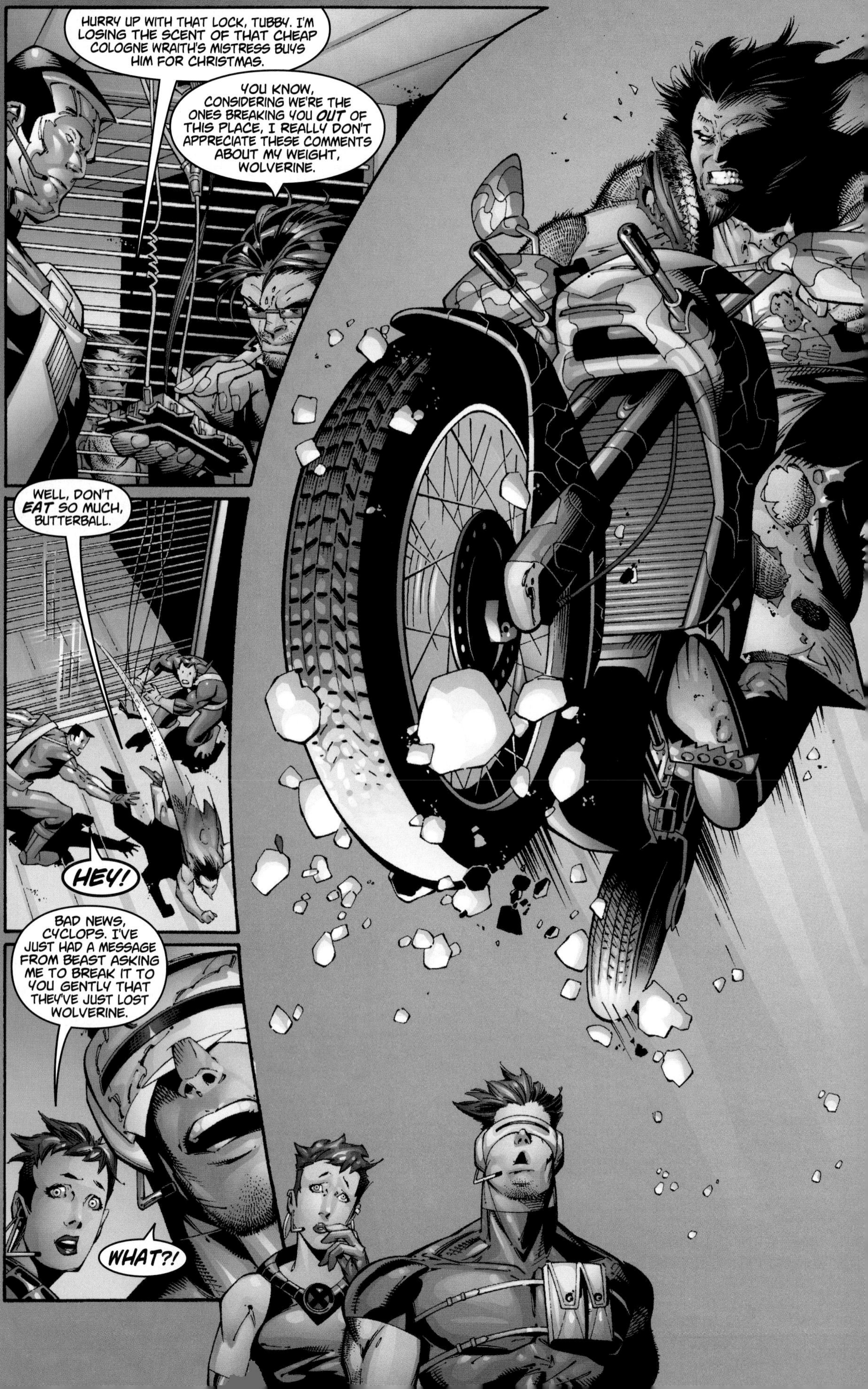
HURRY UP WITH THAT LOCK, TUBBY. I'M LOSING THE SCENT OF THAT CHEAP COLOGNE WRAITH'S MISTRESS BUYS HIM FOR CHRISTMAS.
YOU KNOW, CONSIDERING WE'RE THE ONES BREAKING YOU OUT OF THIS PLACE, I REALLY DON'T APPRECIATE THESE COMMENTS ABOUT MY WEIGHT, WOLVERINE.
WELL, DON'T EAT SO MUCH, BUTTERBALL.
HEY!
BAD NEWS, CYCLOPS. I'VE JUST HAD A MESSAGE FROM BEAST ASKING ME TO BREAK IT TO YOU GENTLY THAT THEY'VE JUST LOST WOLVERINE.
WHAT?!

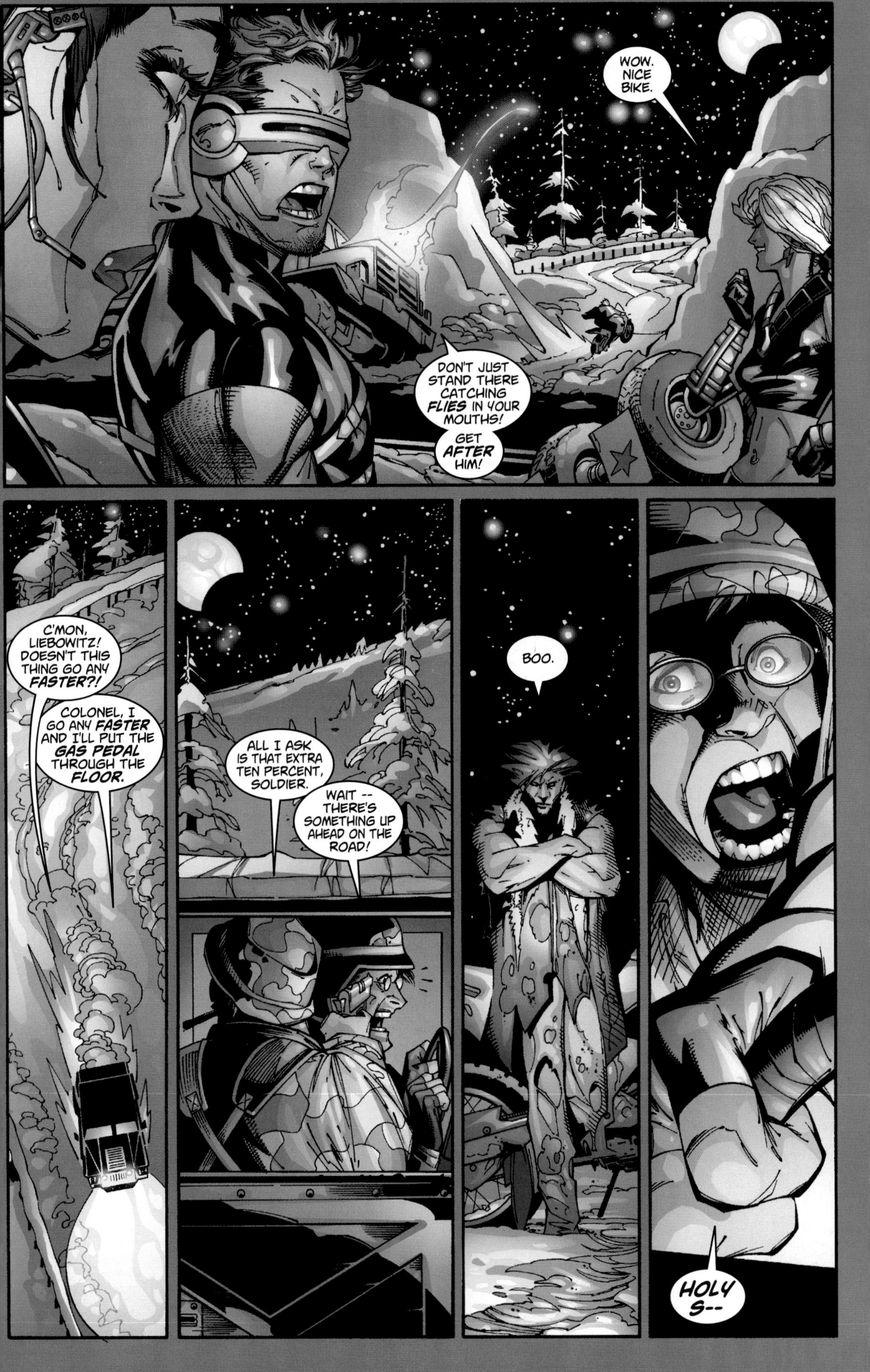
WOW. NICE BIKE.
DON'T JUST STAND THERE CATCHING FLIES IN YOUR MOUTHS!
GET AFTER HIM!
C'MON, LIEBOWITZ! DOESN'T THIS THING GO ANY FASTER?!
COLONEL, I GO ANY FASTER AND I'LL PUT THE GAS PEDAL THROUGH THE FLOOR.
ALL I ASK IS THAT EXTRA TEN PERCENT, SOLDIER.
WAIT -- THERE'S SOMETHING UP AHEAD ON THE ROAD!
BOO.
HOLY S--

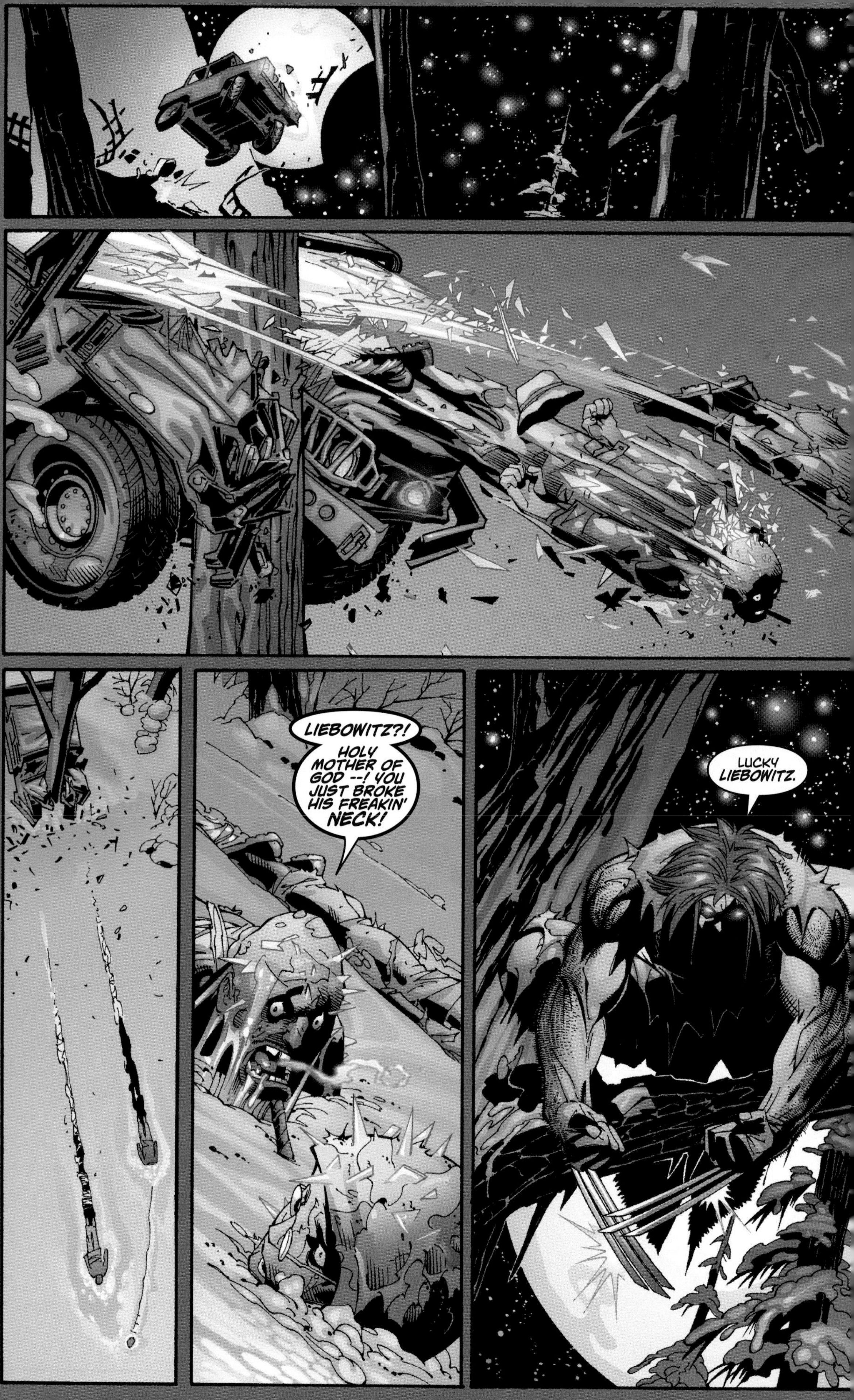
LIEBOWITZ?! HOLY MOTHER OF GOD --! YOU JUST BROKE HIS FREAKIN' NECK!
LUCKY LIEBOWITZ.

WOLVERINE --
NO!

DON'T KILL HIM!

I CAN'T IMAGINE WHAT THAT ANIMAL PUT YOU THROUGH OVER THE YEARS, BUT MURDER HIM OUT HERE LIKE THIS AND ALL YOU'RE GOING TO DO IS PROVE THAT THE PAPERS ARE *RIGHT* ABOUT US.

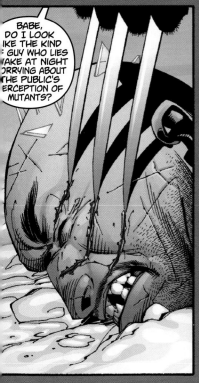

BABE, DO I LOOK LIKE THE KIND OF GUY WHO LIES AWAKE AT NIGHT WORRYING ABOUT THE PUBLIC'S PERCEPTION OF MUTANTS?

YOU'VE HAD A *HARD ENOUGH* DAY, BIG MAN.

DON'T MAKE ME *HURT* YOU.

AND HOW DO YOU PROPOSE TO DO *THAT*, GORGEOUS?

HIT ME WITH A *HIGH-HEEL?* SMACK ME IN THE FACE WITH YOUR *BARBIE* PURSE?

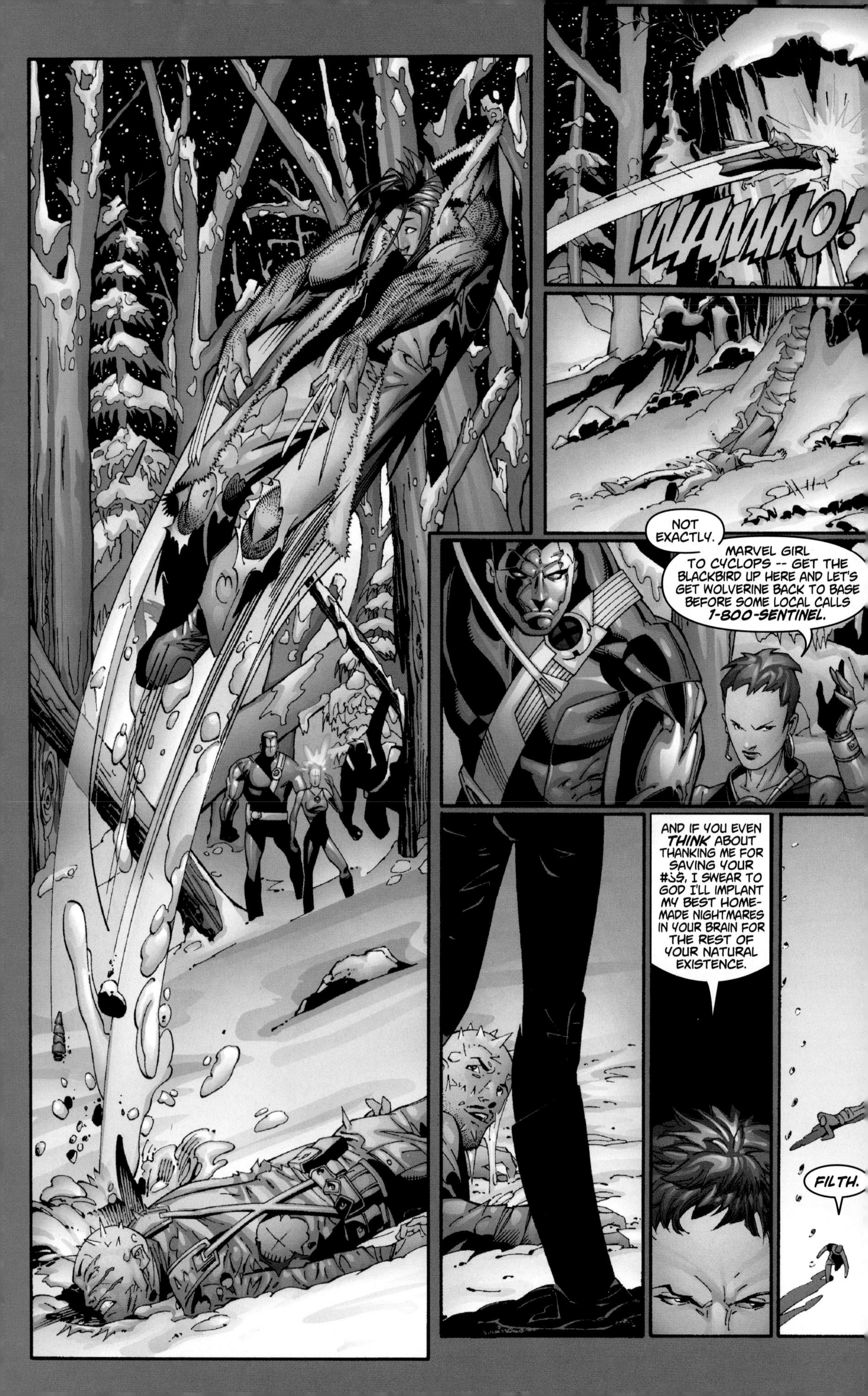
WHAMMO!
NOT EXACTLY.
MARVEL GIRL TO CYCLOPS -- GET THE BLACKBIRD UP HERE AND LET'S GET WOLVERINE BACK TO BASE BEFORE SOME LOCAL CALLS 1-800-SENTINEL.
AND IF YOU EVEN THINK ABOUT THANKING ME FOR SAVING YOUR #$$, I SWEAR TO GOD I'LL IMPLANT MY BEST HOME-MADE NIGHTMARES IN YOUR BRAIN FOR THE REST OF YOUR NATURAL EXISTENCE.
FILTH.

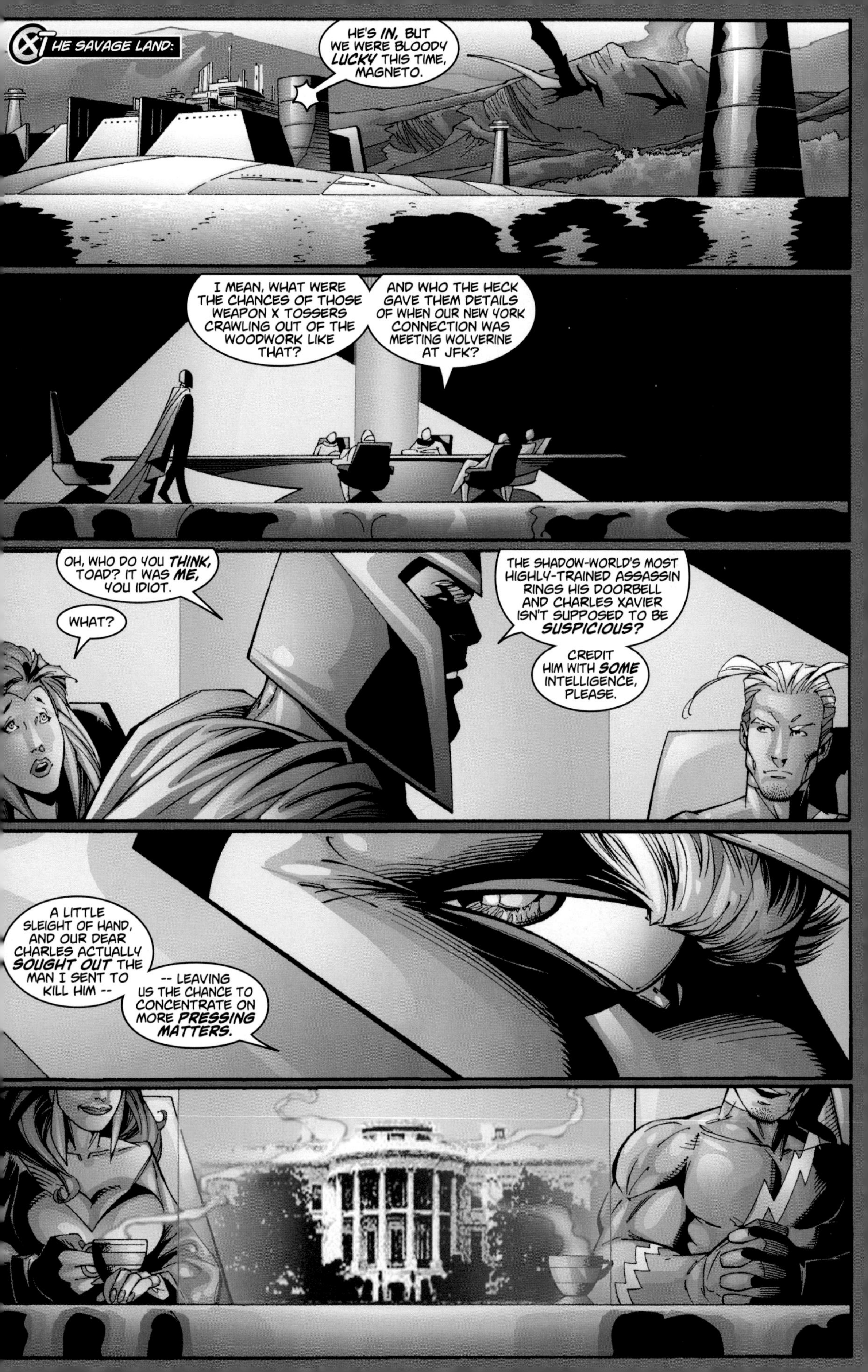
THE SAVAGE LAND:
HE'S IN, BUT WE WERE BLOODY LUCKY THIS TIME, MAGNETO.
I MEAN, WHAT WERE THE CHANCES OF THOSE WEAPON X TOSSERS CRAWLING OUT OF THE WOODWORK LIKE THAT?
AND WHO THE HECK GAVE THEM DETAILS OF WHEN OUR NEW YORK CONNECTION WAS MEETING WOLVERINE AT JFK?
OH, WHO DO YOU THINK, TOAD? IT WAS ME, YOU IDIOT.
WHAT?
THE SHADOW-WORLD'S MOST HIGHLY-TRAINED ASSASSIN RINGS HIS DOORBELL AND CHARLES XAVIER ISN'T SUPPOSED TO BE SUSPICIOUS?
CREDIT HIM WITH SOME INTELLIGENCE, PLEASE.
A LITTLE SLEIGHT OF HAND, AND OUR DEAR CHARLES ACTUALLY SOUGHT OUT THE MAN I SENT TO KILL HIM --
-- LEAVING US THE CHANCE TO CONCENTRATE ON MORE PRESSING MATTERS.

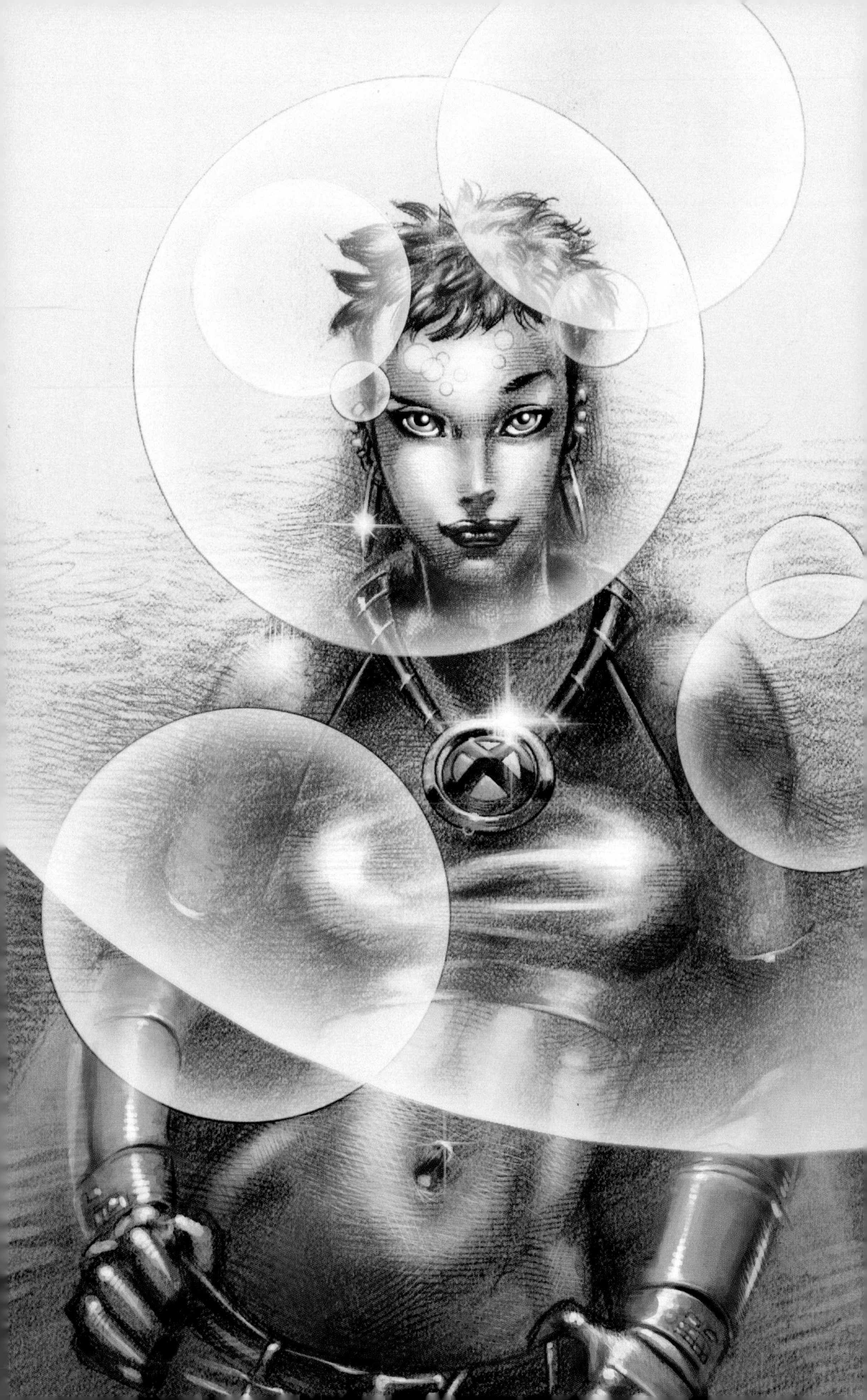

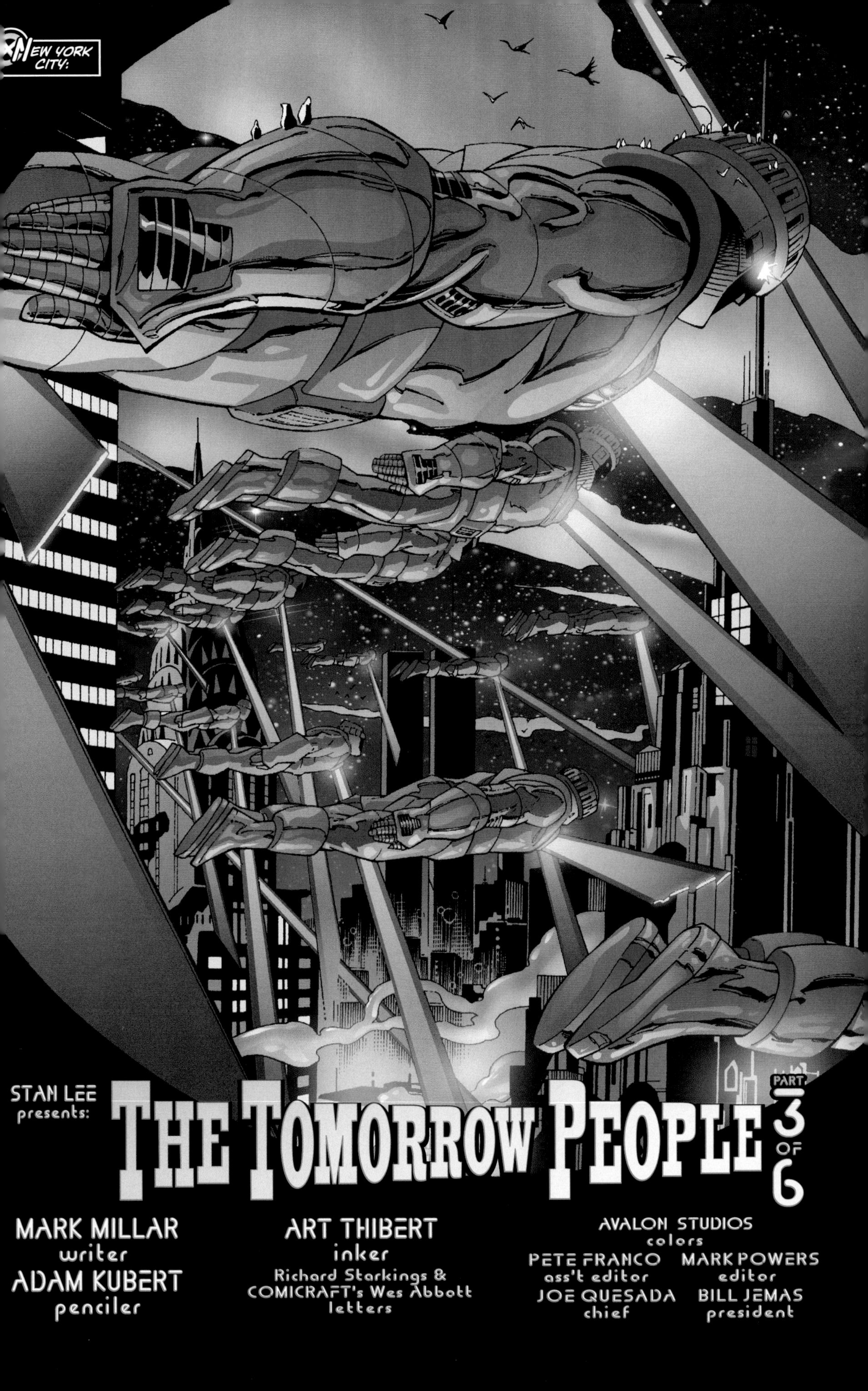

NEW YORK CITY:
STAN LEE presents:
THE TOMORROW PEOPLE PART 3 OF 6
MARK MILLAR writer
ADAM KUBERT penciler
ART THIBERT inker
Richard Starkings & COMICRAFT's Wes Abbott letters
AVALON STUDIOS colors
PETE FRANCO ass't editor
MARK POWERS editor
JOE QUESADA chief
BILL JEMAS president

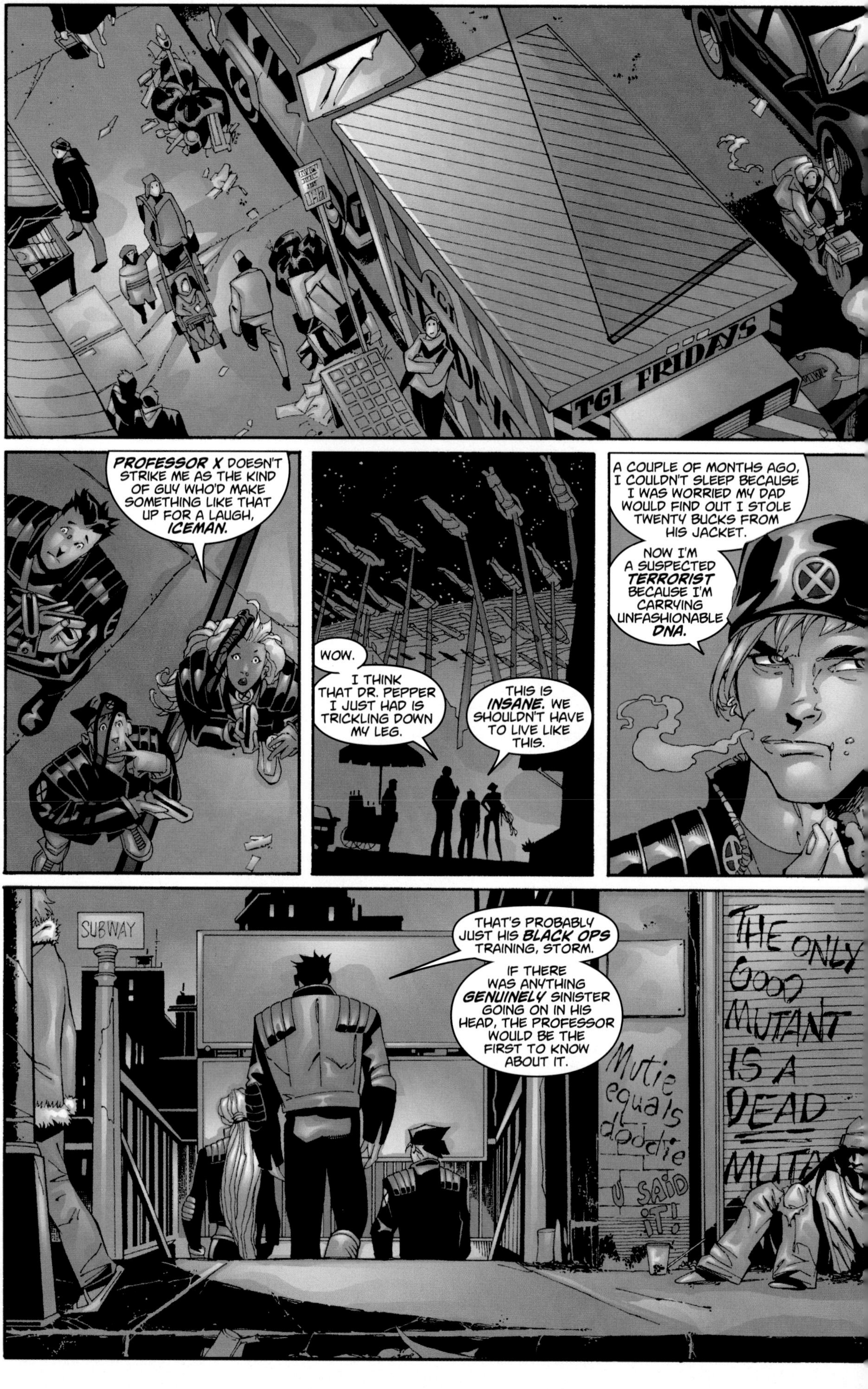
TGI FRIDAYS
PROFESSOR X DOESN'T STRIKE ME AS THE KIND OF GUY WHO'D MAKE SOMETHING LIKE THAT UP FOR A LAUGH, ICEMAN.
WOW.
I THINK THAT DR. PEPPER I JUST HAD IS TRICKLING DOWN MY LEG.
THIS IS INSANE. WE SHOULDN'T HAVE TO LIVE LIKE THIS.
A COUPLE OF MONTHS AGO, I COULDN'T SLEEP BECAUSE I WAS WORRIED MY DAD WOULD FIND OUT I STOLE TWENTY BUCKS FROM HIS JACKET.
NOW I'M A SUSPECTED TERRORIST BECAUSE I'M CARRYING UNFASHIONABLE DNA.
SUBWAY
THAT'S PROBABLY JUST HIS BLACK OPS TRAINING, STORM.
IF THERE WAS ANYTHING GENUINELY SINISTER GOING ON IN HIS HEAD, THE PROFESSOR WOULD BE THE FIRST TO KNOW ABOUT IT.
Mutie equals deadie
U SAID it!
THE ONLY GOOD MUTANT IS A DEAD

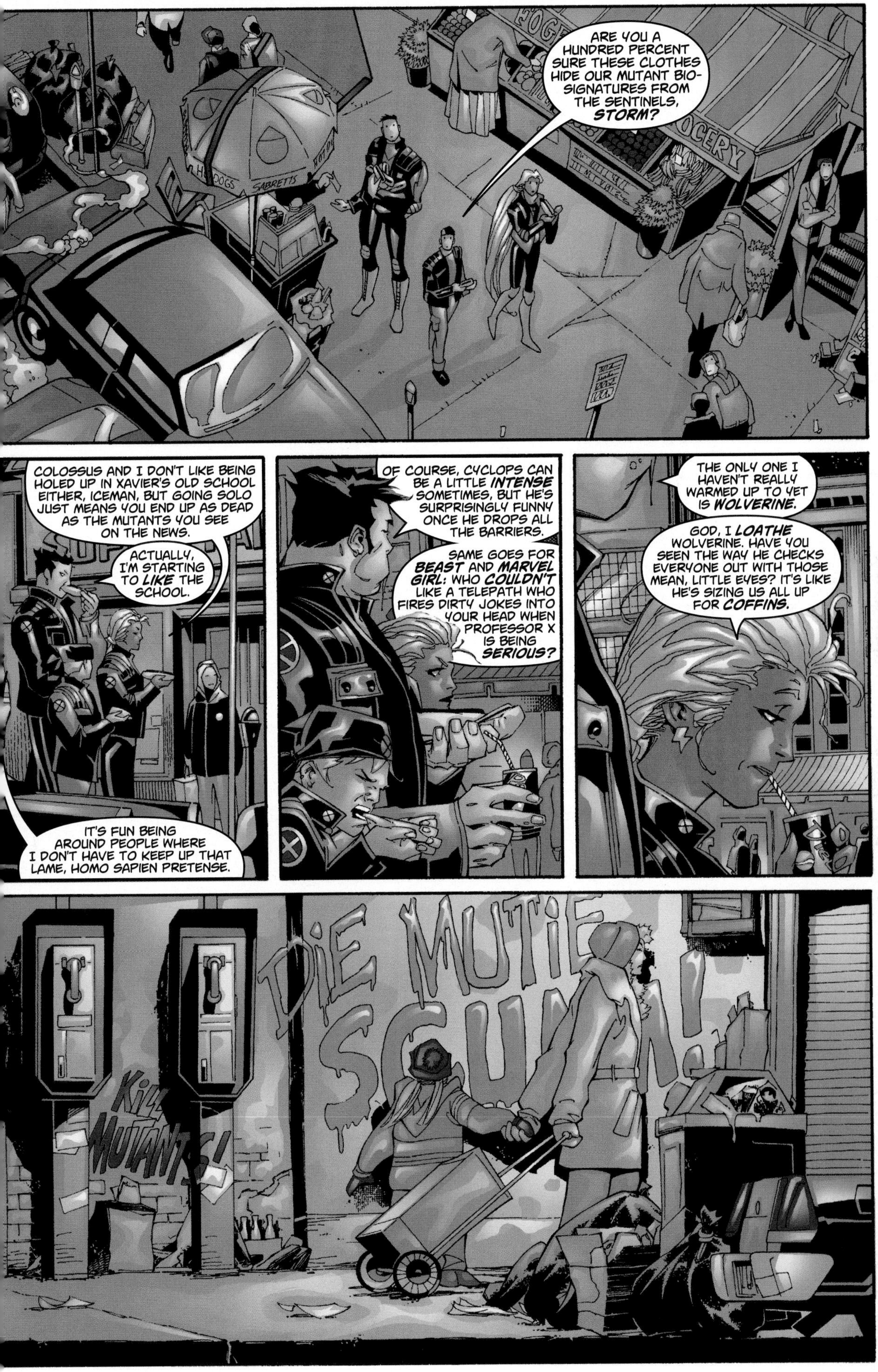
ARE YOU A HUNDRED PERCENT SURE THESE CLOTHES HIDE OUR MUTANT BIO-SIGNATURES FROM THE SENTINELS, STORM?
GROCERY
HOT DOGS
SABRETTS
COLOSSUS AND I DON'T LIKE BEING HOLED UP IN XAVIER'S OLD SCHOOL EITHER, ICEMAN, BUT GOING SOLO JUST MEANS YOU END UP AS DEAD AS THE MUTANTS YOU SEE ON THE NEWS.
ACTUALLY, I'M STARTING TO LIKE THE SCHOOL.
IT'S FUN BEING AROUND PEOPLE WHERE I DON'T HAVE TO KEEP UP THAT LAME, HOMO SAPIEN PRETENSE.
OF COURSE, CYCLOPS CAN BE A LITTLE INTENSE SOMETIMES, BUT HE'S SURPRISINGLY FUNNY ONCE HE DROPS ALL THE BARRIERS.
SAME GOES FOR BEAST AND MARVEL GIRL: WHO COULDN'T LIKE A TELEPATH WHO FIRES DIRTY JOKES INTO YOUR HEAD WHEN PROFESSOR X IS BEING SERIOUS?
THE ONLY ONE I HAVEN'T REALLY WARMED UP TO YET IS WOLVERINE.
GOD, I LOATHE WOLVERINE. HAVE YOU SEEN THE WAY HE CHECKS EVERYONE OUT WITH THOSE MEAN, LITTLE EYES? IT'S LIKE HE'S SIZING US ALL UP FOR COFFINS.
DIE MUTIE SCUM!
KILL MUTANTS!

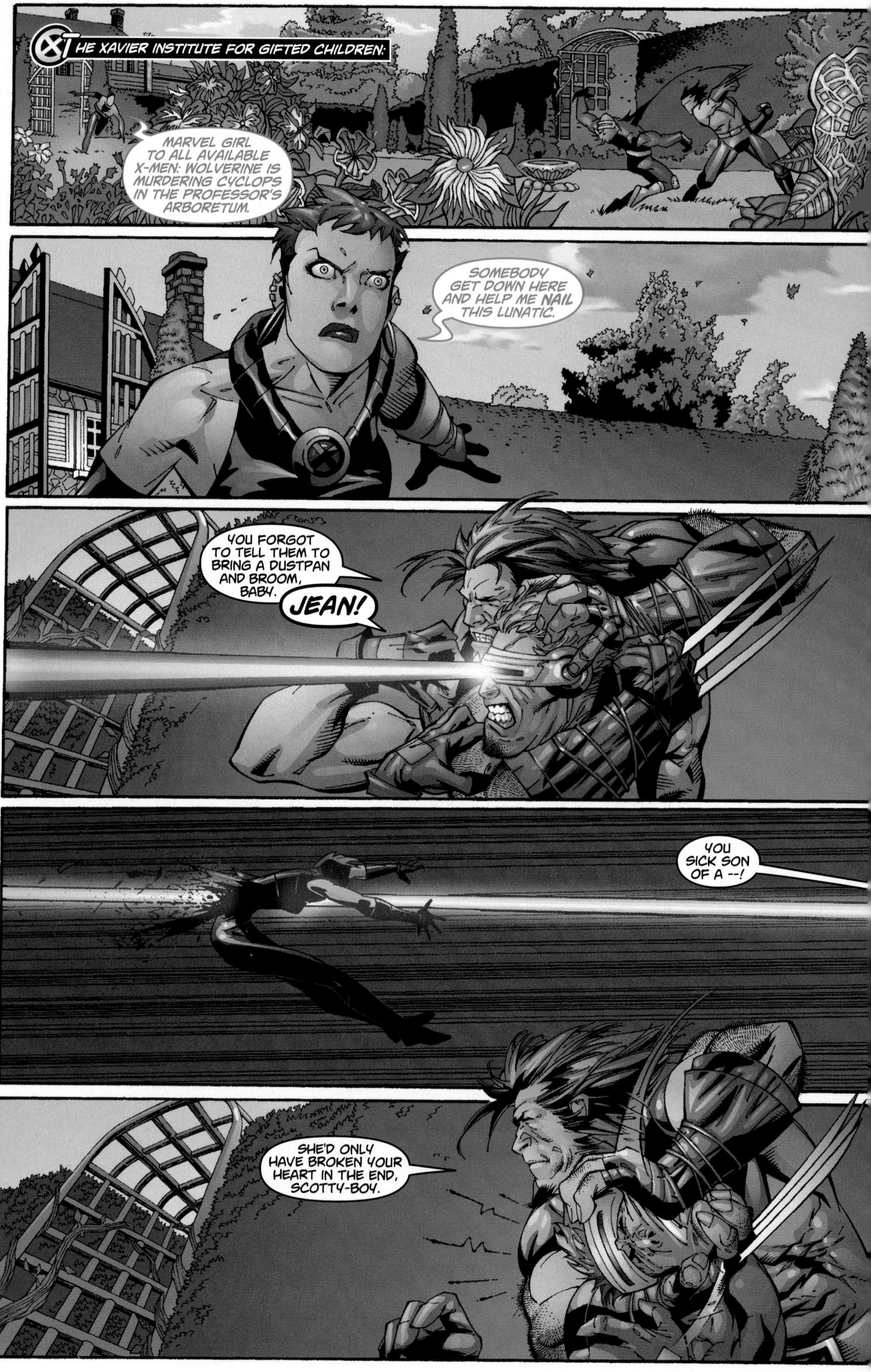
THE XAVIER INSTITUTE FOR GIFTED CHILDREN:
MARVEL GIRL TO ALL AVAILABLE X-MEN: WOLVERINE IS MURDERING CYCLOPS IN THE PROFESSOR'S ARBORETUM.
SOMEBODY GET DOWN HERE AND HELP ME NAIL THIS LUNATIC.
YOU FORGOT TO TELL THEM TO BRING A DUSTPAN AND BROOM, BABY.
JEAN!
YOU SICK SON OF A --!
SHE'D ONLY HAVE BROKEN YOUR HEART IN THE END, SCOTTY-BOY.

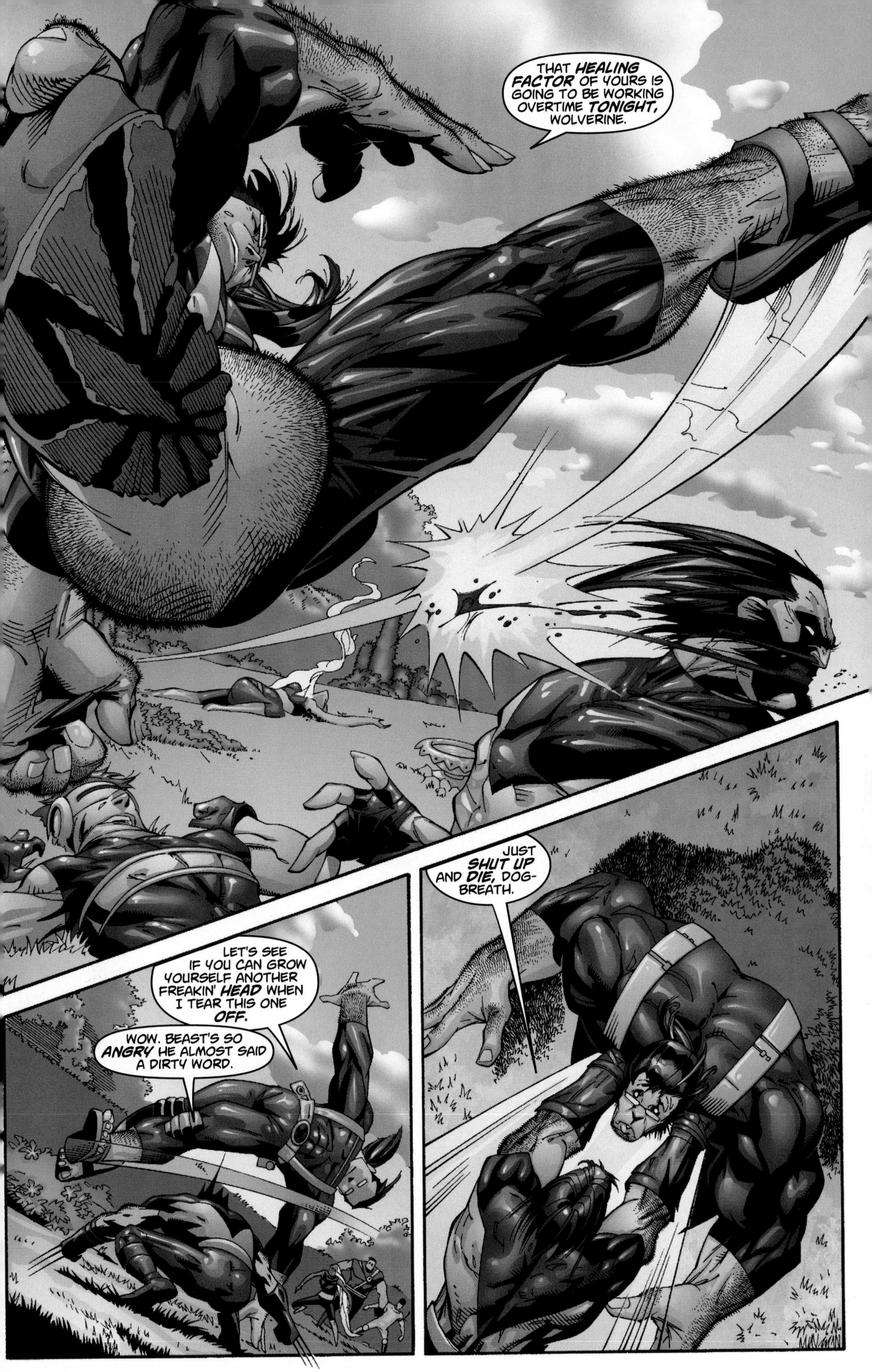
THAT HEALING FACTOR OF YOURS IS GOING TO BE WORKING OVERTIME TONIGHT, WOLVERINE.
LET'S SEE IF YOU CAN GROW YOURSELF ANOTHER FREAKIN' HEAD WHEN I TEAR THIS ONE OFF.
WOW. BEAST'S SO ANGRY HE ALMOST SAID A DIRTY WORD.
JUST SHUT UP AND DIE, DOG-BREATH.

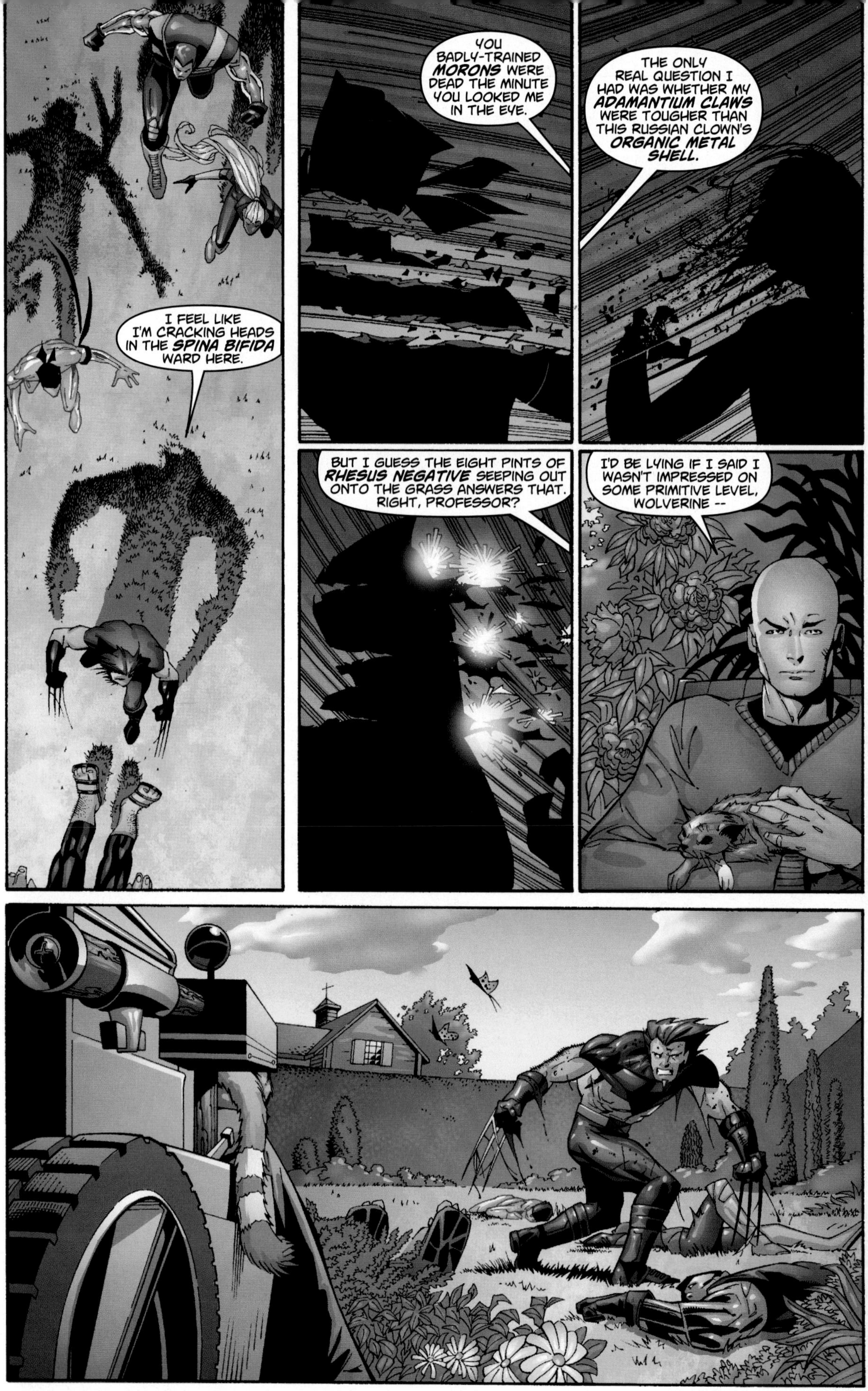

I FEEL LIKE I'M CRACKING HEADS IN THE SPINA BIFIDA WARD HERE.
YOU BADLY-TRAINED MORONS WERE DEAD THE MINUTE YOU LOOKED ME IN THE EYE.
THE ONLY REAL QUESTION I HAD WAS WHETHER MY ADAMANTIUM CLAWS WERE TOUGHER THAN THIS RUSSIAN CLOWN'S ORGANIC METAL SHELL.
BUT I GUESS THE EIGHT PINTS OF RHESUS NEGATIVE SEEPING OUT ONTO THE GRASS ANSWERS THAT. RIGHT, PROFESSOR?
I'D BE LYING IF I SAID I WASN'T IMPRESSED ON SOME PRIMITIVE LEVEL, WOLVERINE --

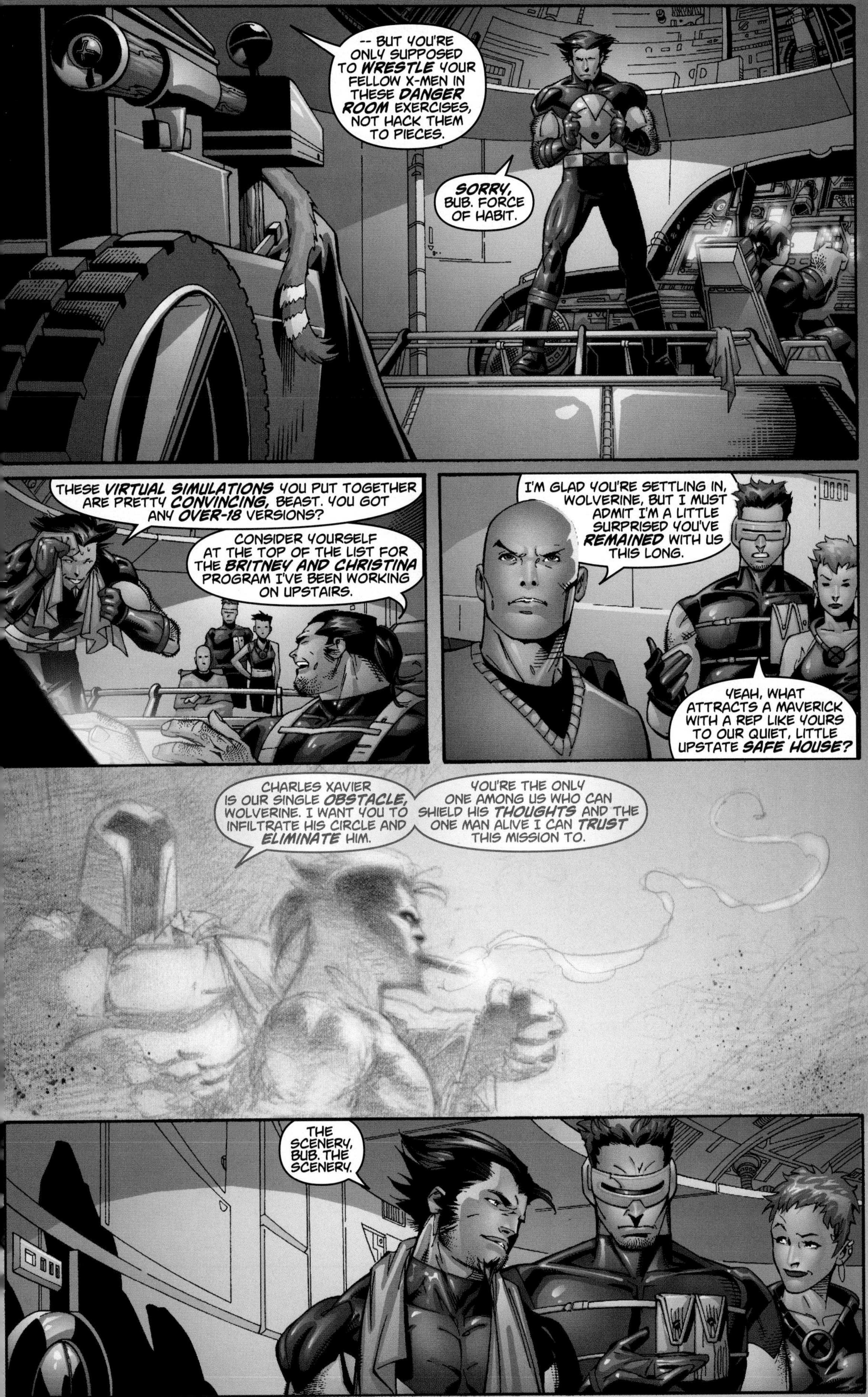
-- BUT YOU'RE ONLY SUPPOSED TO WRESTLE YOUR FELLOW X-MEN IN THESE DANGER ROOM EXERCISES, NOT HACK THEM TO PIECES.
SORRY, BUB. FORCE OF HABIT.
THESE VIRTUAL SIMULATIONS YOU PUT TOGETHER ARE PRETTY CONVINCING, BEAST. YOU GOT ANY OVER-18 VERSIONS?
CONSIDER YOURSELF AT THE TOP OF THE LIST FOR THE BRITNEY AND CHRISTINA PROGRAM I'VE BEEN WORKING ON UPSTAIRS.
I'M GLAD YOU'RE SETTLING IN, WOLVERINE, BUT I MUST ADMIT I'M A LITTLE SURPRISED YOU'VE REMAINED WITH US THIS LONG.
YEAH, WHAT ATTRACTS A MAVERICK WITH A REP LIKE YOURS TO OUR QUIET, LITTLE UPSTATE SAFE HOUSE?
CHARLES XAVIER IS OUR SINGLE OBSTACLE, WOLVERINE. I WANT YOU TO INFILTRATE HIS CIRCLE AND ELIMINATE HIM.
YOU'RE THE ONLY ONE AMONG US WHO CAN SHIELD HIS THOUGHTS AND THE ONE MAN ALIVE I CAN TRUST THIS MISSION TO.
THE SCENERY, BUB. THE SCENERY.

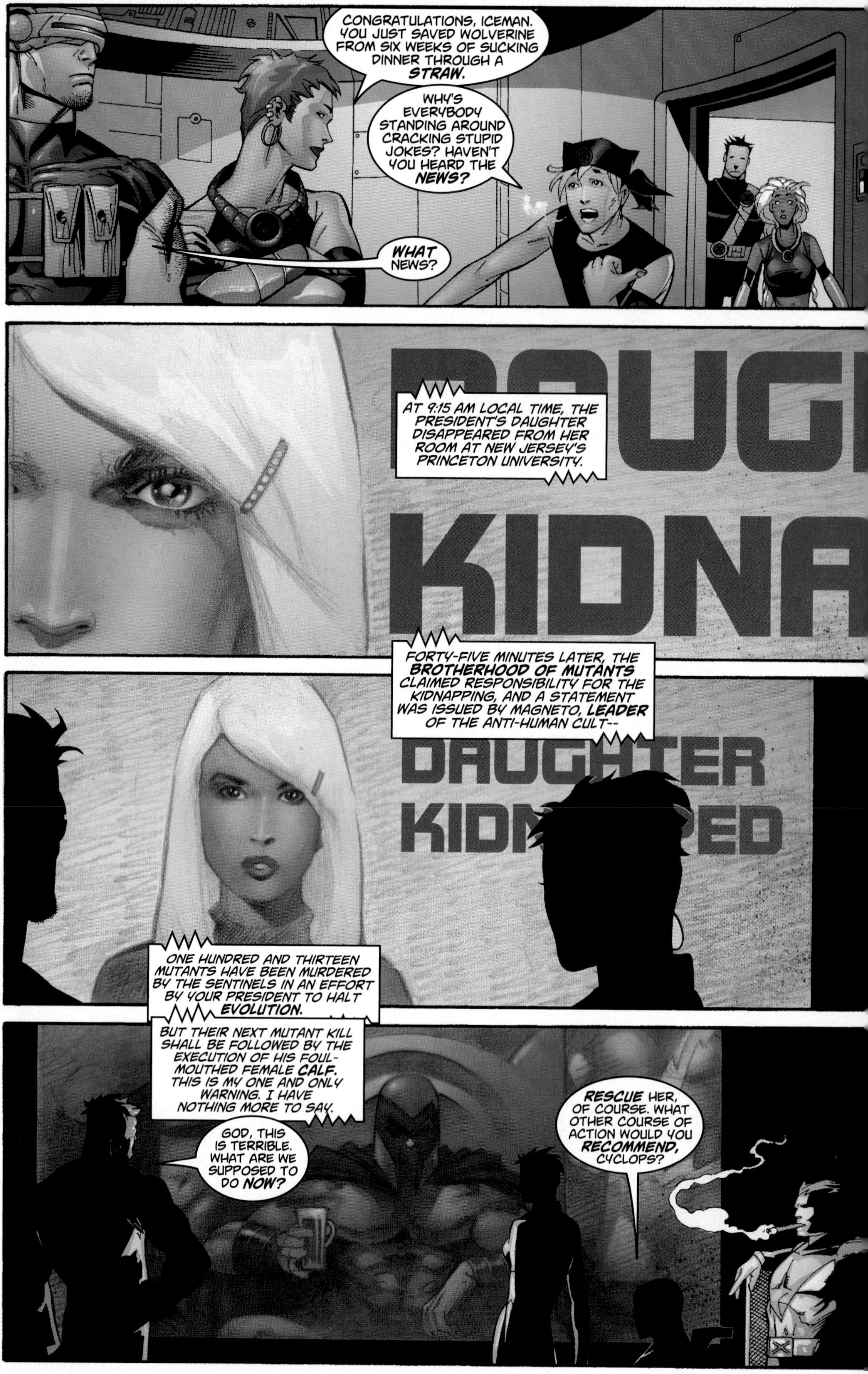

CONGRATULATIONS, ICEMAN. YOU JUST SAVED WOLVERINE FROM SIX WEEKS OF SUCKING DINNER THROUGH A STRAW.
WHY'S EVERYBODY STANDING AROUND CRACKING STUPID JOKES? HAVEN'T YOU HEARD THE NEWS?
WHAT NEWS?
KIDNA
AT 9:15 AM LOCAL TIME, THE PRESIDENT'S DAUGHTER DISAPPEARED FROM HER ROOM AT NEW JERSEY'S PRINCETON UNIVERSITY.
FORTY-FIVE MINUTES LATER, THE BROTHERHOOD OF MUTANTS CLAIMED RESPONSIBILITY FOR THE KIDNAPPING, AND A STATEMENT WAS ISSUED BY MAGNETO, LEADER OF THE ANTI-HUMAN CULT--
DAUGHTER
KIDN PED
ONE HUNDRED AND THIRTEEN MUTANTS HAVE BEEN MURDERED BY THE SENTINELS IN AN EFFORT BY YOUR PRESIDENT TO HALT EVOLUTION.
BUT THEIR NEXT MUTANT KILL SHALL BE FOLLOWED BY THE EXECUTION OF HIS FOUL-MOUTHED FEMALE CALF. THIS IS MY ONE AND ONLY WARNING. I HAVE NOTHING MORE TO SAY.
GOD, THIS IS TERRIBLE. WHAT ARE WE SUPPOSED TO DO NOW?
RESCUE HER, OF COURSE. WHAT OTHER COURSE OF ACTION WOULD YOU RECOMMEND, CYCLOPS?

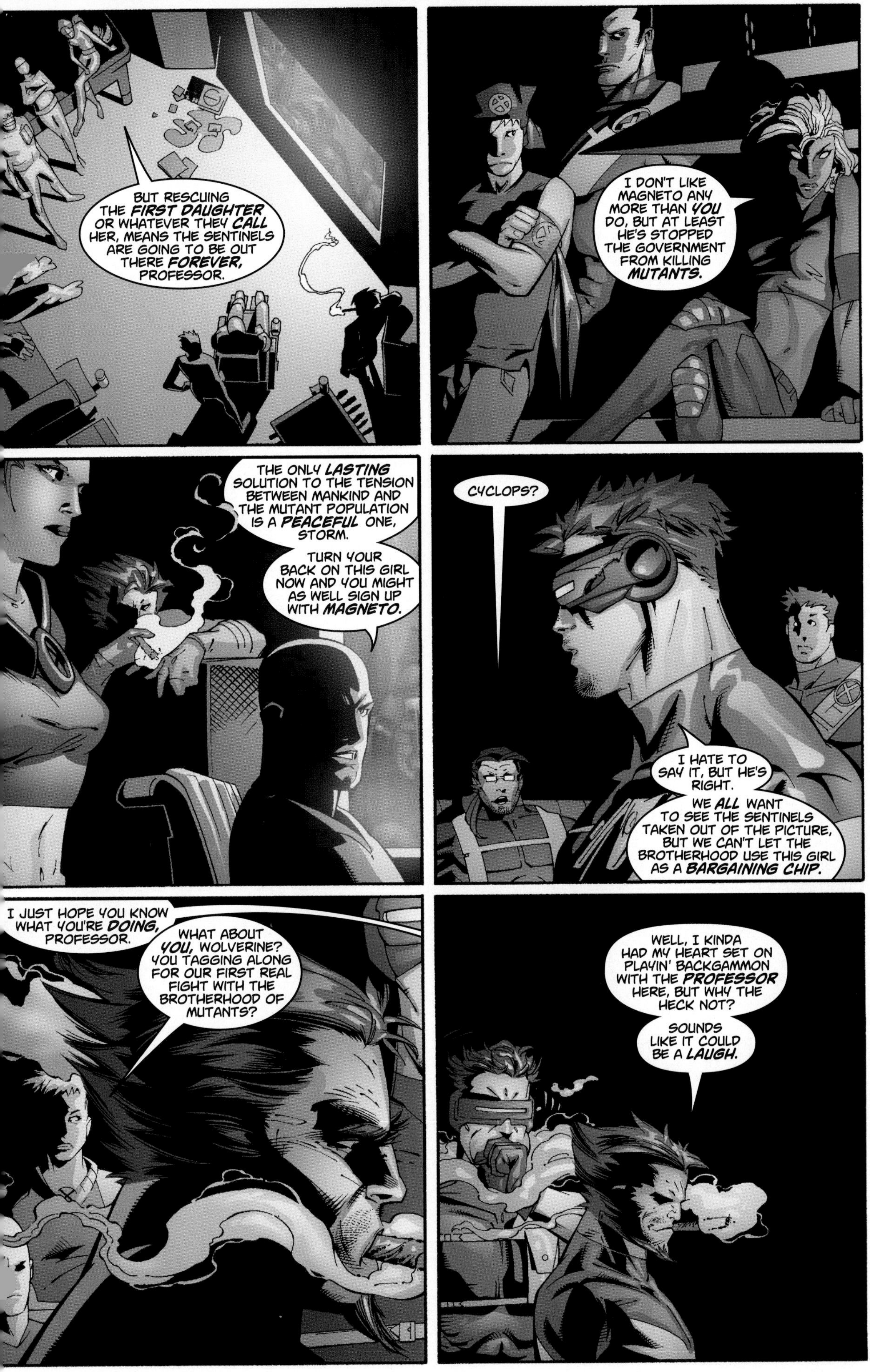
BUT RESCUING THE FIRST DAUGHTER OR WHATEVER THEY CALL HER, MEANS THE SENTINELS ARE GOING TO BE OUT THERE FOREVER, PROFESSOR.
I DON'T LIKE MAGNETO ANY MORE THAN YOU DO, BUT AT LEAST HE'S STOPPED THE GOVERNMENT FROM KILLING MUTANTS.
THE ONLY LASTING SOLUTION TO THE TENSION BETWEEN MANKIND AND THE MUTANT POPULATION IS A PEACEFUL ONE, STORM.
TURN YOUR BACK ON THIS GIRL NOW AND YOU MIGHT AS WELL SIGN UP WITH MAGNETO.
CYCLOPS?
I HATE TO SAY IT, BUT HE'S RIGHT.
WE ALL WANT TO SEE THE SENTINELS TAKEN OUT OF THE PICTURE, BUT WE CAN'T LET THE BROTHERHOOD USE THIS GIRL AS A BARGAINING CHIP.
I JUST HOPE YOU KNOW WHAT YOU'RE DOING, PROFESSOR.
WHAT ABOUT YOU, WOLVERINE? YOU TAGGING ALONG FOR OUR FIRST REAL FIGHT WITH THE BROTHERHOOD OF MUTANTS?
WELL, I KINDA HAD MY HEART SET ON PLAYIN' BACKGAMMON WITH THE PROFESSOR HERE, BUT WHY THE HECK NOT?
SOUNDS LIKE IT COULD BE A LAUGH.

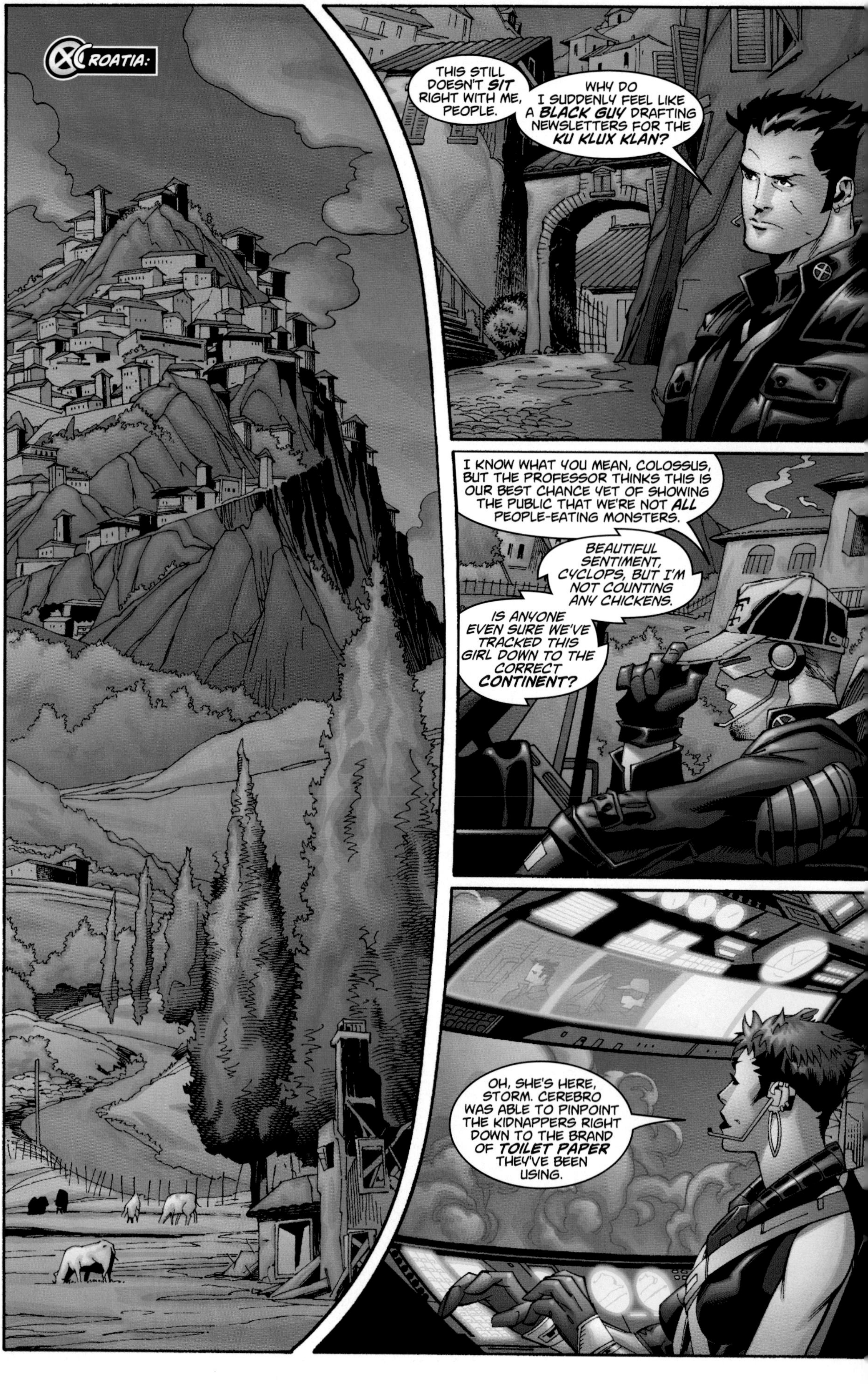
CROATIA:
THIS STILL DOESN'T SIT RIGHT WITH ME, PEOPLE.
WHY DO I SUDDENLY FEEL LIKE A BLACK GUY DRAFTING NEWSLETTERS FOR THE KU KLUX KLAN?
I KNOW WHAT YOU MEAN, COLOSSUS, BUT THE PROFESSOR THINKS THIS IS OUR BEST CHANCE YET OF SHOWING THE PUBLIC THAT WE'RE NOT ALL PEOPLE-EATING MONSTERS.
BEAUTIFUL SENTIMENT, CYCLOPS, BUT I'M NOT COUNTING ANY CHICKENS.
IS ANYONE EVEN SURE WE'VE TRACKED THIS GIRL DOWN TO THE CORRECT CONTINENT?
OH, SHE'S HERE, STORM. CEREBRO WAS ABLE TO PINPOINT THE KIDNAPPERS RIGHT DOWN TO THE BRAND OF TOILET PAPER THEY'VE BEEN USING.

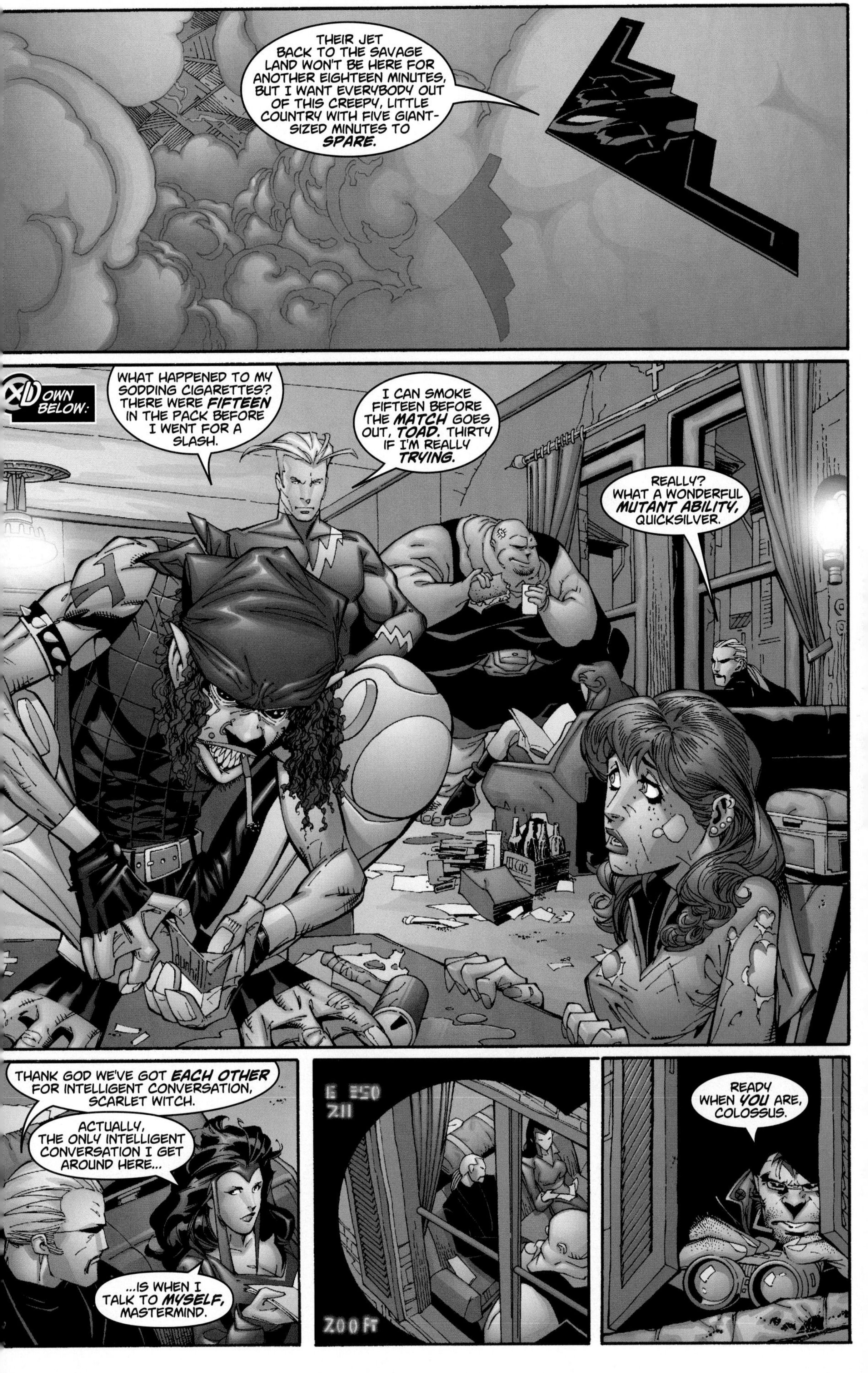
THEIR JET BACK TO THE SAVAGE LAND WON'T BE HERE FOR ANOTHER EIGHTEEN MINUTES, BUT I WANT EVERYBODY OUT OF THIS CREEPY, LITTLE COUNTRY WITH FIVE GIANT-SIZED MINUTES TO SPARE.
DOWN BELOW:
WHAT HAPPENED TO MY SODDING CIGARETTES? THERE WERE FIFTEEN IN THE PACK BEFORE I WENT FOR A SLASH.
I CAN SMOKE FIFTEEN BEFORE THE MATCH GOES OUT, TOAD. THIRTY IF I'M REALLY TRYING.
REALLY? WHAT A WONDERFUL MUTANT ABILITY, QUICKSILVER.
THANK GOD WE'VE GOT EACH OTHER FOR INTELLIGENT CONVERSATION, SCARLET WITCH.
ACTUALLY, THE ONLY INTELLIGENT CONVERSATION I GET AROUND HERE...
...IS WHEN I TALK TO MYSELF, MASTERMIND.
200 FT
READY WHEN YOU ARE, COLOSSUS.

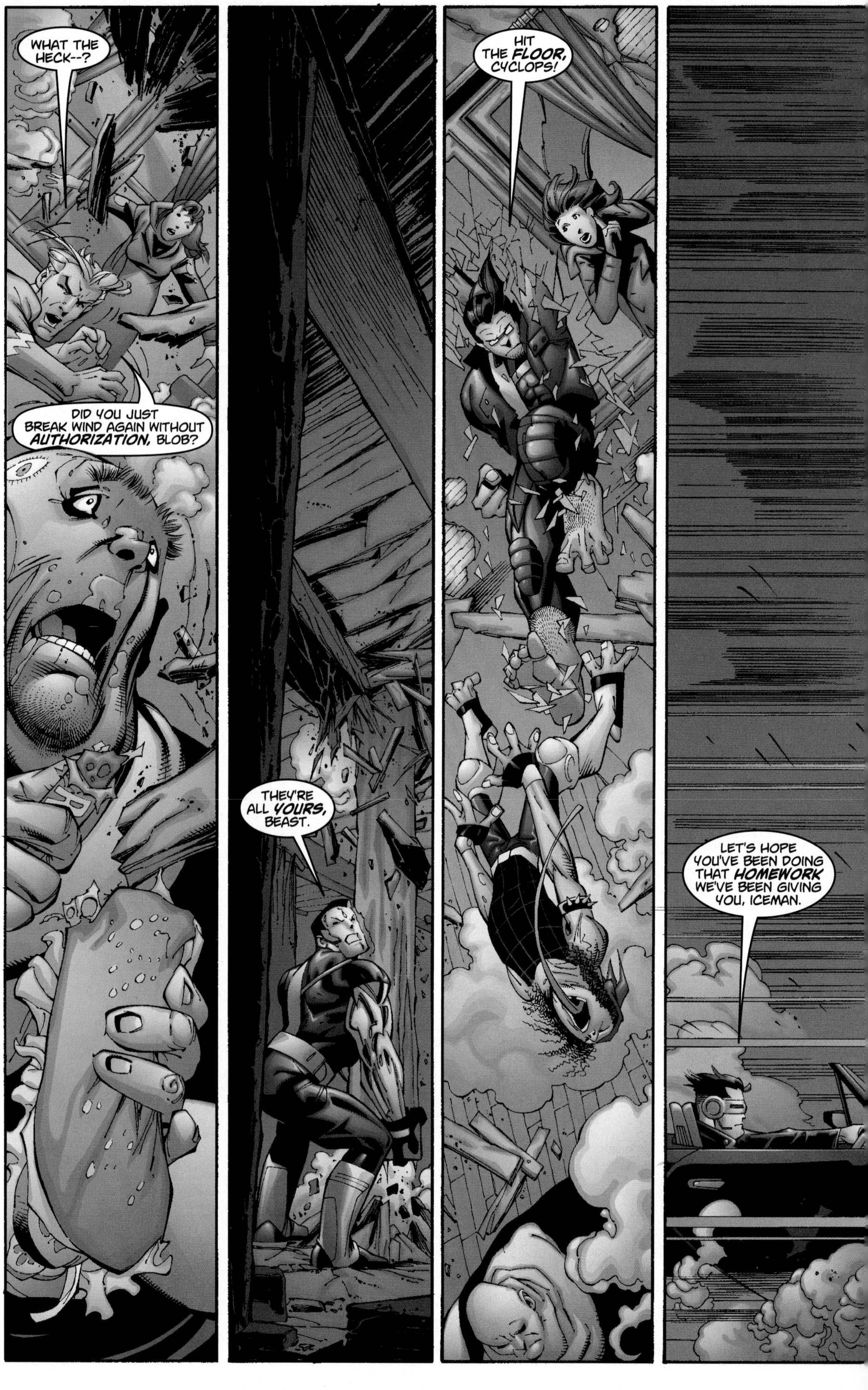
WHAT THE HECK--?
DID YOU JUST BREAK WIND AGAIN WITHOUT AUTHORIZATION, BLOB?
THEY'RE ALL YOURS, BEAST.
HIT THE FLOOR, CYCLOPS!
LET'S HOPE YOU'VE BEEN DOING THAT HOMEWORK WE'VE BEEN GIVING YOU, ICEMAN.

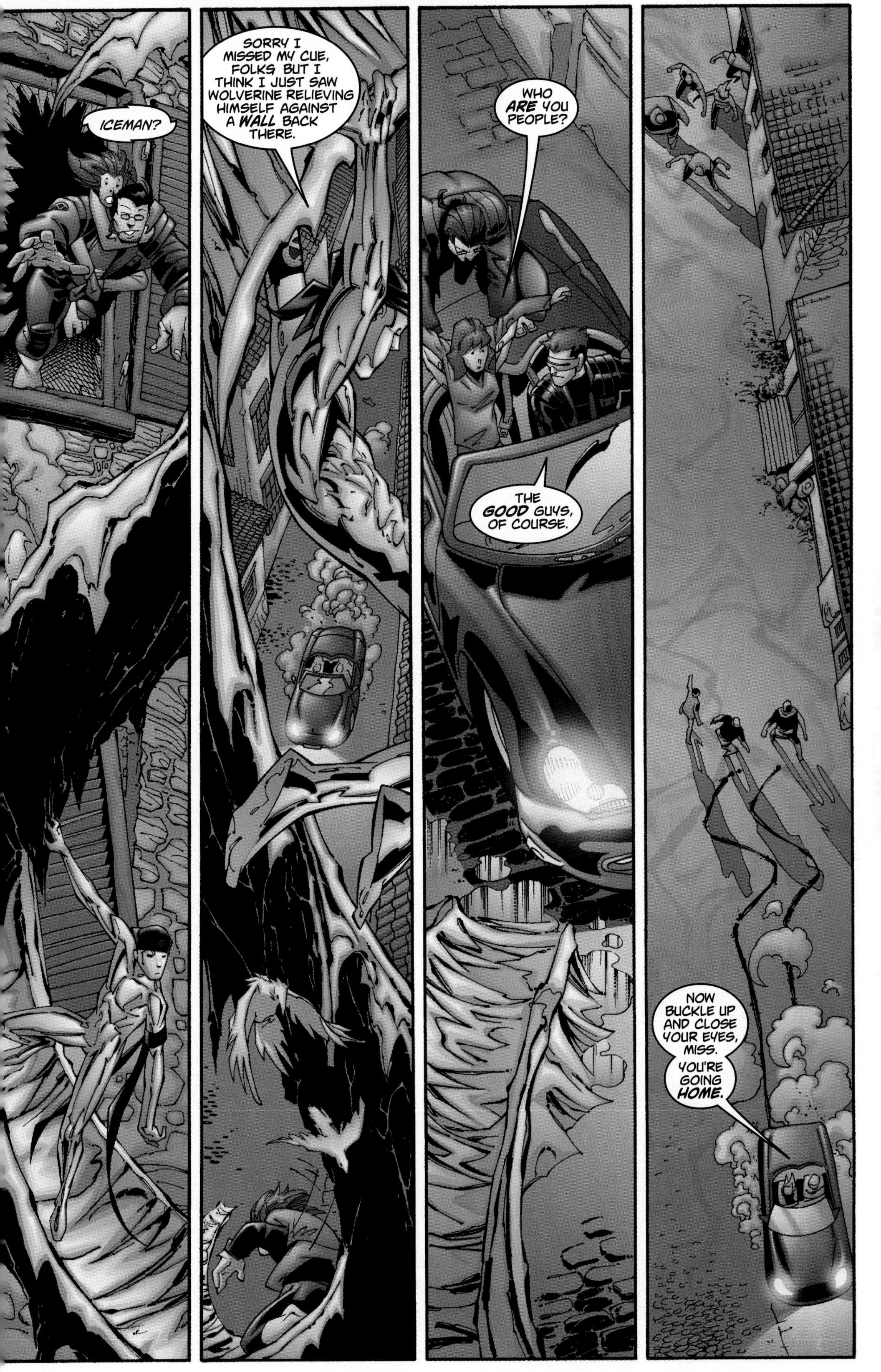
ICEMAN?
SORRY I MISSED MY CUE, FOLKS BUT I THINK I JUST SAW WOLVERINE RELIEVING HIMSELF AGAINST A **WALL** BACK THERE.
WHO **ARE** YOU PEOPLE?
THE **GOOD** GUYS, OF COURSE.
NOW BUCKLE UP AND CLOSE YOUR EYES, MISS.
YOU'RE GOING **HOME**.

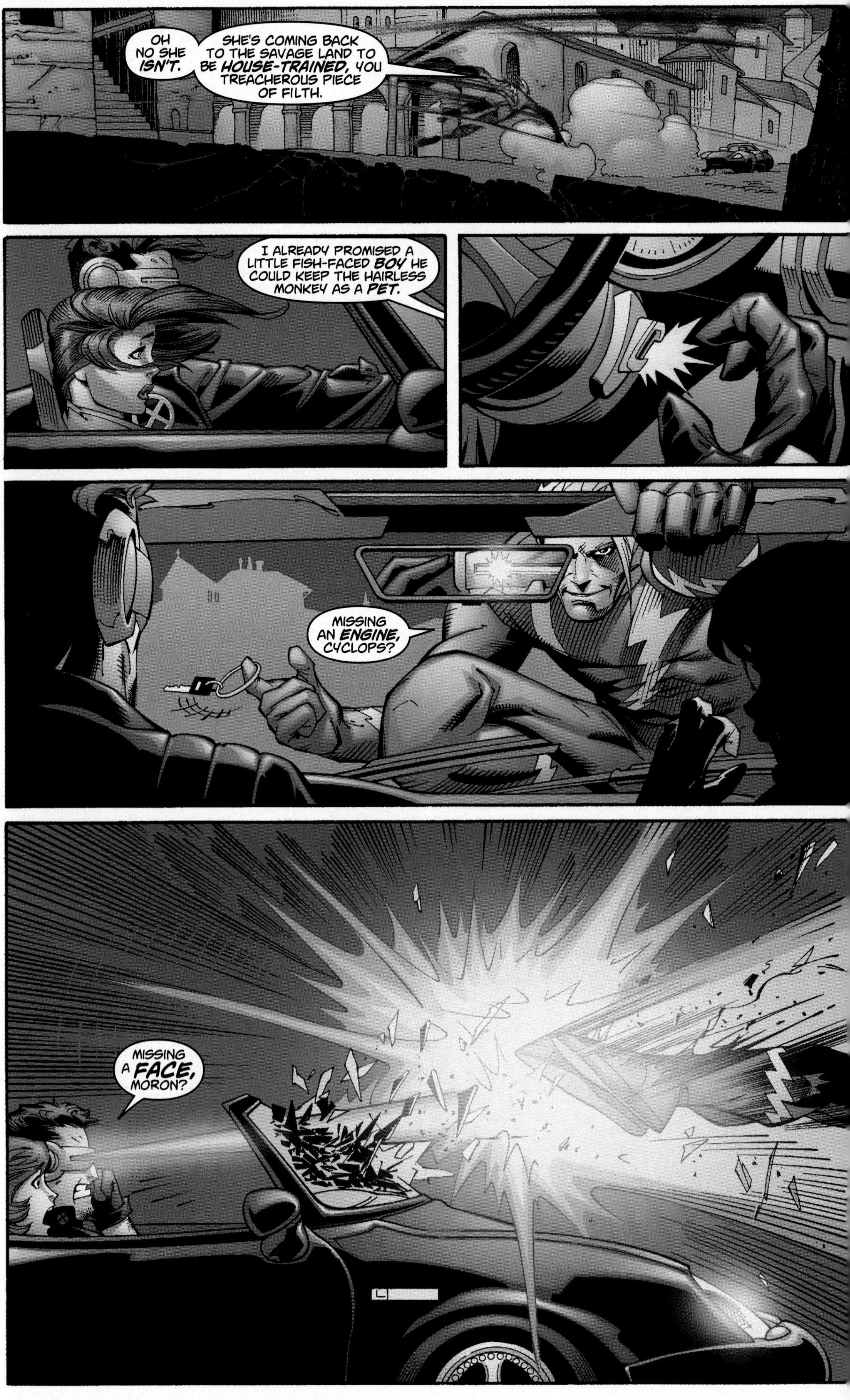

OH NO SHE ISN'T.
SHE'S COMING BACK TO THE SAVAGE LAND TO BE HOUSE-TRAINED, YOU TREACHEROUS PIECE OF FILTH.
I ALREADY PROMISED A LITTLE FISH-FACED BOY HE COULD KEEP THE HAIRLESS MONKEY AS A PET.
MISSING AN ENGINE, CYCLOPS?
MISSING A FACE, MORON?

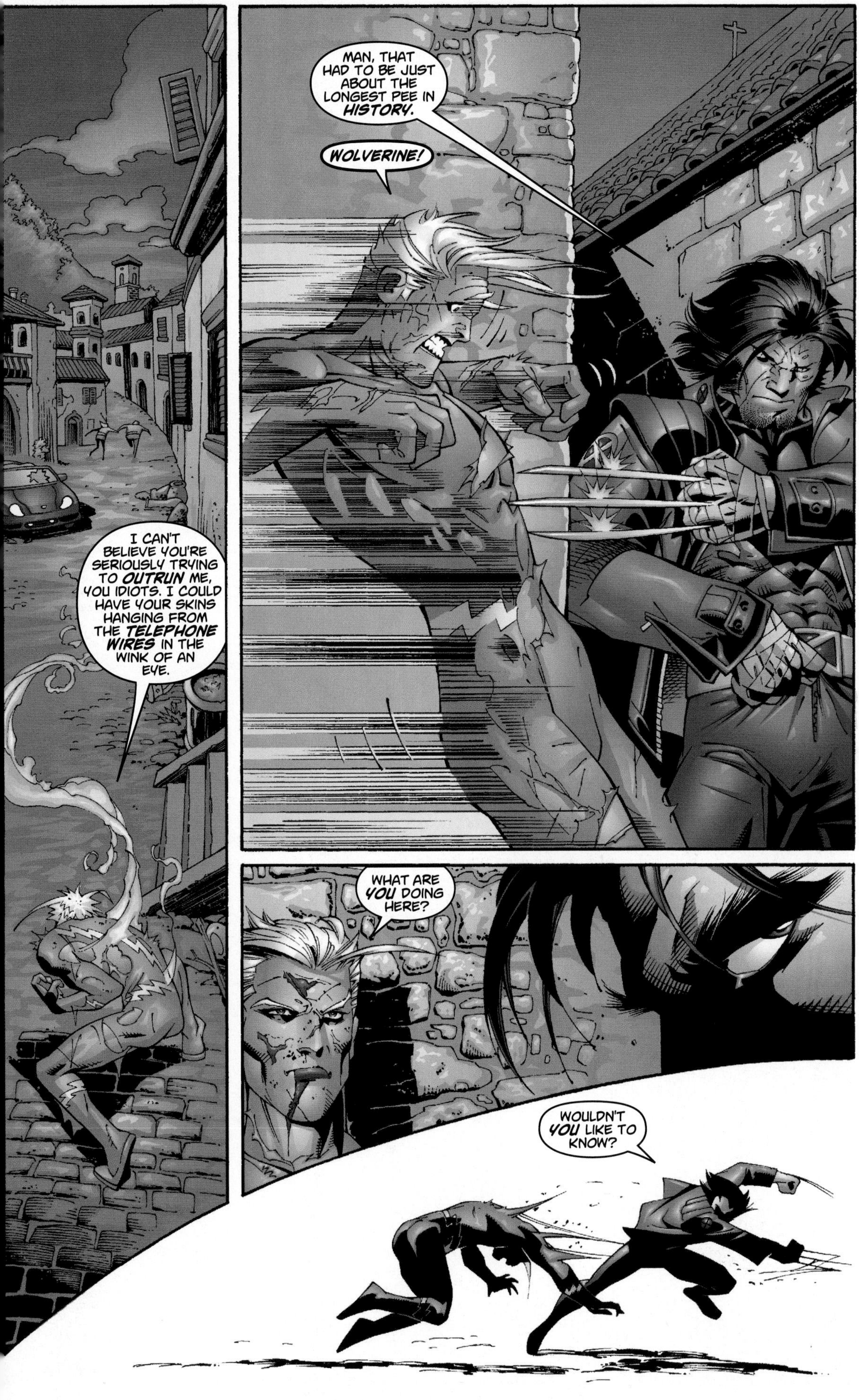
MAN, THAT HAD TO BE JUST ABOUT THE LONGEST PEE IN HISTORY.
WOLVERINE!
I CAN'T BELIEVE YOU'RE SERIOUSLY TRYING TO OUTRUN ME, YOU IDIOTS. I COULD HAVE YOUR SKINS HANGING FROM THE TELEPHONE WIRES IN THE WINK OF AN EYE.
WHAT ARE YOU DOING HERE?
WOULDN'T YOU LIKE TO KNOW?

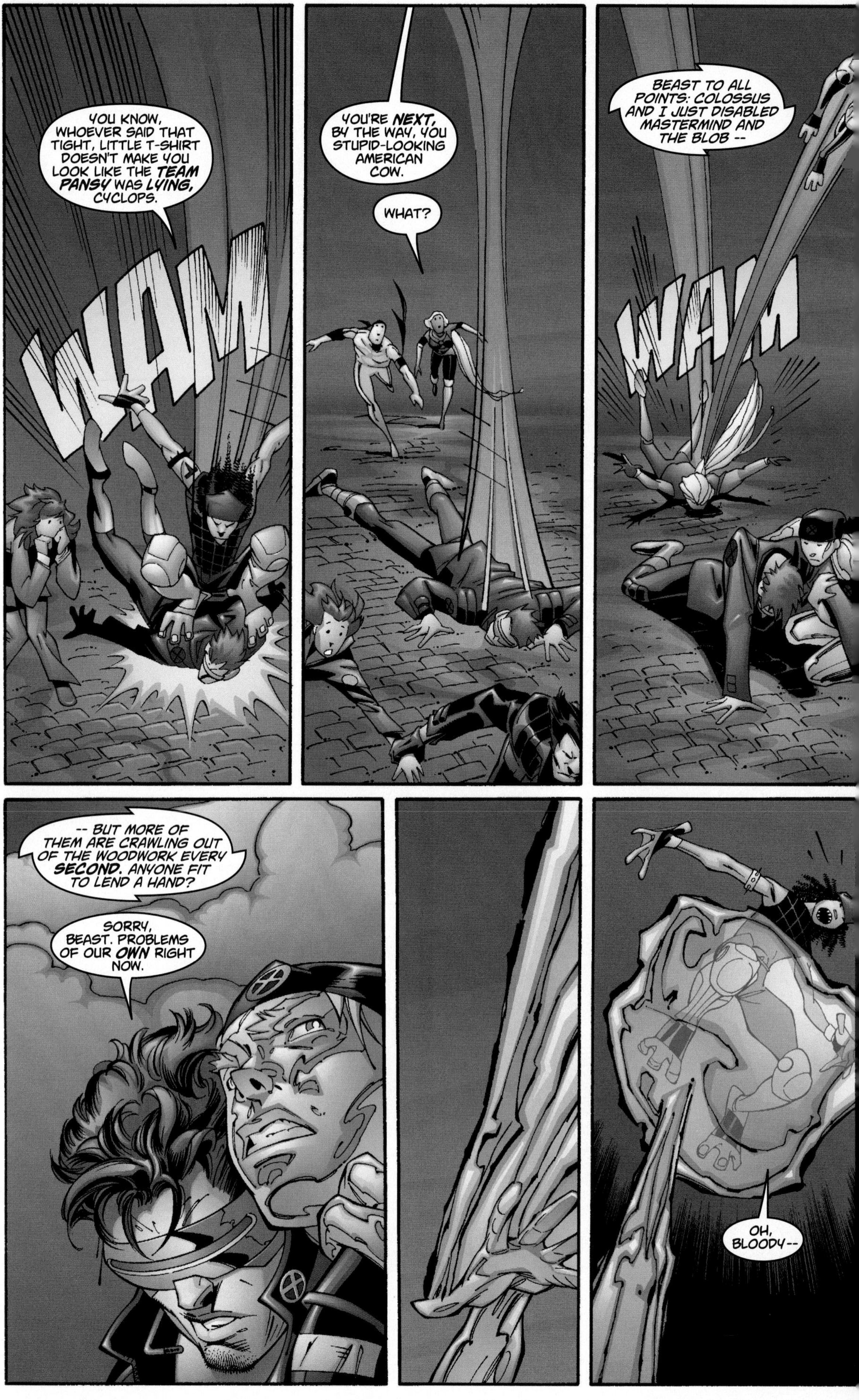
YOU KNOW, WHOEVER SAID THAT TIGHT, LITTLE T-SHIRT DOESN'T MAKE YOU LOOK LIKE THE TEAM PANSY WAS LYING, CYCLOPS.
WAM
YOU'RE NEXT, BY THE WAY, YOU STUPID-LOOKING AMERICAN COW.
WHAT?
BEAST TO ALL POINTS: COLOSSUS AND I JUST DISABLED MASTERMIND AND THE BLOB --
WAM
-- BUT MORE OF THEM ARE CRAWLING OUT OF THE WOODWORK EVERY SECOND. ANYONE FIT TO LEND A HAND?
SORRY, BEAST. PROBLEMS OF OUR OWN RIGHT NOW.
OH, BLOODY--

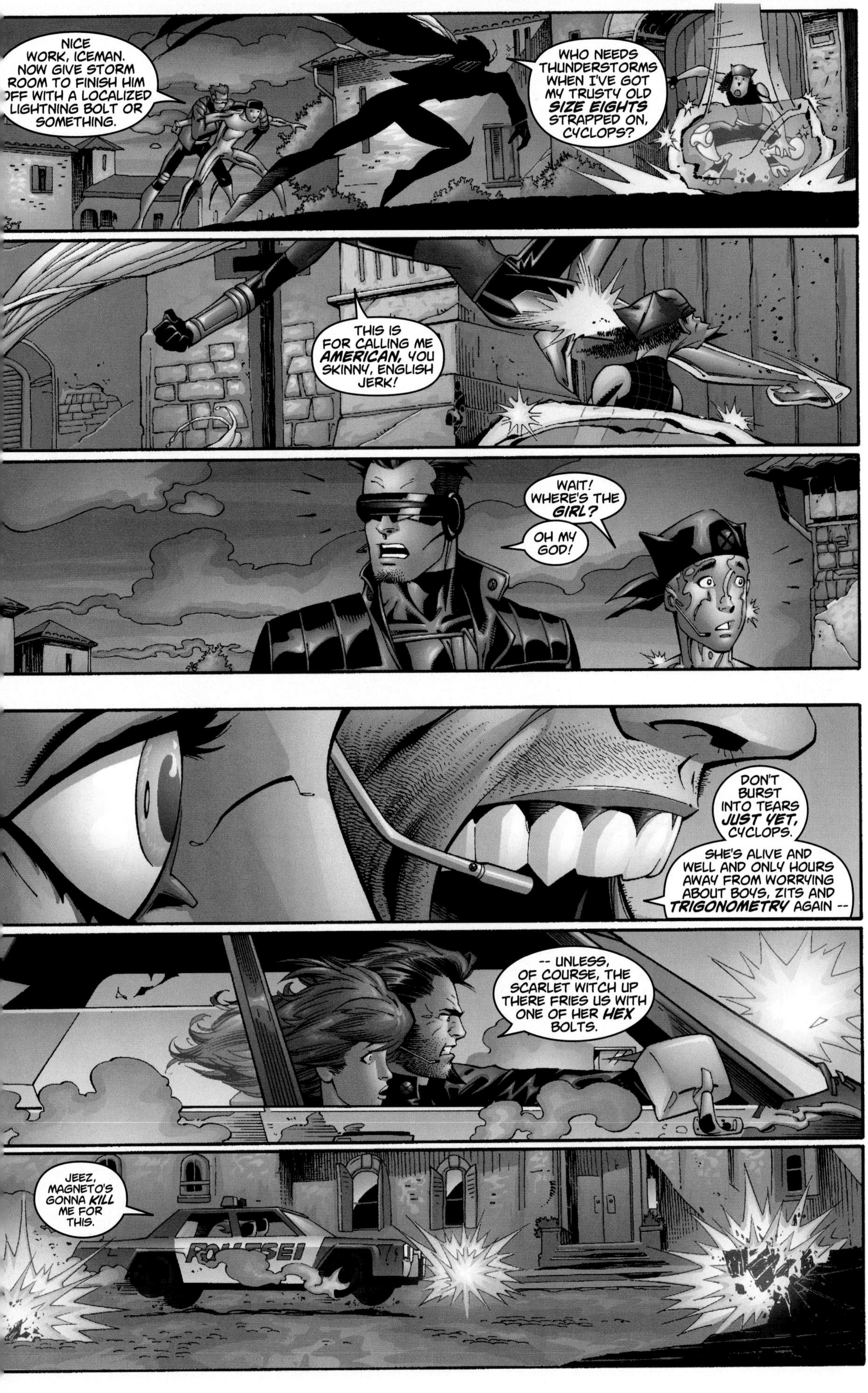
NICE WORK, ICEMAN. NOW GIVE STORM ROOM TO FINISH HIM OFF WITH A LOCALIZED LIGHTNING BOLT OR SOMETHING.
WHO NEEDS THUNDERSTORMS WHEN I'VE GOT MY TRUSTY OLD SIZE EIGHTS STRAPPED ON, CYCLOPS?
THIS IS FOR CALLING ME AMERICAN, YOU SKINNY, ENGLISH JERK!
WAIT! WHERE'S THE GIRL?
OH MY GOD!
DON'T BURST INTO TEARS JUST YET, CYCLOPS.
SHE'S ALIVE AND WELL AND ONLY HOURS AWAY FROM WORRYING ABOUT BOYS, ZITS AND TRIGONOMETRY AGAIN --
-- UNLESS, OF COURSE, THE SCARLET WITCH UP THERE FRIES US WITH ONE OF HER HEX BOLTS.
JEEZ, MAGNETO'S GONNA KILL ME FOR THIS.

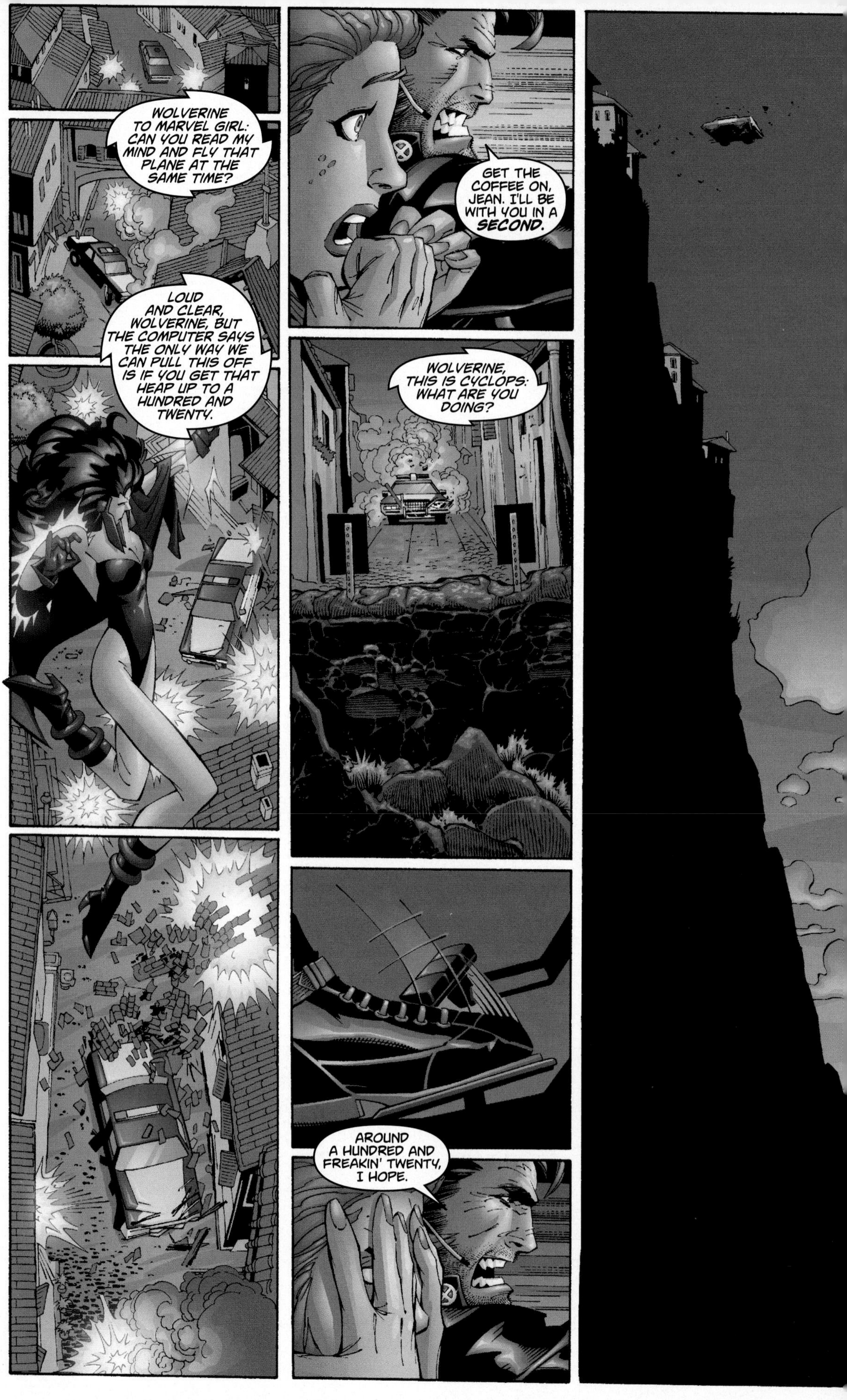

WOLVERINE TO MARVEL GIRL: CAN YOU READ MY MIND AND FLY THAT PLANE AT THE SAME TIME?
LOUD AND CLEAR, WOLVERINE, BUT THE COMPUTER SAYS THE ONLY WAY WE CAN PULL THIS OFF IS IF YOU GET THAT HEAP UP TO A HUNDRED AND TWENTY.
GET THE COFFEE ON, JEAN. I'LL BE WITH YOU IN A SECOND.
WOLVERINE, THIS IS CYCLOPS: WHAT ARE YOU DOING?
AROUND A HUNDRED AND FREAKIN' TWENTY, I HOPE.

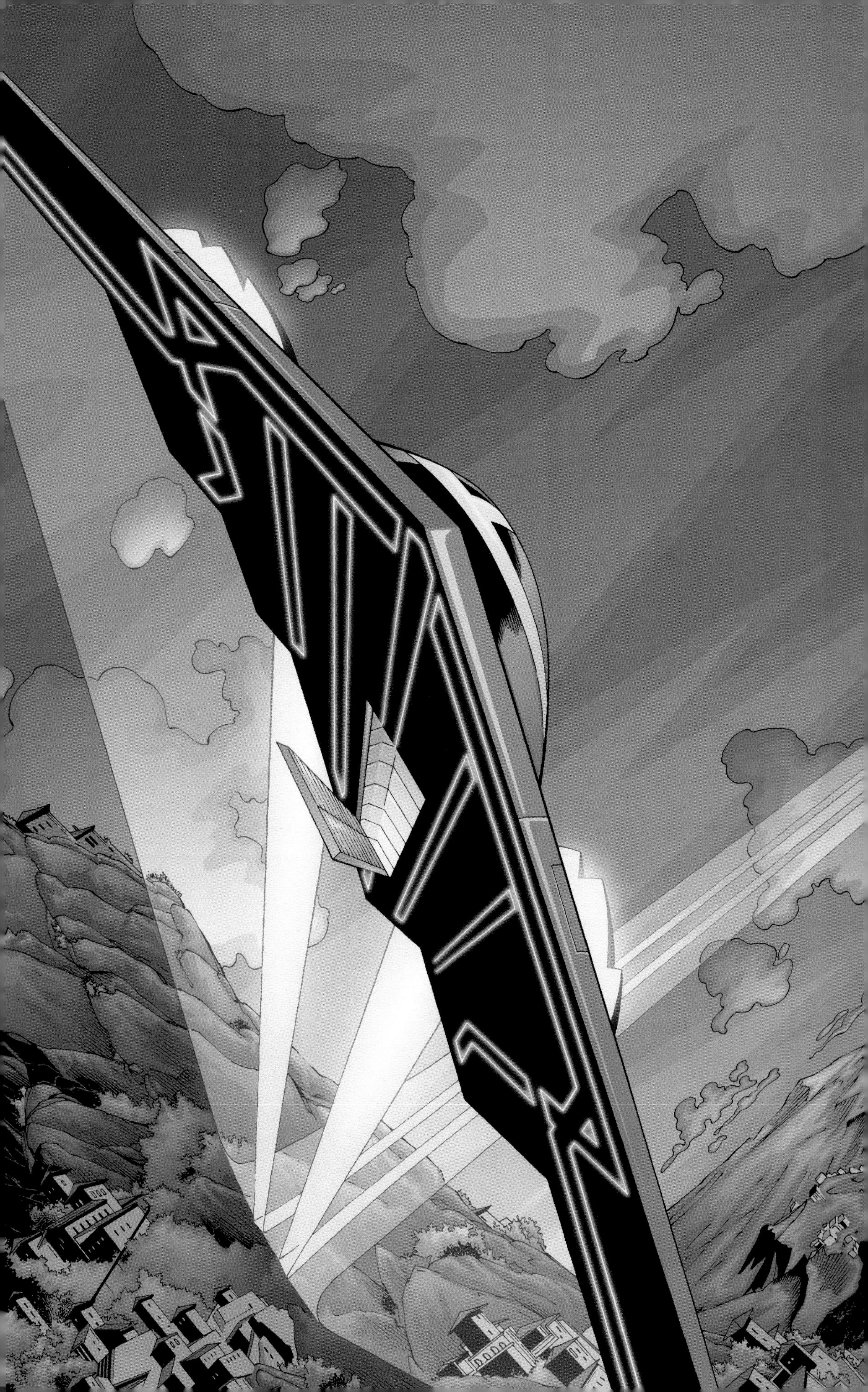

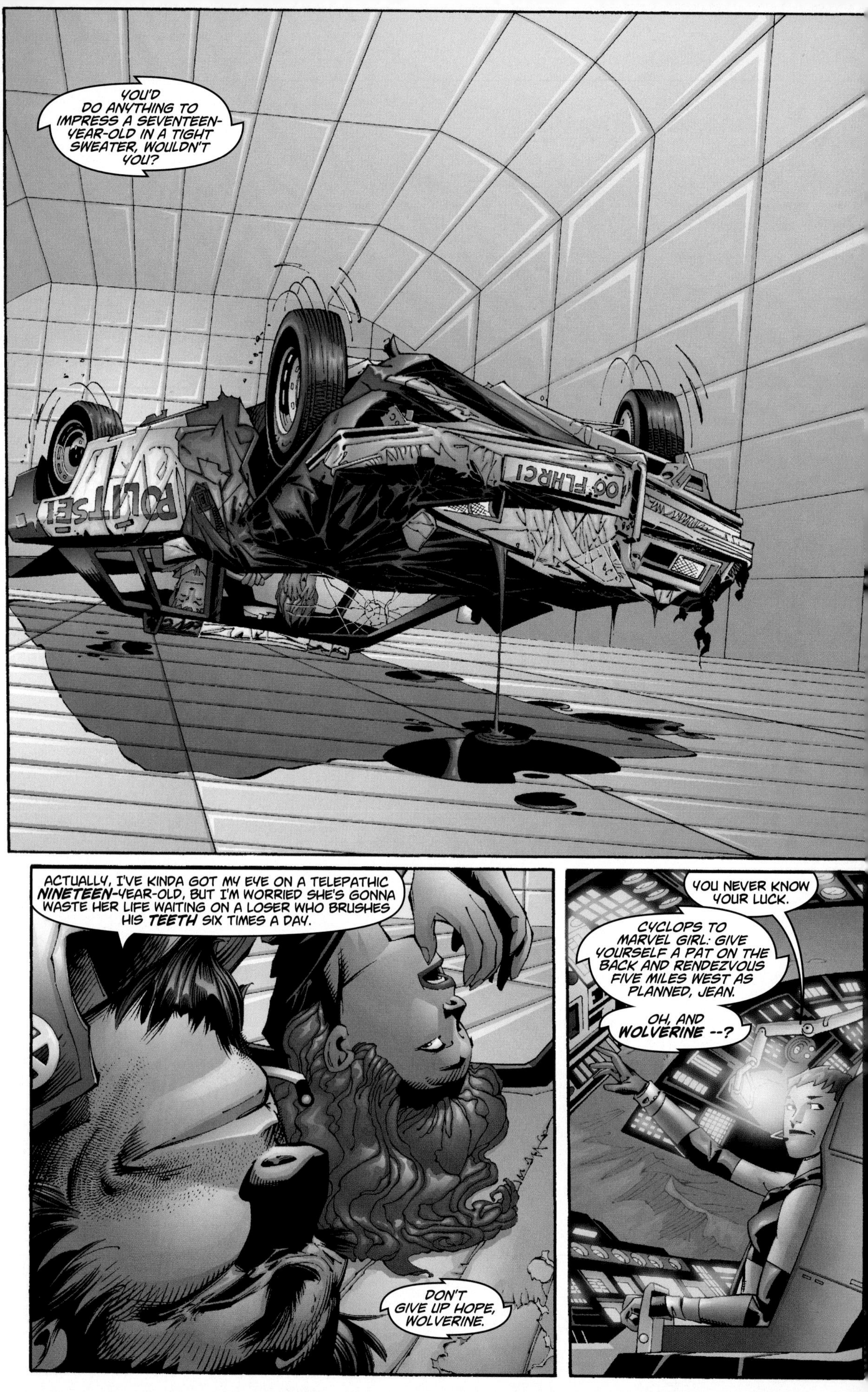
YOU'D DO ANYTHING TO IMPRESS A SEVENTEEN-YEAR-OLD IN A TIGHT SWEATER, WOULDN'T YOU?
ACTUALLY, I'VE KINDA GOT MY EYE ON A TELEPATHIC NINETEEN-YEAR-OLD, BUT I'M WORRIED SHE'S GONNA WASTE HER LIFE WAITING ON A LOSER WHO BRUSHES HIS TEETH SIX TIMES A DAY.
DON'T GIVE UP HOPE, WOLVERINE.
YOU NEVER KNOW YOUR LUCK.
CYCLOPS TO MARVEL GIRL: GIVE YOURSELF A PAT ON THE BACK AND RENDEZVOUS FIVE MILES WEST AS PLANNED, JEAN.
OH, AND WOLVERINE --?

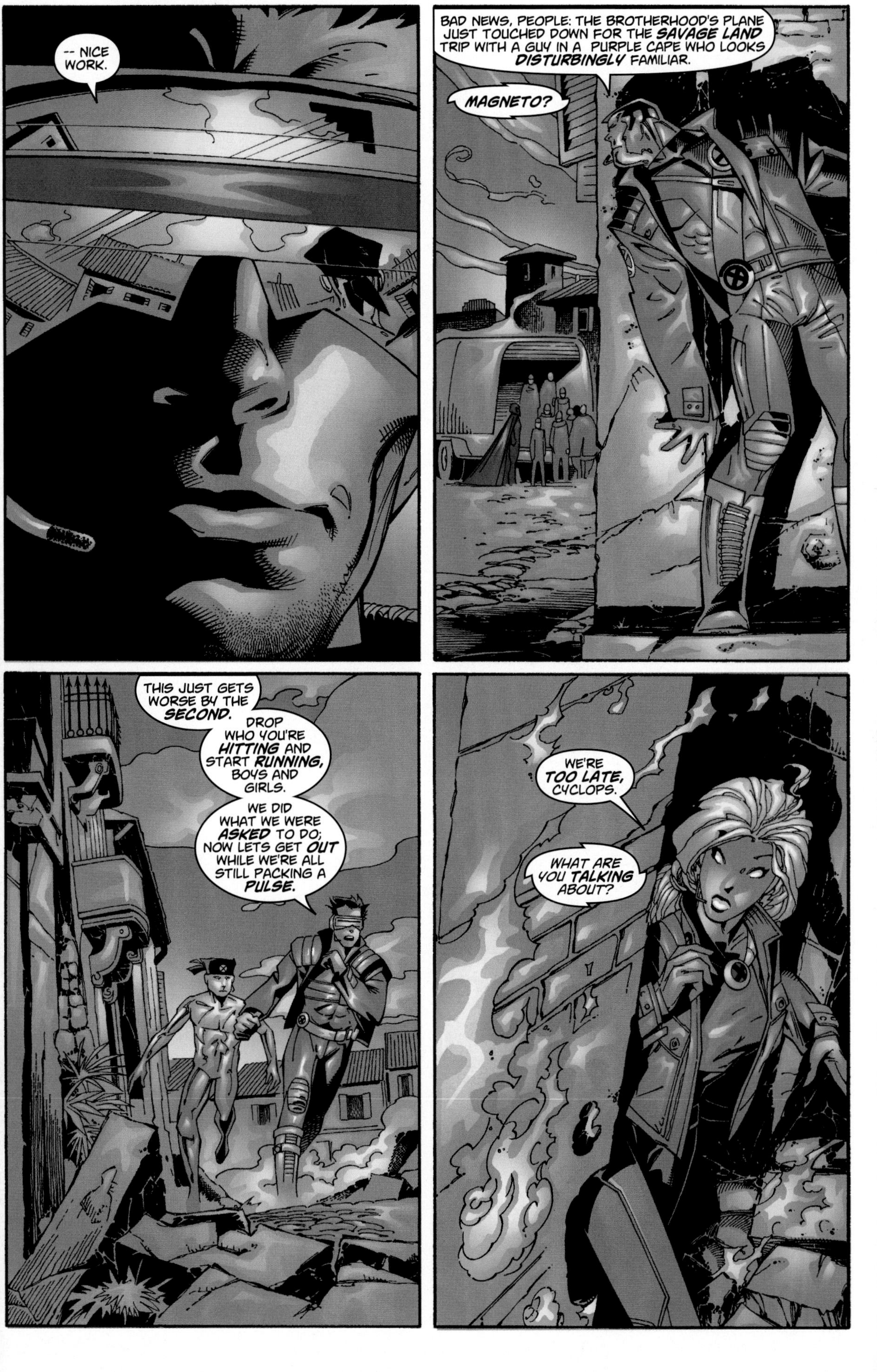
-- NICE WORK.
BAD NEWS, PEOPLE: THE BROTHERHOOD'S PLANE JUST TOUCHED DOWN FOR THE SAVAGE LAND TRIP WITH A GUY IN A PURPLE CAPE WHO LOOKS DISTURBINGLY FAMILIAR.
MAGNETO?
THIS JUST GETS WORSE BY THE SECOND.
DROP WHO YOU'RE HITTING AND START RUNNING, BOYS AND GIRLS.
WE DID WHAT WE WERE ASKED TO DO; NOW LETS GET OUT WHILE WE'RE ALL STILL PACKING A PULSE.
WE'RE TOO LATE, CYCLOPS.
WHAT ARE YOU TALKING ABOUT?

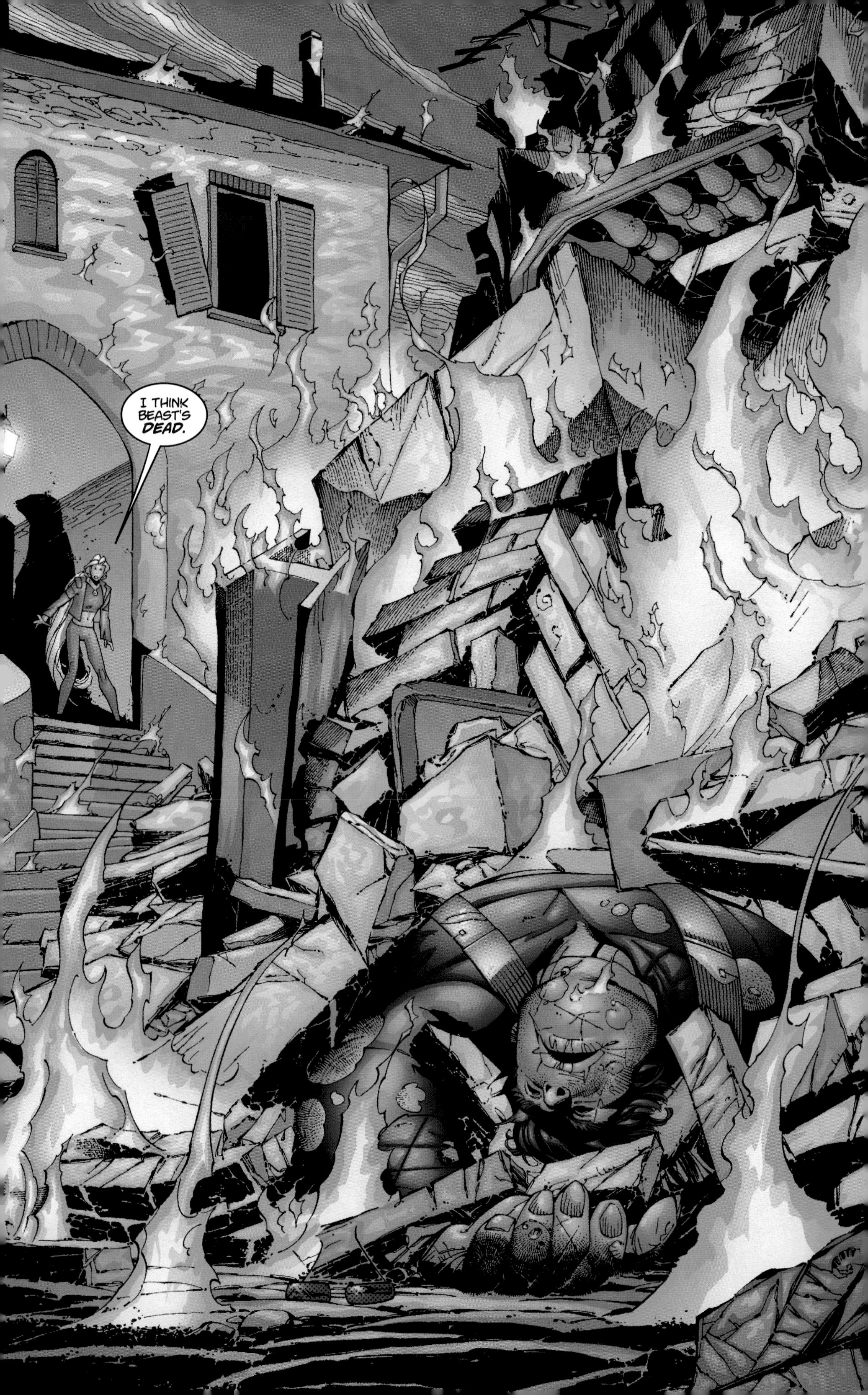
I THINK BEAST'S DEAD.

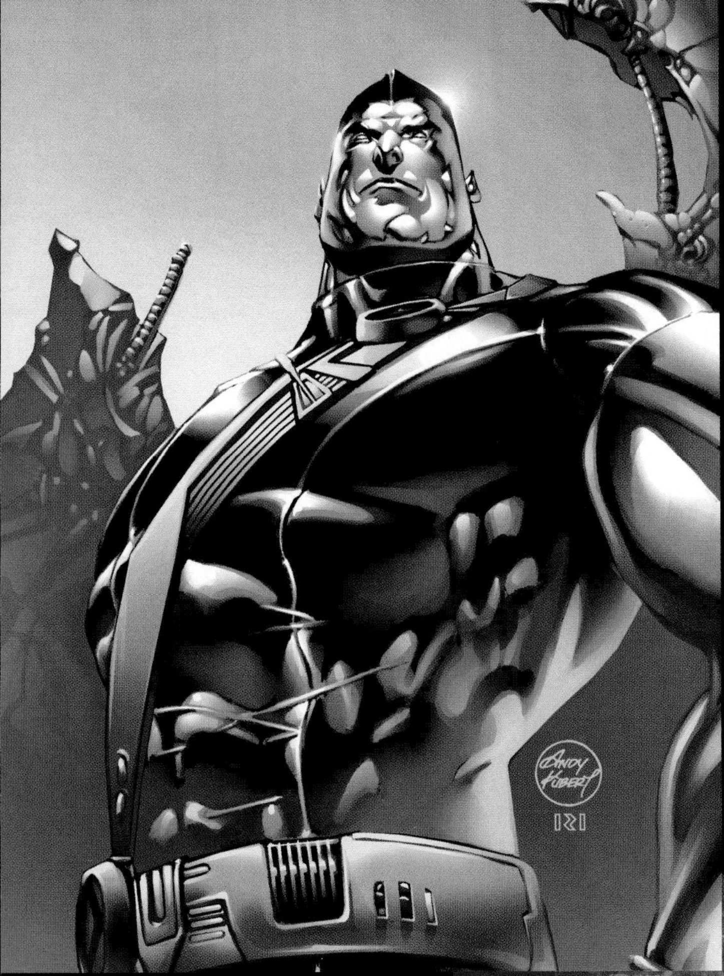

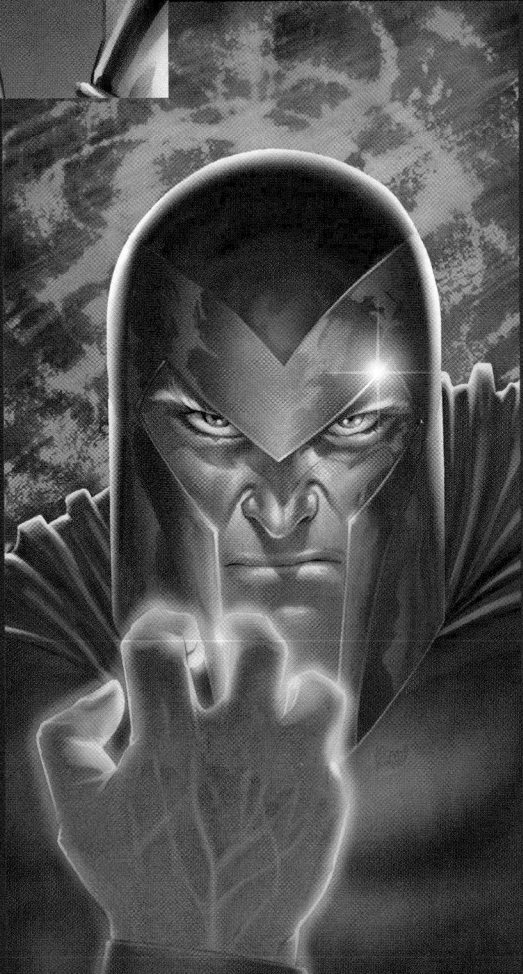

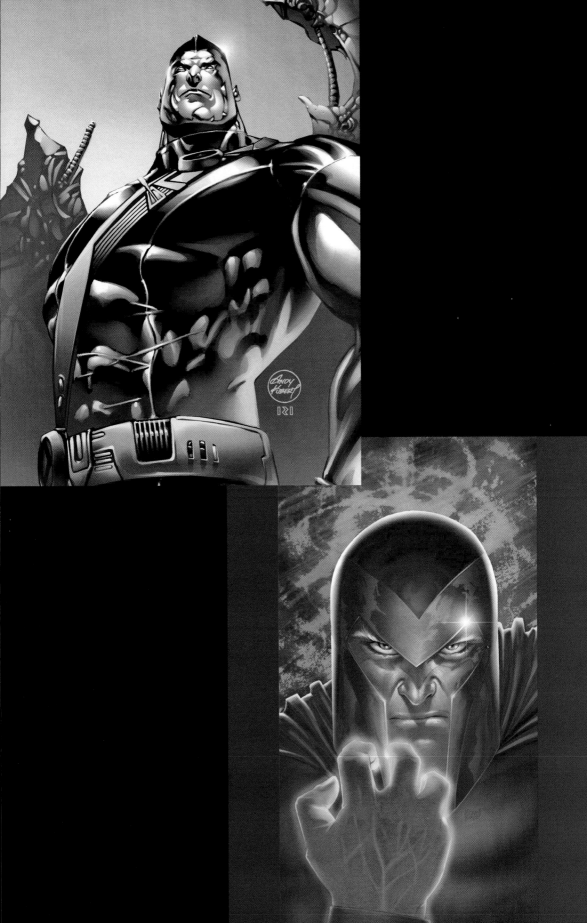

CROATIA.

STORM, THIS IS CYCLOPS. I DON'T THINK WE READ YOUR LAST MESSAGE CORRECTLY.

DID YOU JUST SAY BEAST'S DEAD?

STAN LEE presents:

THE TOMORROW PEOPLE
PART 4 OF 6

MARK MILLAR writer ADAM KUBERT penciler ART THIBERT inker
RICHARD ISANOVE colors Richard Starkings & COMICRAFT's Wes Abbott letters
PETE FRANCO ass't editor MARK POWERS editor JOE QUESADA chief BILL JEMAS president

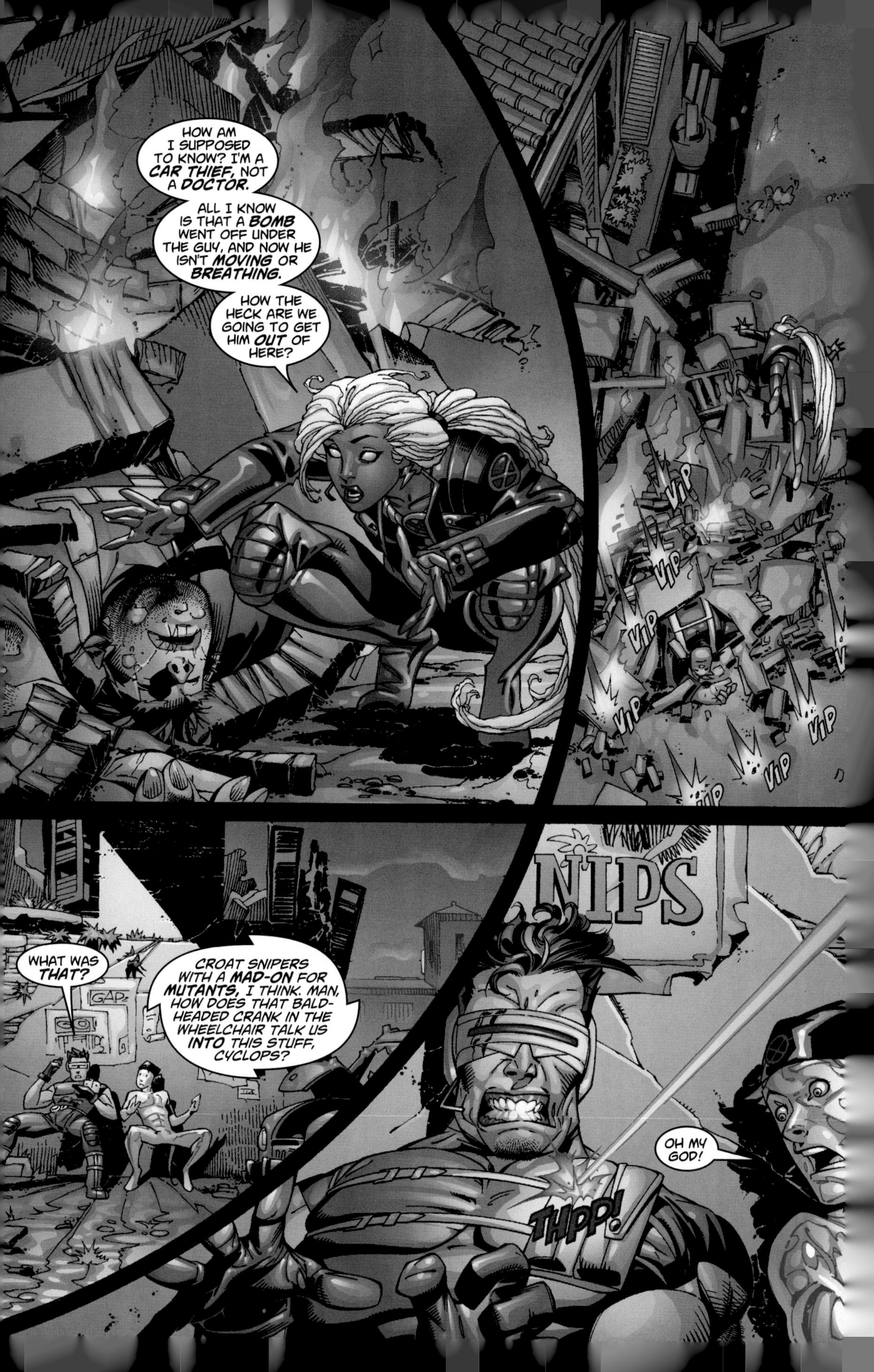
HOW AM I SUPPOSED TO KNOW? I'M A CAR THIEF, NOT A DOCTOR.
ALL I KNOW IS THAT A BOMB WENT OFF UNDER THE GUY, AND NOW HE ISN'T MOVING OR BREATHING.
HOW THE HECK ARE WE GOING TO GET HIM OUT OF HERE?
VIP
VIP
VIP
VIP
VIP
VIP
VIP
WHAT WAS THAT?
CROAT SNIPERS WITH A MAD-ON FOR MUTANTS, I THINK. MAN, HOW DOES THAT BALD-HEADED CRANK IN THE WHEELCHAIR TALK US INTO THIS STUFF, CYCLOPS?
NIPS
THPP!
OH MY GOD!

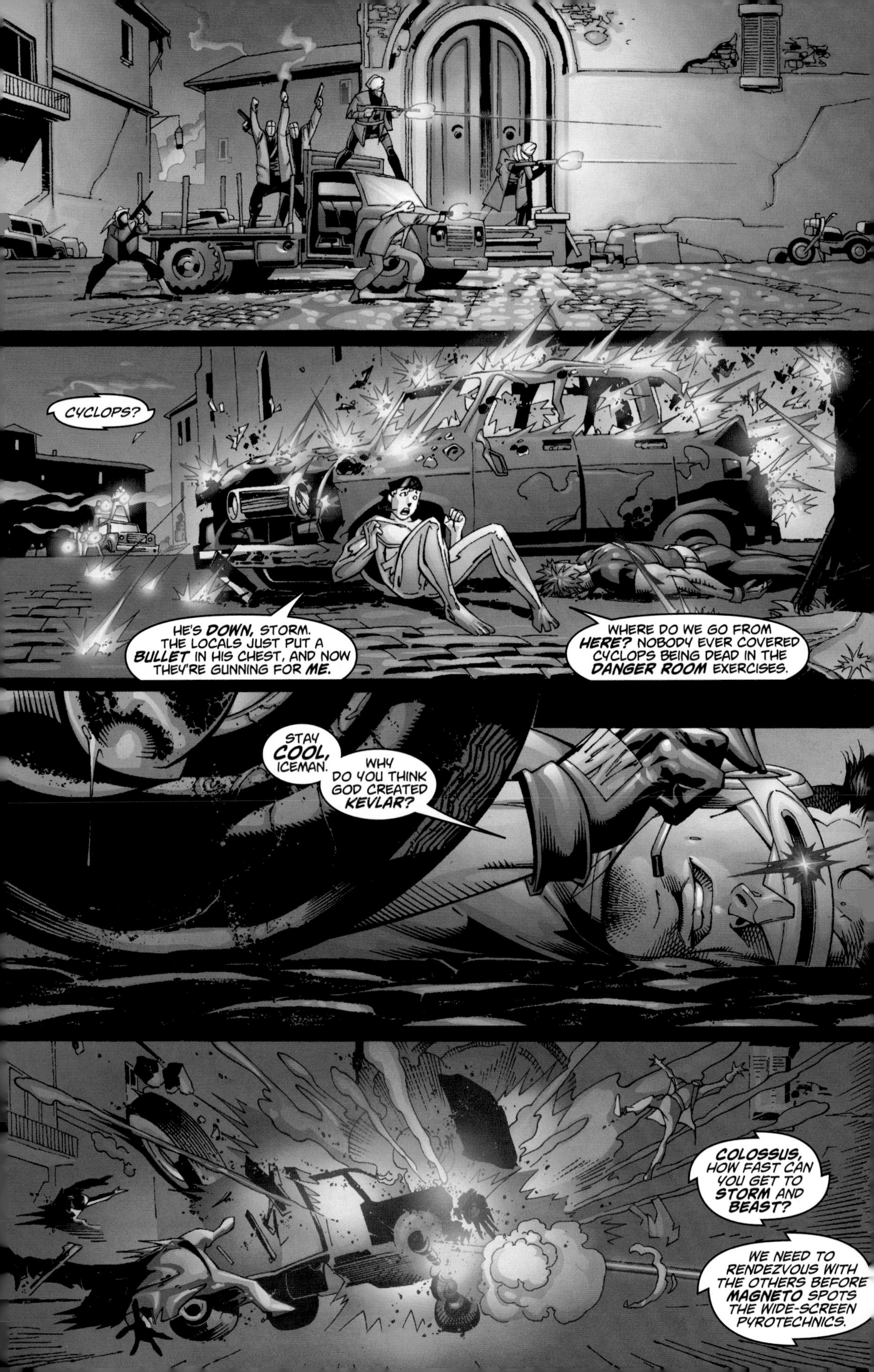
CYCLOPS?
HE'S DOWN, STORM. THE LOCALS JUST PUT A BULLET IN HIS CHEST, AND NOW THEY'RE GUNNING FOR ME.
WHERE DO WE GO FROM HERE? NOBODY EVER COVERED CYCLOPS BEING DEAD IN THE DANGER ROOM EXERCISES.
STAY COOL, ICEMAN.
WHY DO YOU THINK GOD CREATED KEVLAR?
COLOSSUS, HOW FAST CAN YOU GET TO STORM AND BEAST?
WE NEED TO RENDEZVOUS WITH THE OTHERS BEFORE MAGNETO SPOTS THE WIDE-SCREEN PYROTECHNICS.

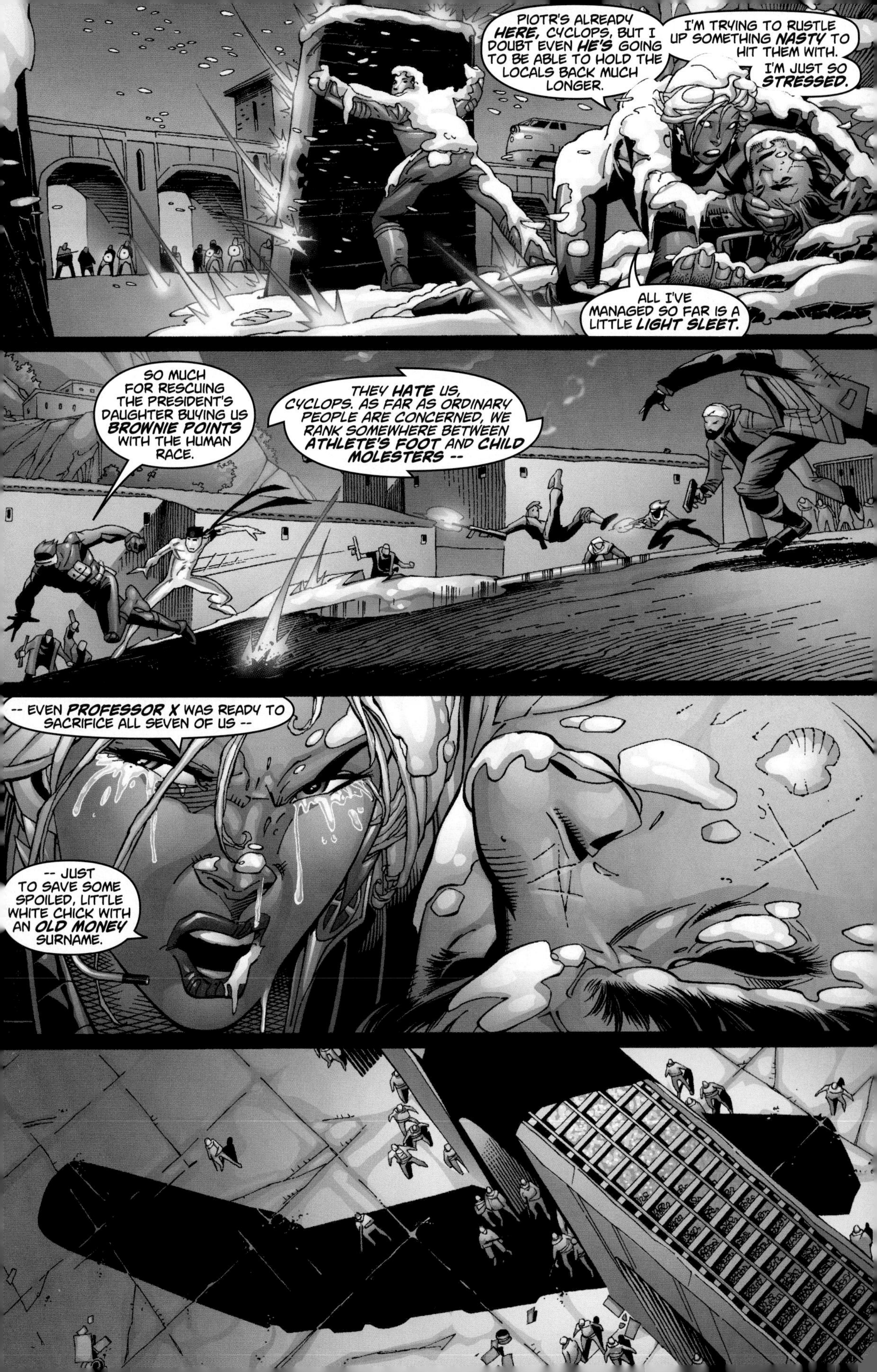
PIOTR'S ALREADY HERE, CYCLOPS, BUT I DOUBT EVEN HE'S GOING TO BE ABLE TO HOLD THE LOCALS BACK MUCH LONGER.
I'M TRYING TO RUSTLE UP SOMETHING NASTY TO HIT THEM WITH.
I'M JUST SO STRESSED.
ALL I'VE MANAGED SO FAR IS A LITTLE LIGHT SLEET.
SO MUCH FOR RESCUING THE PRESIDENT'S DAUGHTER BUYING US BROWNIE POINTS WITH THE HUMAN RACE.
THEY HATE US, CYCLOPS. AS FAR AS ORDINARY PEOPLE ARE CONCERNED, WE RANK SOMEWHERE BETWEEN ATHLETE'S FOOT AND CHILD MOLESTERS --
-- EVEN PROFESSOR X WAS READY TO SACRIFICE ALL SEVEN OF US --
-- JUST TO SAVE SOME SPOILED, LITTLE WHITE CHICK WITH AN OLD MONEY SURNAME.

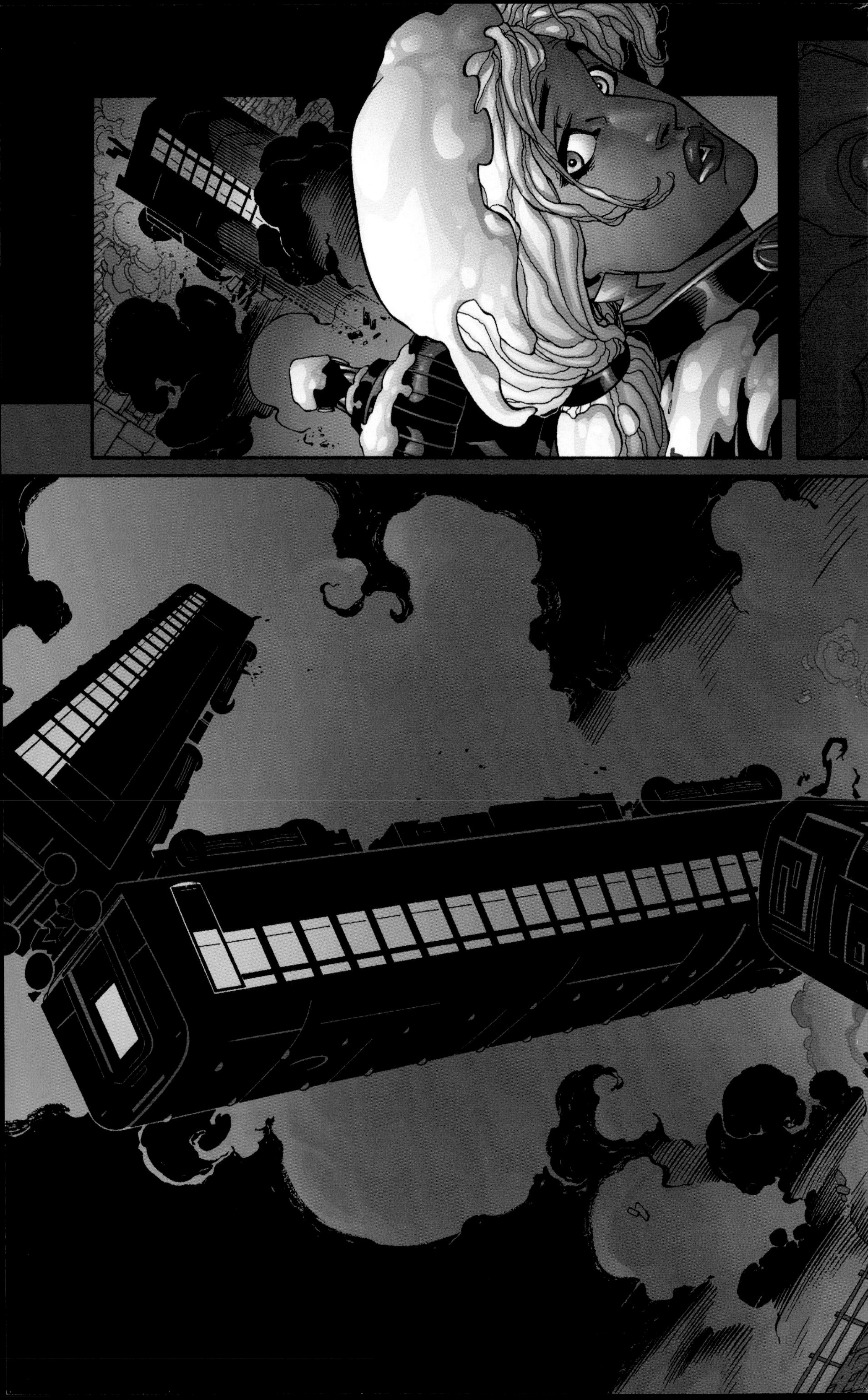

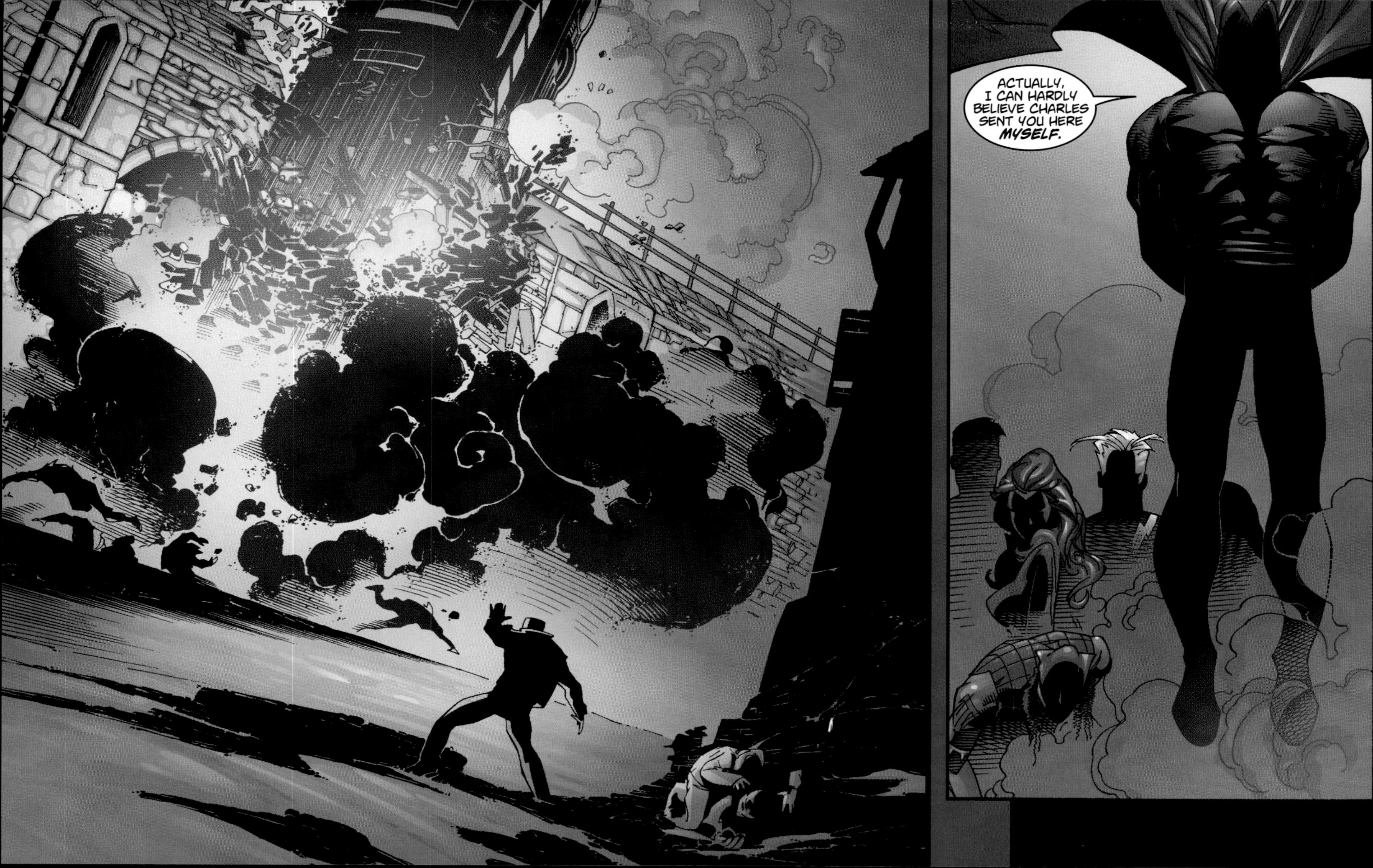
ACTUALLY, I CAN HARDLY BELIEVE CHARLES SENT YOU HERE MYSELF.

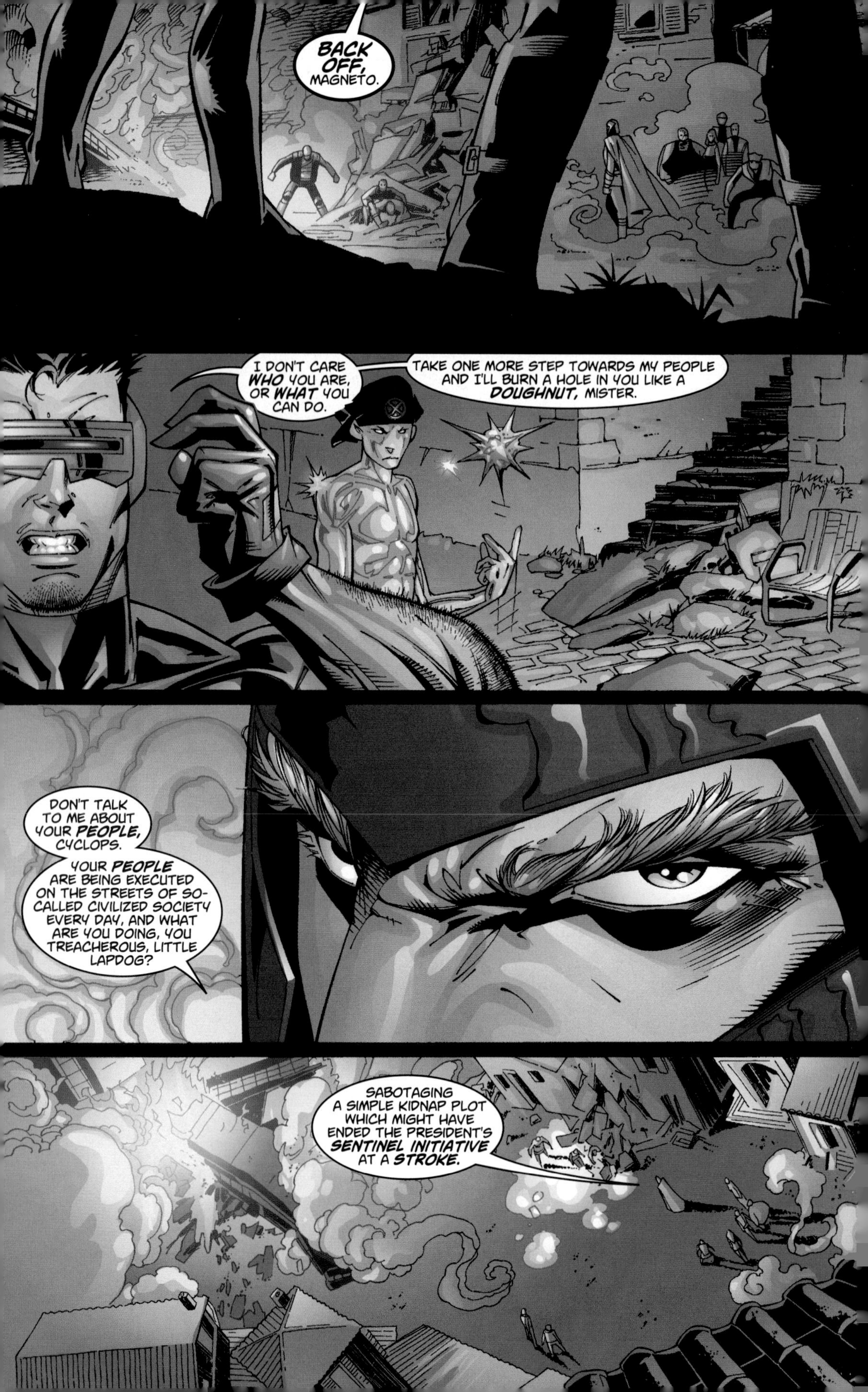

BACK OFF, MAGNETO.
I DON'T CARE WHO YOU ARE, OR WHAT YOU CAN DO.
TAKE ONE MORE STEP TOWARDS MY PEOPLE AND I'LL BURN A HOLE IN YOU LIKE A DOUGHNUT, MISTER.
DON'T TALK TO ME ABOUT YOUR PEOPLE, CYCLOPS.
YOUR PEOPLE ARE BEING EXECUTED ON THE STREETS OF SO-CALLED CIVILIZED SOCIETY EVERY DAY, AND WHAT ARE YOU DOING, YOU TREACHEROUS, LITTLE LAPDOG?
SABOTAGING A SIMPLE KIDNAP PLOT WHICH MIGHT HAVE ENDED THE PRESIDENT'S SENTINEL INITIATIVE AT A STROKE.

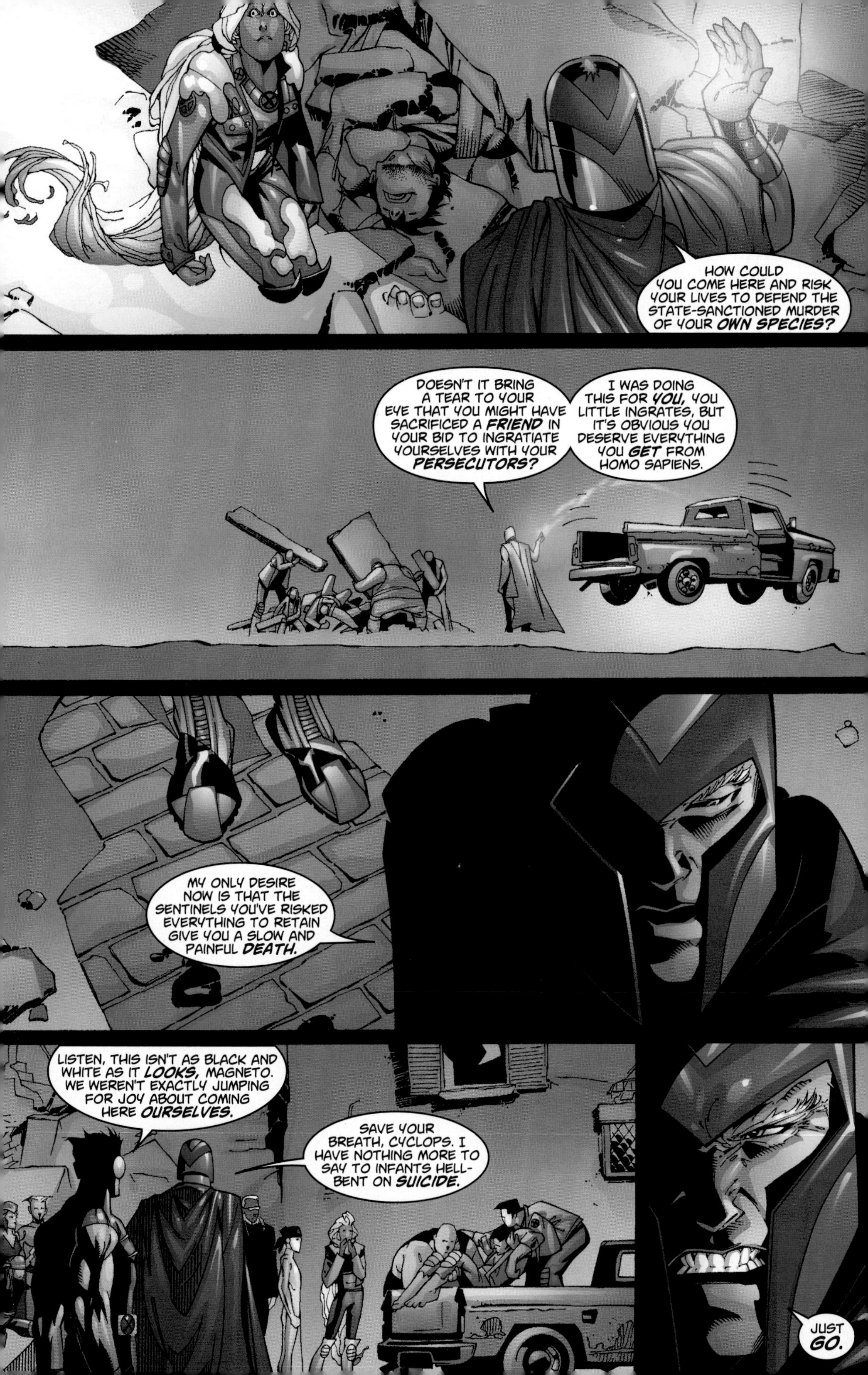
HOW COULD YOU COME HERE AND RISK YOUR LIVES TO DEFEND THE STATE-SANCTIONED MURDER OF YOUR OWN SPECIES?
DOESN'T IT BRING A TEAR TO YOUR EYE THAT YOU MIGHT HAVE SACRIFICED A FRIEND IN YOUR BID TO INGRATIATE YOURSELVES WITH YOUR PERSECUTORS?
I WAS DOING THIS FOR YOU, YOU LITTLE INGRATES, BUT IT'S OBVIOUS YOU DESERVE EVERYTHING YOU GET FROM HOMO SAPIENS.
MY ONLY DESIRE NOW IS THAT THE SENTINELS YOU'VE RISKED EVERYTHING TO RETAIN GIVE YOU A SLOW AND PAINFUL DEATH.
LISTEN, THIS ISN'T AS BLACK AND WHITE AS IT LOOKS, MAGNETO. WE WEREN'T EXACTLY JUMPING FOR JOY ABOUT COMING HERE OURSELVES.
SAVE YOUR BREATH, CYCLOPS. I HAVE NOTHING MORE TO SAY TO INFANTS HELL-BENT ON SUICIDE.
JUST GO.

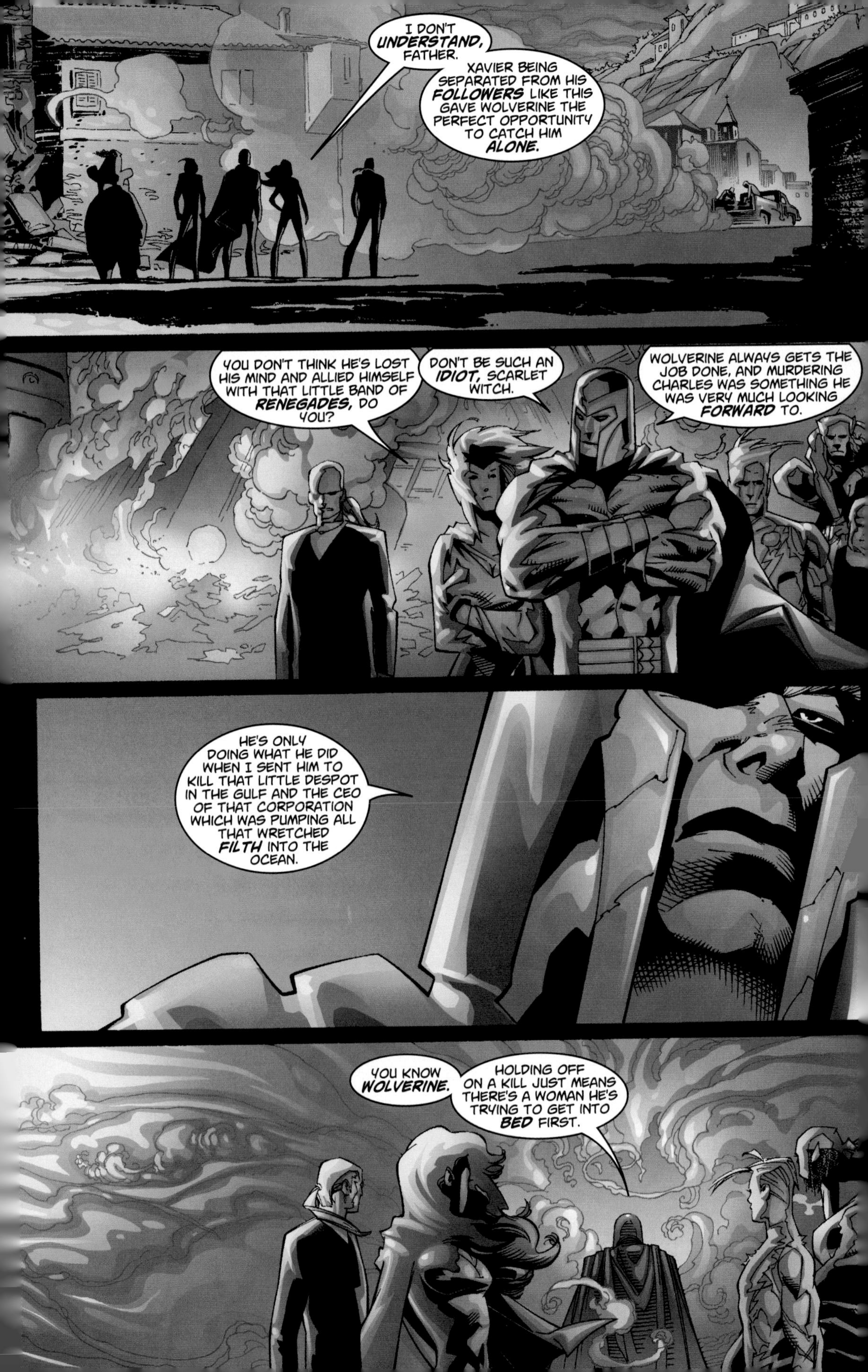
I DON'T UNDERSTAND, FATHER.
XAVIER BEING SEPARATED FROM HIS FOLLOWERS LIKE THIS GAVE WOLVERINE THE PERFECT OPPORTUNITY TO CATCH HIM ALONE.
YOU DON'T THINK HE'S LOST HIS MIND AND ALLIED HIMSELF WITH THAT LITTLE BAND OF RENEGADES, DO YOU?
DON'T BE SUCH AN IDIOT, SCARLET WITCH.
WOLVERINE ALWAYS GETS THE JOB DONE, AND MURDERING CHARLES WAS SOMETHING HE WAS VERY MUCH LOOKING FORWARD TO.
HE'S ONLY DOING WHAT HE DID WHEN I SENT HIM TO KILL THAT LITTLE DESPOT IN THE GULF AND THE CEO OF THAT CORPORATION WHICH WAS PUMPING ALL THAT WRETCHED FILTH INTO THE OCEAN.
YOU KNOW WOLVERINE.
HOLDING OFF ON A KILL JUST MEANS THERE'S A WOMAN HE'S TRYING TO GET INTO BED FIRST.

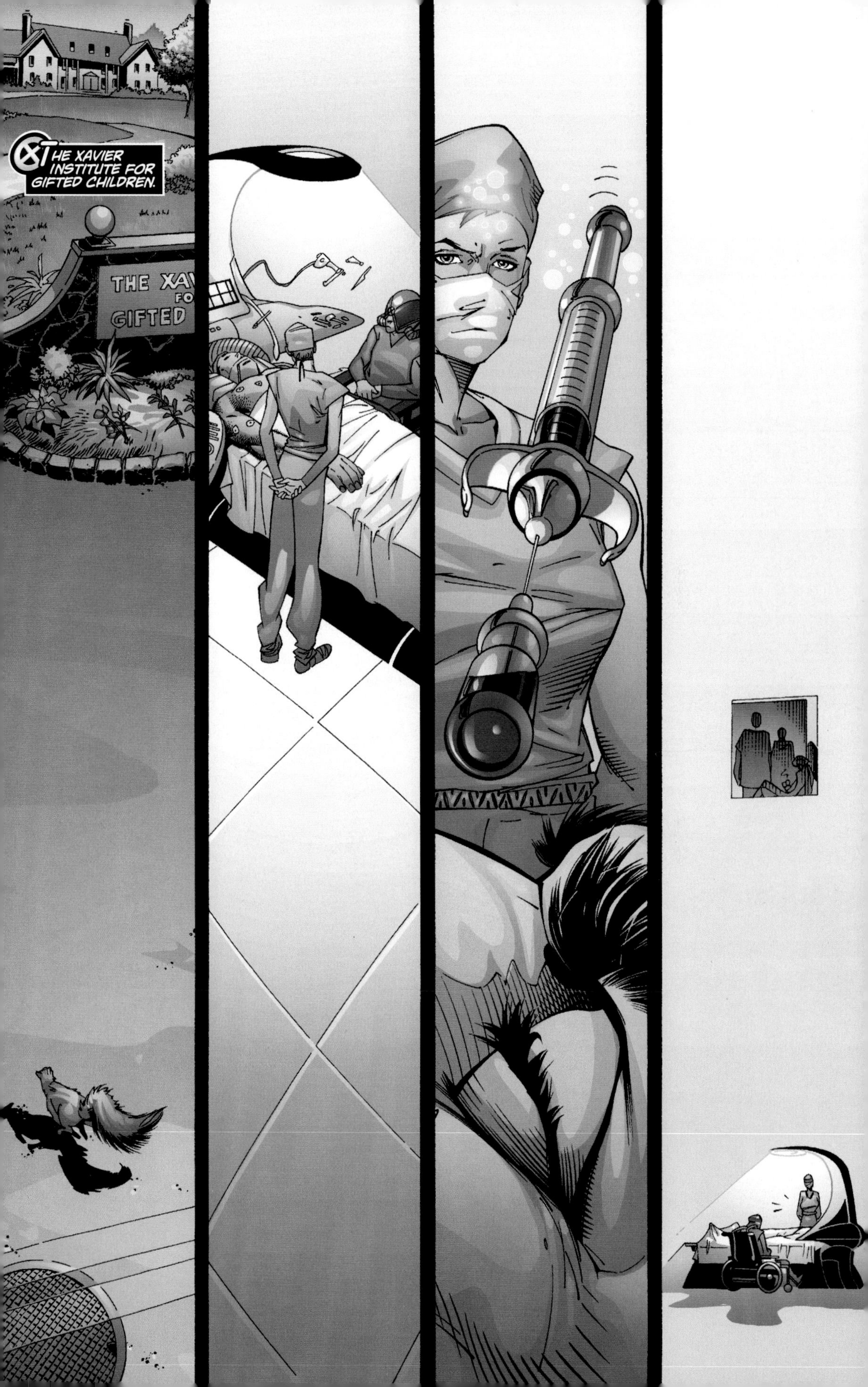
THE XAVIER INSTITUTE FOR GIFTED CHILDREN.
THE XAVI
FO
GIFTED

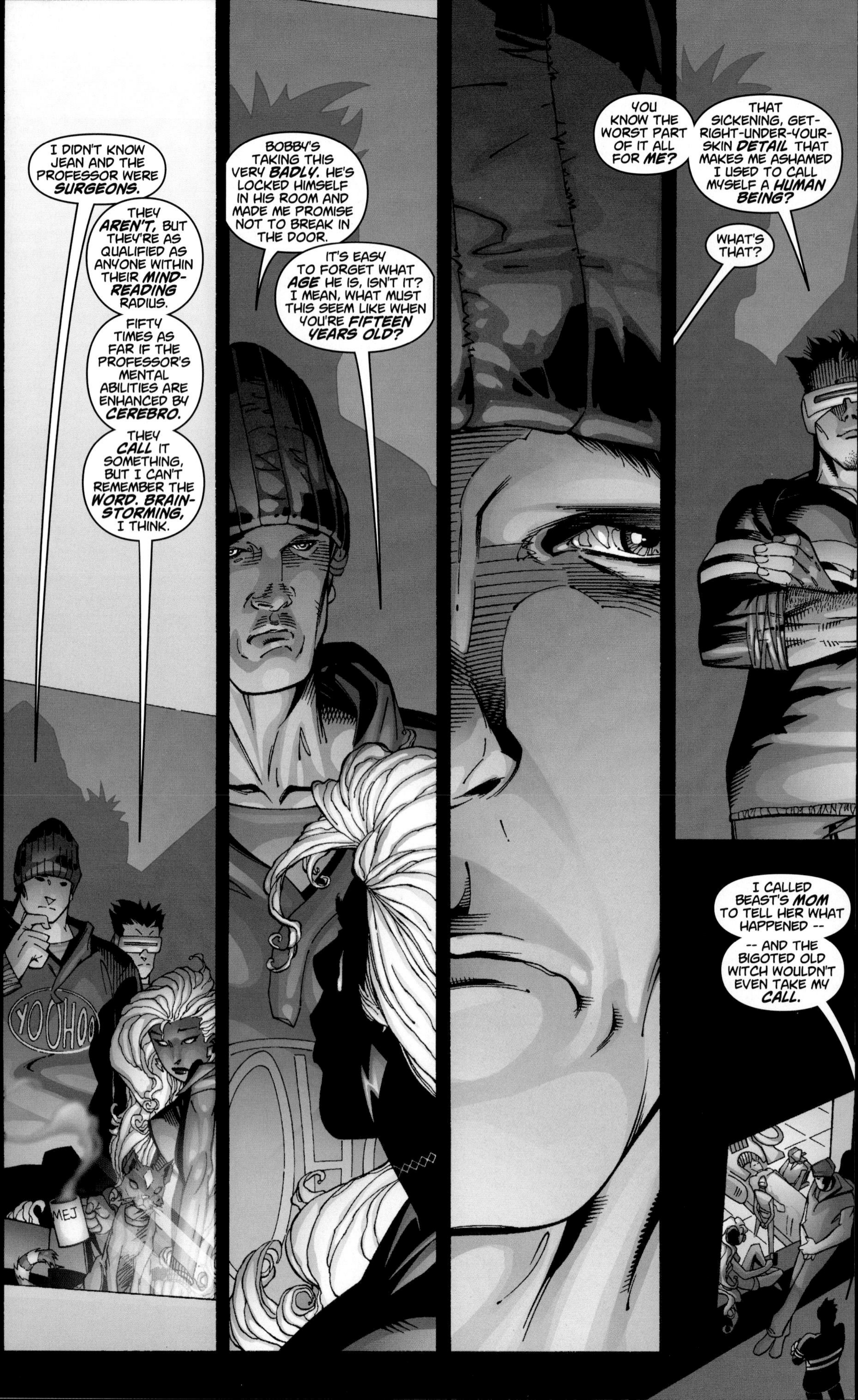
I DIDN'T KNOW JEAN AND THE PROFESSOR WERE SURGEONS.
THEY AREN'T, BUT THEY'RE AS QUALIFIED AS ANYONE WITHIN THEIR MIND-READING RADIUS.
FIFTY TIMES AS FAR IF THE PROFESSOR'S MENTAL ABILITIES ARE ENHANCED BY CEREBRO.
THEY CALL IT SOMETHING, BUT I CAN'T REMEMBER THE WORD. BRAIN-STORMING, I THINK.
BOBBY'S TAKING THIS VERY BADLY. HE'S LOCKED HIMSELF IN HIS ROOM AND MADE ME PROMISE NOT TO BREAK IN THE DOOR.
IT'S EASY TO FORGET WHAT AGE HE IS, ISN'T IT? I MEAN, WHAT MUST THIS SEEM LIKE WHEN YOU'RE FIFTEEN YEARS OLD?
YOU KNOW THE WORST PART OF IT ALL FOR ME?
THAT SICKENING, GET-RIGHT-UNDER-YOUR-SKIN DETAIL THAT MAKES ME ASHAMED I USED TO CALL MYSELF A HUMAN BEING?
WHAT'S THAT?
I CALLED BEAST'S MOM TO TELL HER WHAT HAPPENED --
-- AND THE BIGOTED OLD WITCH WOULDN'T EVEN TAKE MY CALL.
YOOHOO
MEJ

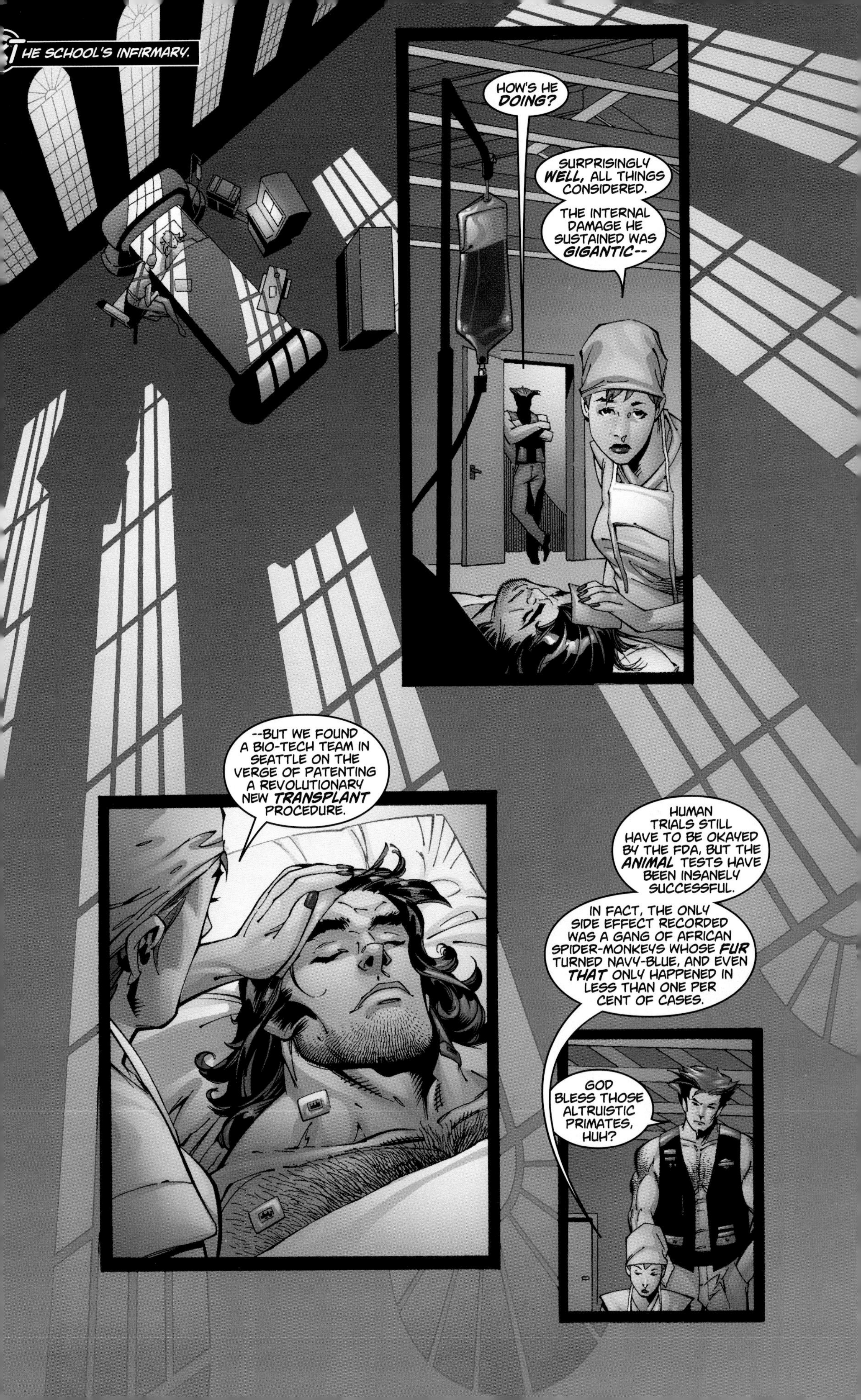
THE SCHOOL'S INFIRMARY.
HOW'S HE DOING?
SURPRISINGLY WELL, ALL THINGS CONSIDERED.
THE INTERNAL DAMAGE HE SUSTAINED WAS GIGANTIC--
--BUT WE FOUND A BIO-TECH TEAM IN SEATTLE ON THE VERGE OF PATENTING A REVOLUTIONARY NEW TRANSPLANT PROCEDURE.
HUMAN TRIALS STILL HAVE TO BE OKAYED BY THE FDA, BUT THE ANIMAL TESTS HAVE BEEN INSANELY SUCCESSFUL.
IN FACT, THE ONLY SIDE EFFECT RECORDED WAS A GANG OF AFRICAN SPIDER-MONKEYS WHOSE FUR TURNED NAVY-BLUE, AND EVEN THAT ONLY HAPPENED IN LESS THAN ONE PER CENT OF CASES.
GOD BLESS THOSE ALTRUISTIC PRIMATES, HUH?

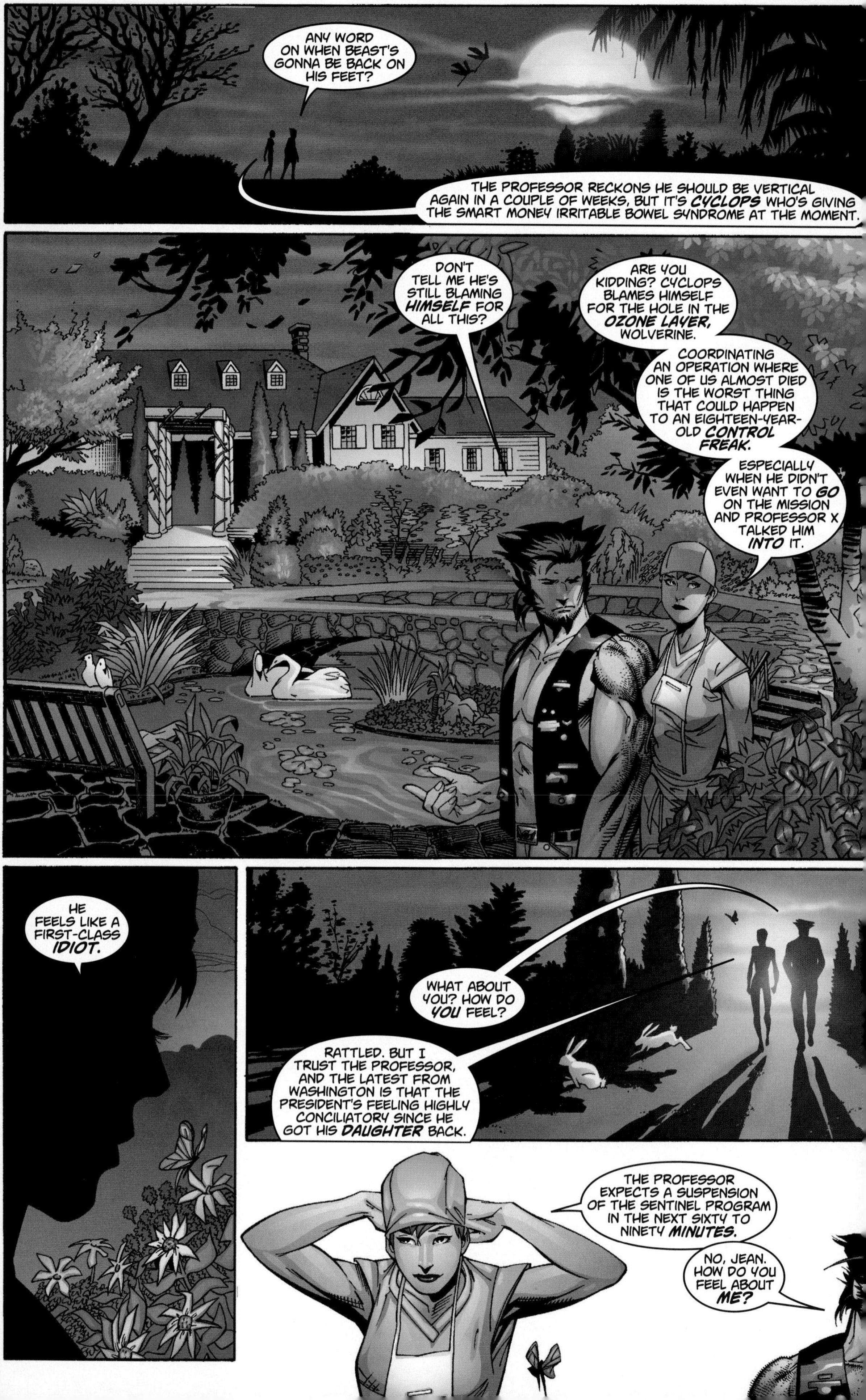
ANY WORD ON WHEN BEAST'S GONNA BE BACK ON HIS FEET?
THE PROFESSOR RECKONS HE SHOULD BE VERTICAL AGAIN IN A COUPLE OF WEEKS, BUT IT'S CYCLOPS WHO'S GIVING THE SMART MONEY IRRITABLE BOWEL SYNDROME AT THE MOMENT.
DON'T TELL ME HE'S STILL BLAMING HIMSELF FOR ALL THIS?
ARE YOU KIDDING? CYCLOPS BLAMES HIMSELF FOR THE HOLE IN THE OZONE LAYER, WOLVERINE.
COORDINATING AN OPERATION WHERE ONE OF US ALMOST DIED IS THE WORST THING THAT COULD HAPPEN TO AN EIGHTEEN-YEAR-OLD CONTROL FREAK.
ESPECIALLY WHEN HE DIDN'T EVEN WANT TO GO ON THE MISSION AND PROFESSOR X TALKED HIM INTO IT.
HE FEELS LIKE A FIRST-CLASS IDIOT.
WHAT ABOUT YOU? HOW DO YOU FEEL?
RATTLED. BUT I TRUST THE PROFESSOR, AND THE LATEST FROM WASHINGTON IS THAT THE PRESIDENT'S FEELING HIGHLY CONCILIATORY SINCE HE GOT HIS DAUGHTER BACK.
THE PROFESSOR EXPECTS A SUSPENSION OF THE SENTINEL PROGRAM IN THE NEXT SIXTY TO NINETY MINUTES.
NO, JEAN. HOW DO YOU FEEL ABOUT ME?

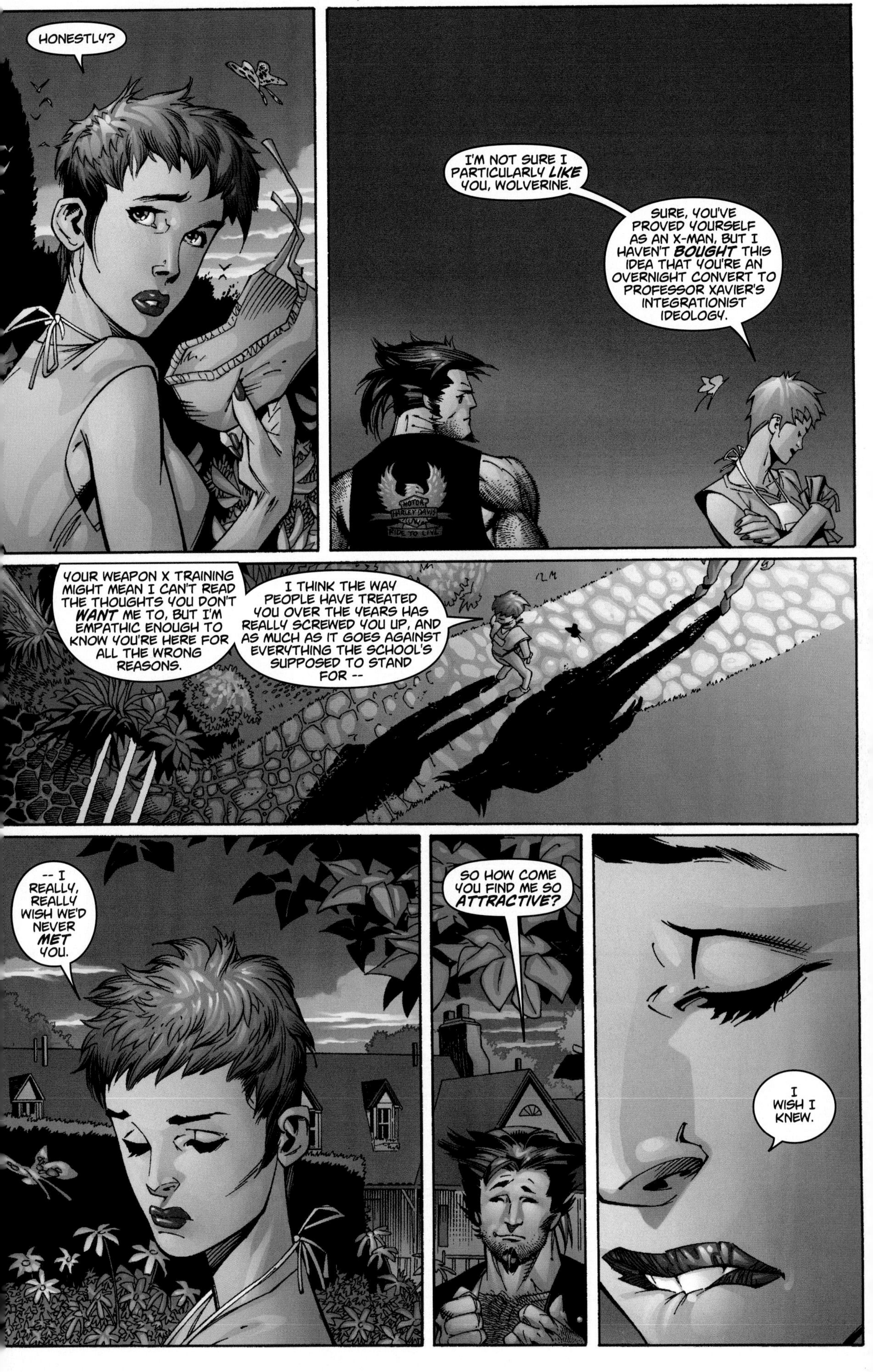
HONESTLY?
I'M NOT SURE I PARTICULARLY *LIKE* YOU, WOLVERINE.
SURE, YOU'VE PROVED YOURSELF AS AN X-MAN, BUT I HAVEN'T *BOUGHT* THIS IDEA THAT YOU'RE AN OVERNIGHT CONVERT TO PROFESSOR XAVIER'S INTEGRATIONIST IDEOLOGY.
YOUR WEAPON X TRAINING MIGHT MEAN I CAN'T READ THE THOUGHTS YOU DON'T *WANT* ME TO, BUT I'M EMPATHIC ENOUGH TO KNOW YOU'RE HERE FOR ALL THE WRONG REASONS.
I THINK THE WAY PEOPLE HAVE TREATED YOU OVER THE YEARS HAS REALLY SCREWED YOU UP, AND AS MUCH AS IT GOES AGAINST EVERYTHING THE SCHOOL'S SUPPOSED TO STAND FOR --
-- I REALLY, REALLY WISH WE'D NEVER *MET* YOU.
SO HOW COME YOU FIND ME SO *ATTRACTIVE?*
I WISH I KNEW.

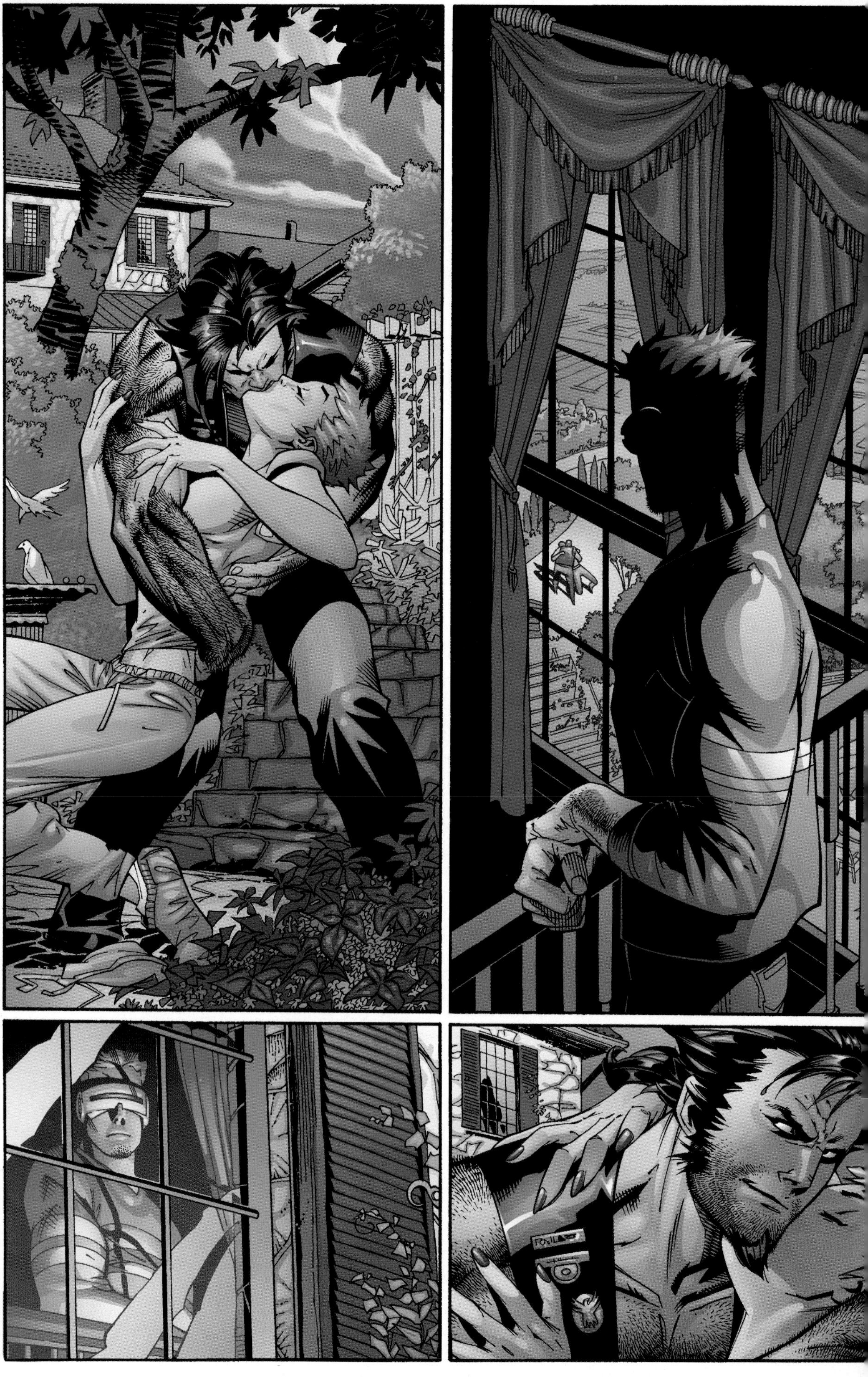

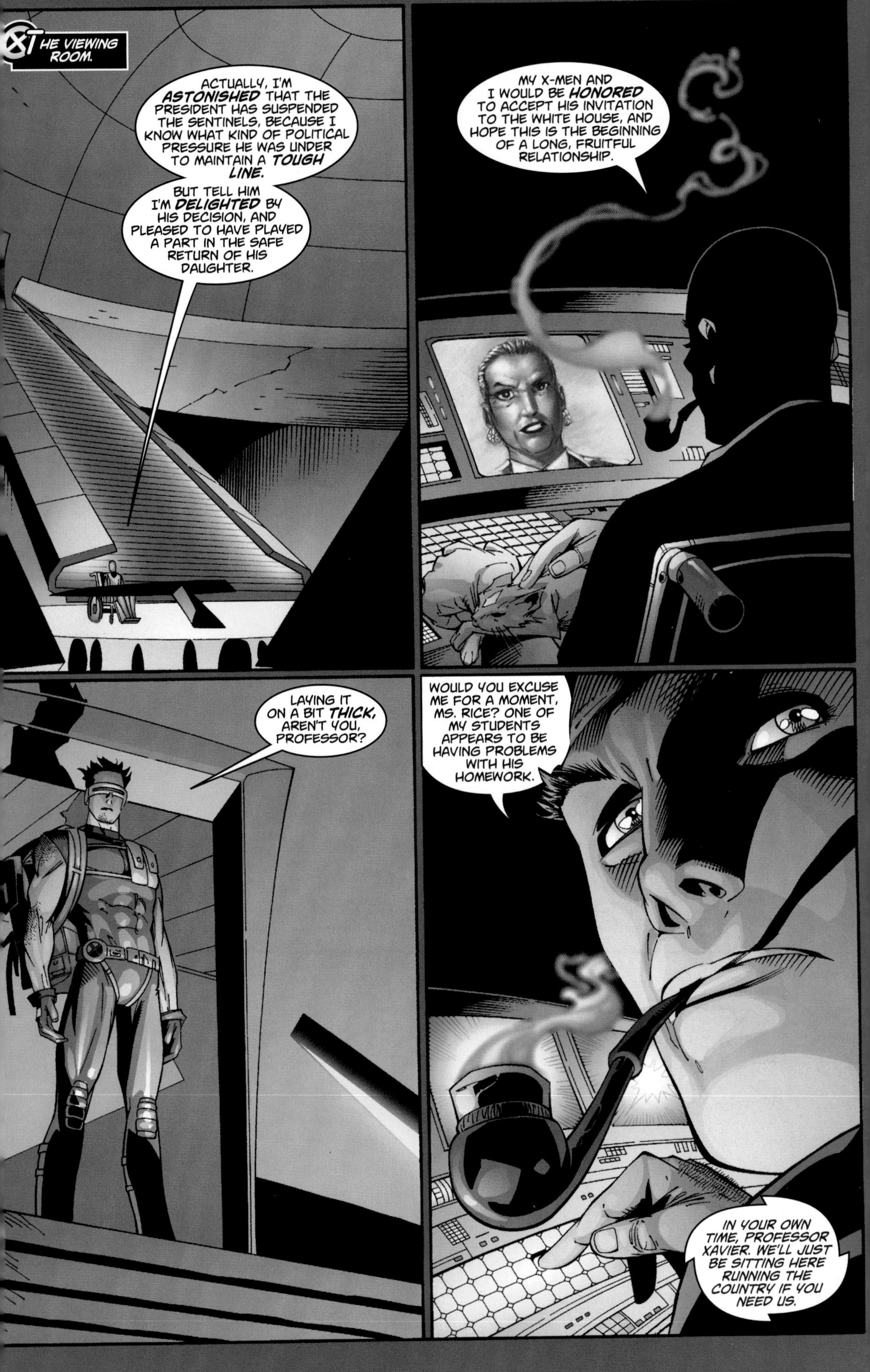
THE VIEWING ROOM.
ACTUALLY, I'M ASTONISHED THAT THE PRESIDENT HAS SUSPENDED THE SENTINELS, BECAUSE I KNOW WHAT KIND OF POLITICAL PRESSURE HE WAS UNDER TO MAINTAIN A TOUGH LINE.
BUT TELL HIM I'M DELIGHTED BY HIS DECISION, AND PLEASED TO HAVE PLAYED A PART IN THE SAFE RETURN OF HIS DAUGHTER.
MY X-MEN AND I WOULD BE HONORED TO ACCEPT HIS INVITATION TO THE WHITE HOUSE, AND HOPE THIS IS THE BEGINNING OF A LONG, FRUITFUL RELATIONSHIP.
LAYING IT ON A BIT THICK, AREN'T YOU, PROFESSOR?
WOULD YOU EXCUSE ME FOR A MOMENT, MS. RICE? ONE OF MY STUDENTS APPEARS TO BE HAVING PROBLEMS WITH HIS HOMEWORK.
IN YOUR OWN TIME, PROFESSOR XAVIER. WE'LL JUST BE SITTING HERE RUNNING THE COUNTRY IF YOU NEED US.

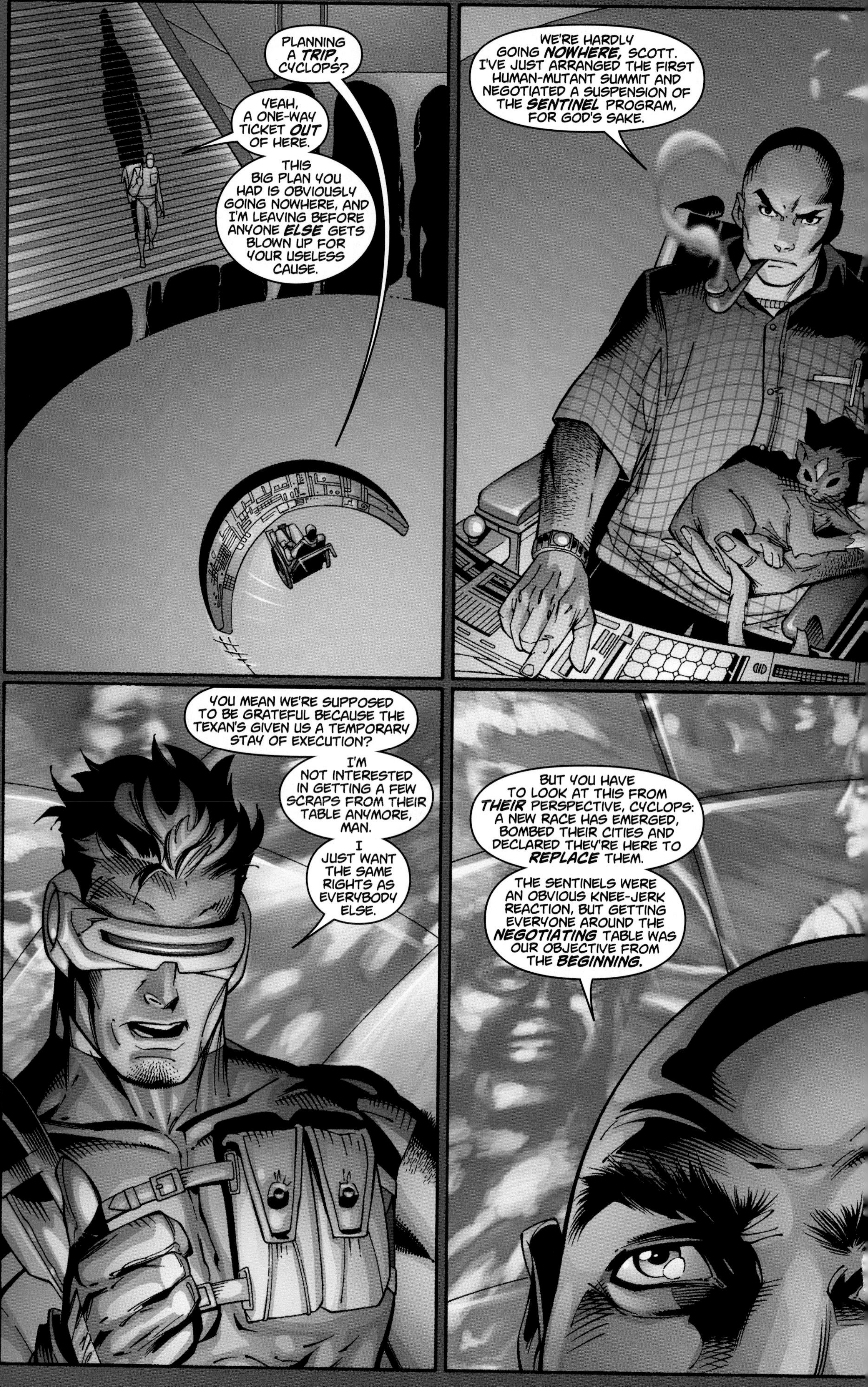
PLANNING A TRIP, CYCLOPS?
YEAH, A ONE-WAY TICKET OUT OF HERE.
THIS BIG PLAN YOU HAD IS OBVIOUSLY GOING NOWHERE, AND I'M LEAVING BEFORE ANYONE ELSE GETS BLOWN UP FOR YOUR USELESS CAUSE.
WE'RE HARDLY GOING NOWHERE, SCOTT. I'VE JUST ARRANGED THE FIRST HUMAN-MUTANT SUMMIT AND NEGOTIATED A SUSPENSION OF THE SENTINEL PROGRAM, FOR GOD'S SAKE.
YOU MEAN WE'RE SUPPOSED TO BE GRATEFUL BECAUSE THE TEXAN'S GIVEN US A TEMPORARY STAY OF EXECUTION?
I'M NOT INTERESTED IN GETTING A FEW SCRAPS FROM THEIR TABLE ANYMORE, MAN.
I JUST WANT THE SAME RIGHTS AS EVERYBODY ELSE.
BUT YOU HAVE TO LOOK AT THIS FROM THEIR PERSPECTIVE, CYCLOPS: A NEW RACE HAS EMERGED, BOMBED THEIR CITIES AND DECLARED THEY'RE HERE TO REPLACE THEM.
THE SENTINELS WERE AN OBVIOUS KNEE-JERK REACTION, BUT GETTING EVERYONE AROUND THE NEGOTIATING TABLE WAS OUR OBJECTIVE FROM THE BEGINNING.

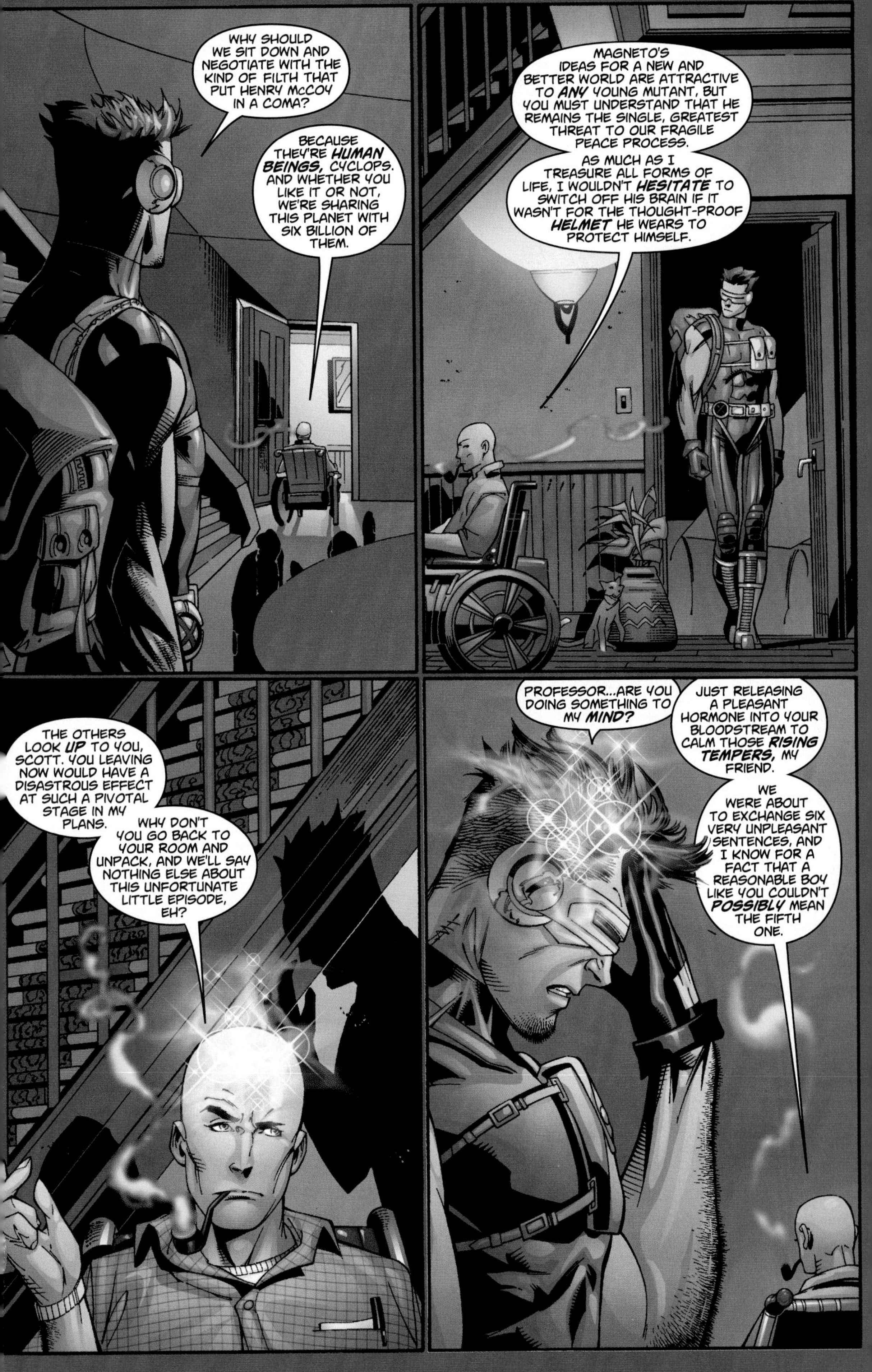
WHY SHOULD WE SIT DOWN AND NEGOTIATE WITH THE KIND OF FILTH THAT PUT HENRY McCOY IN A COMA?
BECAUSE THEY'RE HUMAN BEINGS, CYCLOPS. AND WHETHER YOU LIKE IT OR NOT, WE'RE SHARING THIS PLANET WITH SIX BILLION OF THEM.
MAGNETO'S IDEAS FOR A NEW AND BETTER WORLD ARE ATTRACTIVE TO ANY YOUNG MUTANT, BUT YOU MUST UNDERSTAND THAT HE REMAINS THE SINGLE, GREATEST THREAT TO OUR FRAGILE PEACE PROCESS.
AS MUCH AS I TREASURE ALL FORMS OF LIFE, I WOULDN'T HESITATE TO SWITCH OFF HIS BRAIN IF IT WASN'T FOR THE THOUGHT-PROOF HELMET HE WEARS TO PROTECT HIMSELF.
THE OTHERS LOOK UP TO YOU, SCOTT. YOU LEAVING NOW WOULD HAVE A DISASTROUS EFFECT AT SUCH A PIVOTAL STAGE IN MY PLANS.
WHY DON'T YOU GO BACK TO YOUR ROOM AND UNPACK, AND WE'LL SAY NOTHING ELSE ABOUT THIS UNFORTUNATE LITTLE EPISODE, EH?
PROFESSOR...ARE YOU DOING SOMETHING TO MY MIND?
JUST RELEASING A PLEASANT HORMONE INTO YOUR BLOODSTREAM TO CALM THOSE RISING TEMPERS, MY FRIEND.
WE WERE ABOUT TO EXCHANGE SIX VERY UNPLEASANT SENTENCES, AND I KNOW FOR A FACT THAT A REASONABLE BOY LIKE YOU COULDN'T POSSIBLY MEAN THE FIFTH ONE.

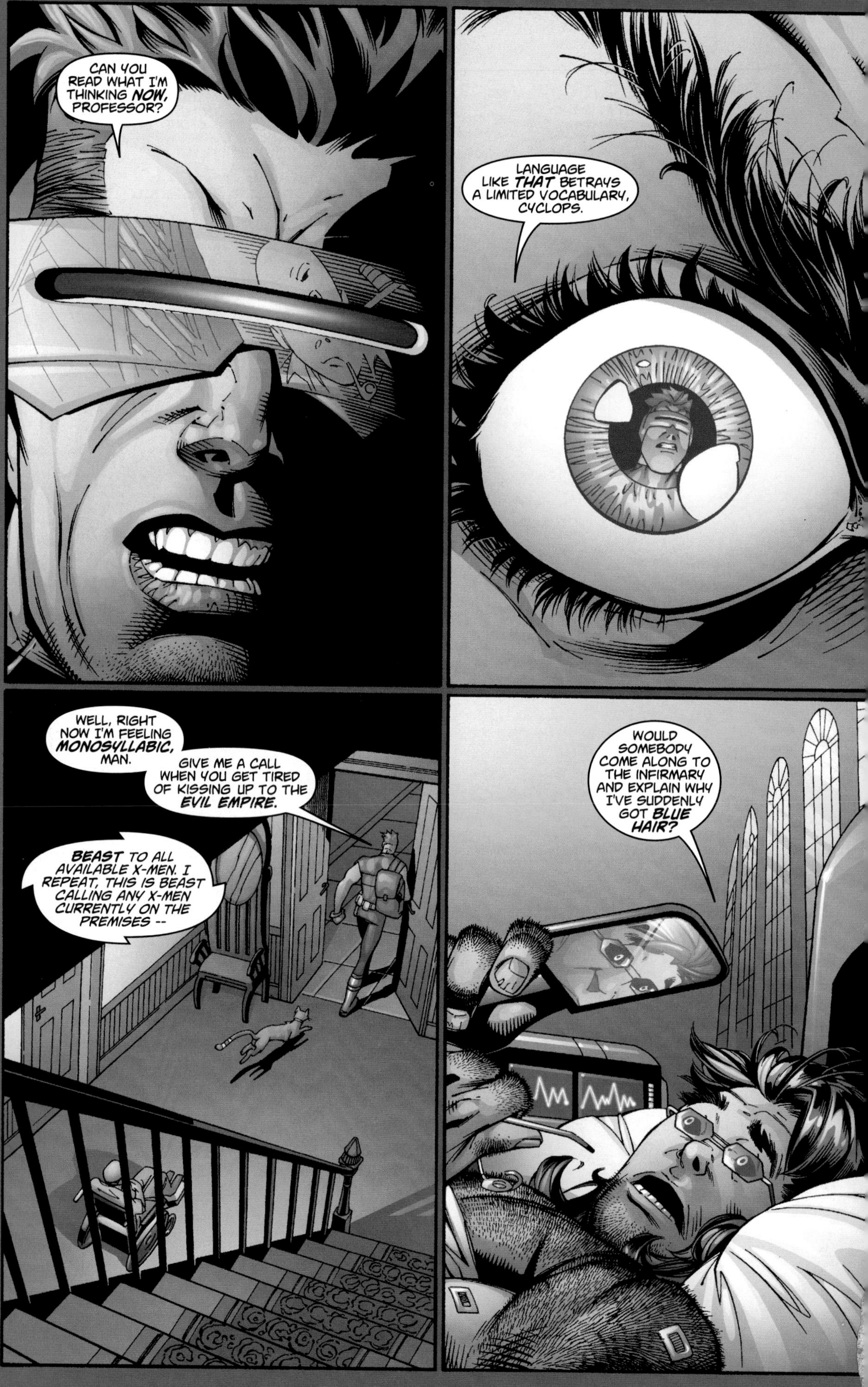
CAN YOU READ WHAT I'M THINKING NOW, PROFESSOR?
LANGUAGE LIKE THAT BETRAYS A LIMITED VOCABULARY, CYCLOPS.
WELL, RIGHT NOW I'M FEELING MONOSYLLABIC, MAN.
GIVE ME A CALL WHEN YOU GET TIRED OF KISSING UP TO THE EVIL EMPIRE.
BEAST TO ALL AVAILABLE X-MEN. I REPEAT, THIS IS BEAST CALLING ANY X-MEN CURRENTLY ON THE PREMISES --
WOULD SOMEBODY COME ALONG TO THE INFIRMARY AND EXPLAIN WHY I'VE SUDDENLY GOT BLUE HAIR?

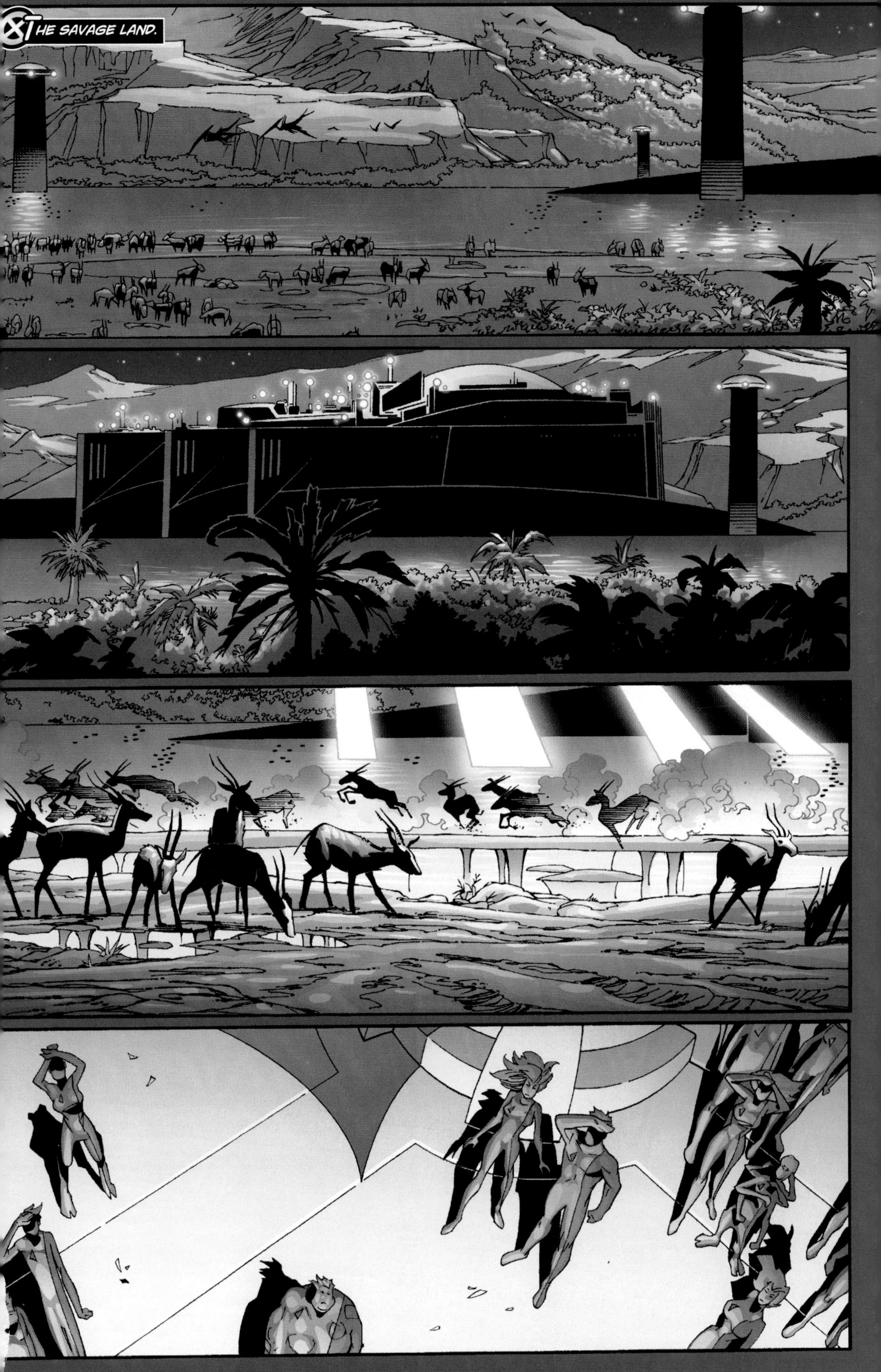
THE SAVAGE LAND.

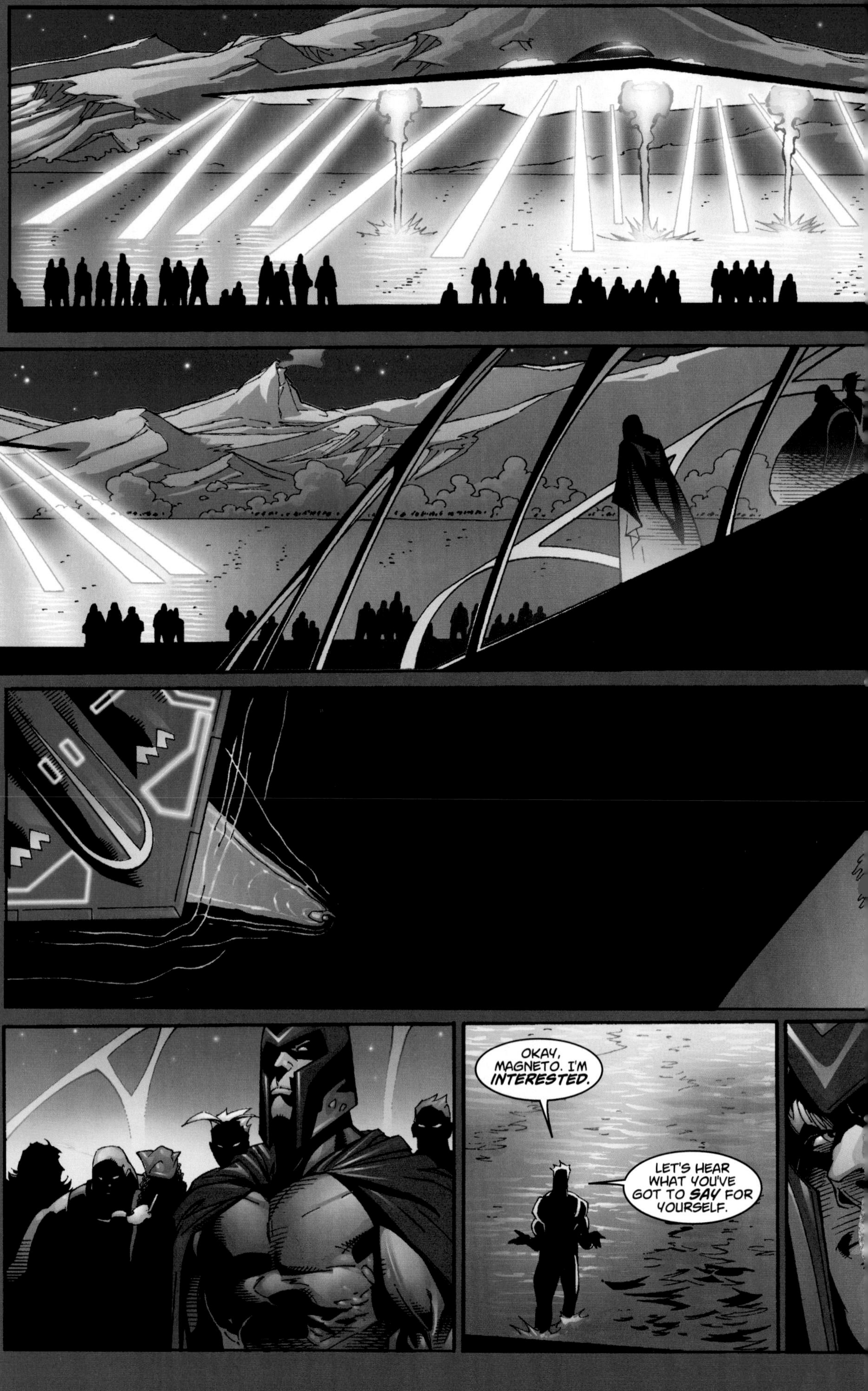
OKAY, MAGNETO. I'M INTERESTED.
LET'S HEAR WHAT YOU'VE GOT TO SAY FOR YOURSELF.

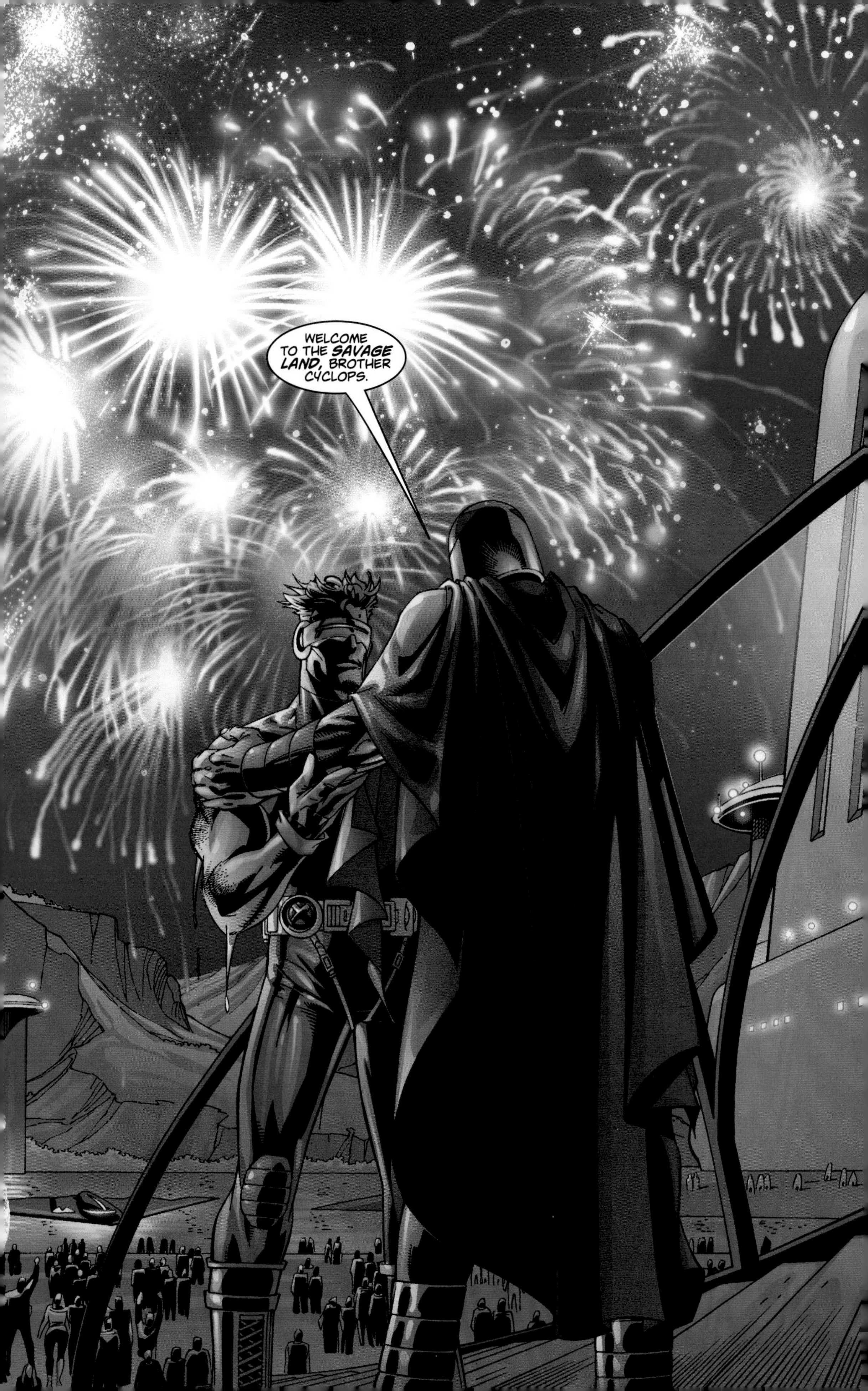
WELCOME TO THE SAVAGE LAND, BROTHER CYCLOPS.

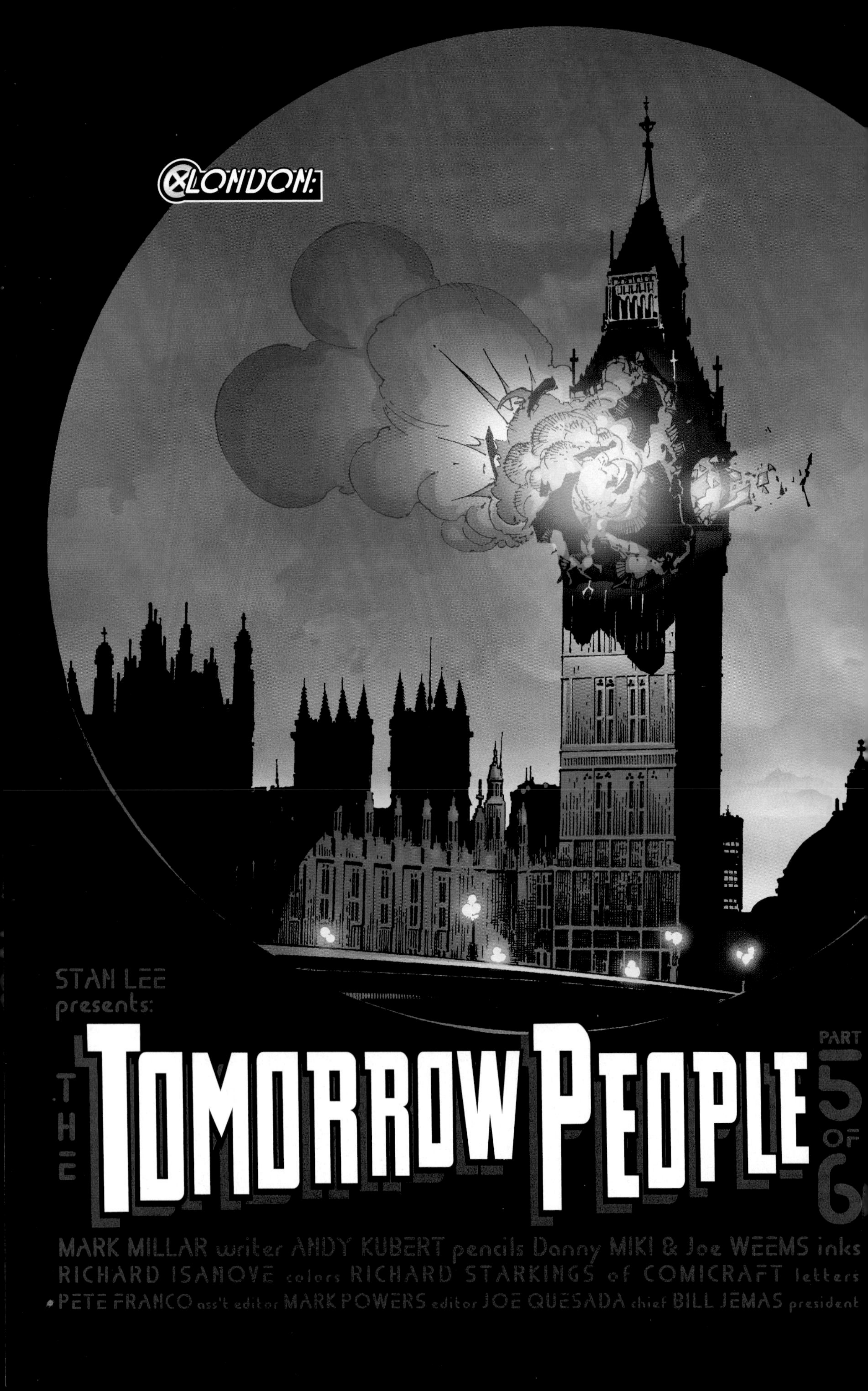
LONDON:
STAN LEE presents:
THE TOMORROW PEOPLE
PART 5 OF 6
MARK MILLAR writer ANDY KUBERT pencils Danny MIKI & Joe WEEMS inks
RICHARD ISANOVE colors RICHARD STARKINGS of COMICRAFT letters
PETE FRANCO ass't editor MARK POWERS editor JOE QUESADA chief BILL JEMAS president

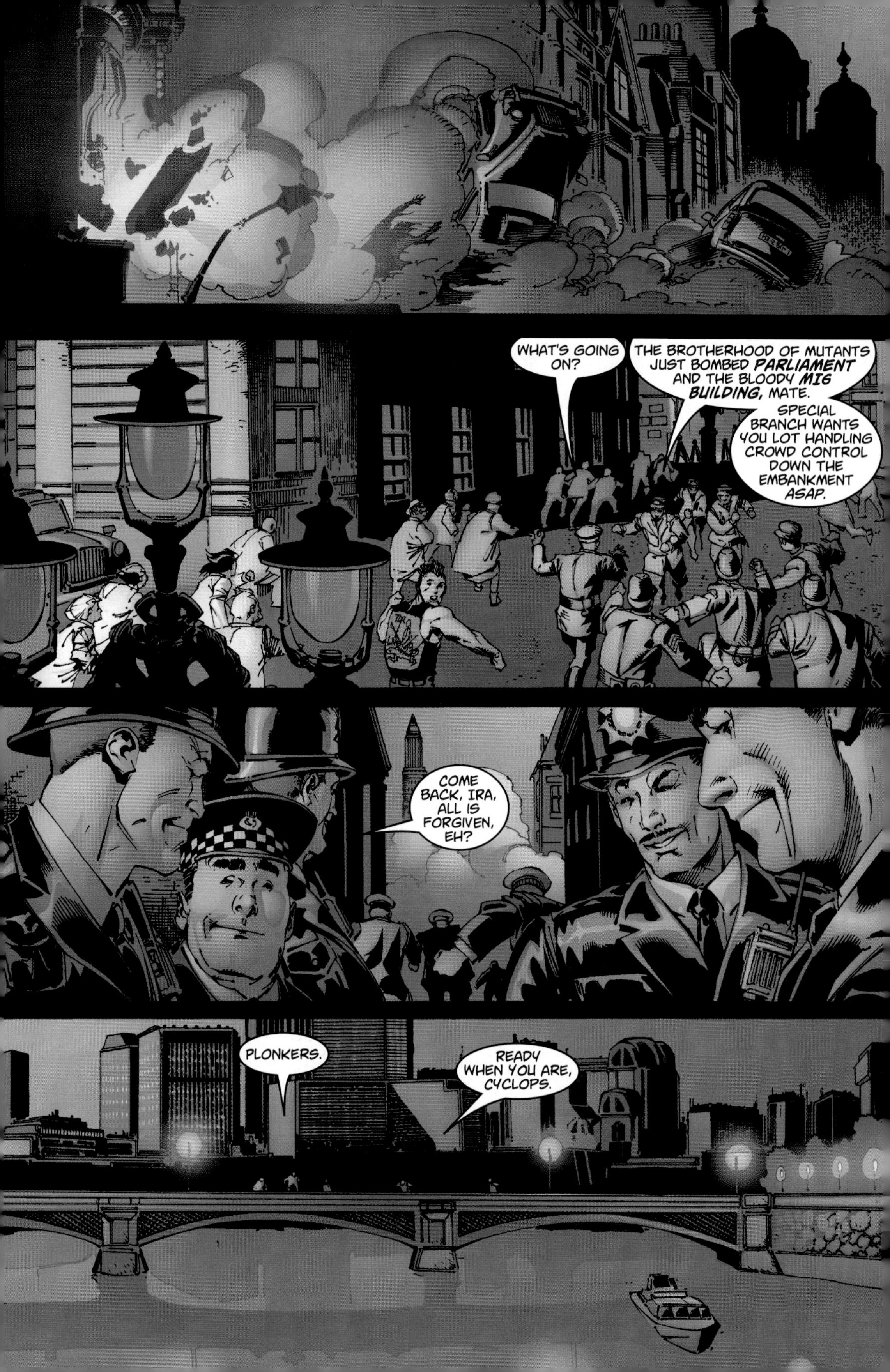
WHAT'S GOING ON?
THE BROTHERHOOD OF MUTANTS JUST BOMBED PARLIAMENT AND THE BLOODY MI6 BUILDING, MATE.
SPECIAL BRANCH WANTS YOU LOT HANDLING CROWD CONTROL DOWN THE EMBANKMENT ASAP.
COME BACK, IRA, ALL IS FORGIVEN, EH?
PLONKERS.
READY WHEN YOU ARE, CYCLOPS.

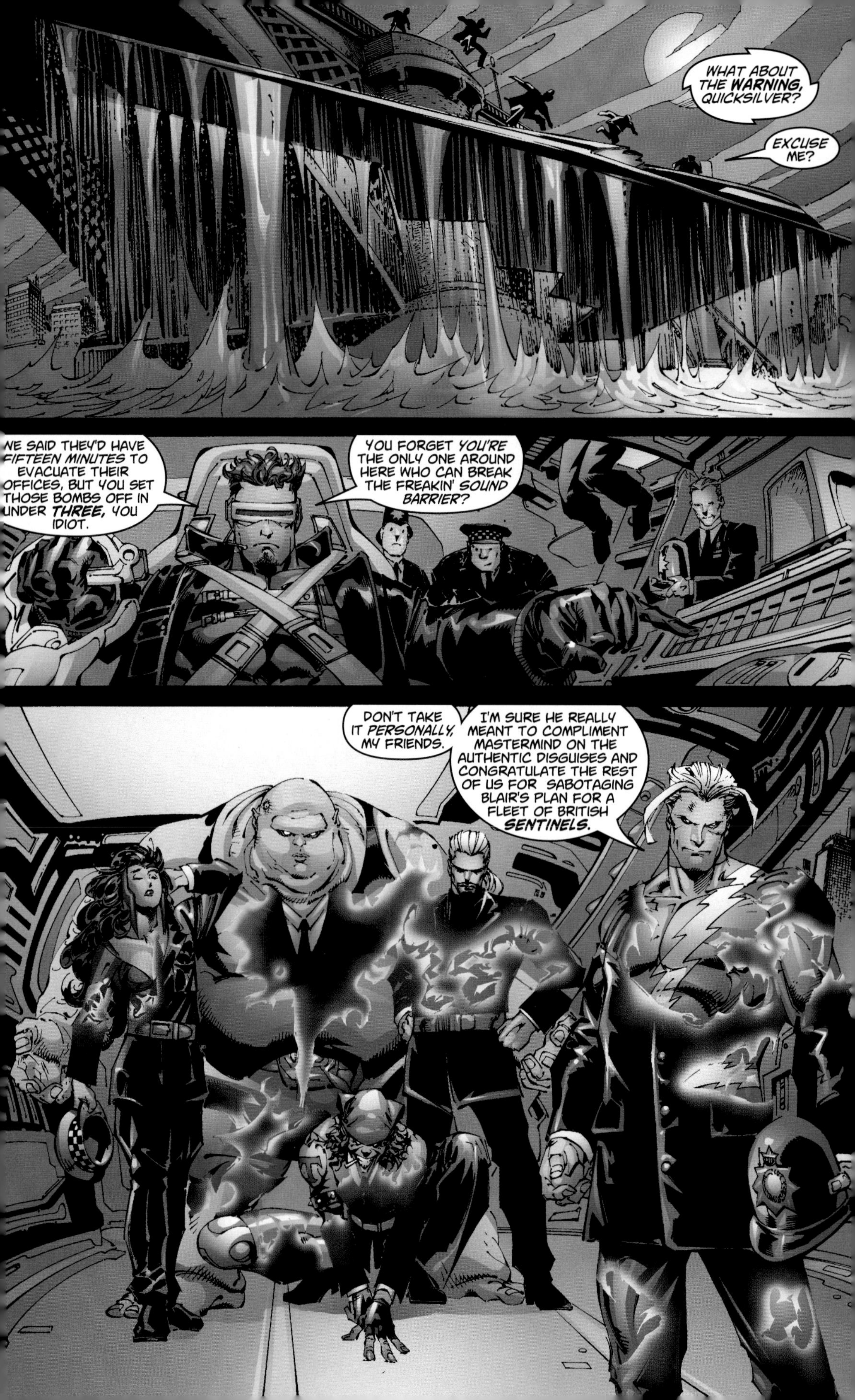
WHAT ABOUT THE **WARNING,** QUICKSILVER?
EXCUSE ME?
WE SAID THEY'D HAVE *FIFTEEN MINUTES* TO EVACUATE THEIR OFFICES, BUT YOU SET THOSE BOMBS OFF IN UNDER **THREE,** YOU IDIOT.
YOU FORGET *YOU'RE* THE ONLY ONE AROUND HERE WHO CAN BREAK THE FREAKIN' *SOUND* BARRIER?
DON'T TAKE IT *PERSONALLY,* MY FRIENDS.
I'M SURE HE REALLY MEANT TO COMPLIMENT MASTERMIND ON THE AUTHENTIC DISGUISES AND CONGRATULATE THE REST OF US FOR SABOTAGING BLAIR'S PLAN FOR A FLEET OF BRITISH ***SENTINELS.***

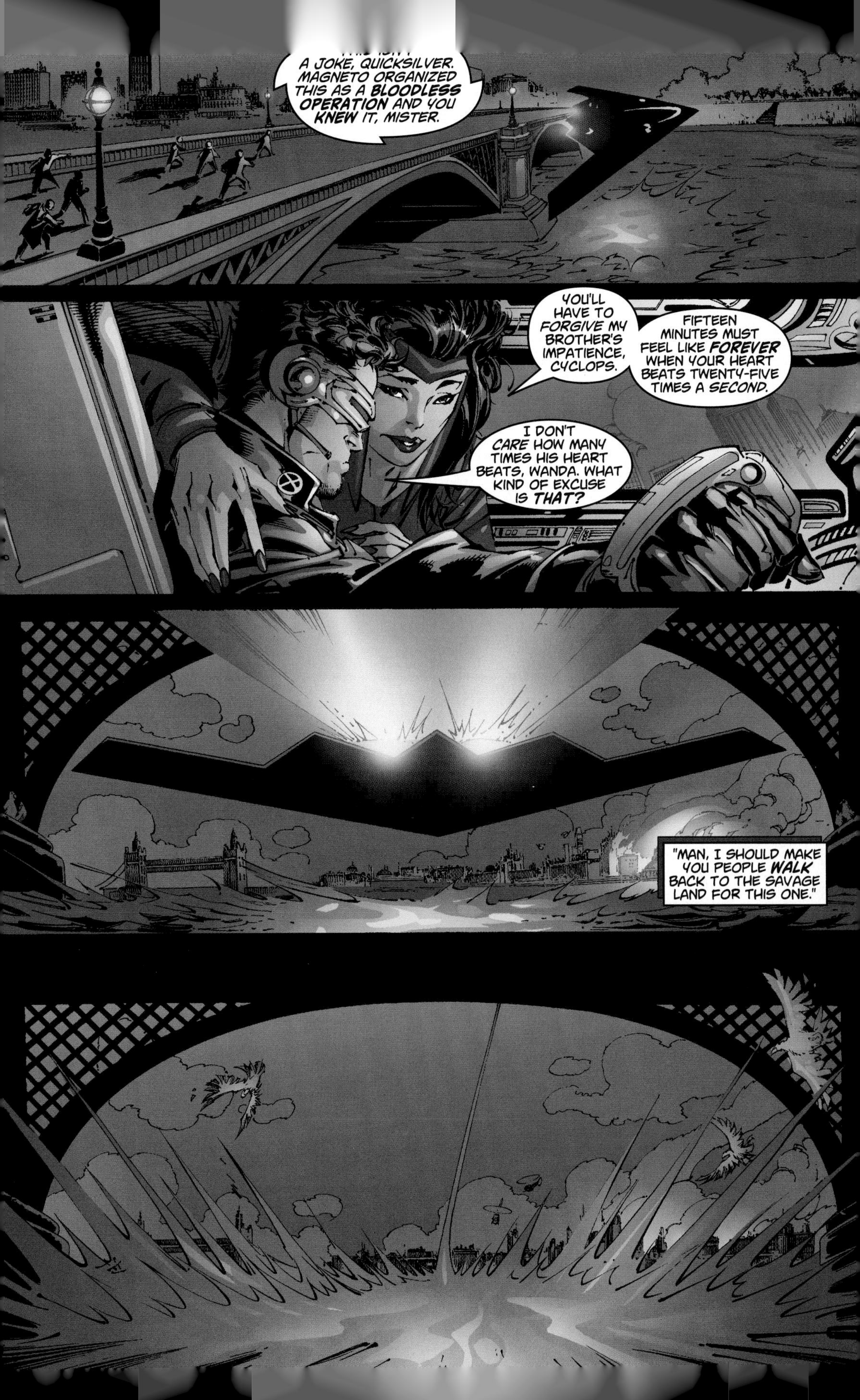
A JOKE, QUICKSILVER. MAGNETO ORGANIZED THIS AS A BLOODLESS OPERATION AND YOU KNEW IT, MISTER.
YOU'LL HAVE TO FORGIVE MY BROTHER'S IMPATIENCE, CYCLOPS.
FIFTEEN MINUTES MUST FEEL LIKE FOREVER WHEN YOUR HEART BEATS TWENTY-FIVE TIMES A SECOND.
I DON'T CARE HOW MANY TIMES HIS HEART BEATS, WANDA. WHAT KIND OF EXCUSE IS THAT?
"MAN, I SHOULD MAKE YOU PEOPLE WALK BACK TO THE SAVAGE LAND FOR THIS ONE."

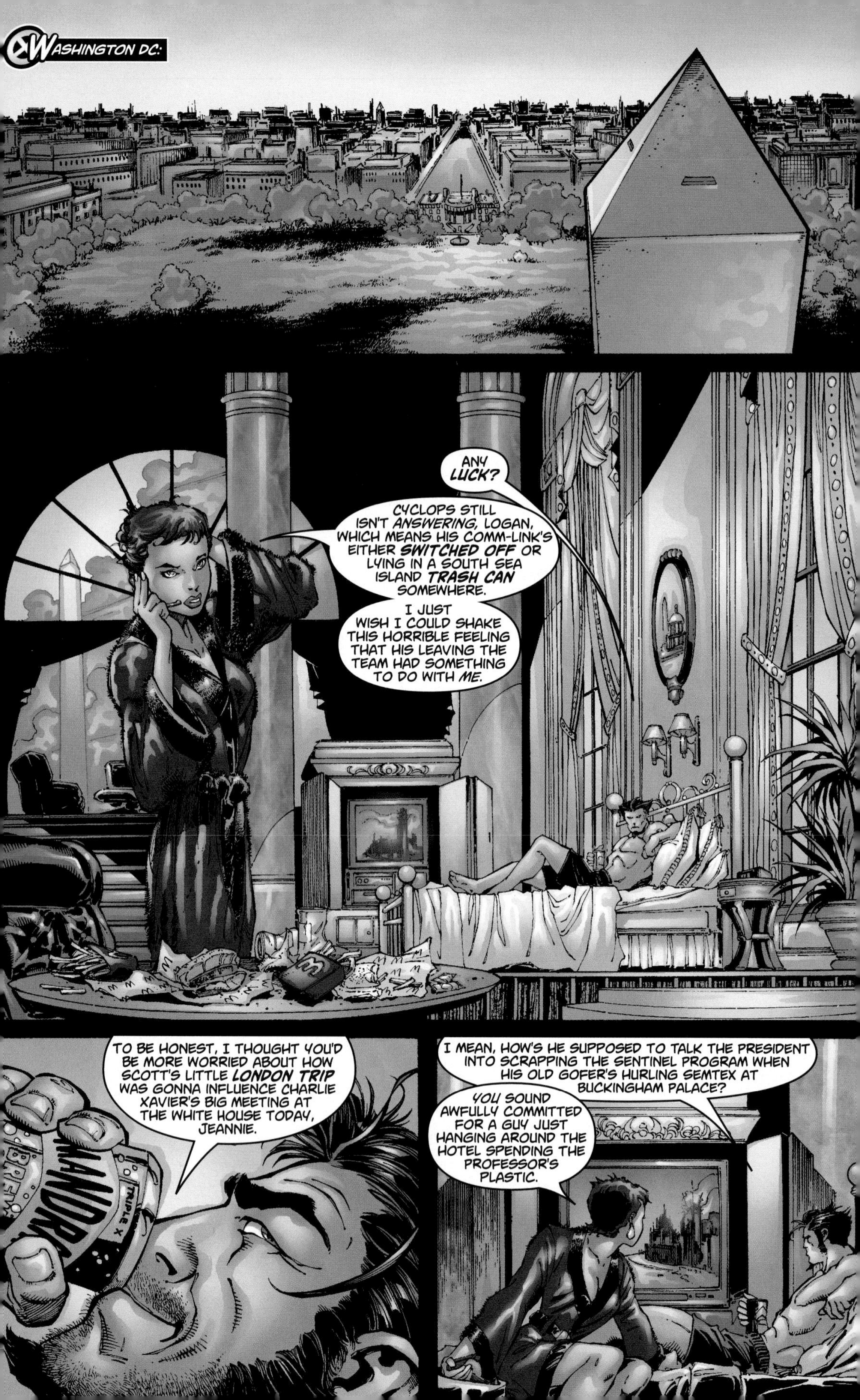
WASHINGTON DC:
ANY LUCK?
CYCLOPS STILL ISN'T ANSWERING, LOGAN, WHICH MEANS HIS COMM-LINK'S EITHER SWITCHED OFF OR LYING IN A SOUTH SEA ISLAND TRASH CAN SOMEWHERE.
I JUST WISH I COULD SHAKE THIS HORRIBLE FEELING THAT HIS LEAVING THE TEAM HAD SOMETHING TO DO WITH ME.
TO BE HONEST, I THOUGHT YOU'D BE MORE WORRIED ABOUT HOW SCOTT'S LITTLE LONDON TRIP WAS GONNA INFLUENCE CHARLIE XAVIER'S BIG MEETING AT THE WHITE HOUSE TODAY, JEANNIE.
I MEAN, HOW'S HE SUPPOSED TO TALK THE PRESIDENT INTO SCRAPPING THE SENTINEL PROGRAM WHEN HIS OLD GOFER'S HURLING SEMTEX AT BUCKINGHAM PALACE?
YOU SOUND AWFULLY COMMITTED FOR A GUY JUST HANGING AROUND THE HOTEL SPENDING THE PROFESSOR'S PLASTIC.
TRIPLE X

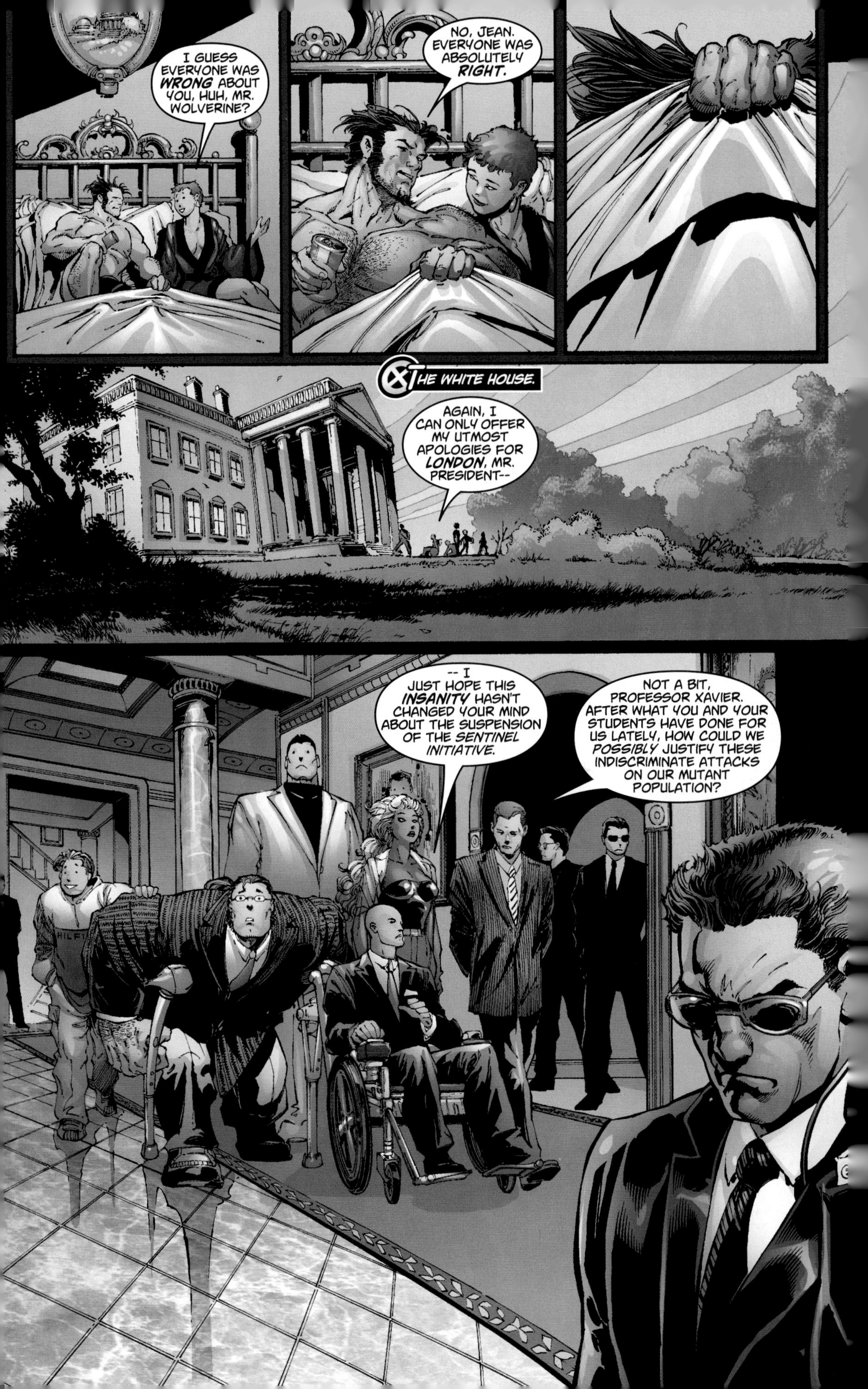
I GUESS EVERYONE WAS WRONG ABOUT YOU, HUH, MR. WOLVERINE?
NO, JEAN. EVERYONE WAS ABSOLUTELY RIGHT.
THE WHITE HOUSE.
AGAIN, I CAN ONLY OFFER MY UTMOST APOLOGIES FOR LONDON, MR. PRESIDENT--
-- I JUST HOPE THIS INSANITY HASN'T CHANGED YOUR MIND ABOUT THE SUSPENSION OF THE SENTINEL INITIATIVE.
NOT A BIT, PROFESSOR XAVIER. AFTER WHAT YOU AND YOUR STUDENTS HAVE DONE FOR US LATELY, HOW COULD WE POSSIBLY JUSTIFY THESE INDISCRIMINATE ATTACKS ON OUR MUTANT POPULATION?
HILFI

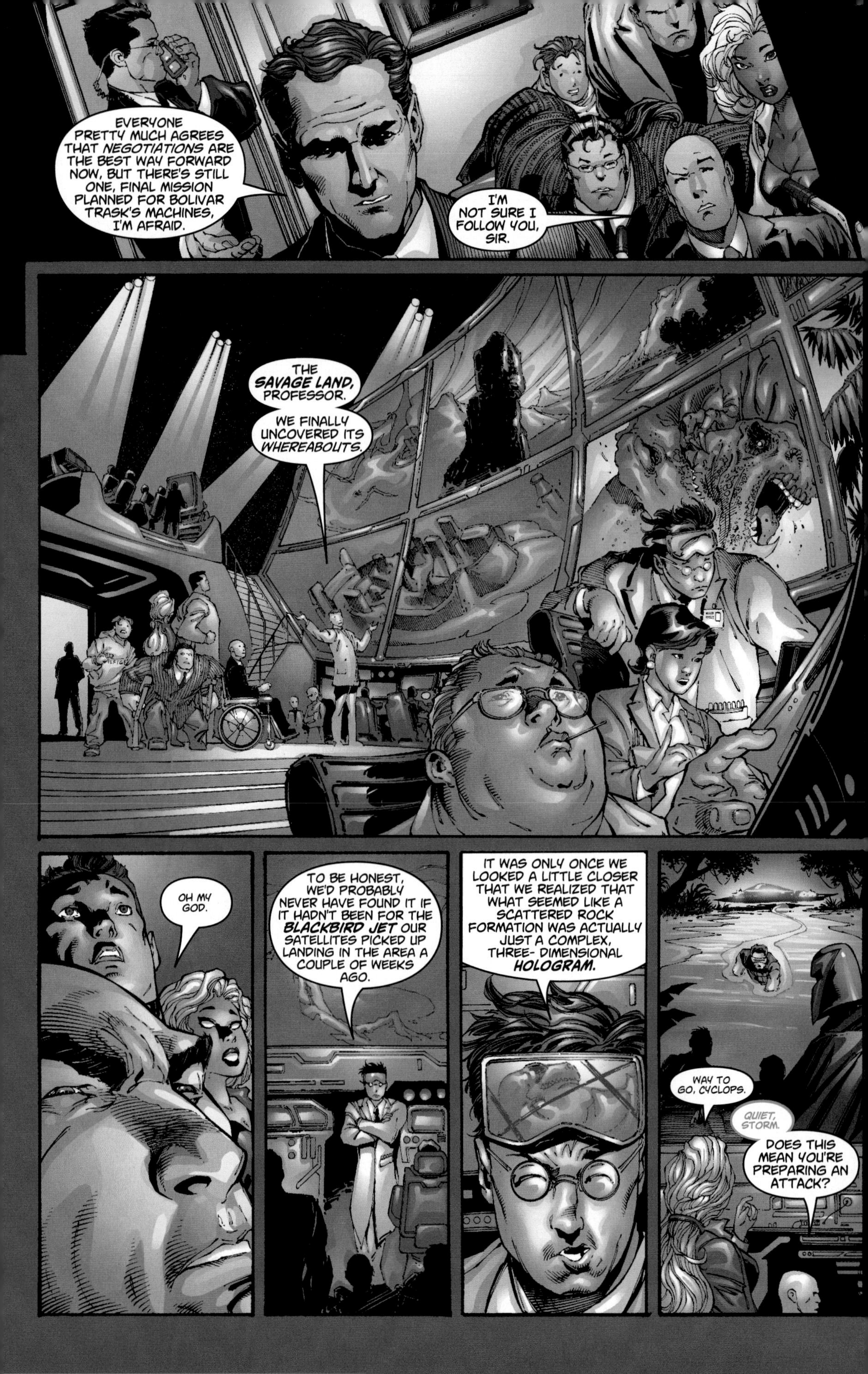
EVERYONE PRETTY MUCH AGREES THAT *NEGOTIATIONS* ARE THE BEST WAY FORWARD NOW, BUT THERE'S STILL ONE, FINAL MISSION PLANNED FOR BOLIVAR TRASK'S MACHINES, I'M AFRAID.
I'M NOT SURE I FOLLOW YOU, SIR.
THE ***SAVAGE LAND,*** PROFESSOR.
WE FINALLY UNCOVERED ITS *WHEREABOUTS.*
OH MY GOD.
TO BE HONEST, WE'D PROBABLY NEVER HAVE FOUND IT IF IT HADN'T BEEN FOR THE ***BLACKBIRD JET*** OUR SATELLITES PICKED UP LANDING IN THE AREA A COUPLE OF WEEKS AGO.
IT WAS ONLY ONCE WE LOOKED A LITTLE CLOSER THAT WE REALIZED THAT WHAT SEEMED LIKE A SCATTERED ROCK FORMATION WAS ACTUALLY JUST A COMPLEX, THREE- DIMENSIONAL **HOLOGRAM.**
WAY TO GO, CYCLOPS.
QUIET, STORM.
DOES THIS MEAN YOU'RE PREPARING AN ATTACK?

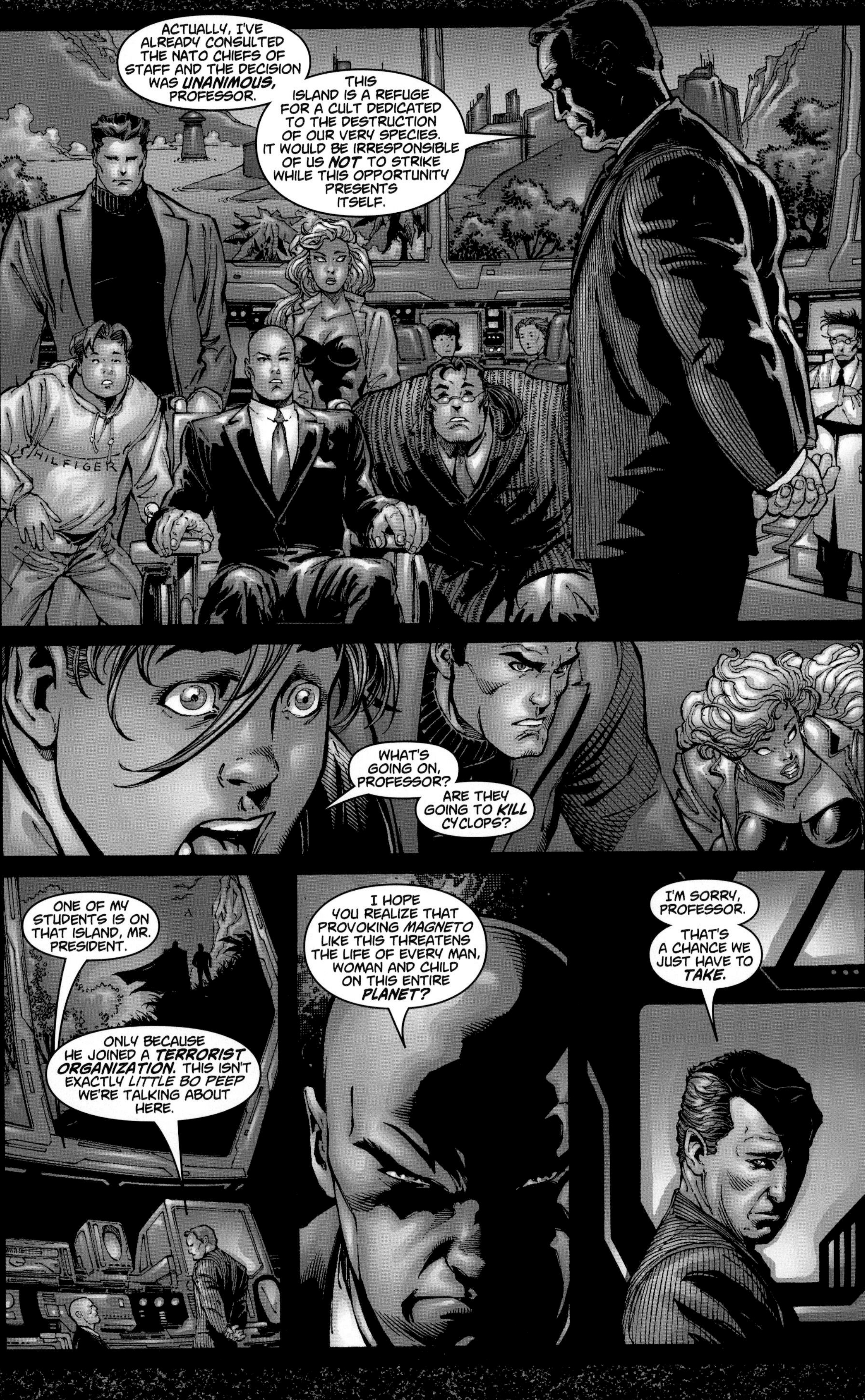
ACTUALLY, I'VE ALREADY CONSULTED THE NATO CHIEFS OF STAFF AND THE DECISION WAS UNANIMOUS, PROFESSOR.
THIS ISLAND IS A REFUGE FOR A CULT DEDICATED TO THE DESTRUCTION OF OUR VERY SPECIES. IT WOULD BE IRRESPONSIBLE OF US NOT TO STRIKE WHILE THIS OPPORTUNITY PRESENTS ITSELF.
WHAT'S GOING ON, PROFESSOR?
ARE THEY GOING TO KILL CYCLOPS?
ONE OF MY STUDENTS IS ON THAT ISLAND, MR. PRESIDENT.
ONLY BECAUSE HE JOINED A TERRORIST ORGANIZATION. THIS ISN'T EXACTLY LITTLE BO PEEP WE'RE TALKING ABOUT HERE.
I HOPE YOU REALIZE THAT PROVOKING MAGNETO LIKE THIS THREATENS THE LIFE OF EVERY MAN, WOMAN AND CHILD ON THIS ENTIRE PLANET?
I'M SORRY, PROFESSOR.
THAT'S A CHANCE WE JUST HAVE TO TAKE.
HILFIGER

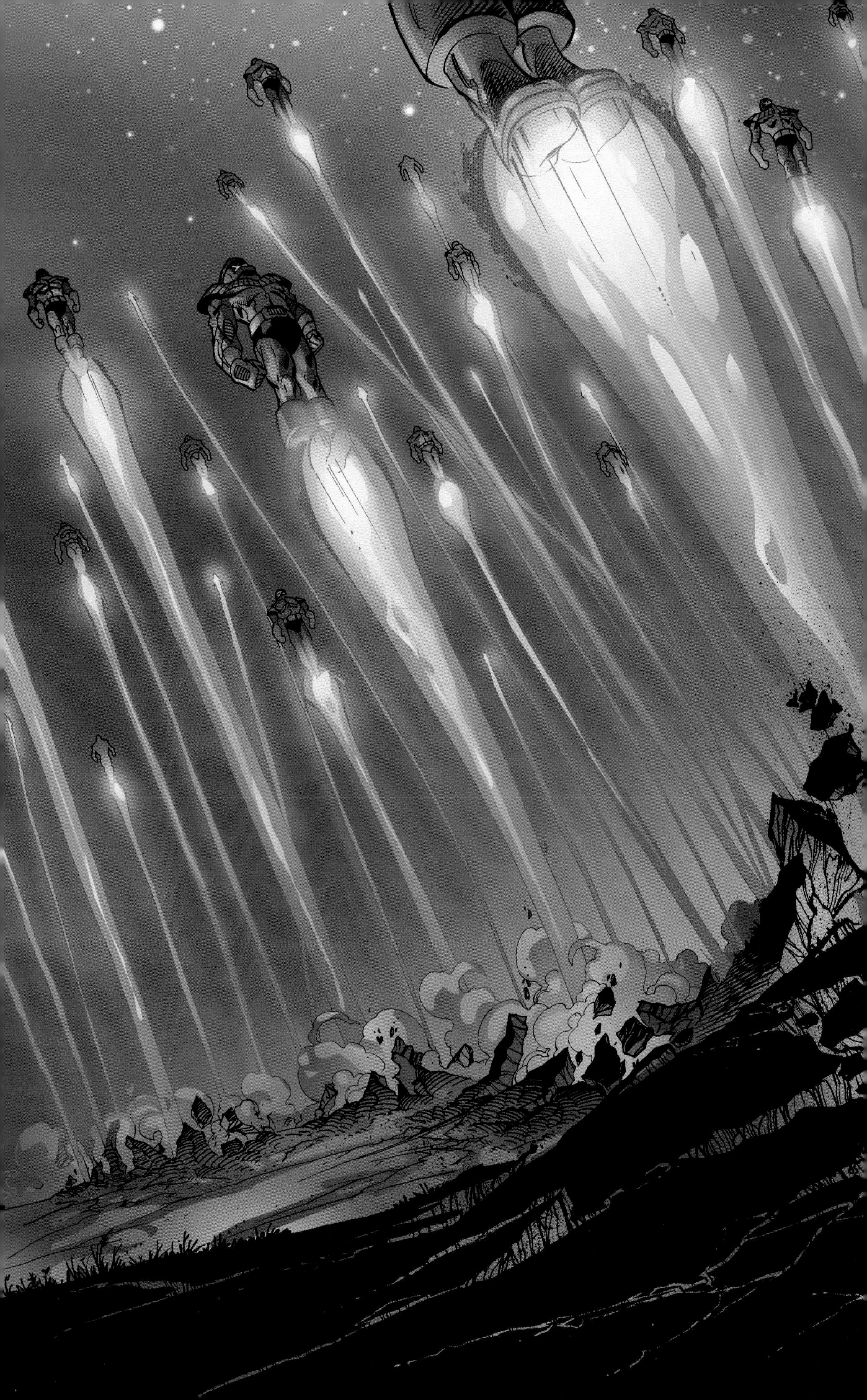

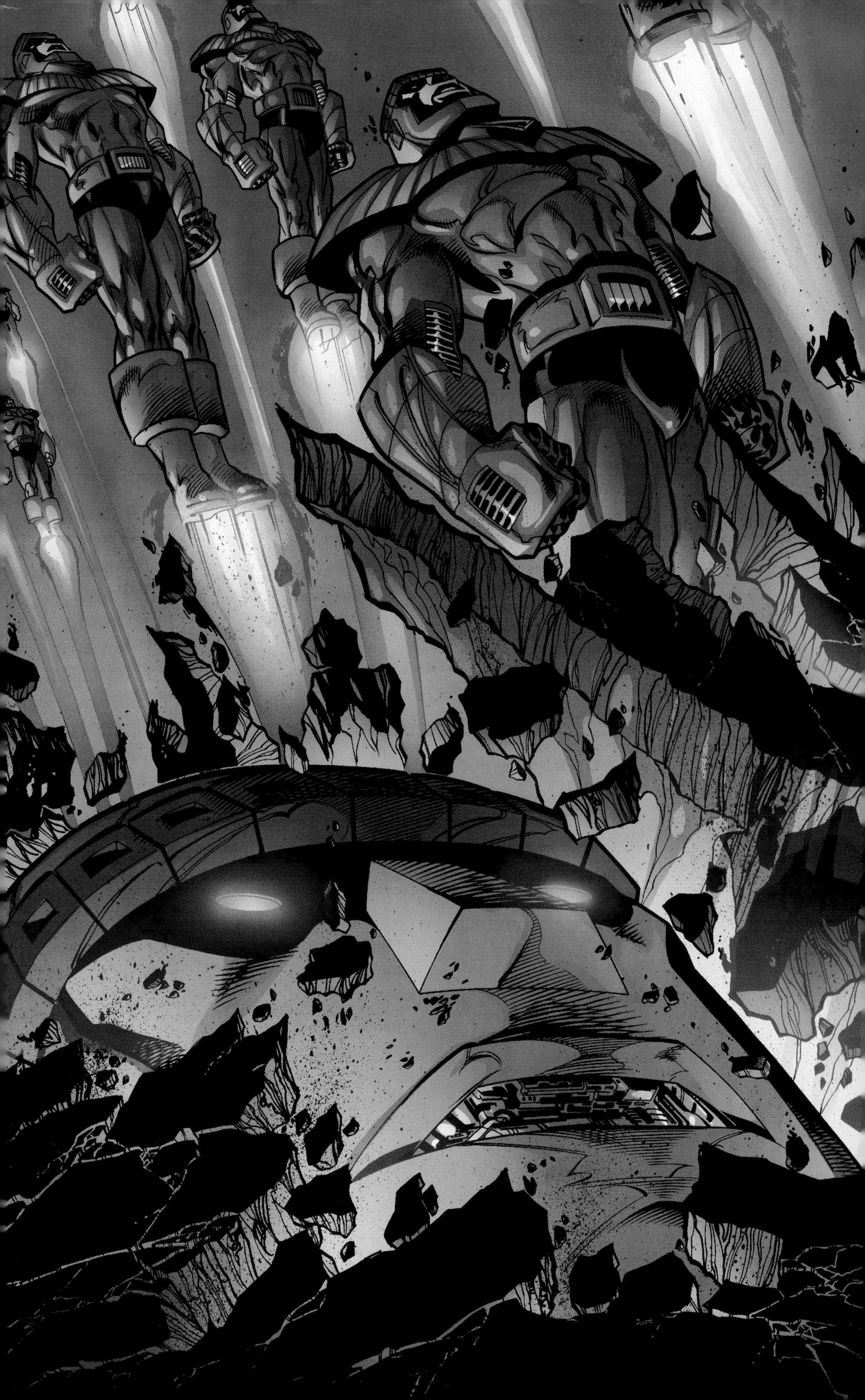

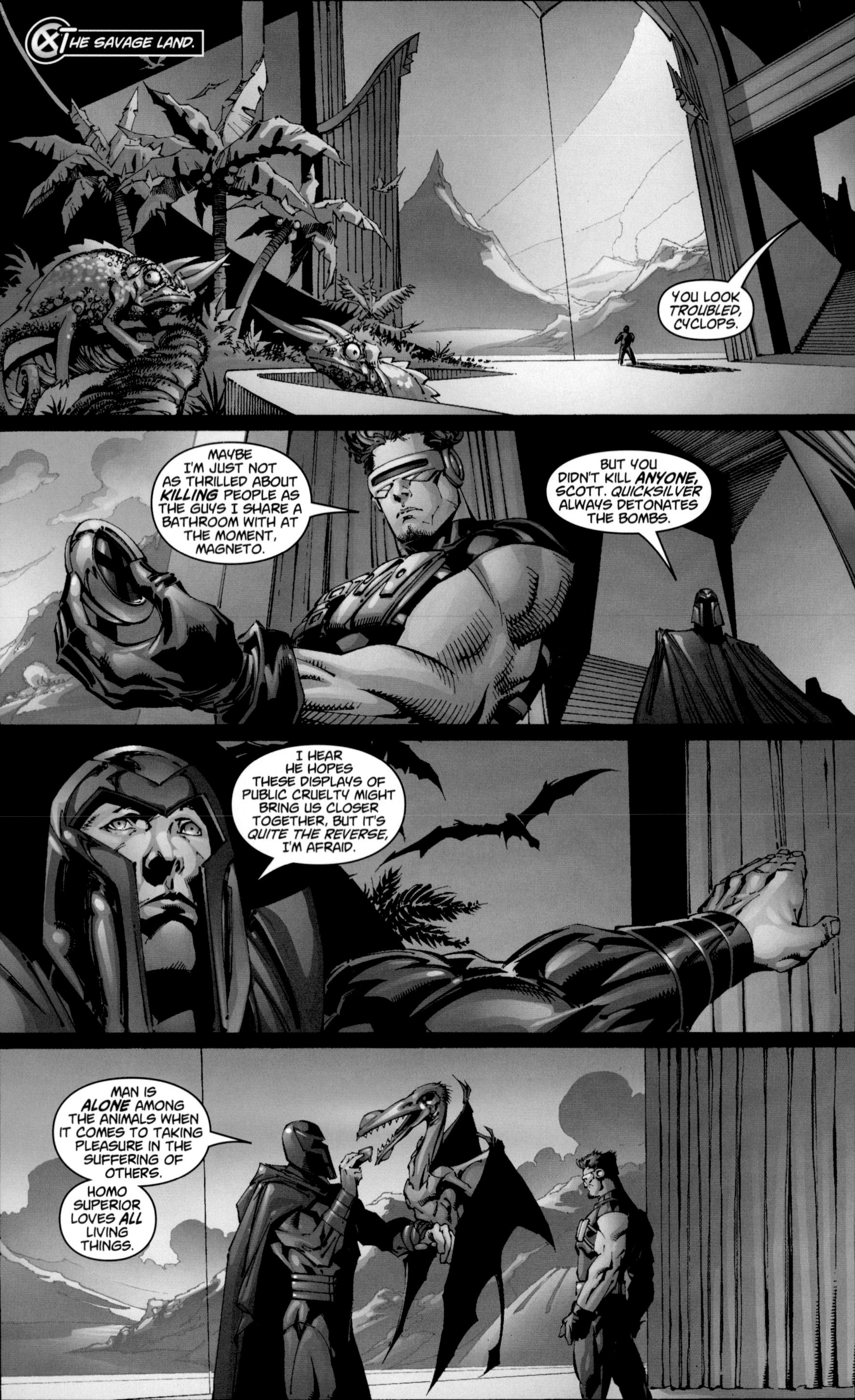
THE SAVAGE LAND.
YOU LOOK TROUBLED, CYCLOPS.
MAYBE I'M JUST NOT AS THRILLED ABOUT KILLING PEOPLE AS THE GUYS I SHARE A BATHROOM WITH AT THE MOMENT, MAGNETO.
BUT YOU DIDN'T KILL ANYONE, SCOTT. QUICKSILVER ALWAYS DETONATES THE BOMBS.
I HEAR HE HOPES THESE DISPLAYS OF PUBLIC CRUELTY MIGHT BRING US CLOSER TOGETHER, BUT IT'S QUITE THE REVERSE, I'M AFRAID.
MAN IS ALONE AMONG THE ANIMALS WHEN IT COMES TO TAKING PLEASURE IN THE SUFFERING OF OTHERS.
HOMO SUPERIOR LOVES ALL LIVING THINGS.

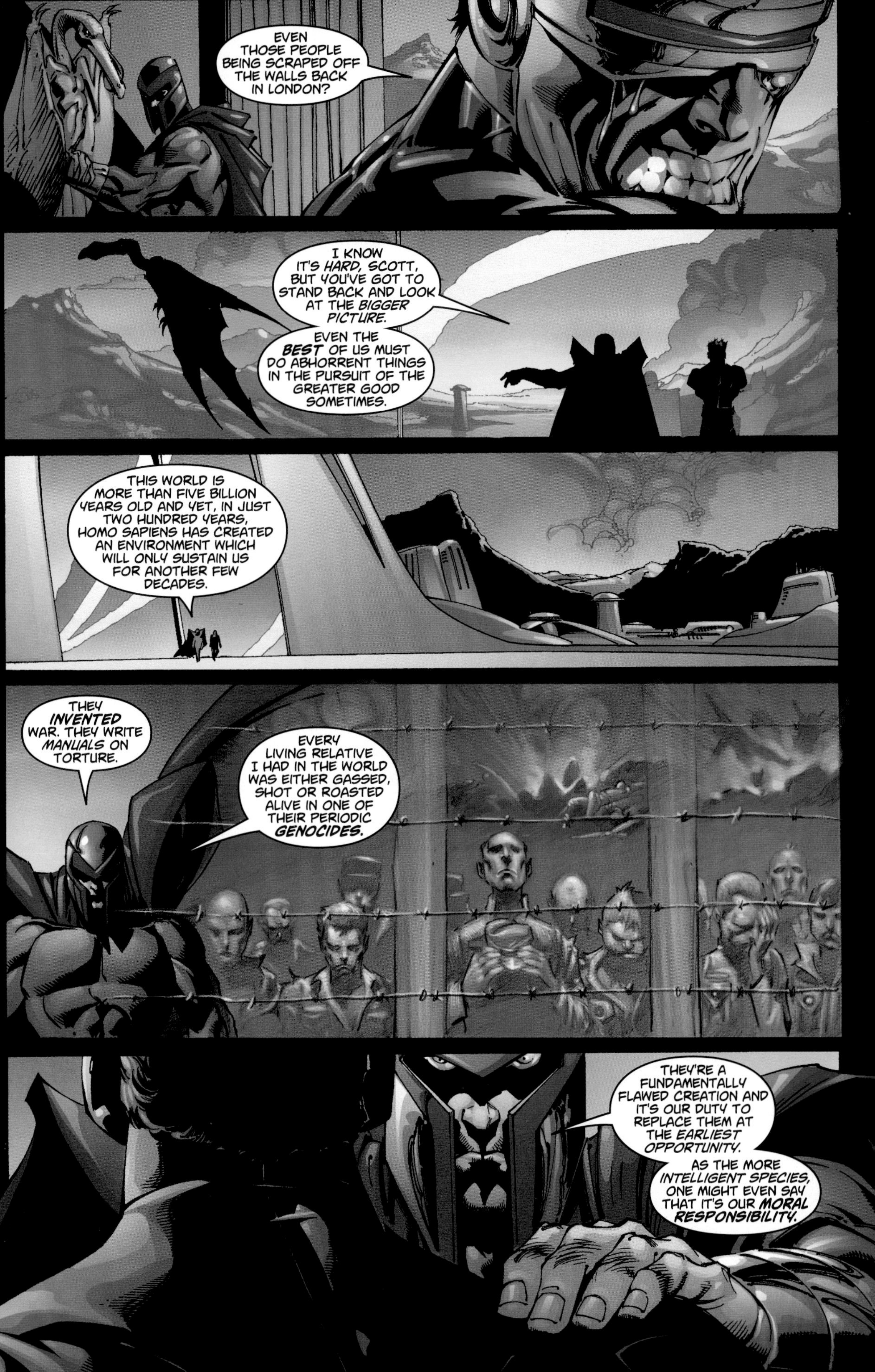
EVEN THOSE PEOPLE BEING SCRAPED OFF THE WALLS BACK IN LONDON?
I KNOW IT'S *HARD*, SCOTT, BUT YOU'VE GOT TO STAND BACK AND LOOK AT THE *BIGGER PICTURE*.
EVEN THE **BEST** OF US MUST DO ABHORRENT THINGS IN THE PURSUIT OF THE GREATER GOOD SOMETIMES.
THIS WORLD IS MORE THAN FIVE BILLION YEARS OLD AND YET, IN JUST TWO HUNDRED YEARS, HOMO SAPIENS HAS CREATED AN ENVIRONMENT WHICH WILL ONLY SUSTAIN US FOR ANOTHER FEW DECADES.
THEY ***INVENTED*** WAR. THEY WRITE *MANUALS* ON TORTURE.
EVERY LIVING RELATIVE I HAD IN THE WORLD WAS EITHER GASSED, SHOT OR ROASTED ALIVE IN ONE OF THEIR PERIODIC ***GENOCIDES***.
THEY'RE A FUNDAMENTALLY FLAWED CREATION AND IT'S OUR DUTY TO REPLACE THEM AT THE *EARLIEST OPPORTUNITY*.
AS THE MORE *INTELLIGENT SPECIES*, ONE MIGHT EVEN SAY THAT IT'S OUR ***MORAL RESPONSIBILITY***.

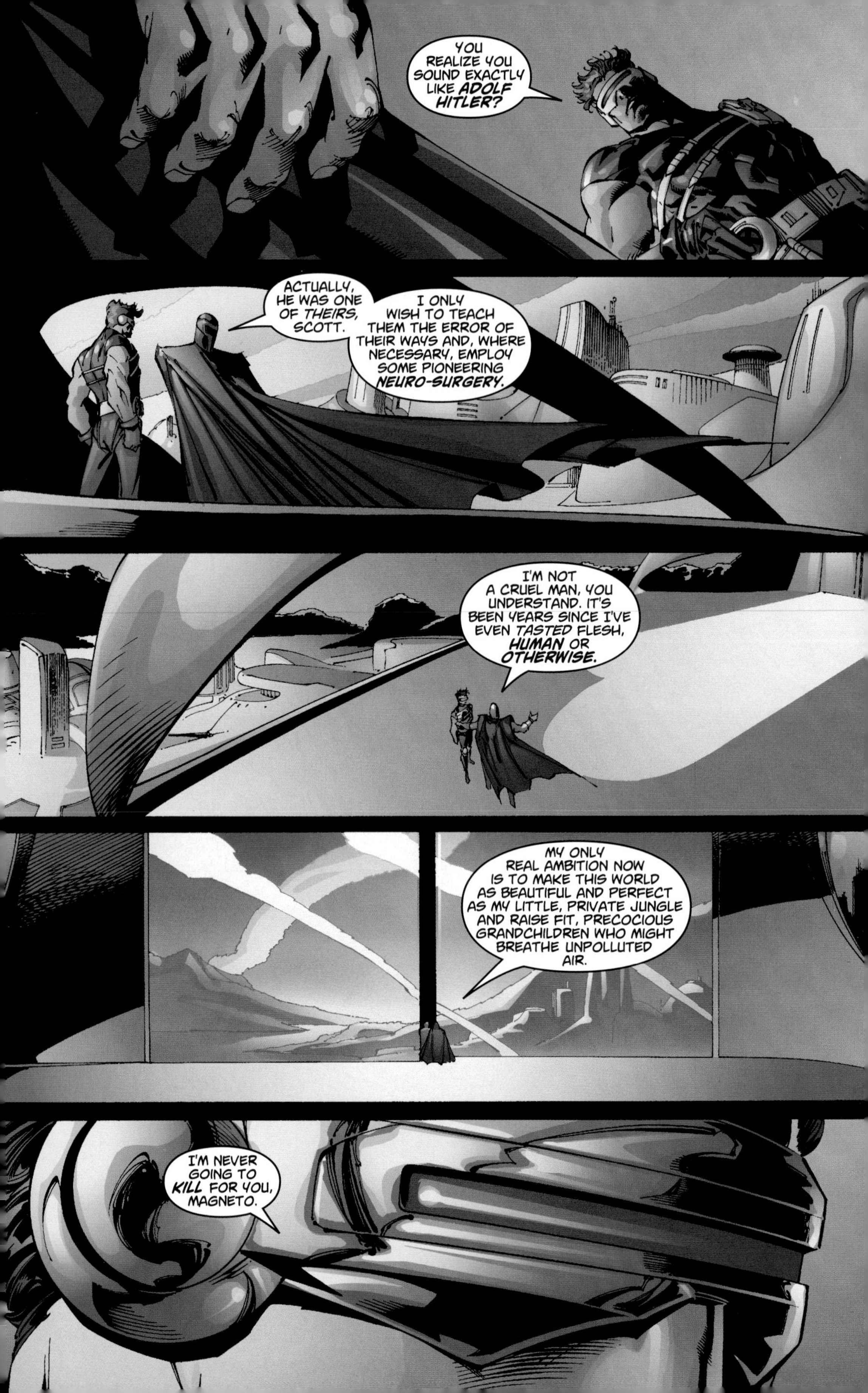
YOU REALIZE YOU SOUND EXACTLY LIKE ADOLF HITLER?
ACTUALLY, HE WAS ONE OF THEIRS, SCOTT.
I ONLY WISH TO TEACH THEM THE ERROR OF THEIR WAYS AND, WHERE NECESSARY, EMPLOY SOME PIONEERING NEURO-SURGERY.
I'M NOT A CRUEL MAN, YOU UNDERSTAND. IT'S BEEN YEARS SINCE I'VE EVEN TASTED FLESH, HUMAN OR OTHERWISE.
MY ONLY REAL AMBITION NOW IS TO MAKE THIS WORLD AS BEAUTIFUL AND PERFECT AS MY LITTLE, PRIVATE JUNGLE AND RAISE FIT, PRECOCIOUS GRANDCHILDREN WHO MIGHT BREATHE THE UNPOLLUTED AIR.
I'M NEVER GOING TO KILL FOR YOU, MAGNETO.

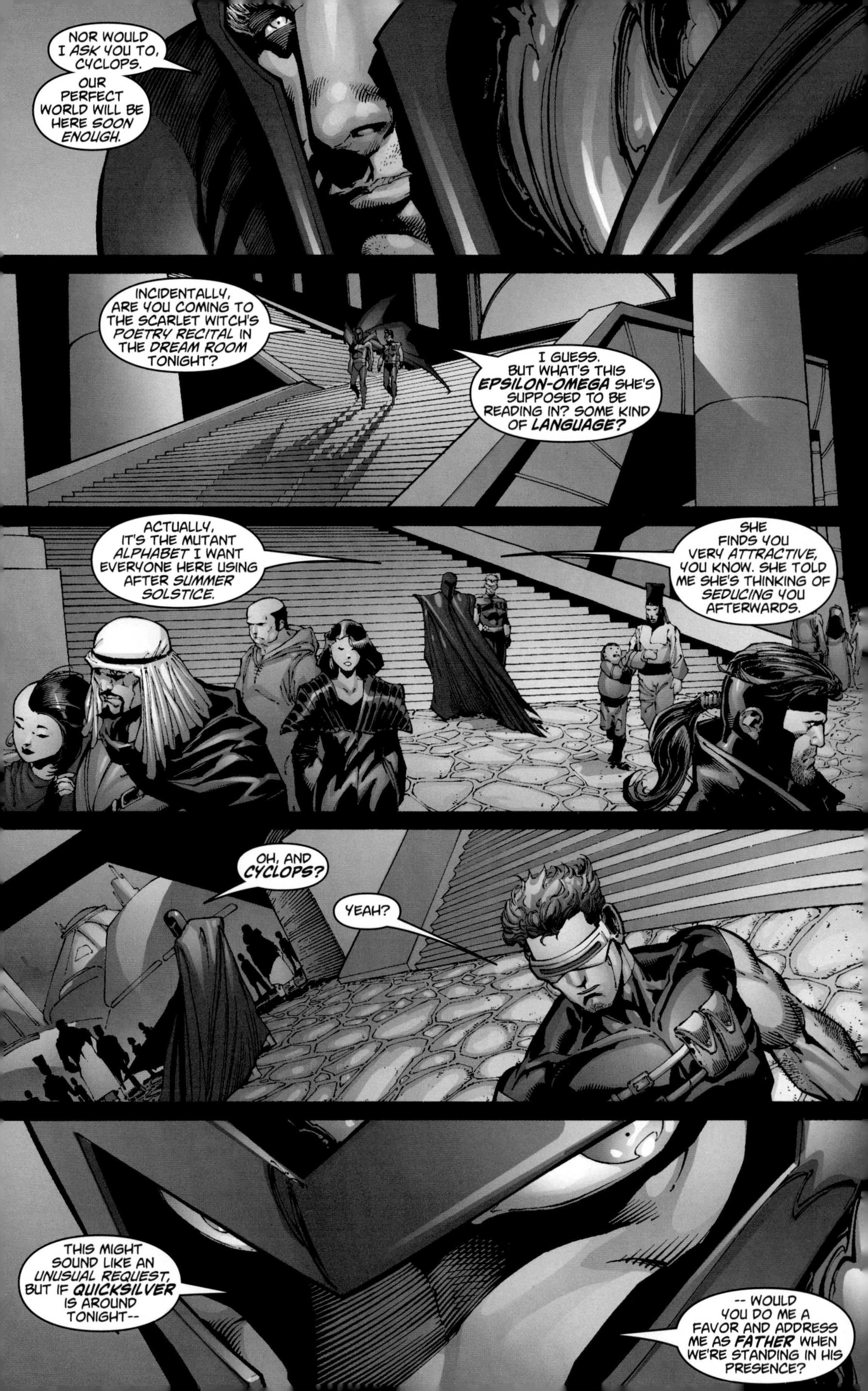
NOR WOULD I ASK YOU TO, CYCLOPS.
OUR PERFECT WORLD WILL BE HERE SOON ENOUGH.
INCIDENTALLY, ARE YOU COMING TO THE SCARLET WITCH'S POETRY RECITAL IN THE DREAM ROOM TONIGHT?
I GUESS. BUT WHAT'S THIS EPSILON-OMEGA SHE'S SUPPOSED TO BE READING IN? SOME KIND OF LANGUAGE?
ACTUALLY, IT'S THE MUTANT ALPHABET I WANT EVERYONE HERE USING AFTER SUMMER SOLSTICE.
SHE FINDS YOU VERY ATTRACTIVE, YOU KNOW. SHE TOLD ME SHE'S THINKING OF SEDUCING YOU AFTERWARDS.
OH, AND CYCLOPS?
YEAH?
THIS MIGHT SOUND LIKE AN UNUSUAL REQUEST, BUT IF QUICKSILVER IS AROUND TONIGHT--
-- WOULD YOU DO ME A FAVOR AND ADDRESS ME AS FATHER WHEN WE'RE STANDING IN HIS PRESENCE?

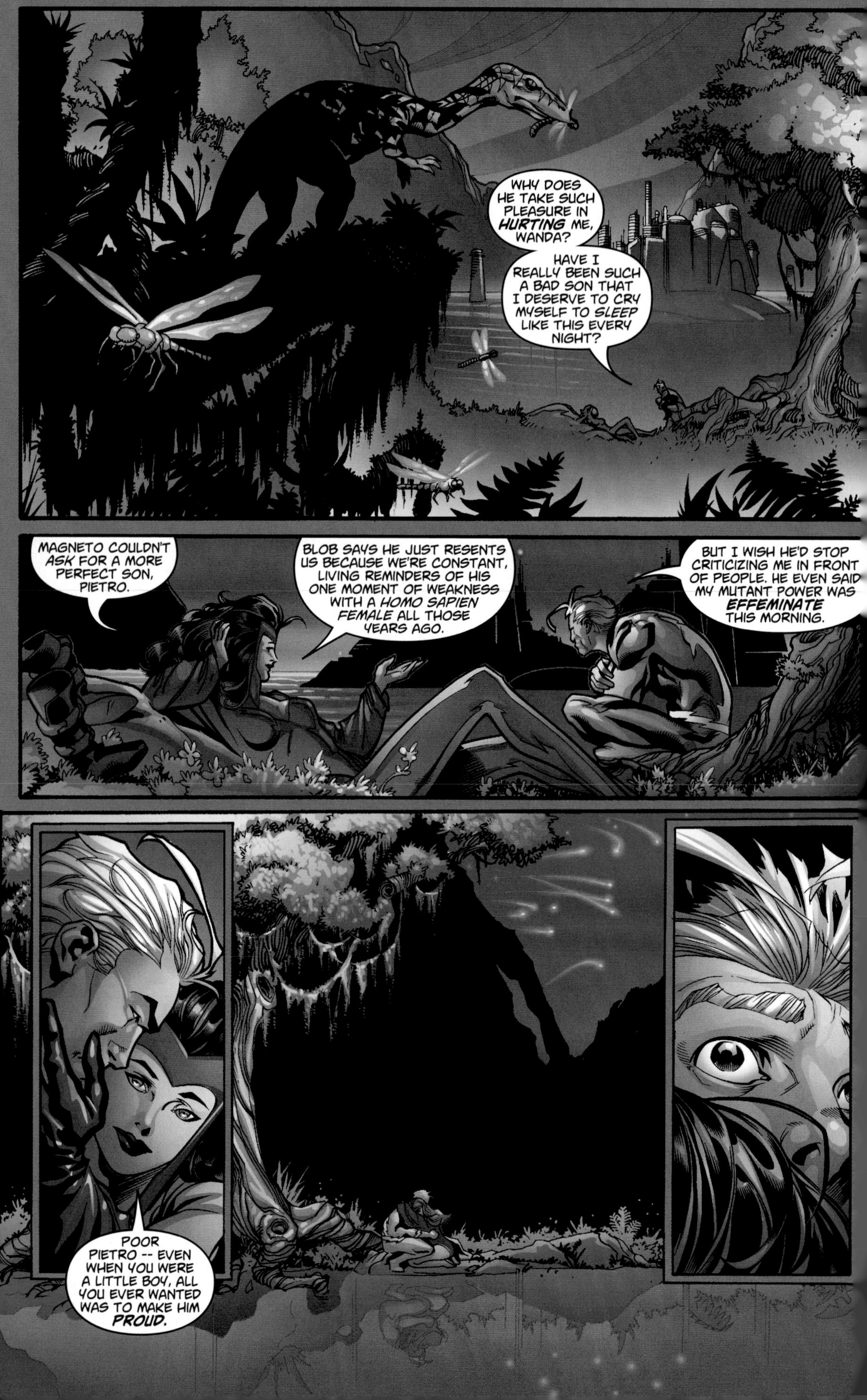
WHY DOES HE TAKE SUCH PLEASURE IN HURTING ME, WANDA?
HAVE I REALLY BEEN SUCH A BAD SON THAT I DESERVE TO CRY MYSELF TO SLEEP LIKE THIS EVERY NIGHT?
MAGNETO COULDN'T ASK FOR A MORE PERFECT SON, PIETRO.
BLOB SAYS HE JUST RESENTS US BECAUSE WE'RE CONSTANT, LIVING REMINDERS OF HIS ONE MOMENT OF WEAKNESS WITH A HOMO SAPIEN FEMALE ALL THOSE YEARS AGO.
BUT I WISH HE'D STOP CRITICIZING ME IN FRONT OF PEOPLE. HE EVEN SAID MY MUTANT POWER WAS EFFEMINATE THIS MORNING.
POOR PIETRO -- EVEN WHEN YOU WERE A LITTLE BOY, ALL YOU EVER WANTED WAS TO MAKE HIM PROUD.

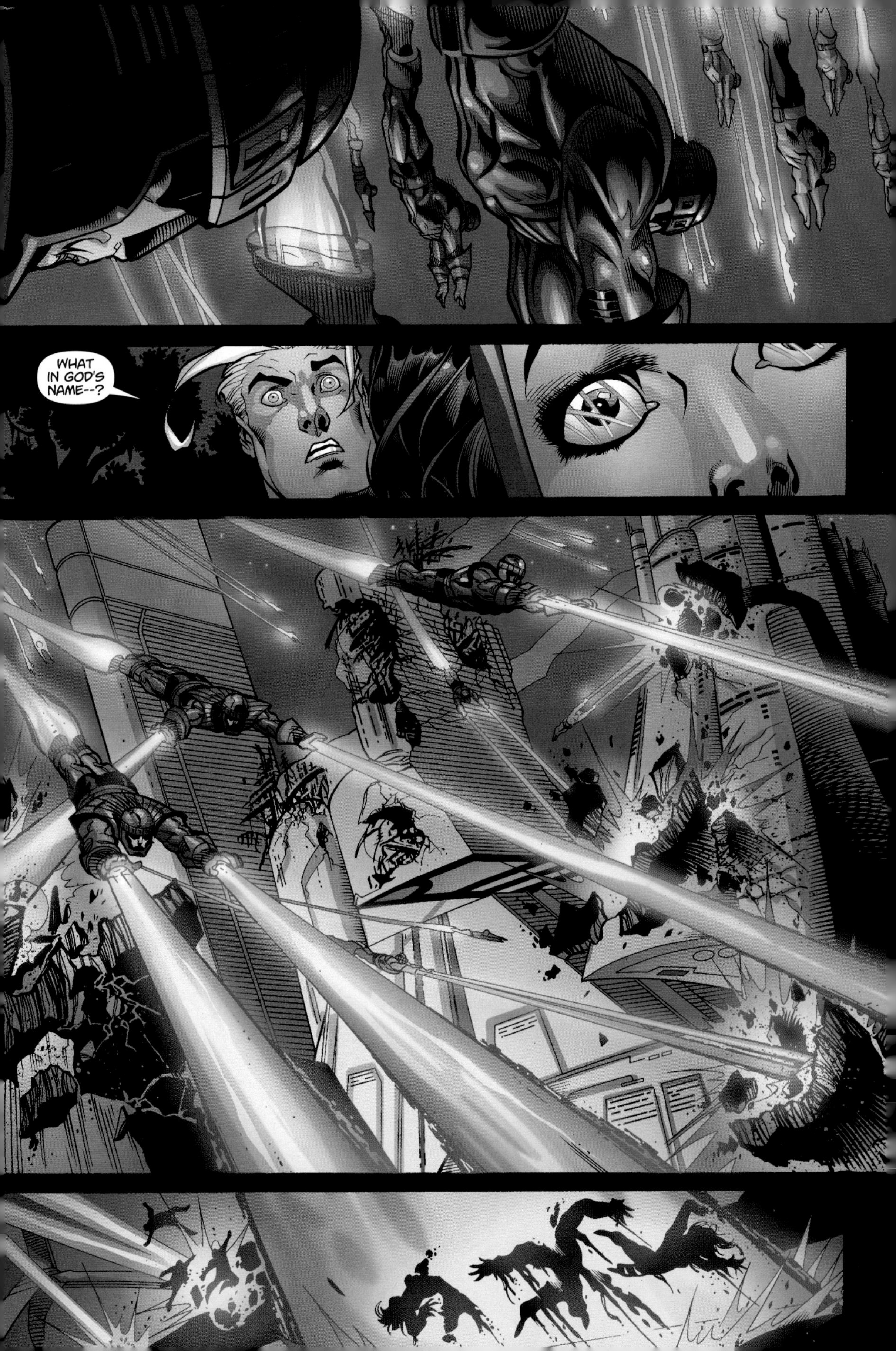
WHAT IN GOD'S NAME--?

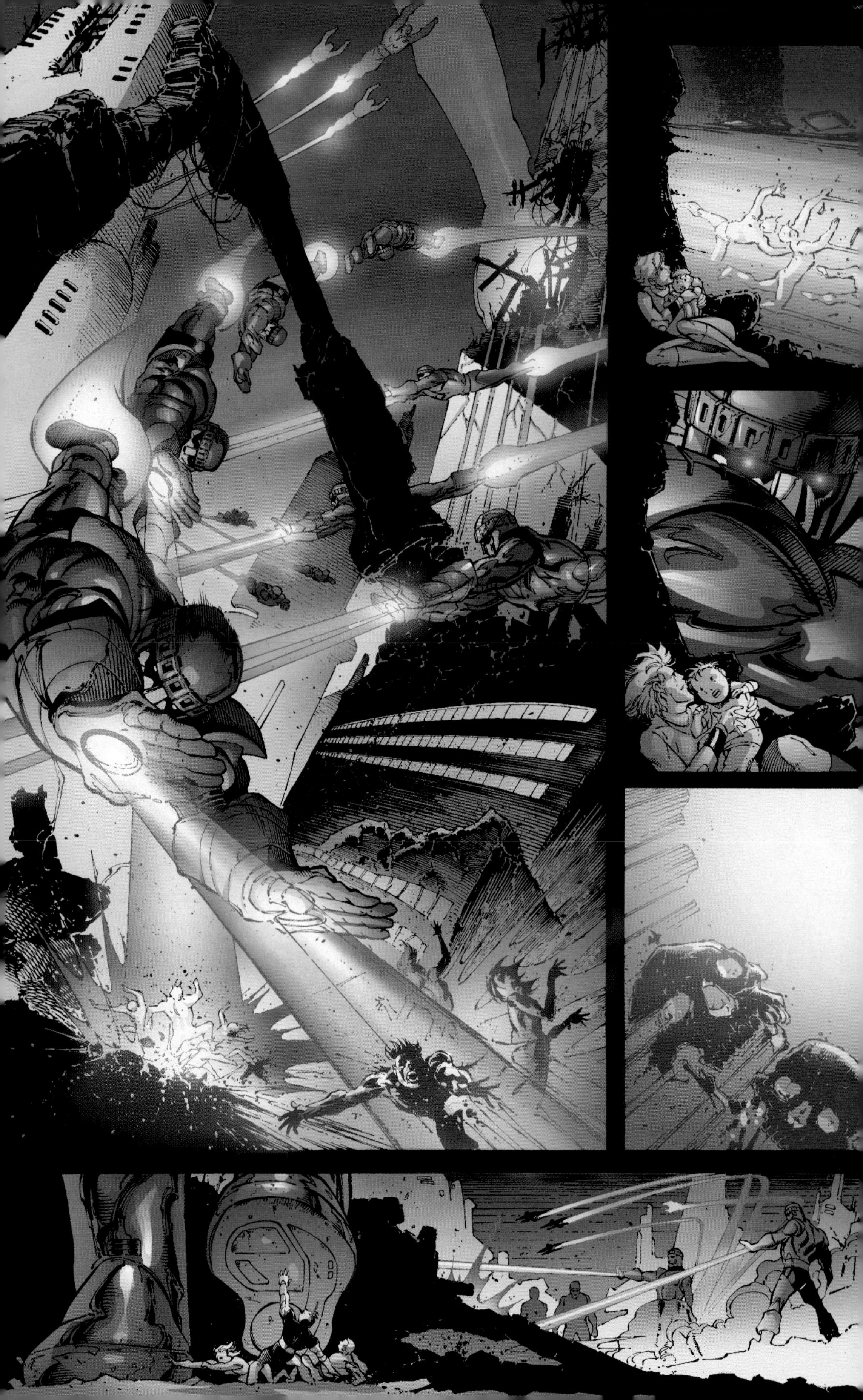

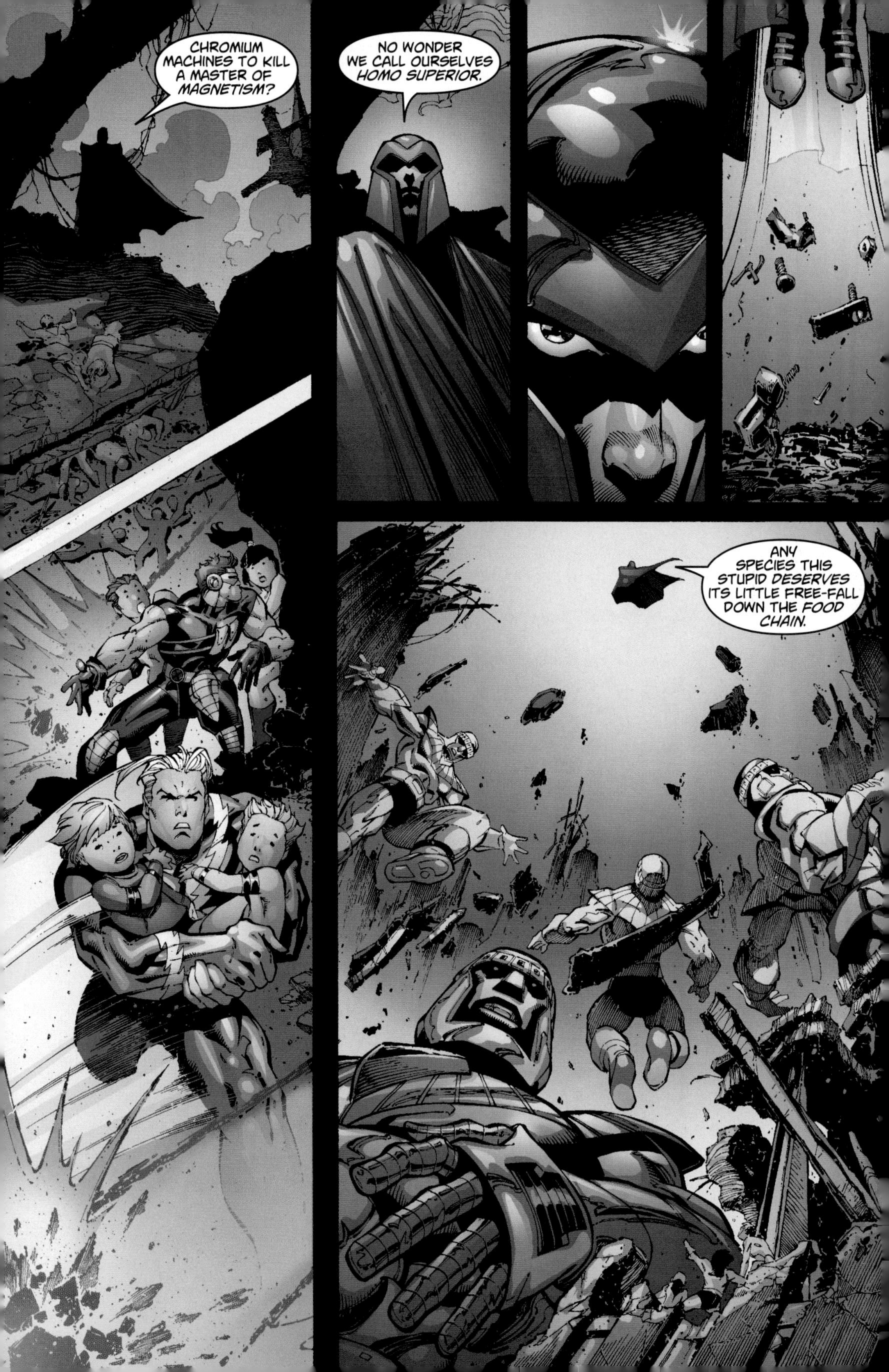
CHROMIUM MACHINES TO KILL A MASTER OF MAGNETISM?
NO WONDER WE CALL OURSELVES HOMO SUPERIOR.
ANY SPECIES THIS STUPID DESERVES ITS LITTLE FREE-FALL DOWN THE FOOD CHAIN.

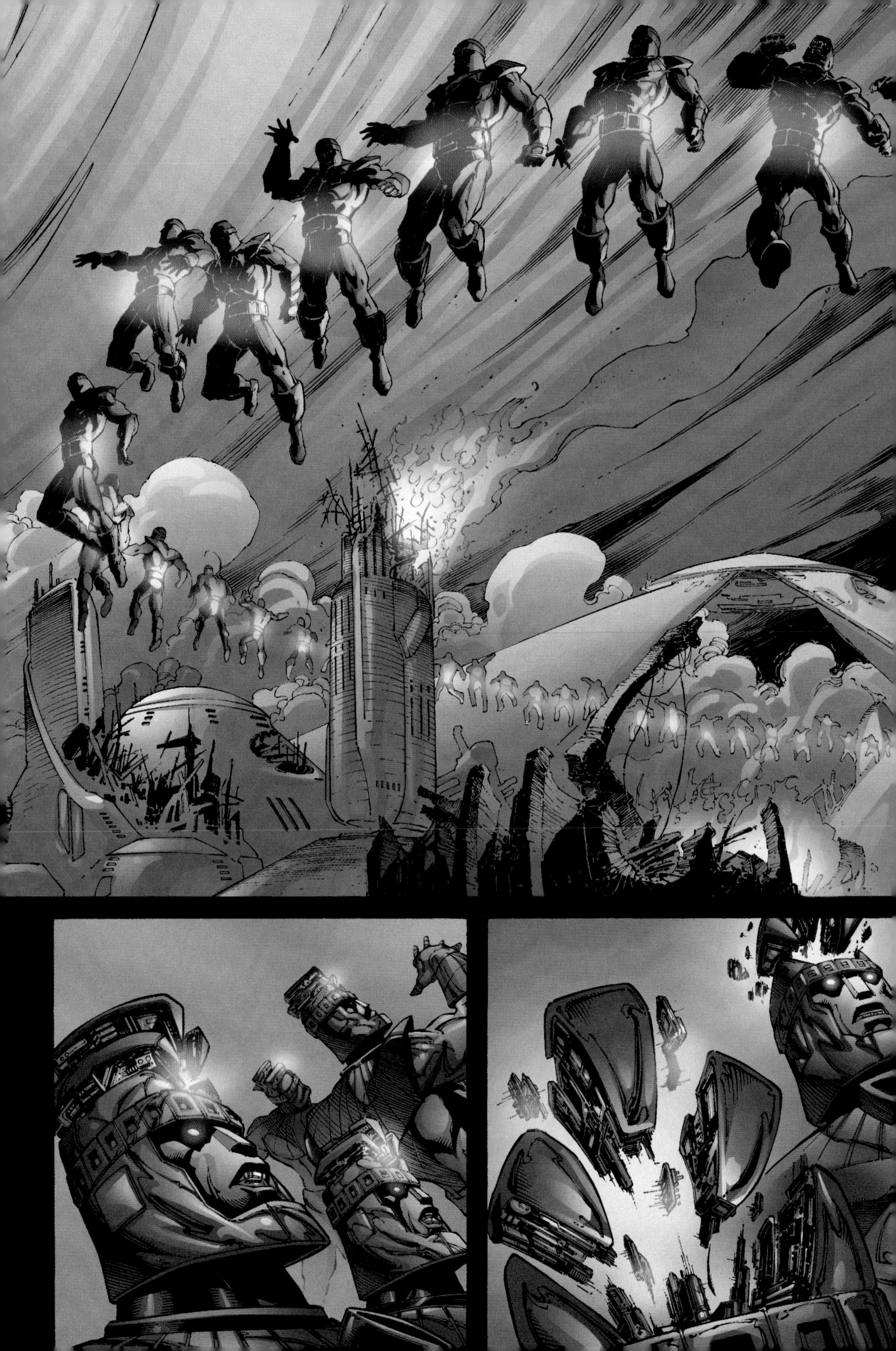

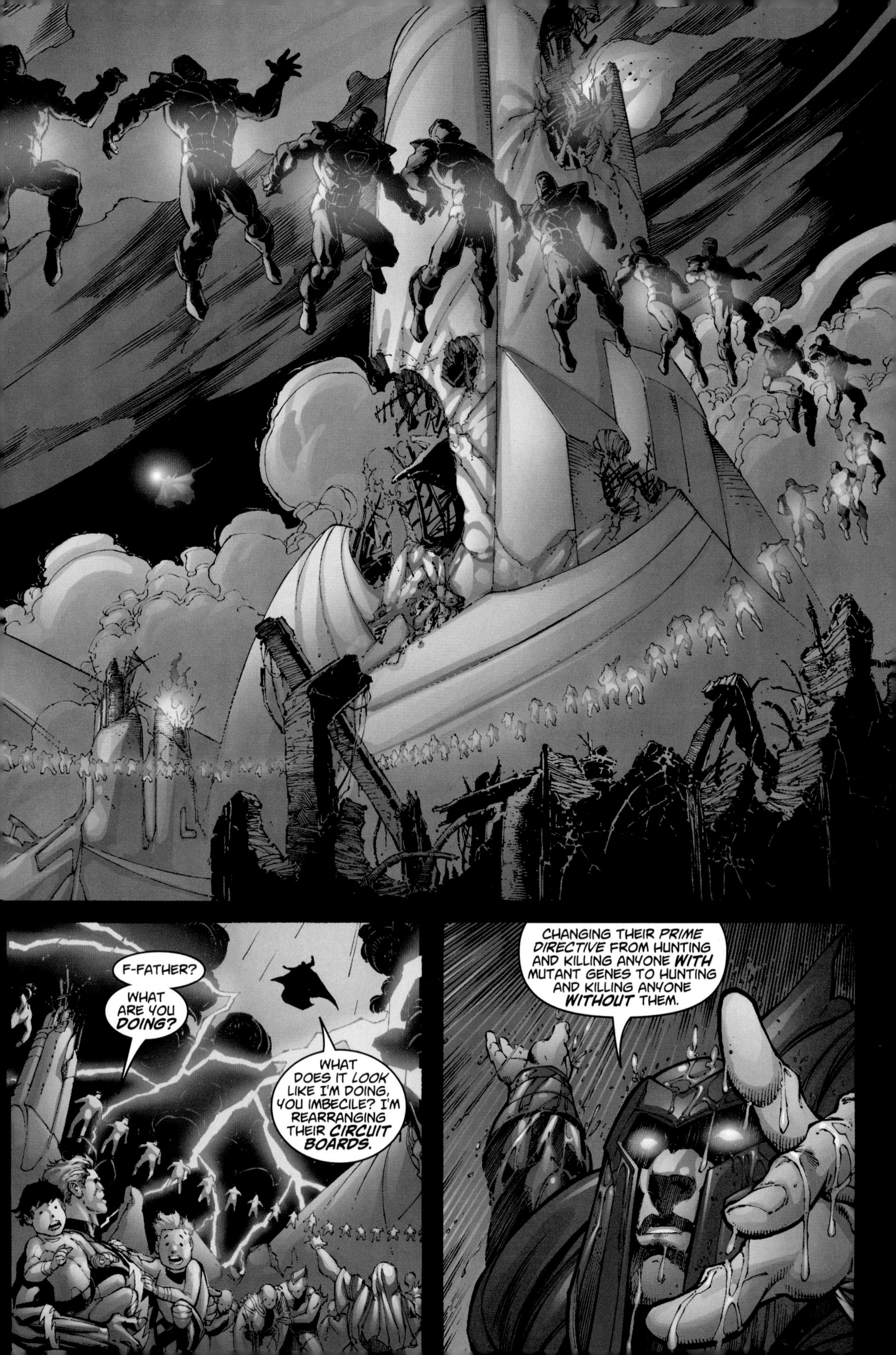

F-FATHER?
WHAT ARE YOU DOING?
WHAT DOES IT LOOK LIKE I'M DOING, YOU IMBECILE? I'M REARRANGING THEIR CIRCUIT BOARDS.
CHANGING THEIR PRIME DIRECTIVE FROM HUNTING AND KILLING ANYONE WITH MUTANT GENES TO HUNTING AND KILLING ANYONE WITHOUT THEM.

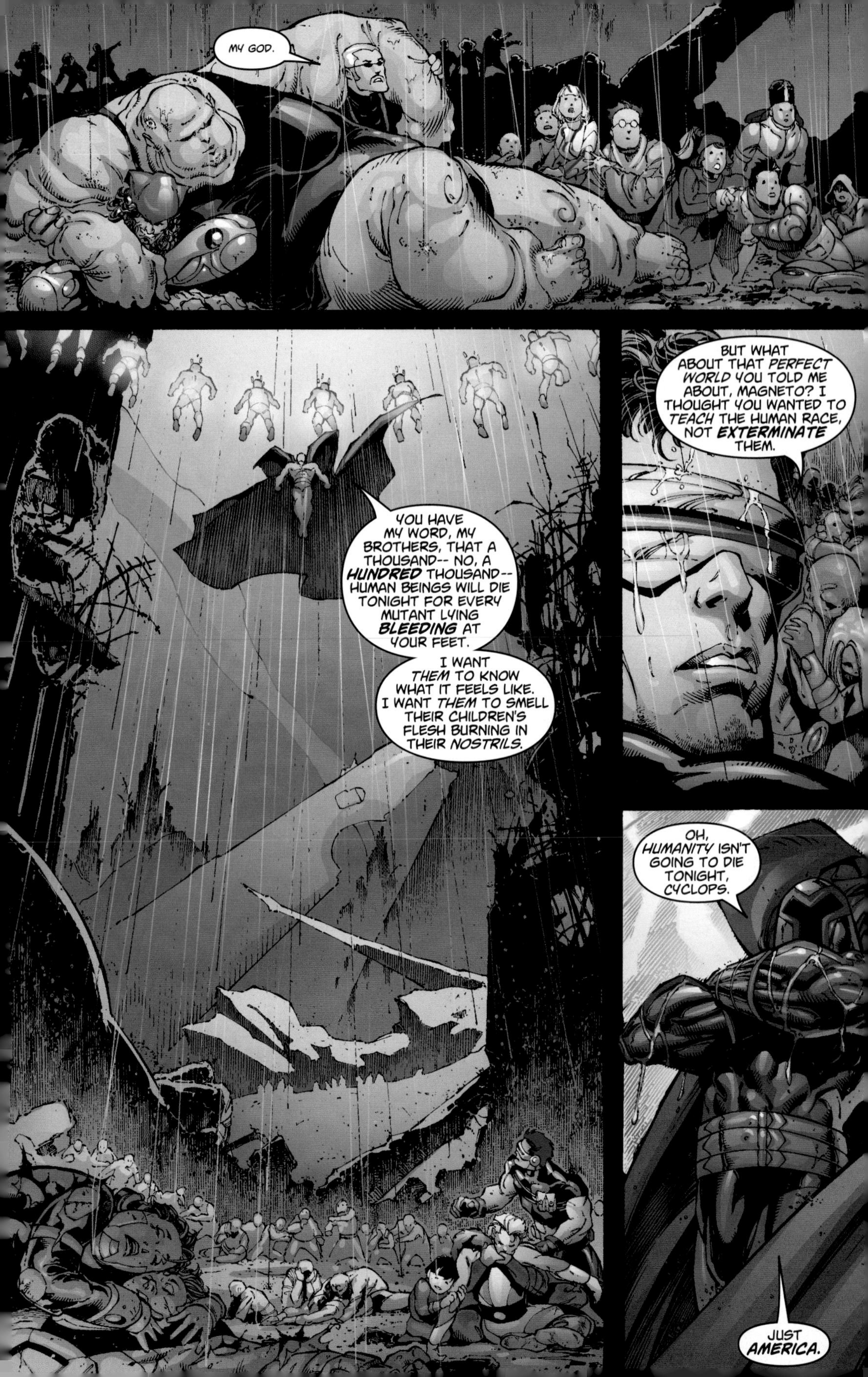
MY GOD.
BUT WHAT ABOUT THAT PERFECT WORLD YOU TOLD ME ABOUT, MAGNETO? I THOUGHT YOU WANTED TO TEACH THE HUMAN RACE, NOT EXTERMINATE THEM.
YOU HAVE MY WORD, MY BROTHERS, THAT A THOUSAND-- NO, A HUNDRED THOUSAND-- HUMAN BEINGS WILL DIE TONIGHT FOR EVERY MUTANT LYING BLEEDING AT YOUR FEET.
I WANT THEM TO KNOW WHAT IT FEELS LIKE. I WANT THEM TO SMELL THEIR CHILDREN'S FLESH BURNING IN THEIR NOSTRILS.
OH, HUMANITY ISN'T GOING TO DIE TONIGHT, CYCLOPS.
JUST AMERICA.

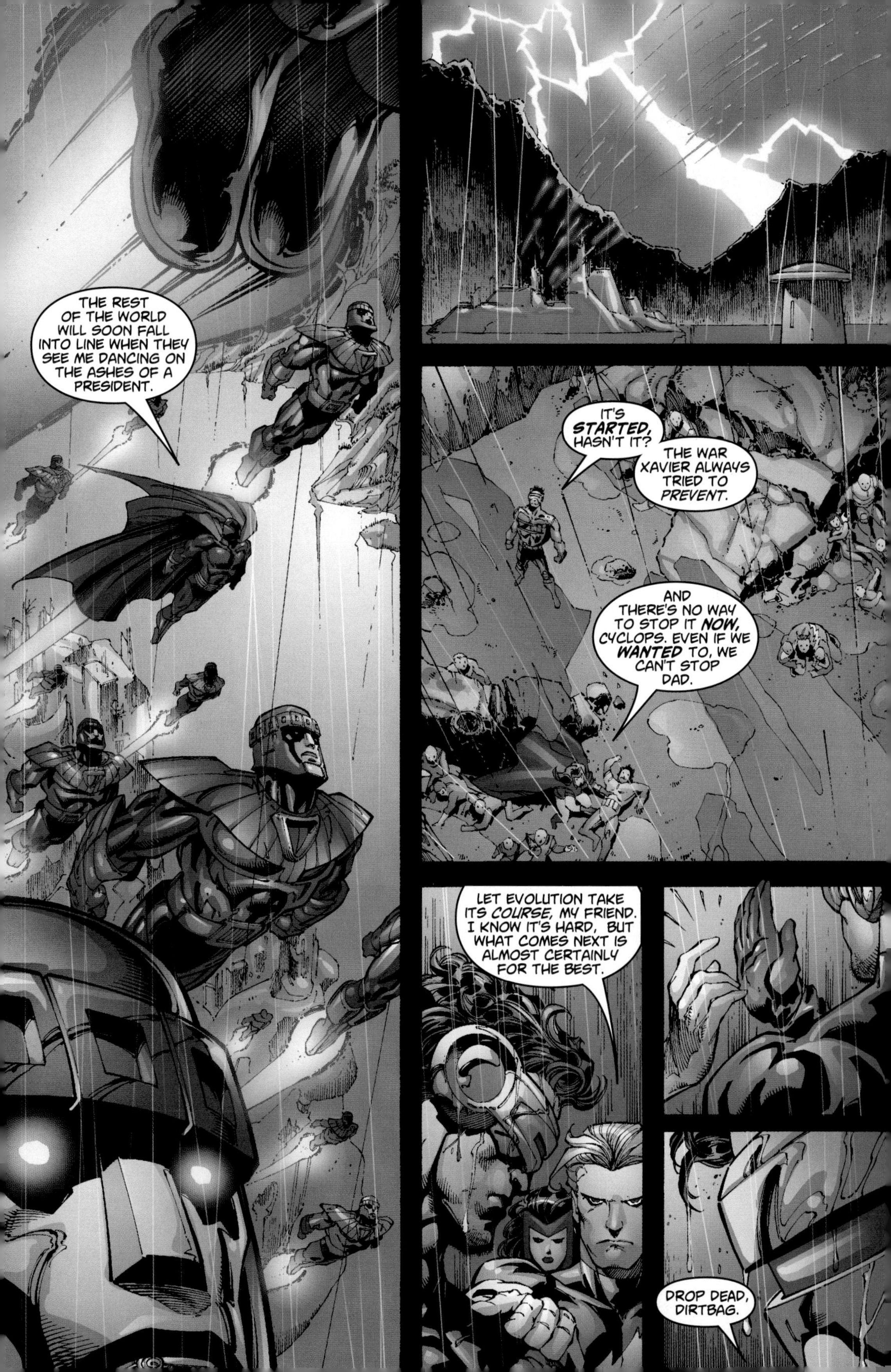
THE REST OF THE WORLD WILL SOON FALL INTO LINE WHEN THEY SEE ME DANCING ON THE ASHES OF A PRESIDENT.
IT'S STARTED, HASN'T IT?
THE WAR XAVIER ALWAYS TRIED TO PREVENT.
AND THERE'S NO WAY TO STOP IT NOW, CYCLOPS. EVEN IF WE WANTED TO, WE CAN'T STOP DAD.
LET EVOLUTION TAKE ITS COURSE, MY FRIEND. I KNOW IT'S HARD, BUT WHAT COMES NEXT IS ALMOST CERTAINLY FOR THE BEST.
DROP DEAD, DIRTBAG.

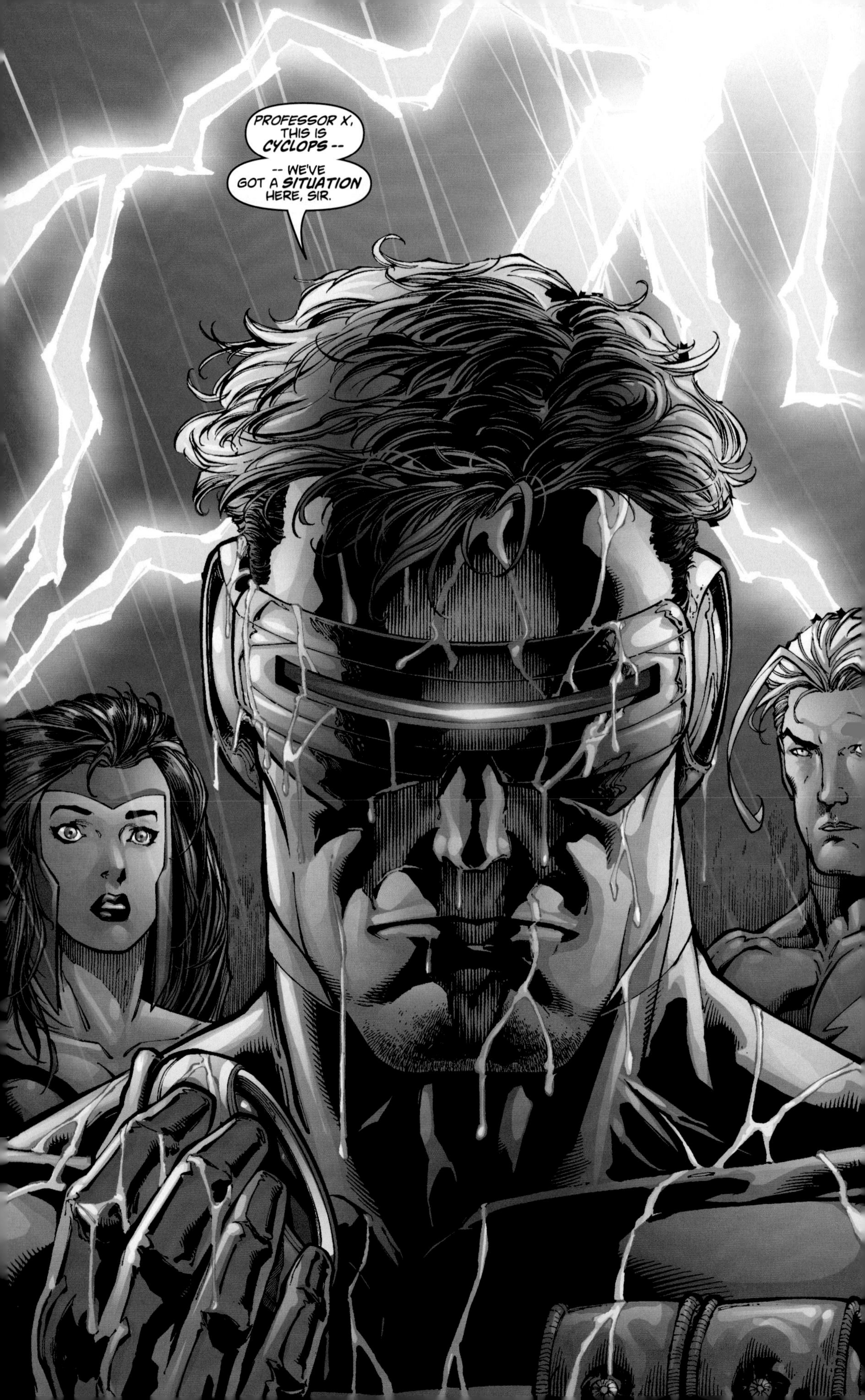
PROFESSOR X, THIS IS CYCLOPS --
-- WE'VE GOT A SITUATION HERE, SIR.

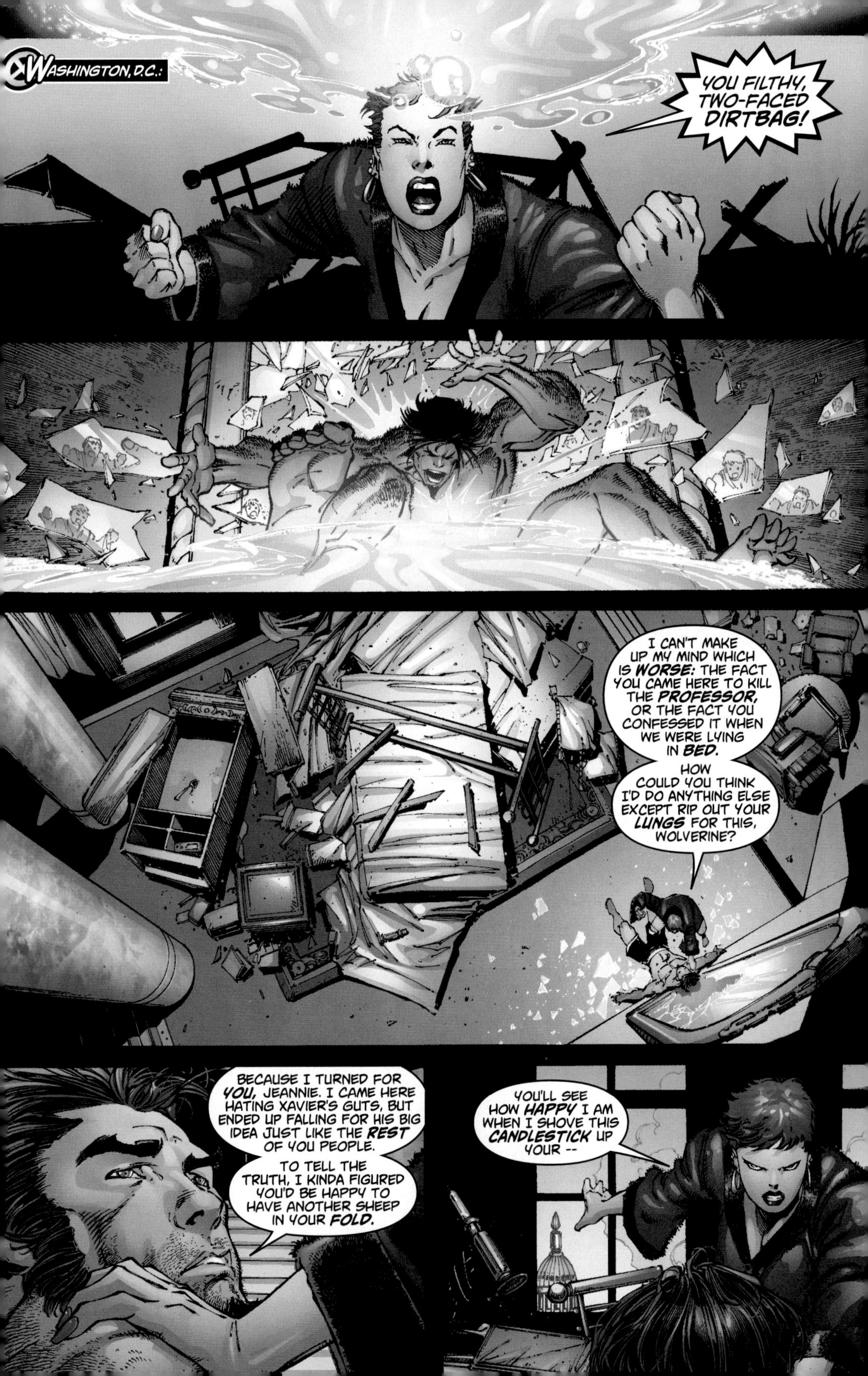
WASHINGTON, D.C.:
YOU FILTHY, TWO-FACED DIRTBAG!
I CAN'T MAKE UP MY MIND WHICH IS WORSE: THE FACT YOU CAME HERE TO KILL THE PROFESSOR, OR THE FACT YOU CONFESSED IT WHEN WE WERE LYING IN BED.
HOW COULD YOU THINK I'D DO ANYTHING ELSE EXCEPT RIP OUT YOUR LUNGS FOR THIS, WOLVERINE?
BECAUSE I TURNED FOR YOU, JEANNIE. I CAME HERE HATING XAVIER'S GUTS, BUT ENDED UP FALLING FOR HIS BIG IDEA JUST LIKE THE REST OF YOU PEOPLE.
TO TELL THE TRUTH, I KINDA FIGURED YOU'D BE HAPPY TO HAVE ANOTHER SHEEP IN YOUR FOLD.
YOU'LL SEE HOW HAPPY I AM WHEN I SHOVE THIS CANDLESTICK UP YOUR --

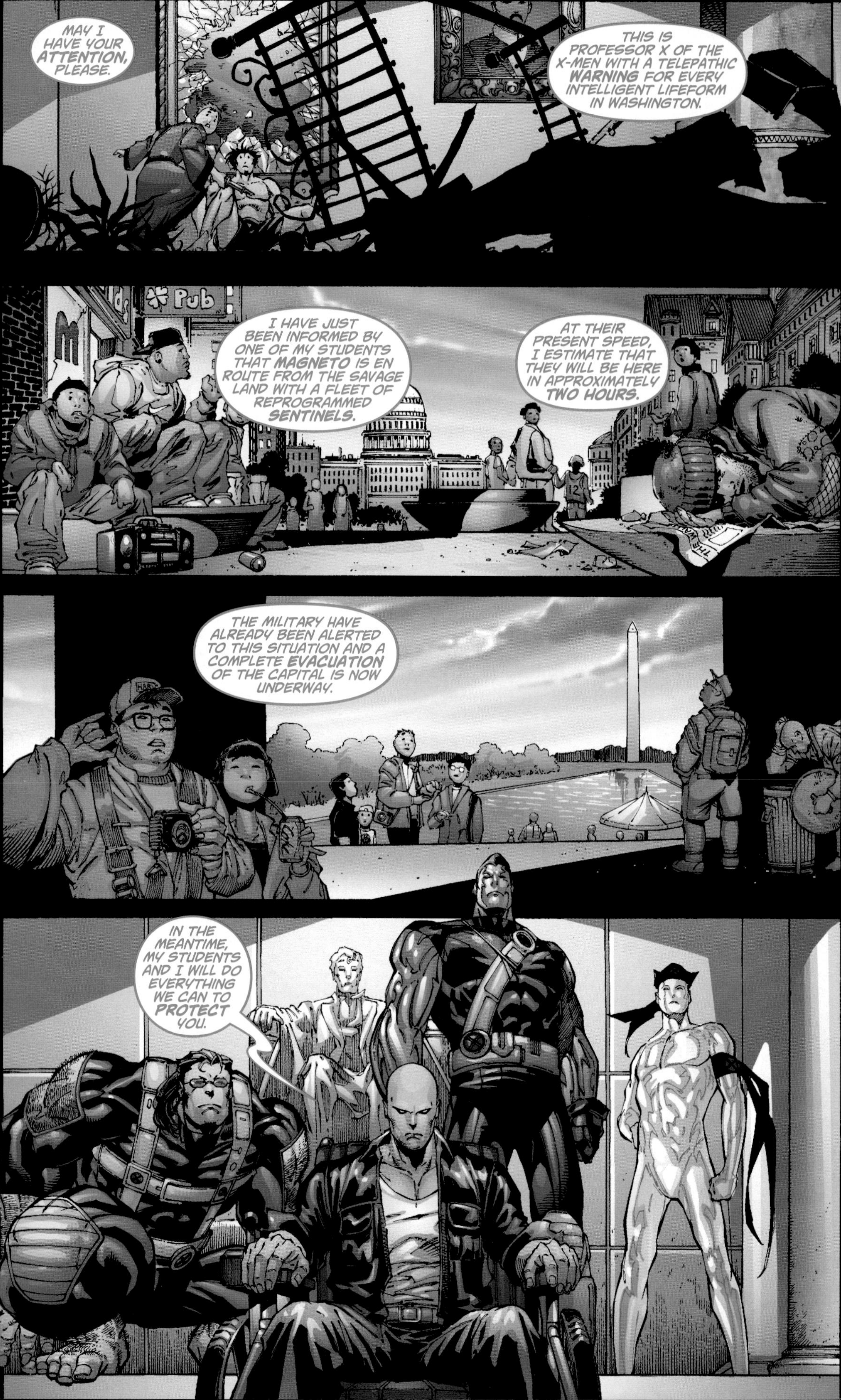

MAY I HAVE YOUR ATTENTION, PLEASE.
THIS IS PROFESSOR X OF THE X-MEN WITH A TELEPATHIC WARNING FOR EVERY INTELLIGENT LIFEFORM IN WASHINGTON.
Pub
I HAVE JUST BEEN INFORMED BY ONE OF MY STUDENTS THAT MAGNETO IS EN ROUTE FROM THE SAVAGE LAND WITH A FLEET OF REPROGRAMMED SENTINELS.
AT THEIR PRESENT SPEED, I ESTIMATE THAT THEY WILL BE HERE IN APPROXIMATELY TWO HOURS.
THE MILITARY HAVE ALREADY BEEN ALERTED TO THIS SITUATION AND A COMPLETE EVACUATION OF THE CAPITAL IS NOW UNDERWAY.
IN THE MEANTIME, MY STUDENTS AND I WILL DO EVERYTHING WE CAN TO PROTECT YOU.

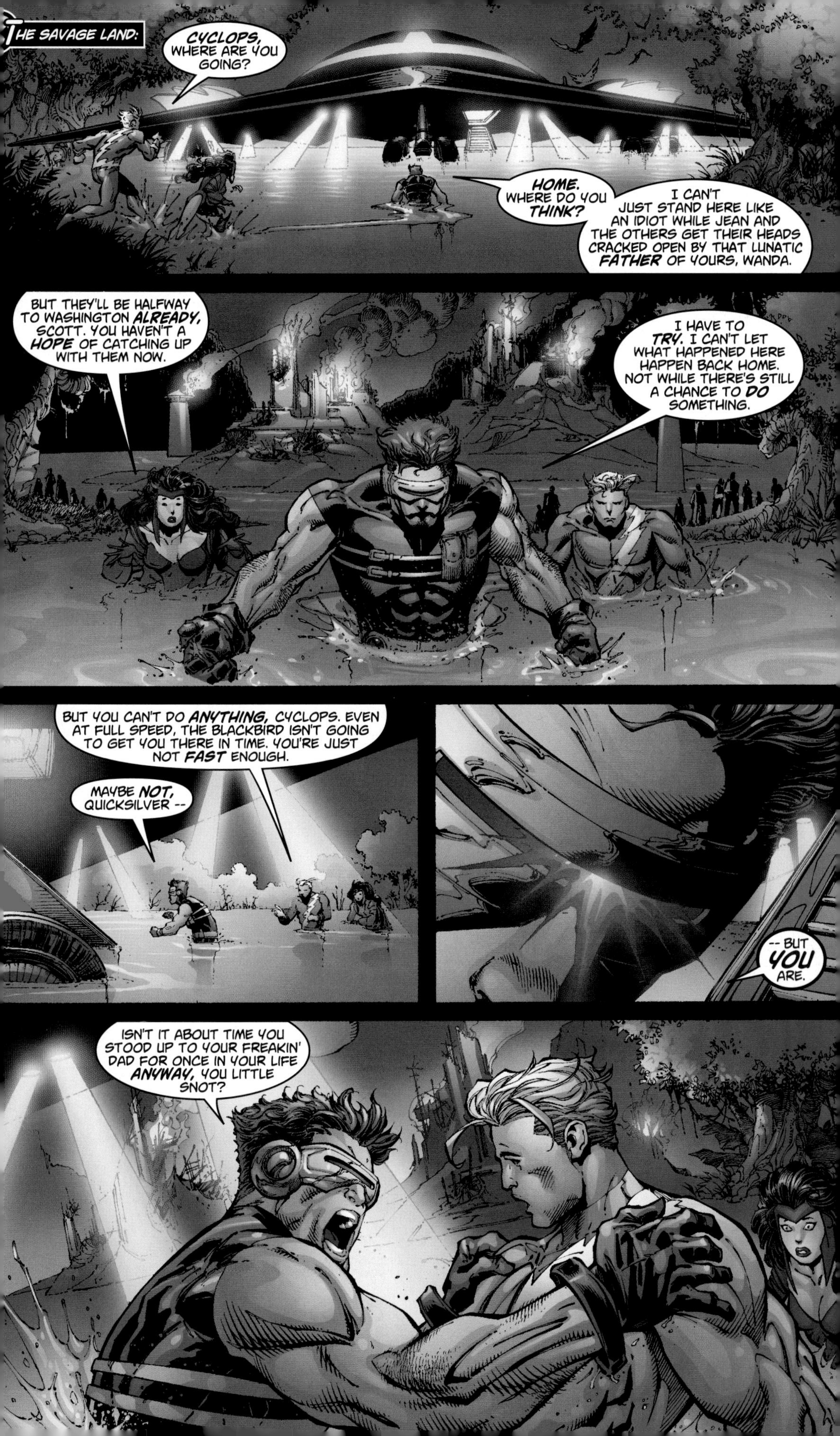
THE SAVAGE LAND:
CYCLOPS, WHERE ARE YOU GOING?
HOME. WHERE DO YOU THINK?
I CAN'T JUST STAND HERE LIKE AN IDIOT WHILE JEAN AND THE OTHERS GET THEIR HEADS CRACKED OPEN BY THAT LUNATIC FATHER OF YOURS, WANDA.
BUT THEY'LL BE HALFWAY TO WASHINGTON ALREADY, SCOTT. YOU HAVEN'T A HOPE OF CATCHING UP WITH THEM NOW.
I HAVE TO TRY. I CAN'T LET WHAT HAPPENED HERE HAPPEN BACK HOME. NOT WHILE THERE'S STILL A CHANCE TO DO SOMETHING.
BUT YOU CAN'T DO ANYTHING, CYCLOPS. EVEN AT FULL SPEED, THE BLACKBIRD ISN'T GOING TO GET YOU THERE IN TIME. YOU'RE JUST NOT FAST ENOUGH.
MAYBE NOT, QUICKSILVER --
-- BUT YOU ARE.
ISN'T IT ABOUT TIME YOU STOOD UP TO YOUR FREAKIN' DAD FOR ONCE IN YOUR LIFE ANYWAY, YOU LITTLE SNOT?

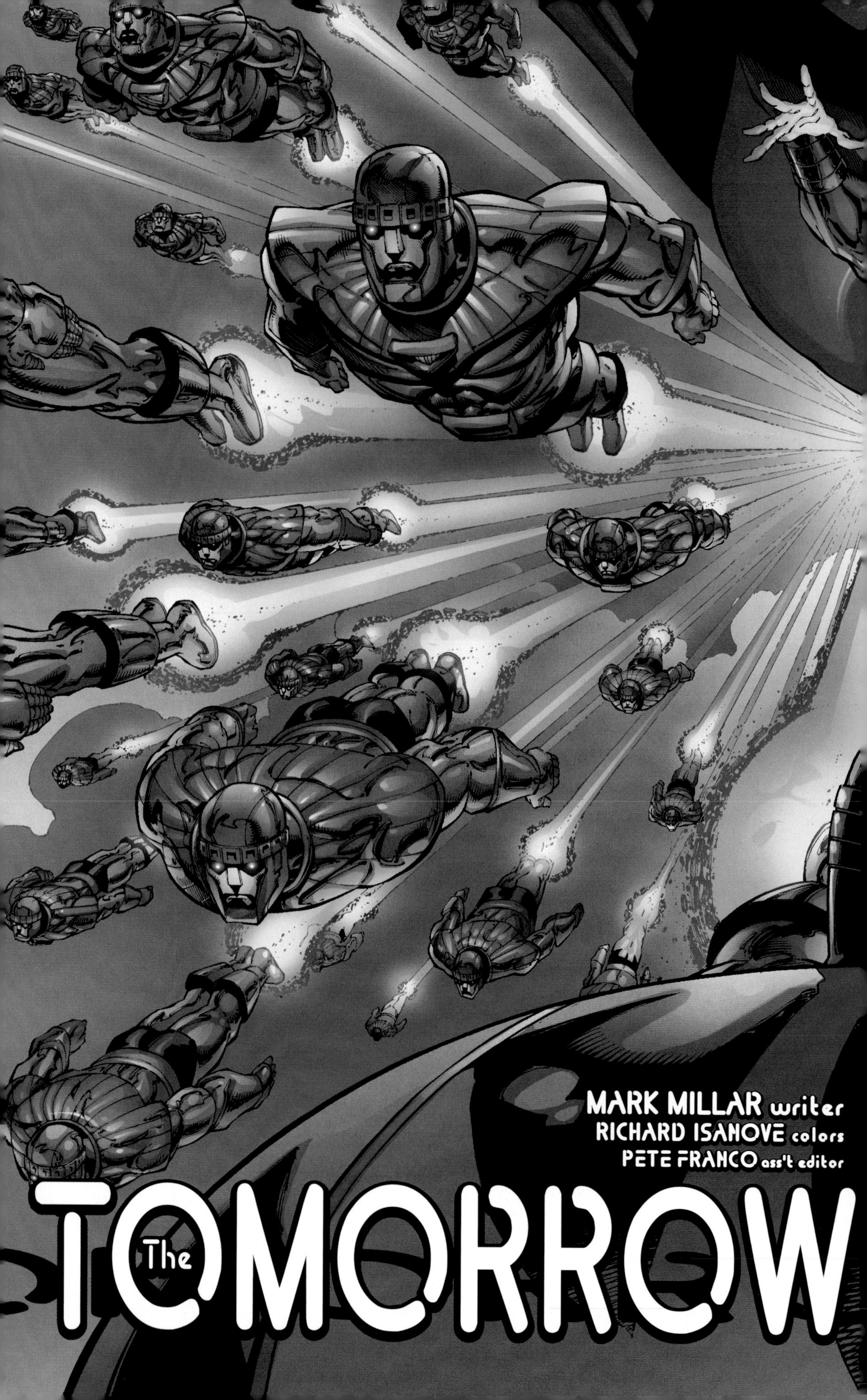
MARK MILLAR writer
RICHARD ISANOVE colors
PETE FRANCO ass't editor
The TOMORROW

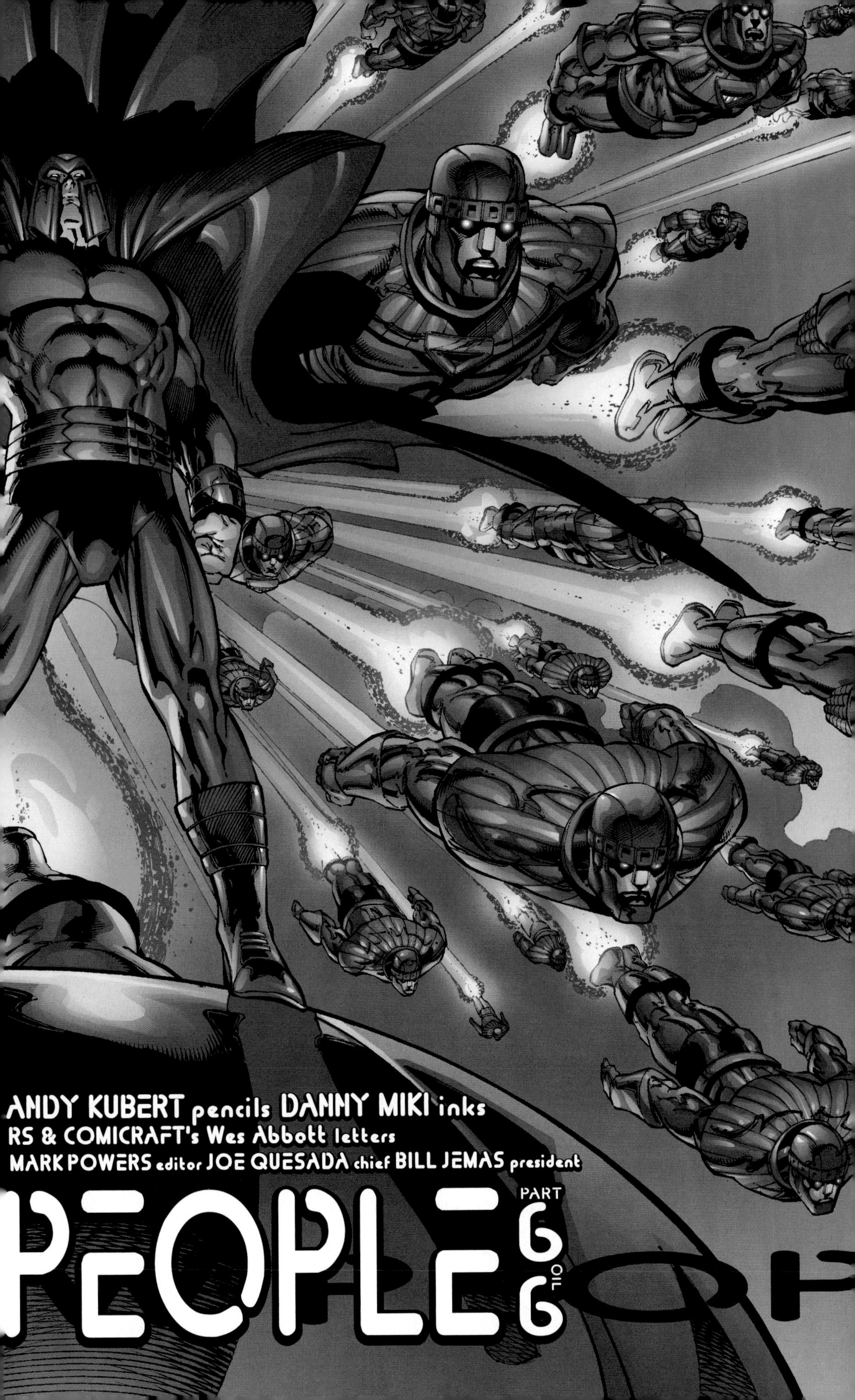
ANDY KUBERT pencils DANNY MIKI inks
RS & COMICRAFT's Wes Abbott letters
MARK POWERS editor JOE QUESADA chief BILL JEMAS president
PEOPLE
PART 6 OF 6

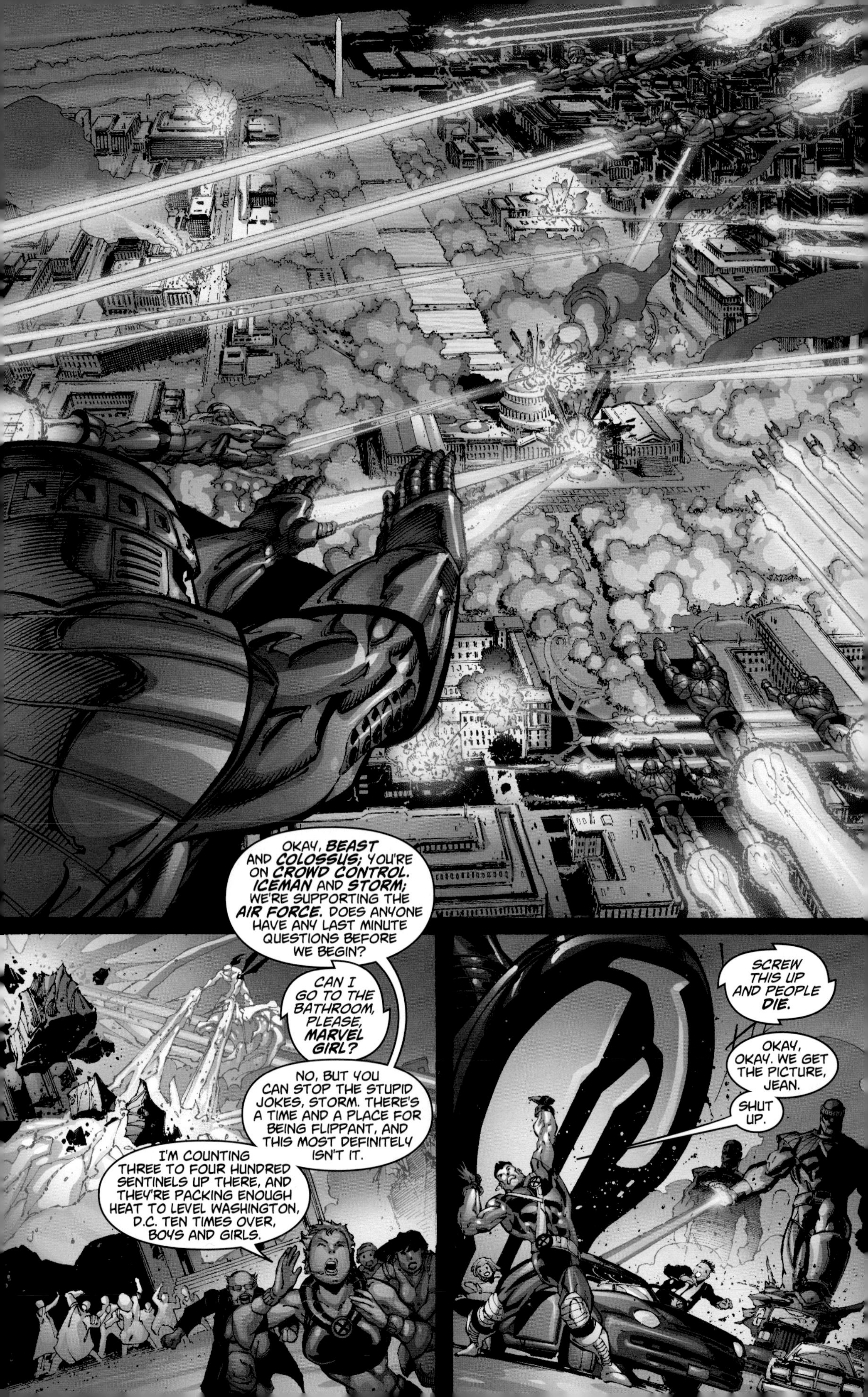
OKAY, BEAST AND COLOSSUS; YOU'RE ON CROWD CONTROL. ICEMAN AND STORM; WE'RE SUPPORTING THE AIR FORCE. DOES ANYONE HAVE ANY LAST MINUTE QUESTIONS BEFORE WE BEGIN?
CAN I GO TO THE BATHROOM, PLEASE, MARVEL GIRL?
NO, BUT YOU CAN STOP THE STUPID JOKES, STORM. THERE'S A TIME AND A PLACE FOR BEING FLIPPANT, AND THIS MOST DEFINITELY ISN'T IT.
I'M COUNTING THREE TO FOUR HUNDRED SENTINELS UP THERE, AND THEY'RE PACKING ENOUGH HEAT TO LEVEL WASHINGTON, D.C. TEN TIMES OVER, BOYS AND GIRLS.
SCREW THIS UP AND PEOPLE DIE.
OKAY, OKAY. WE GET THE PICTURE, JEAN.
SHUT UP.

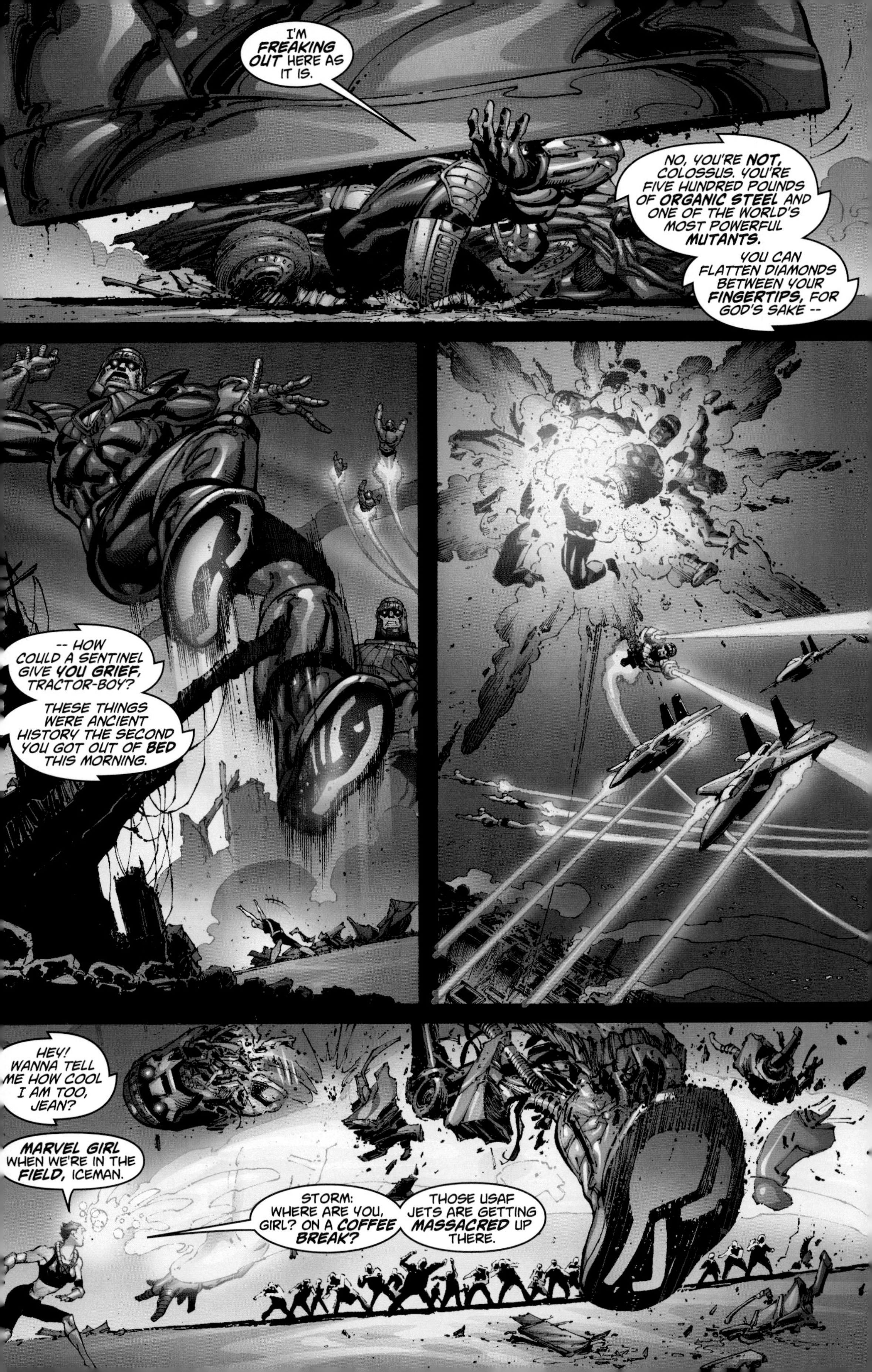
I'M FREAKING OUT HERE AS IT IS.
NO, YOU'RE NOT, COLOSSUS. YOU'RE FIVE HUNDRED POUNDS OF ORGANIC STEEL AND ONE OF THE WORLD'S MOST POWERFUL MUTANTS.
YOU CAN FLATTEN DIAMONDS BETWEEN YOUR FINGERTIPS, FOR GOD'S SAKE --
-- HOW COULD A SENTINEL GIVE YOU GRIEF, TRACTOR-BOY?
THESE THINGS WERE ANCIENT HISTORY THE SECOND YOU GOT OUT OF BED THIS MORNING.
HEY! WANNA TELL ME HOW COOL I AM TOO, JEAN?
MARVEL GIRL WHEN WE'RE IN THE FIELD, ICEMAN.
STORM: WHERE ARE YOU, GIRL? ON A COFFEE BREAK?
THOSE USAF JETS ARE GETTING MASSACRED UP THERE.

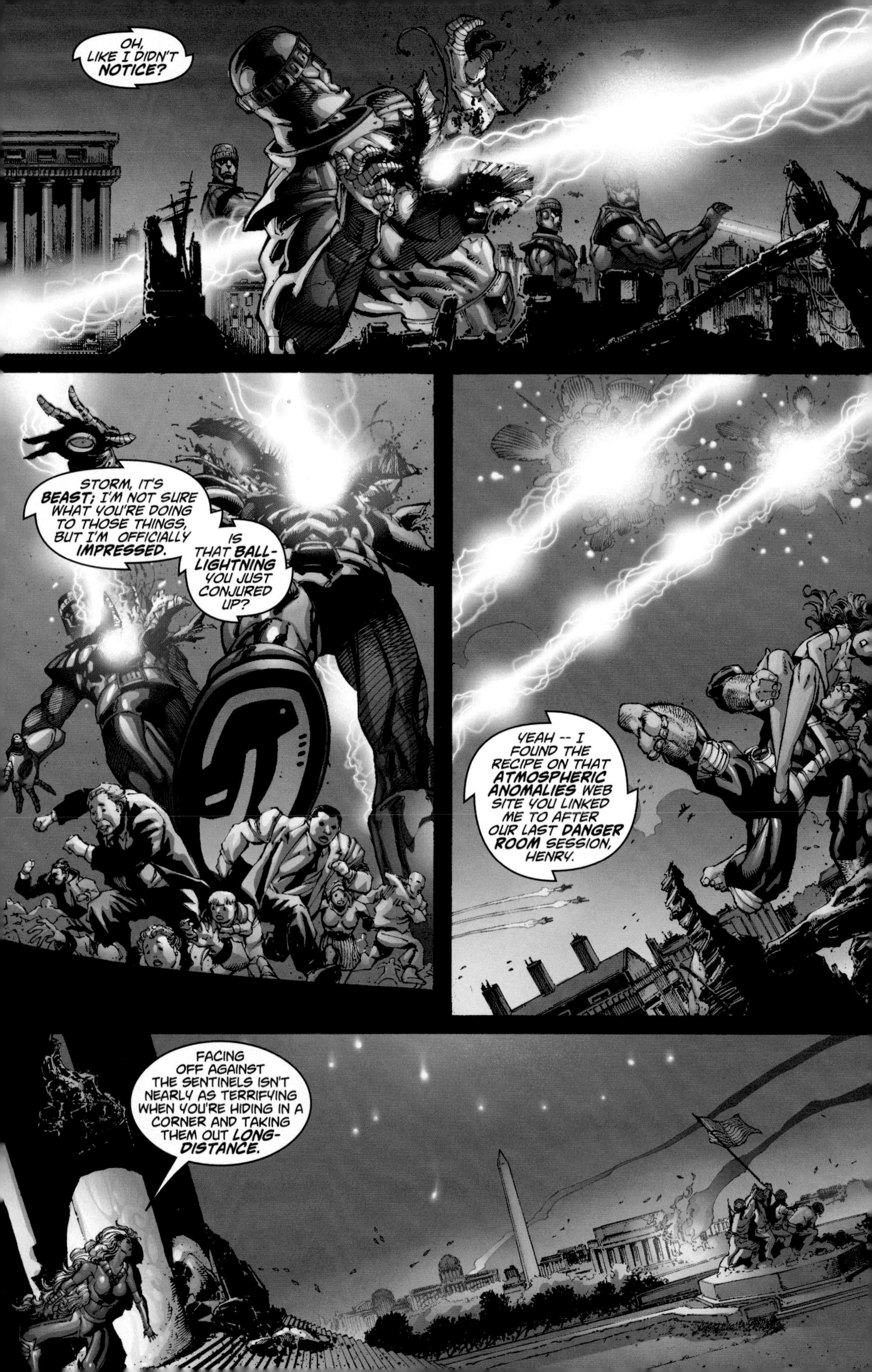
OH, LIKE I DIDN'T NOTICE?
STORM, IT'S BEAST; I'M NOT SURE WHAT YOU'RE DOING TO THOSE THINGS, BUT I'M OFFICIALLY IMPRESSED.
IS THAT BALL-LIGHTNING YOU JUST CONJURED UP?
YEAH -- I FOUND THE RECIPE ON THAT ATMOSPHERIC ANOMALIES WEB SITE YOU LINKED ME TO AFTER OUR LAST DANGER ROOM SESSION, HENRY.
FACING OFF AGAINST THE SENTINELS ISN'T NEARLY AS TERRIFYING WHEN YOU'RE HIDING IN A CORNER AND TAKING THEM OUT LONG-DISTANCE.

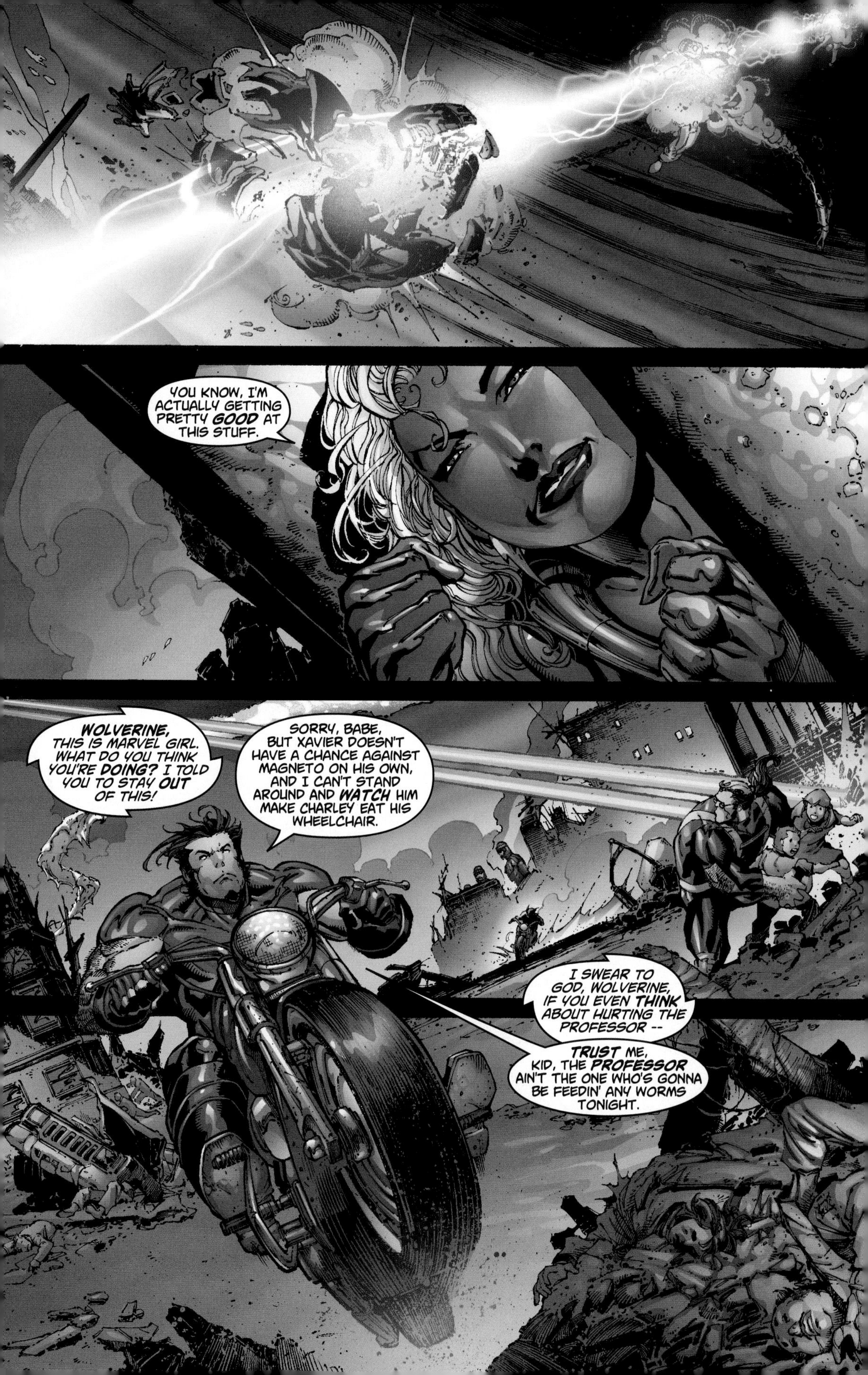
YOU KNOW, I'M ACTUALLY GETTING PRETTY GOOD AT THIS STUFF.
WOLVERINE, THIS IS MARVEL GIRL. WHAT DO YOU THINK YOU'RE DOING? I TOLD YOU TO STAY OUT OF THIS!
SORRY, BABE, BUT XAVIER DOESN'T HAVE A CHANCE AGAINST MAGNETO ON HIS OWN, AND I CAN'T STAND AROUND AND WATCH HIM MAKE CHARLEY EAT HIS WHEELCHAIR.
I SWEAR TO GOD, WOLVERINE, IF YOU EVEN THINK ABOUT HURTING THE PROFESSOR --
TRUST ME, KID, THE PROFESSOR AIN'T THE ONE WHO'S GONNA BE FEEDIN' ANY WORMS TONIGHT.

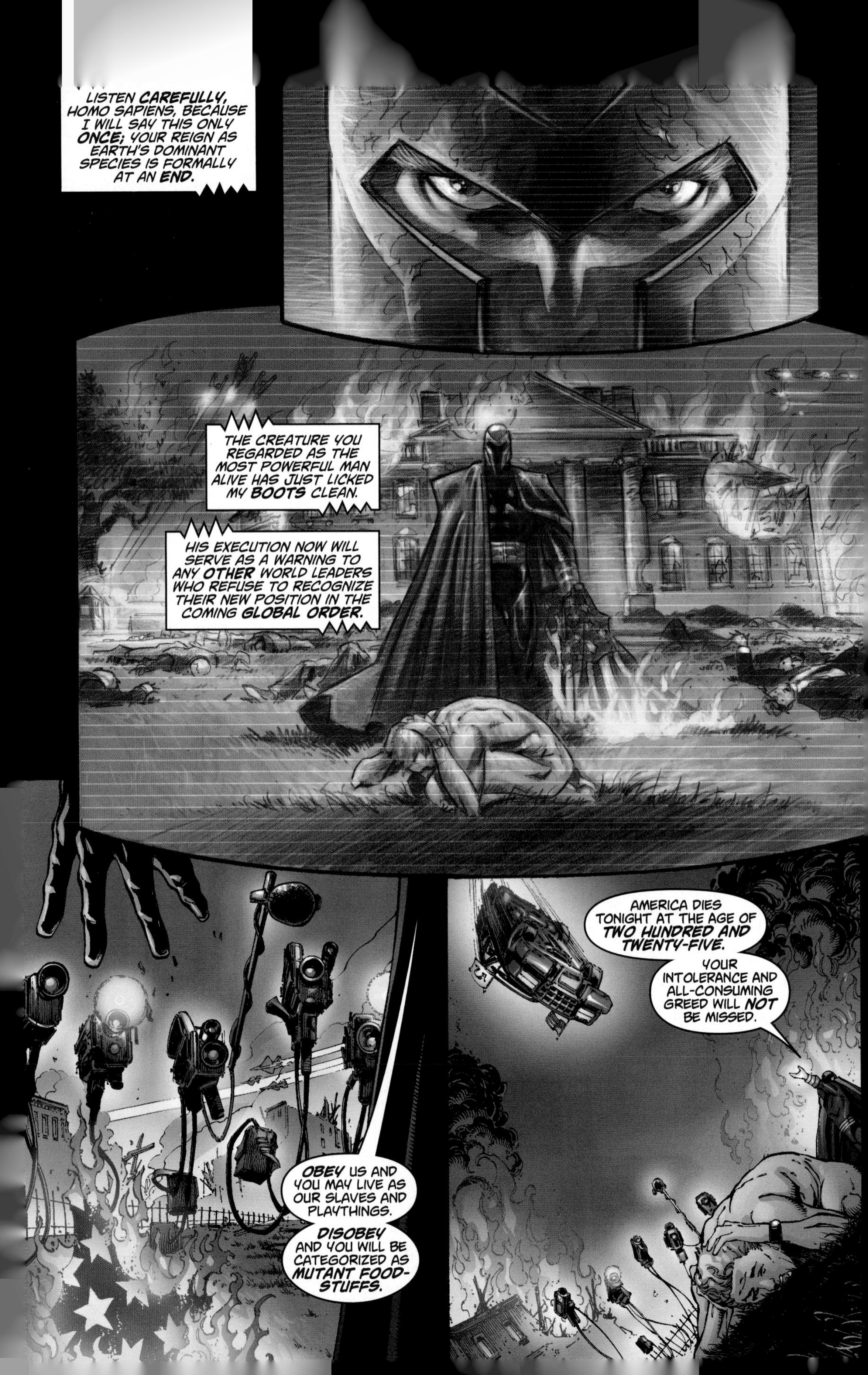

LISTEN CAREFULLY, HOMO SAPIENS, BECAUSE I WILL SAY THIS ONLY ONCE: YOUR REIGN AS EARTH'S DOMINANT SPECIES IS FORMALLY AT AN END.
THE CREATURE YOU REGARDED AS THE MOST POWERFUL MAN ALIVE HAS JUST LICKED MY BOOTS CLEAN.
HIS EXECUTION NOW WILL SERVE AS A WARNING TO ANY OTHER WORLD LEADERS WHO REFUSE TO RECOGNIZE THEIR NEW POSITION IN THE COMING GLOBAL ORDER.
OBEY US AND YOU MAY LIVE AS OUR SLAVES AND PLAYTHINGS.
DISOBEY AND YOU WILL BE CATEGORIZED AS MUTANT FOOD-STUFFS.
AMERICA DIES TONIGHT AT THE AGE OF TWO HUNDRED AND TWENTY-FIVE.
YOUR INTOLERANCE AND ALL-CONSUMING GREED WILL NOT BE MISSED.

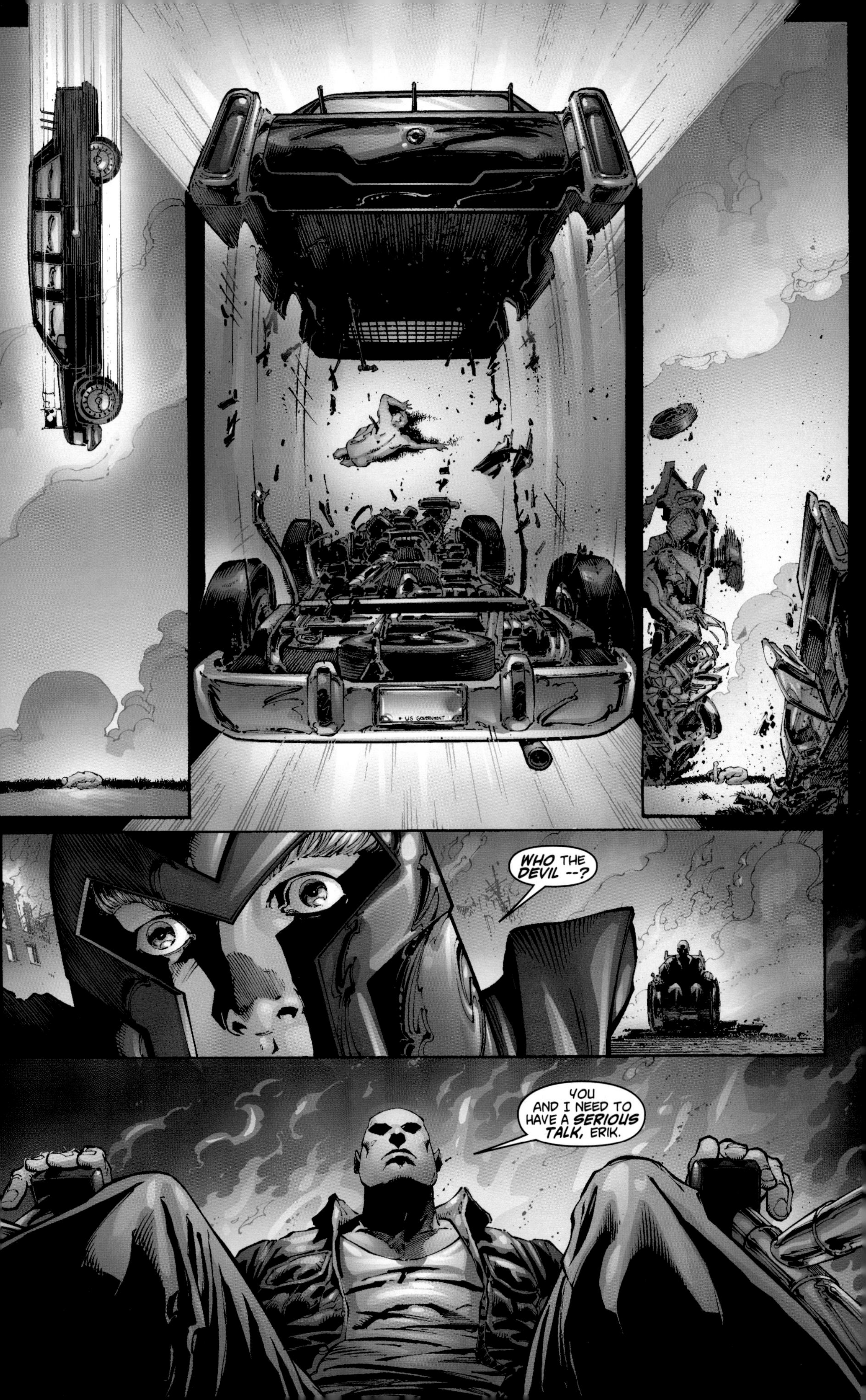
U.S. GOVERNMENT
WHO THE DEVIL --?
YOU AND I NEED TO HAVE A SERIOUS TALK, ERIK.

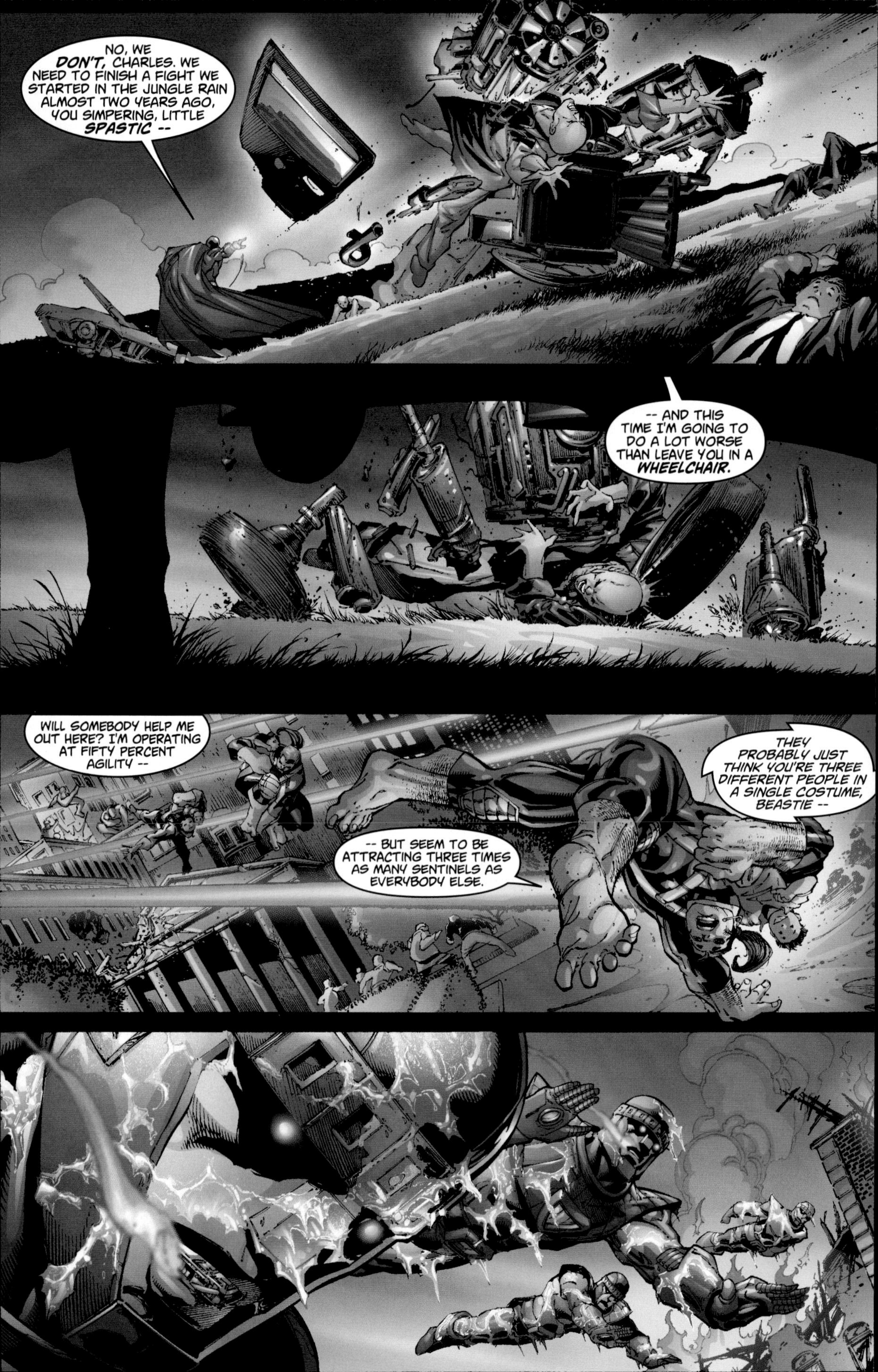
NO, WE DON'T, CHARLES. WE NEED TO FINISH A FIGHT WE STARTED IN THE JUNGLE RAIN ALMOST TWO YEARS AGO, YOU SIMPERING, LITTLE SPASTIC --
-- AND THIS TIME I'M GOING TO DO A LOT WORSE THAN LEAVE YOU IN A WHEELCHAIR.
WILL SOMEBODY HELP ME OUT HERE? I'M OPERATING AT FIFTY PERCENT AGILITY --
-- BUT SEEM TO BE ATTRACTING THREE TIMES AS MANY SENTINELS AS EVERYBODY ELSE.
THEY PROBABLY JUST THINK YOU'RE THREE DIFFERENT PEOPLE IN A SINGLE COSTUME, BEASTIE --

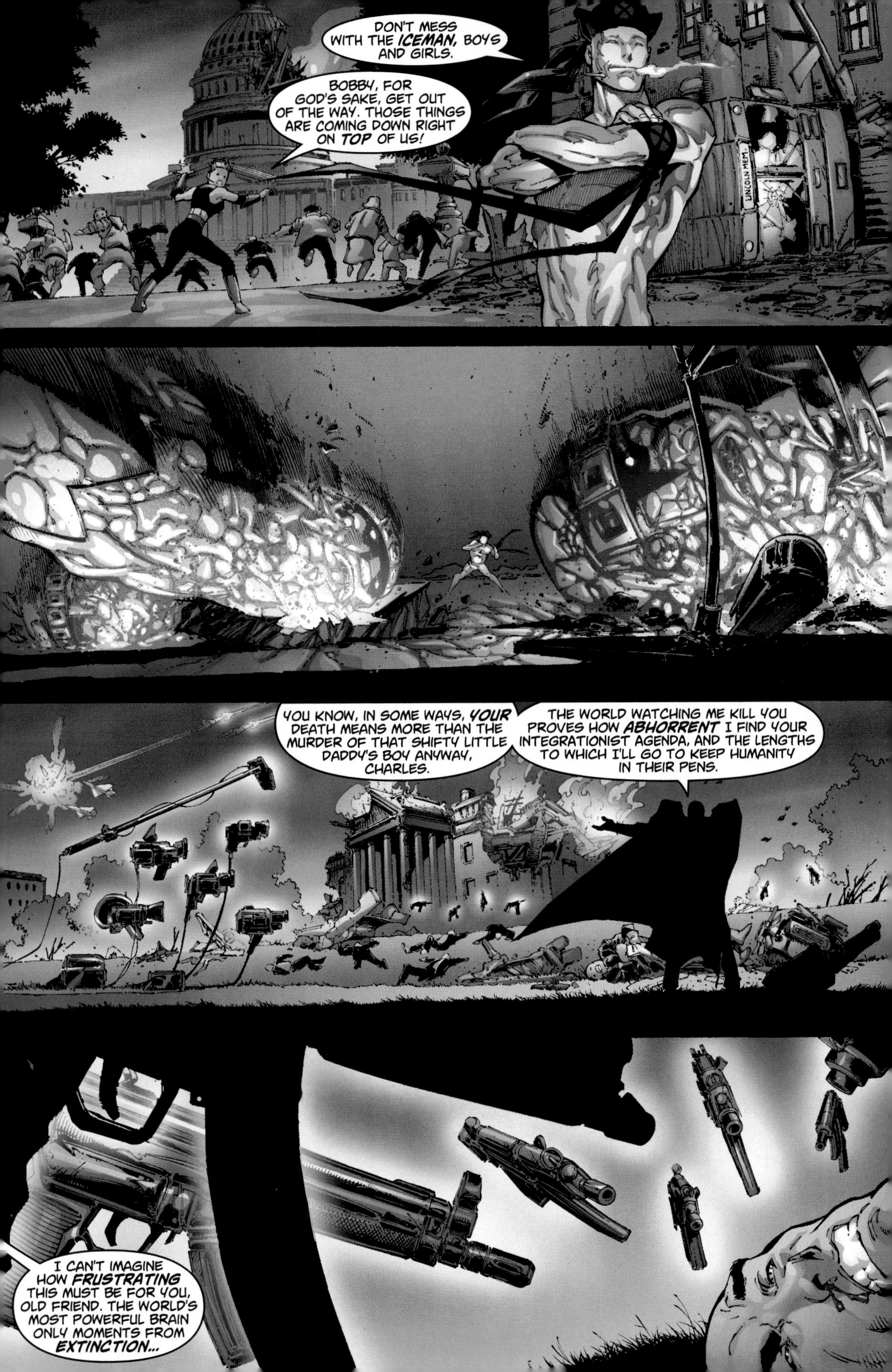
DON'T MESS WITH THE ICEMAN, BOYS AND GIRLS.
BOBBY, FOR GOD'S SAKE, GET OUT OF THE WAY. THOSE THINGS ARE COMING DOWN RIGHT ON TOP OF US!
LINCOLN MEM.
YOU KNOW, IN SOME WAYS, YOUR DEATH MEANS MORE THAN THE MURDER OF THAT SHIFTY LITTLE DADDY'S BOY ANYWAY, CHARLES.
THE WORLD WATCHING ME KILL YOU PROVES HOW ABHORRENT I FIND YOUR INTEGRATIONIST AGENDA, AND THE LENGTHS TO WHICH I'LL GO TO KEEP HUMANITY IN THEIR PENS.
I CAN'T IMAGINE HOW FRUSTRATING THIS MUST BE FOR YOU, OLD FRIEND. THE WORLD'S MOST POWERFUL BRAIN ONLY MOMENTS FROM EXTINCTION...

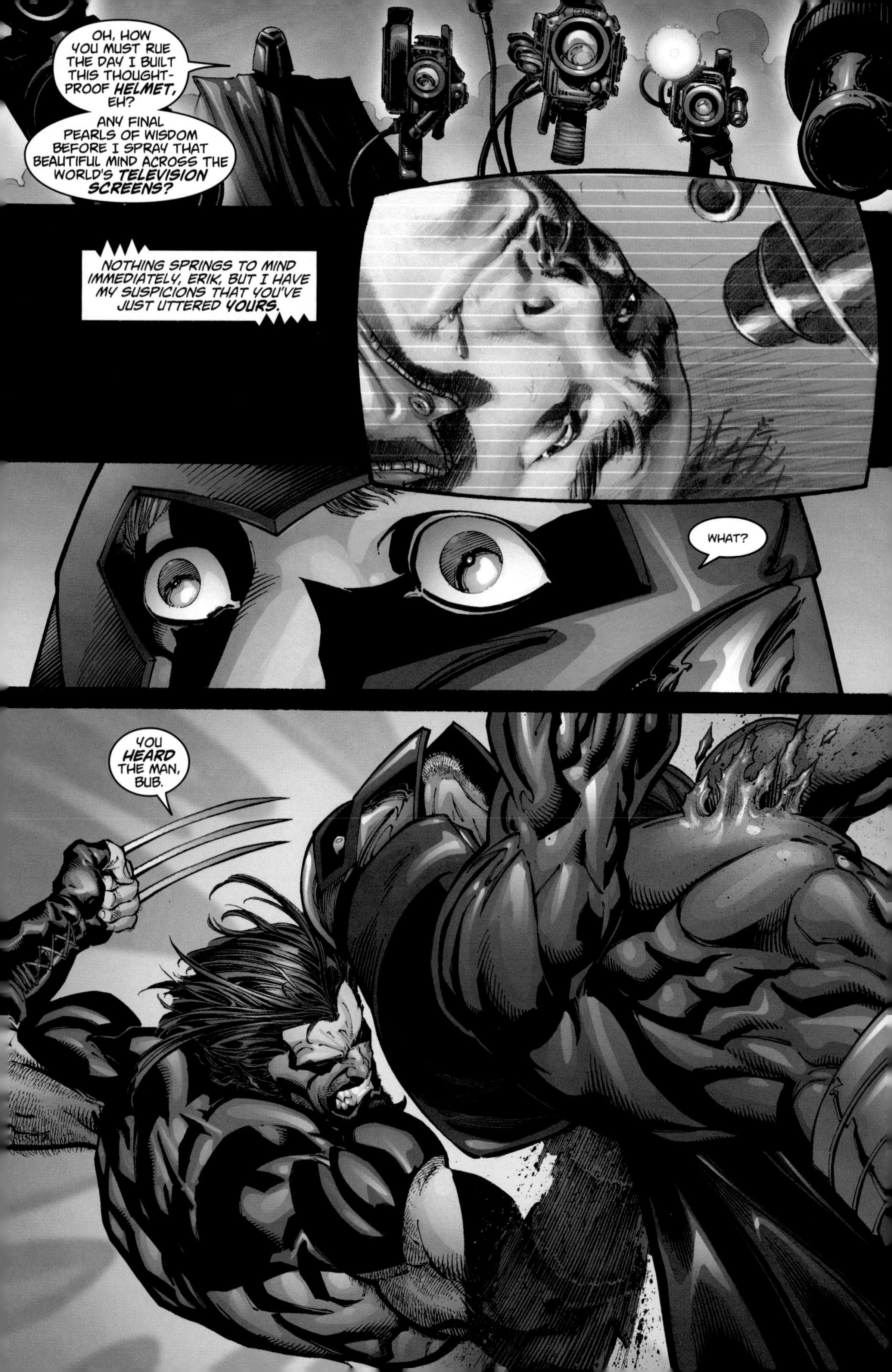
OH, HOW YOU MUST RUE THE DAY I BUILT THIS THOUGHT-PROOF HELMET, EH?
ANY FINAL PEARLS OF WISDOM BEFORE I SPRAY THAT BEAUTIFUL MIND ACROSS THE WORLD'S TELEVISION SCREENS?
NOTHING SPRINGS TO MIND IMMEDIATELY, ERIK, BUT I HAVE MY SUSPICIONS THAT YOU'VE JUST UTTERED YOURS.
WHAT?
YOU HEARD THE MAN, BUB.

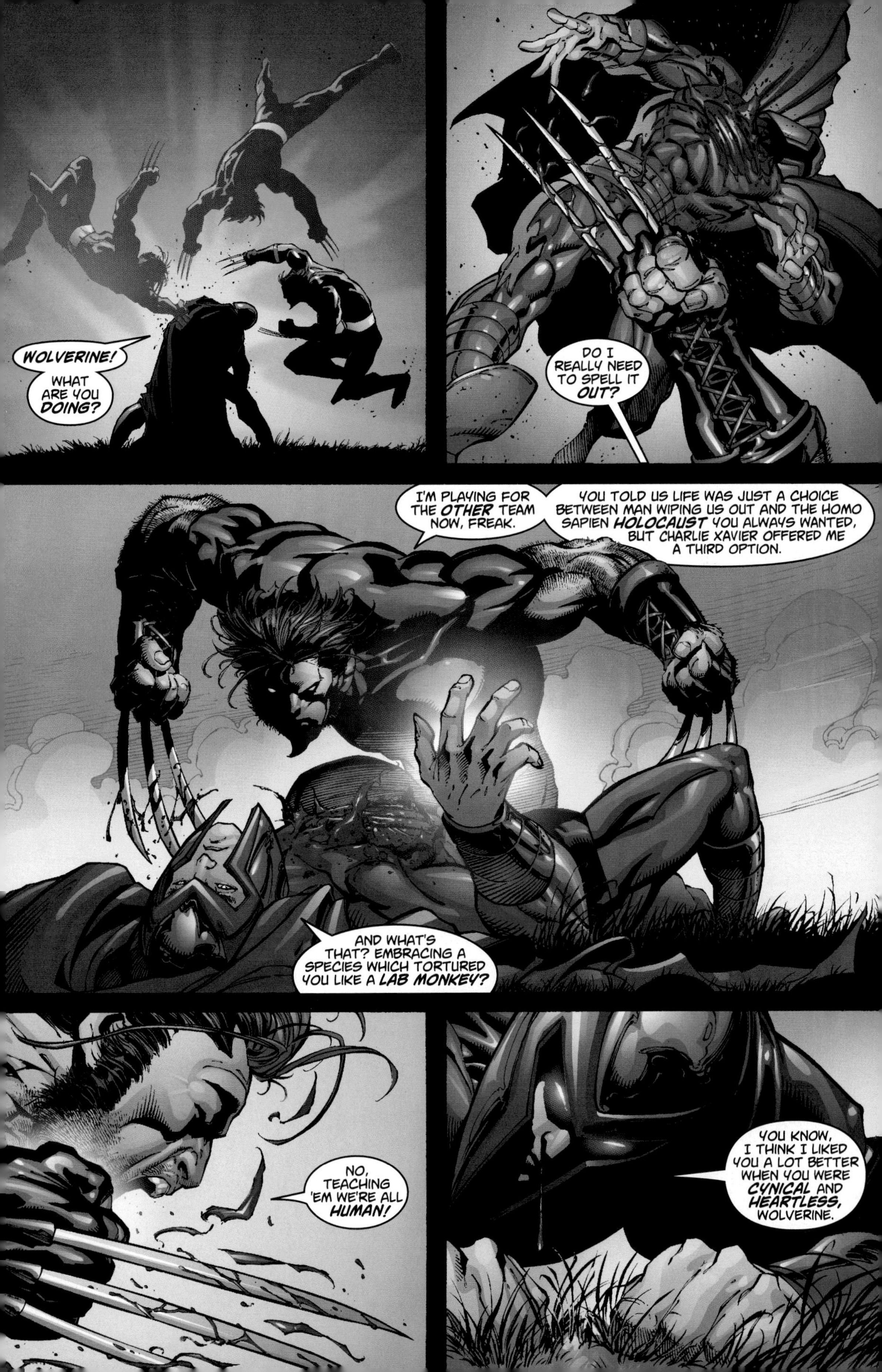
WOLVERINE! WHAT ARE YOU DOING?
DO I REALLY NEED TO SPELL IT OUT?
I'M PLAYING FOR THE OTHER TEAM NOW, FREAK.
YOU TOLD US LIFE WAS JUST A CHOICE BETWEEN MAN WIPING US OUT AND THE HOMO SAPIEN HOLOCAUST YOU ALWAYS WANTED, BUT CHARLIE XAVIER OFFERED ME A THIRD OPTION.
AND WHAT'S THAT? EMBRACING A SPECIES WHICH TORTURED YOU LIKE A LAB MONKEY?
NO, TEACHING 'EM WE'RE ALL HUMAN!
YOU KNOW, I THINK I LIKED YOU A LOT BETTER WHEN YOU WERE CYNICAL AND HEARTLESS, WOLVERINE.

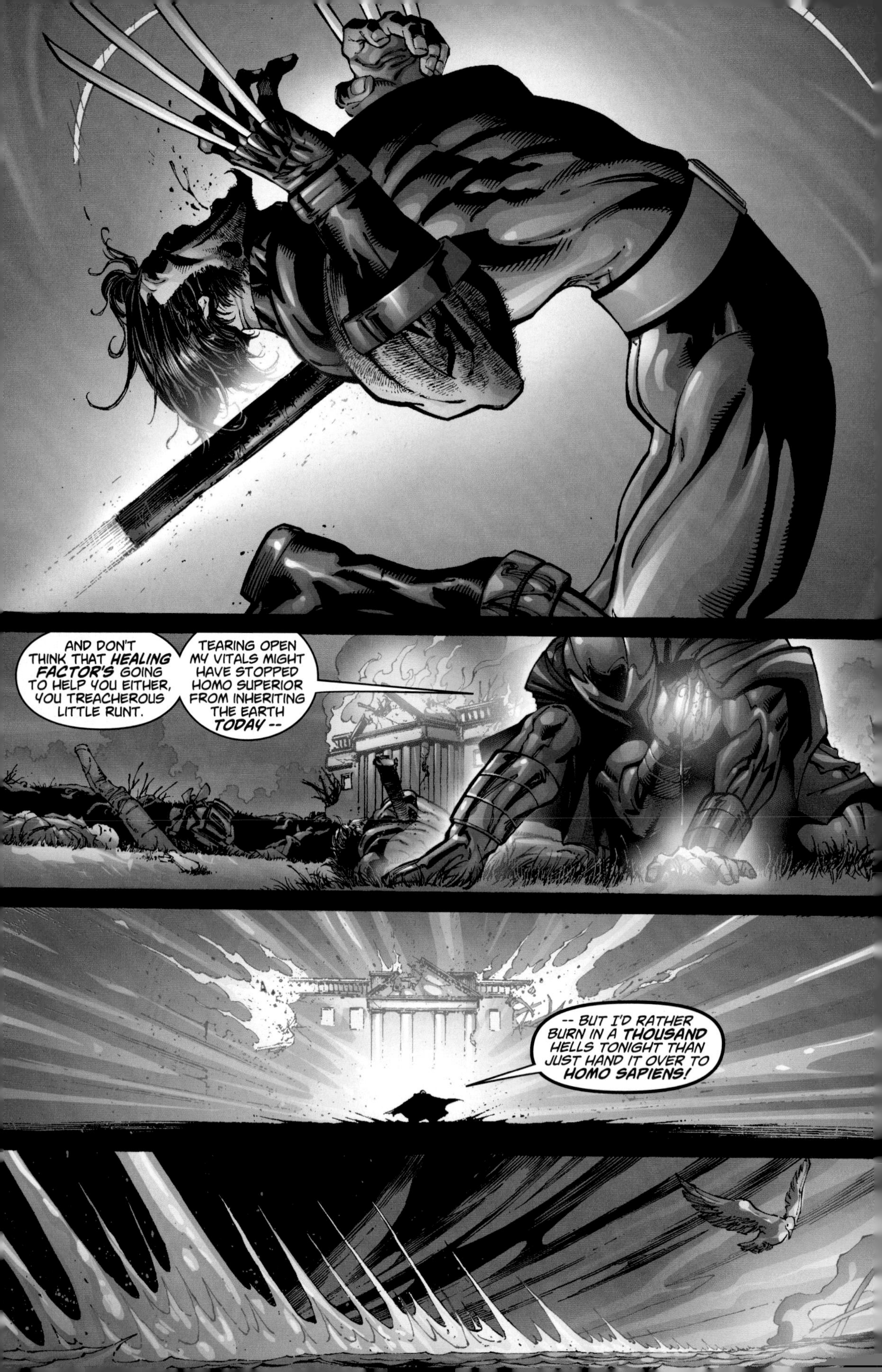
AND DON'T THINK THAT HEALING FACTOR'S GOING TO HELP YOU EITHER, YOU TREACHEROUS LITTLE RUNT.
TEARING OPEN MY VITALS MIGHT HAVE STOPPED HOMO SUPERIOR FROM INHERITING THE EARTH TODAY --
-- BUT I'D RATHER BURN IN A THOUSAND HELLS TONIGHT THAN JUST HAND IT OVER TO HOMO SAPIENS!

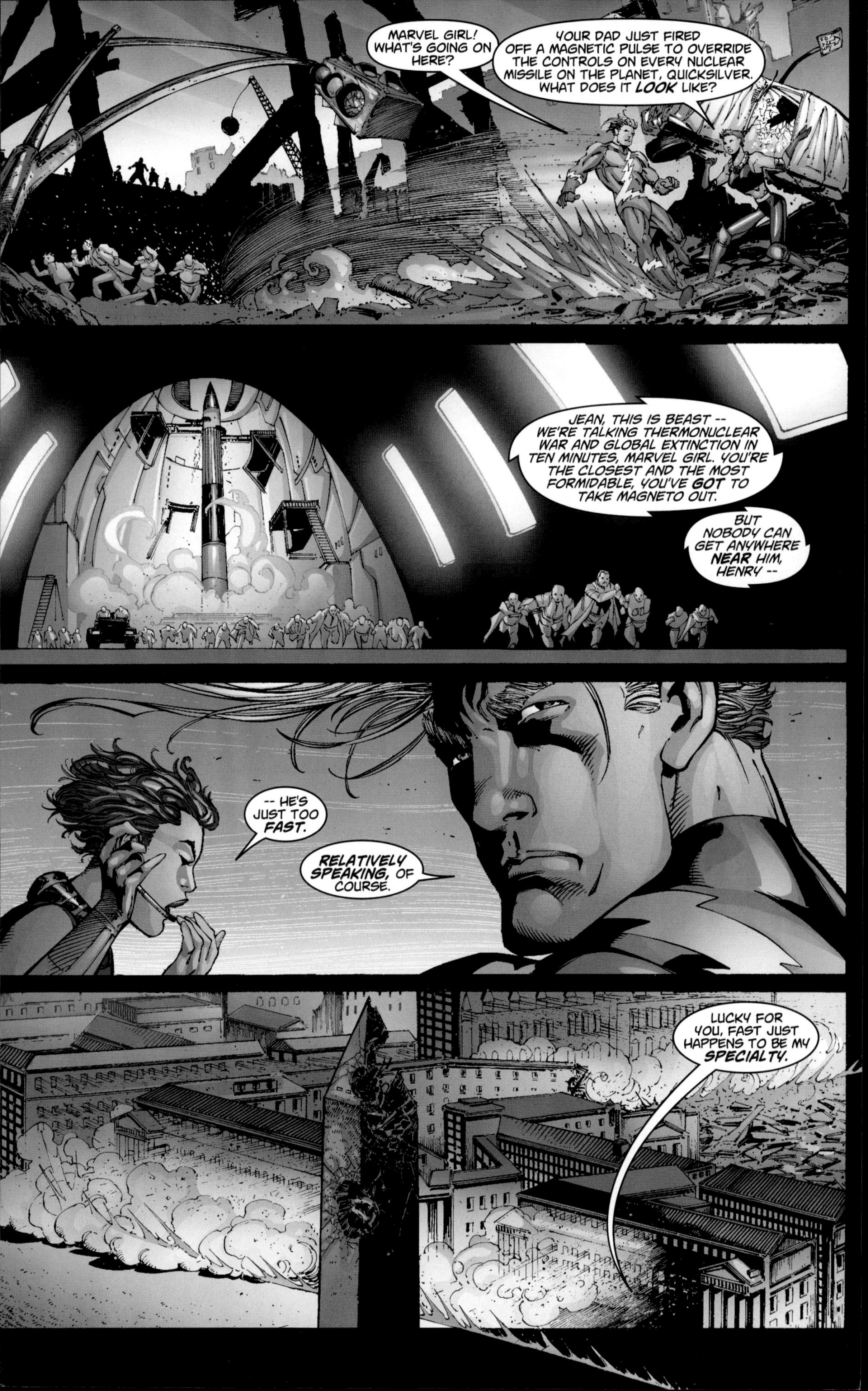
MARVEL GIRL! WHAT'S GOING ON HERE?
YOUR DAD JUST FIRED OFF A MAGNETIC PULSE TO OVERRIDE THE CONTROLS ON EVERY NUCLEAR MISSILE ON THE PLANET, QUICKSILVER. WHAT DOES IT LOOK LIKE?
JEAN, THIS IS BEAST -- WE'RE TALKING THERMONUCLEAR WAR AND GLOBAL EXTINCTION IN TEN MINUTES, MARVEL GIRL. YOU'RE THE CLOSEST AND THE MOST FORMIDABLE, YOU'VE GOT TO TAKE MAGNETO OUT.
BUT NOBODY CAN GET ANYWHERE NEAR HIM, HENRY --
-- HE'S JUST TOO FAST.
RELATIVELY SPEAKING, OF COURSE.
LUCKY FOR YOU, FAST JUST HAPPENS TO BE MY SPECIALTY.

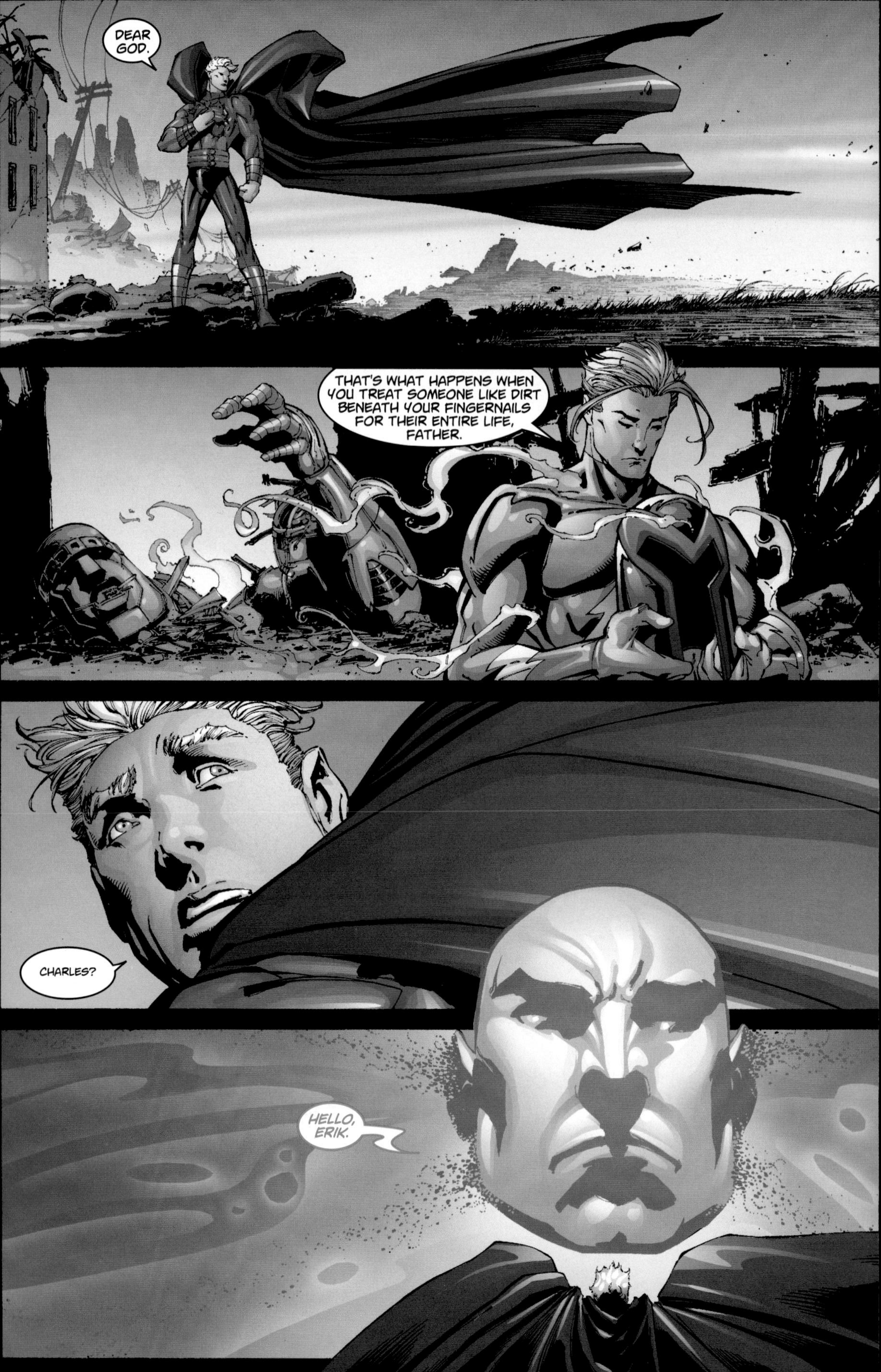
DEAR GOD.
THAT'S WHAT HAPPENS WHEN YOU TREAT SOMEONE LIKE DIRT BENEATH YOUR FINGERNAILS FOR THEIR ENTIRE LIFE, FATHER.
CHARLES?
HELLO, ERIK.

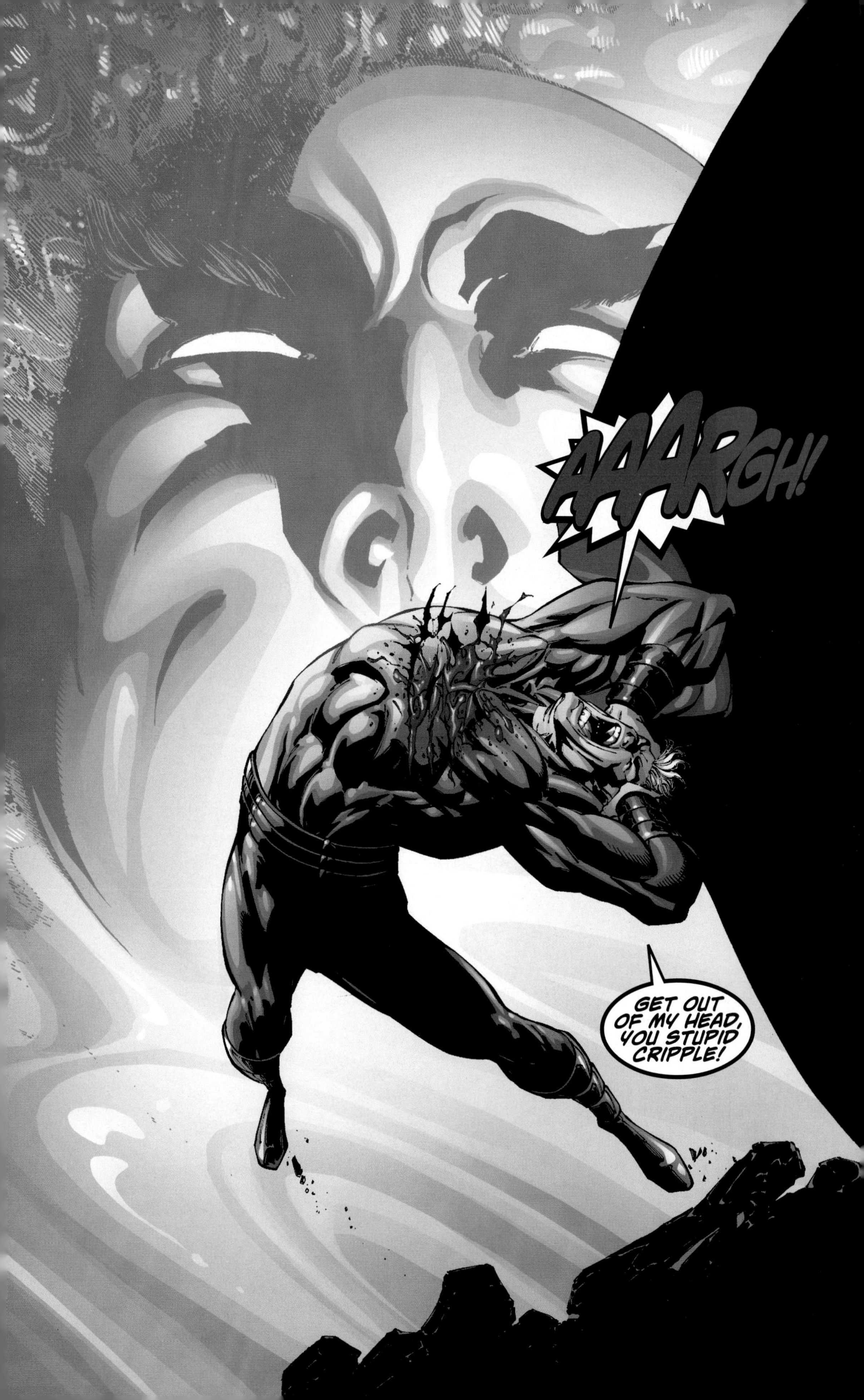
AAARGH!
GET OUT OF MY HEAD, YOU STUPID CRIPPLE!

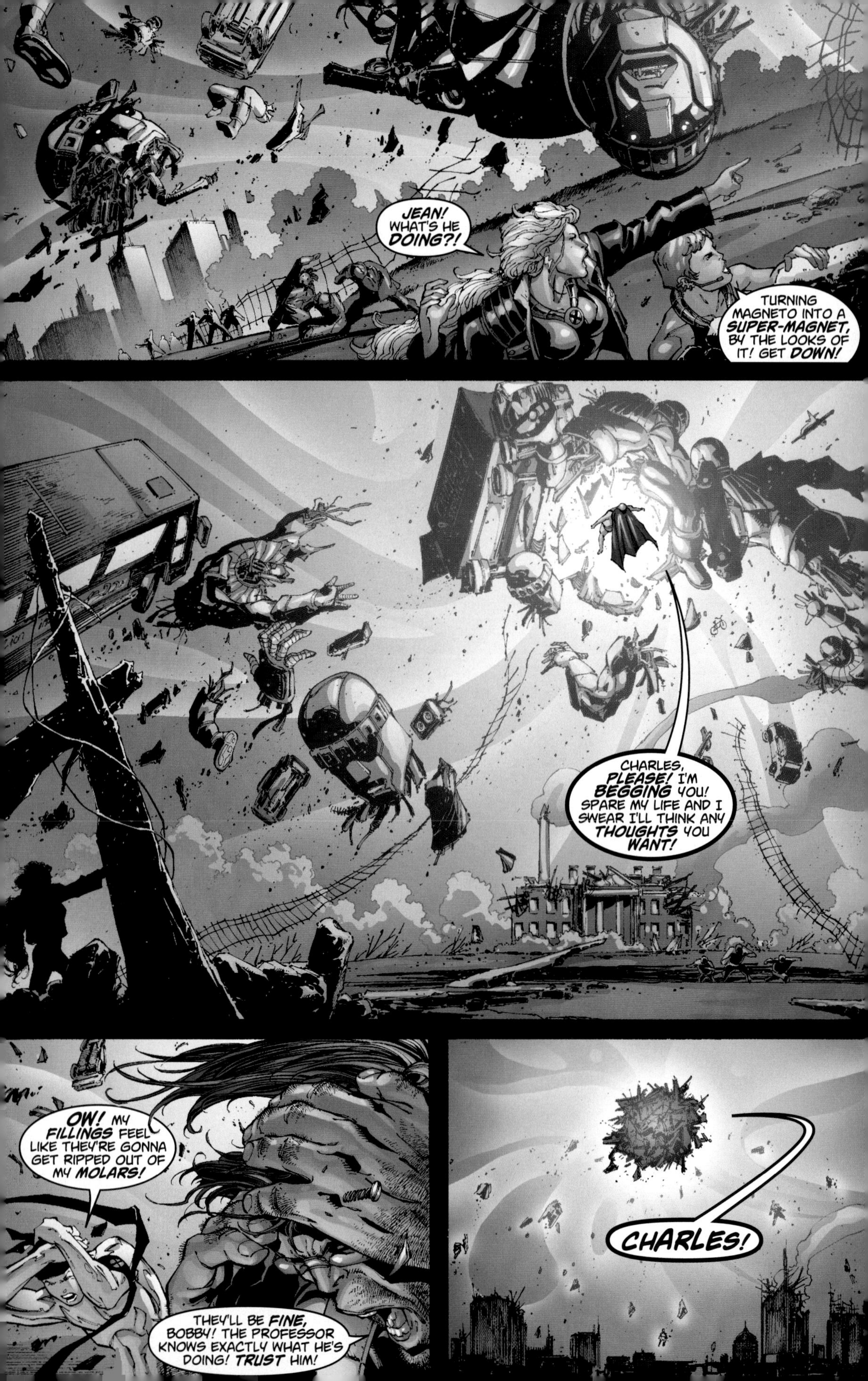
JEAN! WHAT'S HE DOING?!
TURNING MAGNETO INTO A SUPER-MAGNET, BY THE LOOKS OF IT! GET DOWN!
CHARLES, PLEASE! I'M BEGGING YOU! SPARE MY LIFE AND I SWEAR I'LL THINK ANY THOUGHTS YOU WANT!
OW! MY FILLINGS FEEL LIKE THEY'RE GONNA GET RIPPED OUT OF MY MOLARS!
THEY'LL BE FINE, BOBBY! THE PROFESSOR KNOWS EXACTLY WHAT HE'S DOING! TRUST HIM!
CHARLES!

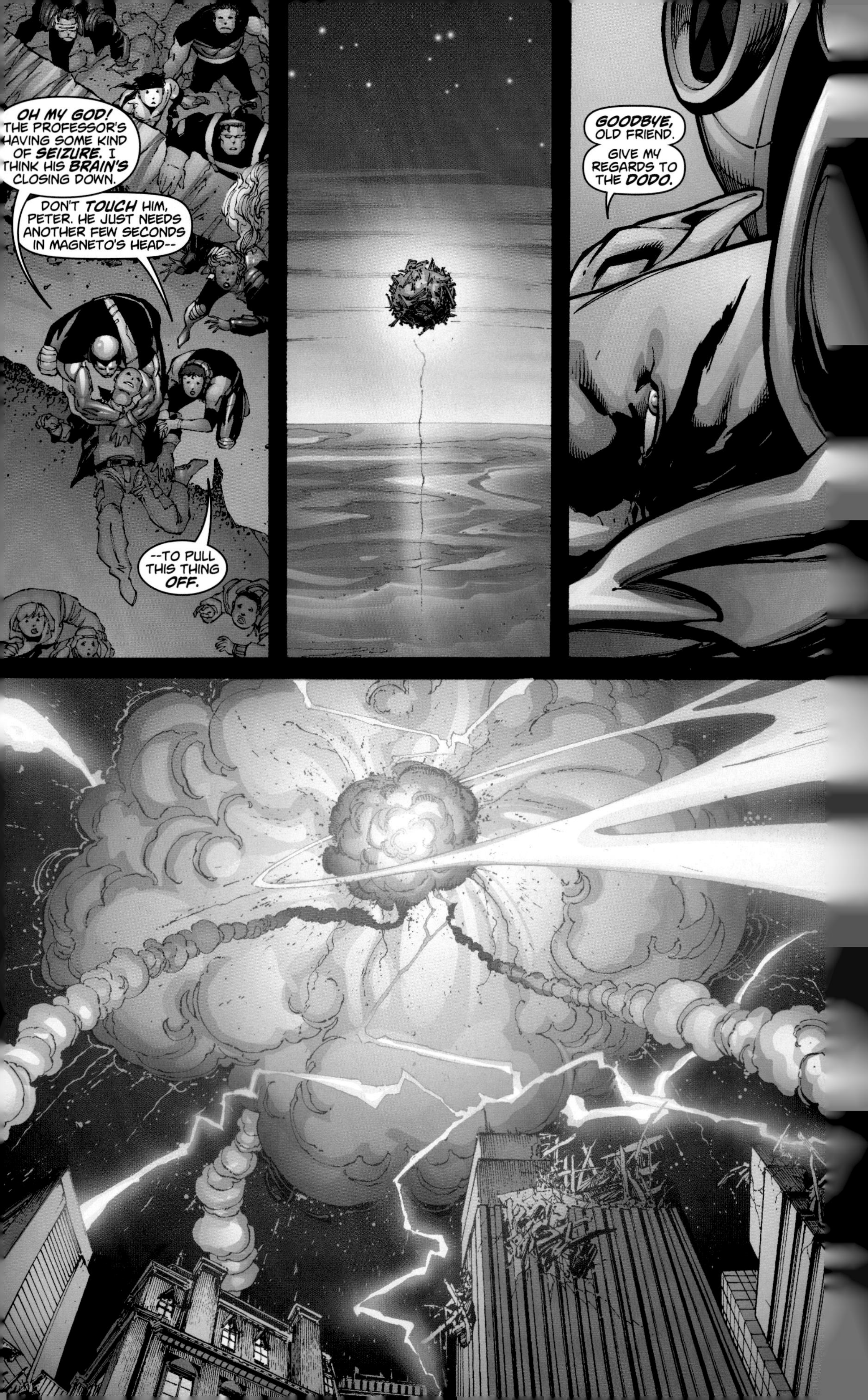
OH MY GOD! THE PROFESSOR'S HAVING SOME KIND OF SEIZURE. I THINK HIS BRAIN'S CLOSING DOWN.
DON'T TOUCH HIM, PETER. HE JUST NEEDS ANOTHER FEW SECONDS IN MAGNETO'S HEAD--
--TO PULL THIS THING OFF.
GOODBYE, OLD FRIEND.
GIVE MY REGARDS TO THE DODO.

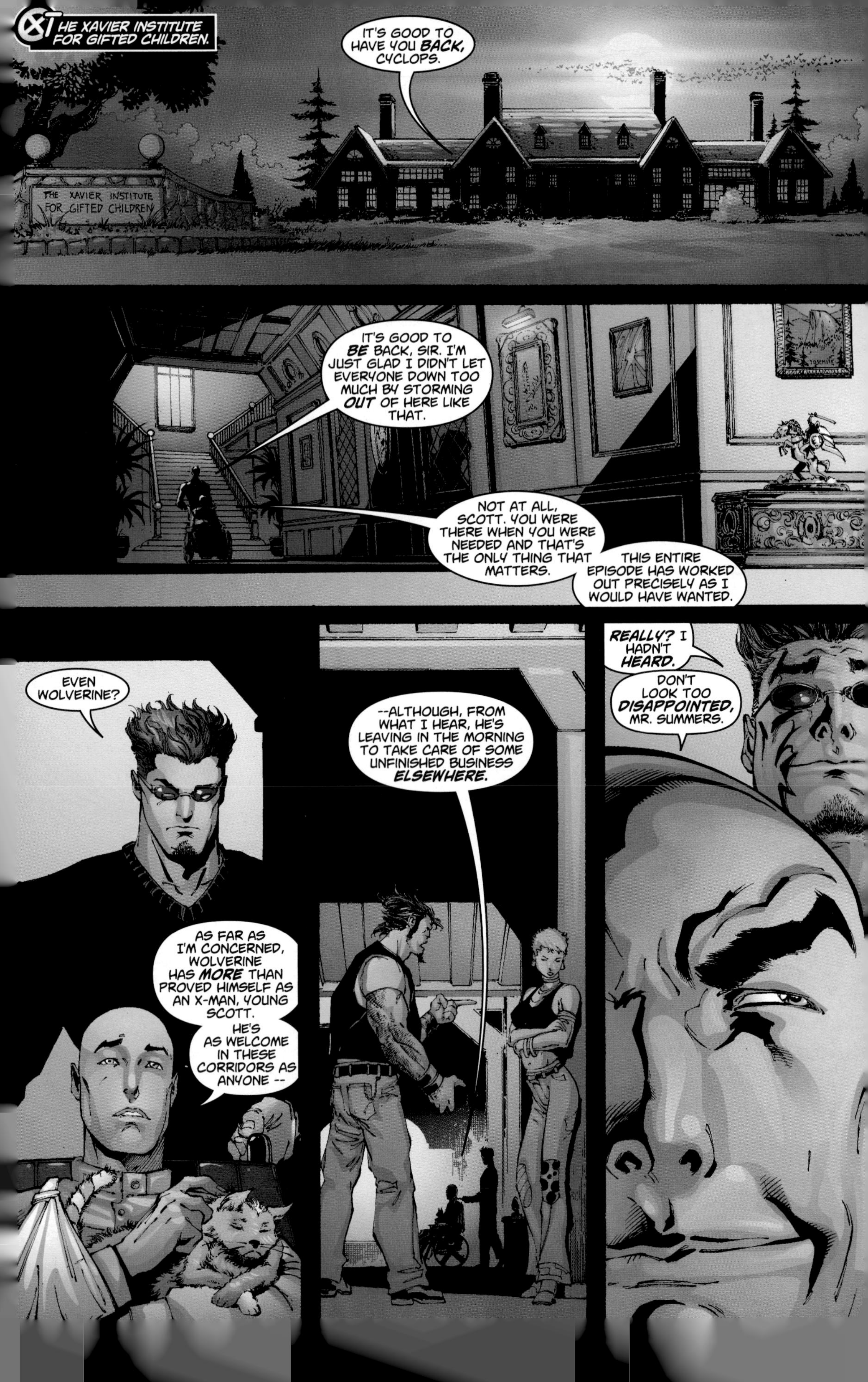
THE XAVIER INSTITUTE FOR GIFTED CHILDREN.
IT'S GOOD TO HAVE YOU BACK, CYCLOPS.
THE XAVIER INSTITUTE FOR GIFTED CHILDREN
IT'S GOOD TO BE BACK, SIR. I'M JUST GLAD I DIDN'T LET EVERYONE DOWN TOO MUCH BY STORMING OUT OF HERE LIKE THAT.
NOT AT ALL, SCOTT. YOU WERE THERE WHEN YOU WERE NEEDED AND THAT'S THE ONLY THING THAT MATTERS.
THIS ENTIRE EPISODE HAS WORKED OUT PRECISELY AS I WOULD HAVE WANTED.
EVEN WOLVERINE?
AS FAR AS I'M CONCERNED, WOLVERINE HAS MORE THAN PROVED HIMSELF AS AN X-MAN, YOUNG SCOTT.
HE'S AS WELCOME IN THESE CORRIDORS AS ANYONE --
--ALTHOUGH, FROM WHAT I HEAR, HE'S LEAVING IN THE MORNING TO TAKE CARE OF SOME UNFINISHED BUSINESS ELSEWHERE.
REALLY? I HADN'T HEARD.
DON'T LOOK TOO DISAPPOINTED, MR. SUMMERS.

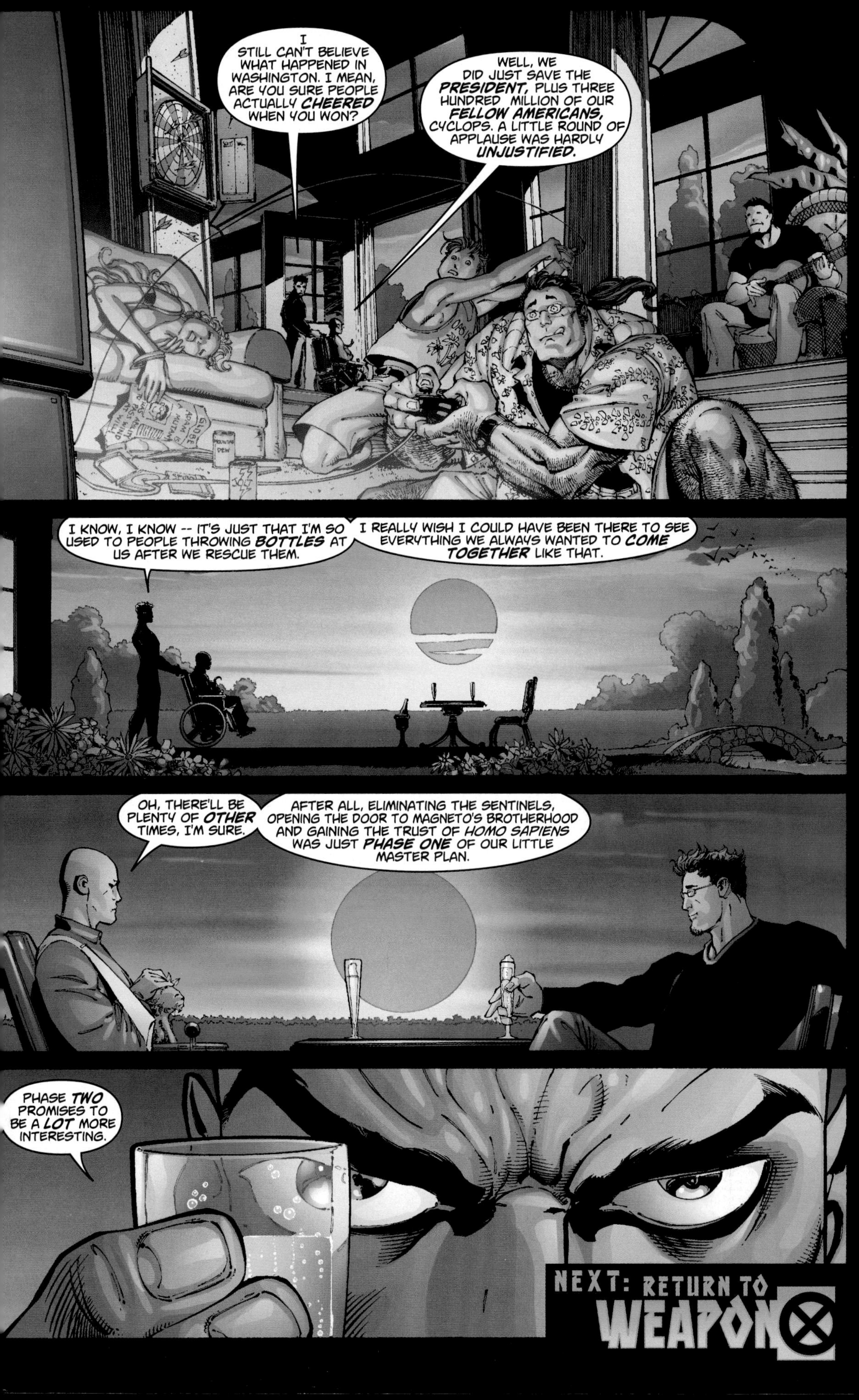
I STILL CAN'T BELIEVE WHAT HAPPENED IN WASHINGTON. I MEAN, ARE YOU SURE PEOPLE ACTUALLY CHEERED WHEN YOU WON?
WELL, WE DID JUST SAVE THE PRESIDENT, PLUS THREE HUNDRED MILLION OF OUR FELLOW AMERICANS, CYCLOPS. A LITTLE ROUND OF APPLAUSE WAS HARDLY UNJUSTIFIED.
I KNOW, I KNOW -- IT'S JUST THAT I'M SO USED TO PEOPLE THROWING BOTTLES AT US AFTER WE RESCUE THEM.
I REALLY WISH I COULD HAVE BEEN THERE TO SEE EVERYTHING WE ALWAYS WANTED TO COME TOGETHER LIKE THAT.
OH, THERE'LL BE PLENTY OF OTHER TIMES, I'M SURE.
AFTER ALL, ELIMINATING THE SENTINELS, OPENING THE DOOR TO MAGNETO'S BROTHERHOOD AND GAINING THE TRUST OF HOMO SAPIENS WAS JUST PHASE ONE OF OUR LITTLE MASTER PLAN.
PHASE TWO PROMISES TO BE A LOT MORE INTERESTING.
NEXT: RETURN TO WEAPON X

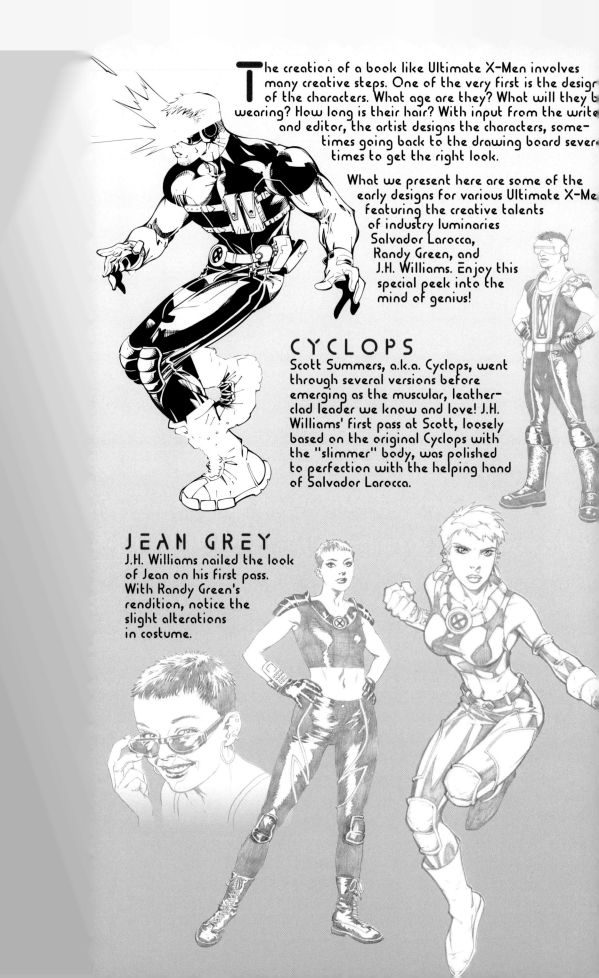

The creation of a book like Ultimate X-Men involves many creative steps. One of the very first is the design of the characters. What age are they? What will they be wearing? How long is their hair? With input from the writer and editor, the artist designs the characters, sometimes going back to the drawing board several times to get the right look.

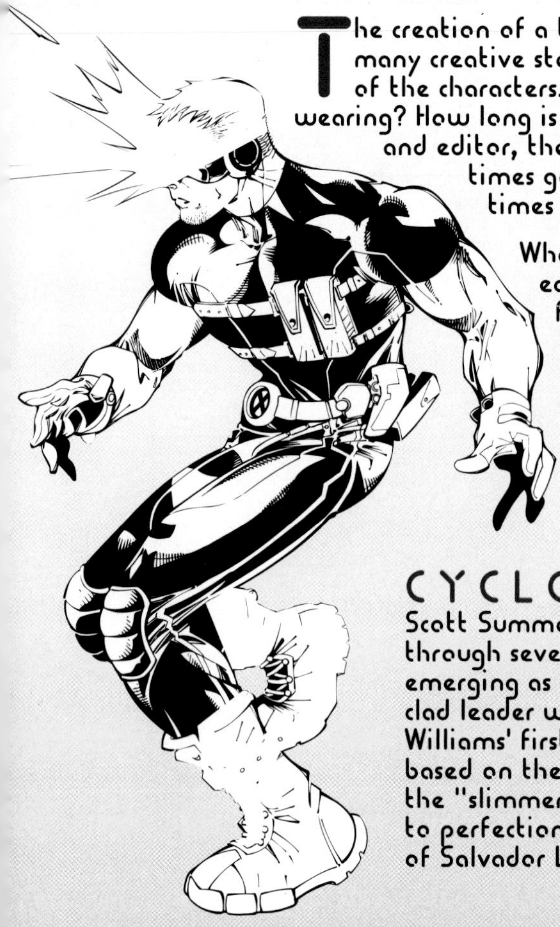

What we present here are some of the early designs for various Ultimate X-Men featuring the creative talents of industry luminaries Salvador Larocca, Randy Green, and J.H. Williams. Enjoy this special peek into the mind of genius!

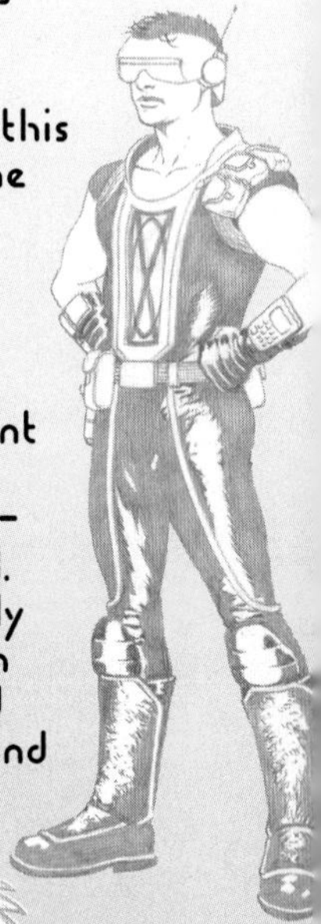

CYCLOPS

Scott Summers, a.k.a. Cyclops, went through several versions before emerging as the muscular, leather-clad leader we know and love! J.H. Williams' first pass at Scott, loosely based on the original Cyclops with the "slimmer" body, was polished to perfection with the helping hand of Salvador Larocca.

JEAN GREY

J.H. Williams nailed the look of Jean on his first pass. With Randy Green's rendition, notice the slight alterations in costume.

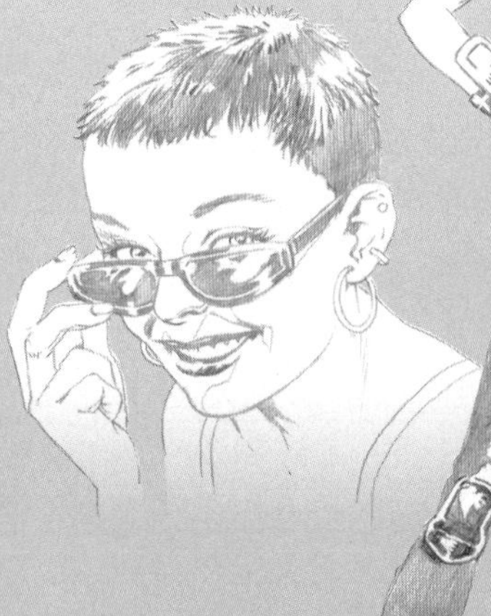

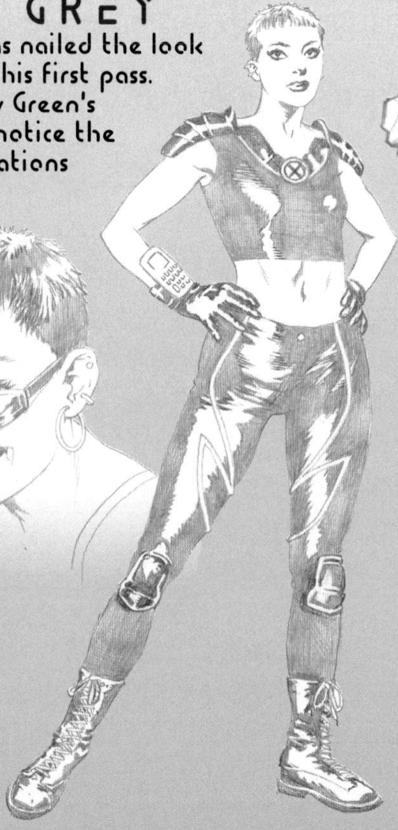

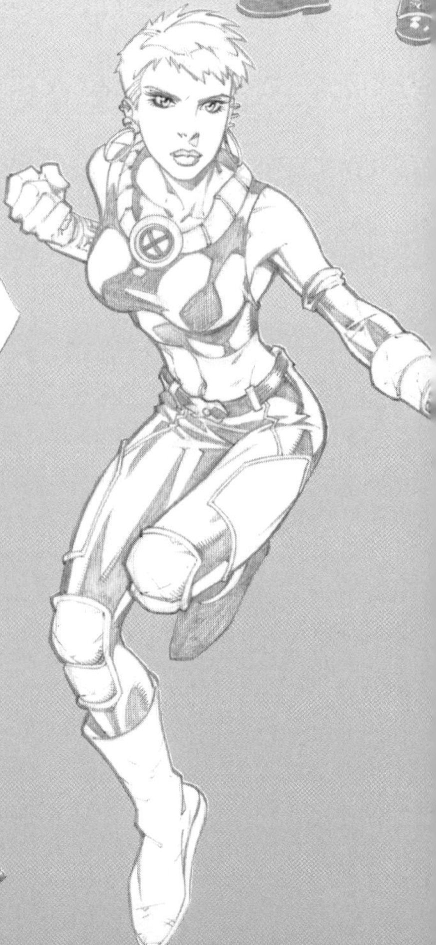

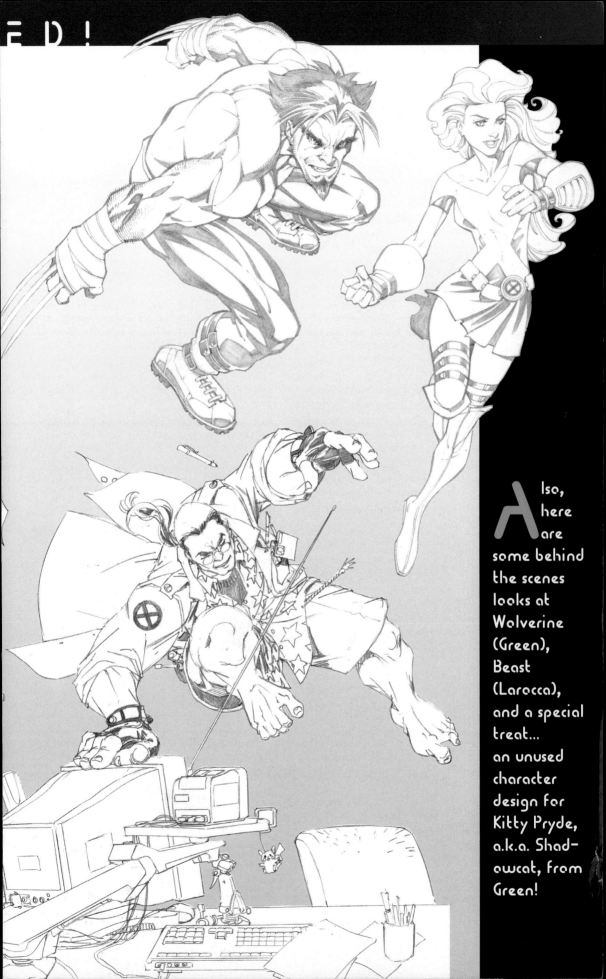

Also, here are some behind the scenes looks at Wolverine (Green), Beast (Larocca), and a special treat... an unused character design for Kitty Pryde, a.k.a. Shadowcat, from Green!

THE MARVEL UNIVERSE MAY BE THE LONGEST-RUNNING CONTINUOUS STORY IN MODERN HISTORY.

Stan Lee and his creative team laid a strong base of characters and themes. Then, every year, for the last four decades, each Marvel comic has been placed carefully upon that foundation. Well over 20,000 books -- produced by thousands of writers, artists, and editors -- form the universal story structure we call "continuity." The strength of Marvel comics is that our loyal fans, our "True Believers," fully embrace our complex and rich continuity.

But, Ultimate X-Men has nearly nothing to do with any of that.

Joe Quesada and I started the Ultimate books because we wanted Marvel to get back in touch with kids. We wanted Marvel's great teen heroes -- Spidey and the X-Men -- to star in comics for 2001 kids. Everybody knows kids and teens like reading about kids and teens, but Marvel's teen stars went and got old. In our mainline books, our former teen stars are pushing 30 years old, many are married, and some have kids of their own. Moreover, the "continuity" stood as a huge barrier to entry for readers of any age. With every comic crafted to fit in with 20,000 others, no one book was easy for a new reader to pick up and read.

In the past, Marvel editors rarely messed around with the continuity, for fear of "betraying" the vocal members of our loyal adult fan base who complain about everything that contradicts the stories they have been reading for 10, 20 or 30 years. Frankly, the sheer fear of adult-fan backlash forced Marvel editors into dozens of lame teen-publishing programs. These fell into four basic categories:

1. "Untold Stories": Turn back the clock to 1962 and tell stories that had not yet been "revealed." In other words, we forced Cyclops and Phoenix into skinny ties and bobby socks, and made them fight giant ants created by atomic-bomb testing.

2. "Adventures": Publish comics based on Marvel kids' cartoons. In other words, we forced comic creators to use the simplistic artistic and storytelling styles that couldn't possibly work anywhere else but in action animation.

3. "What if": Give the writers and artists creative freedom to write and draw the characters they love in modern, real world, settings. But, put some nim "Alternate universe" label on the covers so fans know the books really "don't count."

4. "Packs": Create all new kids' teams, -- i.e., Marvel's own XFL.

And then, Marvel management had the real challenge of trying to look surprised when all those publishing programs flat out failed.

But now, here is Ultimate X-Men -- no backstory, no turning back the clock, no hands tied behind the creators' backs, no apology, and no fear -- just the real X-Men portrayed as teenagers in the real world. This six-issue story arc hit the comic industry like six tons of bricks, launching as the No. 1 book in the business and growing in readership with each new release.

And here is the wonderful surprise for this Marvel management team: success. Not just among new readers, but among Marvel's loyal adult following. It turns out true Marvel fans are not just "True Believers" in the old stories. They gladly embrace great work, even if it is not tied to the old story lines.

Mark Millar captured lightning in a bottle: the spirit and essence of the X-Men as teenagers. Then, he unpopped the cork on this incredible moral and military struggle for global domination. Marvel's most popular pencilers, Adam and Andy Kubert, have raised their craft to an all-time high -- splashing the story across page after page in their uniquely bold and clear graphic style. Inkers, Art Thibert and Danny Miki, along with colorists, Richard Isanove and Brian Haberlin, made outstanding contributions to the look of this book. Mark Powers and Peter Franco have kept all of the moving parts together, and managed to translate my complaints into creative input for Millar and the Kuberts. Combined with Brian Bendis and Mark Bagley on Spider-Man, Ultimate Marvel has been an unqualified hit.

And now, I would like to make an unusual dedication for Marvel's hottest teen book. Ultimate X-Men is dedicated to our adult fans, who have opened their hearts and minds to our new Marvel Universe.

BILL JEMAS
PRESIDENT, MARVEL ENTERPRISES

APRIL 28, 200